Global Shifts

Earth System Governance

Frank Biermann and Oran R. Young, series editors

Oran R. Young, *Institutional Dynamics: Emergent Patterns in International Environmental Governance*

Frank Biermann and Philipp Pattberg, eds., *Global Environmental Governance Reconsidered*

Olav Schram Stokke, *Disaggregating International Regimes: A New Approach to Evaluation and Comparison*

Aarti Gupta and Michael Mason, eds., *Transparency in Global Environmental Governance: Critical Perspectives*

Sikina Jinnah, *Post-Treaty Politics: Secretariat Influence in Global Environmental Governance*

Frank Biermann, *Earth System Governance: World Politics in the Anthropocene*

Walter F. Baber and Robert B. Bartlett, *Consensus in Global Environmental Governance: Deliberative Democracy in Nature's Regime*

Diarmuid Torney, *European Climate Leadership in Question: Policies toward China and India*

David Ciplet, J. Timmons Roberts, and Mizan R. Khan, *Power in a Warming World: The New Global Politics of Climate Change and the Remaking of Environmental Inequality*

Simon Nicholson and Sikina Jinnah, eds., *New Earth Politics: Essays from the Anthropocene*

Norichika Kanie and Frank Biermann, eds., *Governing through Goals: Sustainable Development Goals as Governance Innovation*

Oran R. Young, *Governing Complex Systems: Social Capital for the Anthropocene*

Susan Park and Teresa Kramarz, eds., *Global Environmental Governance and the Accountability Trap*

Teresa Kramarz, *Forgotten Values: The World Bank and Its Partnerships for the Environment*

Lena Partzsch, *Alternatives to Multilateralism: New Forms of Social and Environmental Governance*

Katharina Rietig, *Learning in Governance: Climate Policy Integration in the European Union*

Yixian Sun, *Certifying China: The Rise and Limits of Transnational Sustainability Governance in Emerging Economies*

Philip Schleifer, *Global Shifts: Business, Politics, and Deforestation in a Changing World Economy*

Global Shifts

Business, Politics, and Deforestation in a Changing World Economy

Philip Schleifer

The MIT Press
Cambridge, Massachusetts
London, England

© 2023 Massachusetts Institute of Technology

This work is subject to a Creative Commons CC-BY-NC-ND license.

Subject to such license, all rights are reserved.

The MIT Press would like to thank the anonymous peer reviewers who provided comments on drafts of this book. The generous work of academic experts is essential for establishing the authority and quality of our publications. We acknowledge with gratitude the contributions of these otherwise uncredited readers.

This book was set in Stone Serif and Stone Sans by Westchester Publishing Services. Printed and bound in the United States of America.

Library of Congress Cataloging-in-Publication Data

Names: Schleifer, Philip, author.
Title: Global shifts : business, politics, and deforestation in a changing world economy / Philip Schleifer.
Description: Cambridge, Massachusetts : The MIT Press, [2023] | Series: Earth system governance | Includes bibliographical references and index.
Identifiers: LCCN 2022033273 (print) | LCCN 2022033274 (ebook) |
 ISBN 9780262545532 (paperback) | ISBN 9780262374439 (epub) |
 ISBN 9780262374446 (pdf)
Subjects: LCSH: Deforestation—Economic aspects. | Deforestation—Political aspects. | Farm supply industries.
Classification: LCC SD418 .S35 2023 (print) | LCC SD418 (ebook) |
 DDC 333.75—dc23/eng/20220829
LC record available at https://lccn.loc.gov/2022033273
LC ebook record available at https://lccn.loc.gov/2022033274

10 9 8 7 6 5 4 3 2 1

To Simone and Oskar

Contents

Series Foreword ix
Acknowledgments xi
List of Abbreviations xv

1 Introduction: A Failed Market Transformation 1
2 Varieties of Political Economy Analysis: A Framework 25
3 Global Shifts and the Zero-Deforestation Regime Complex 47
4 The Comparative Politics of Sustainable Markets 73
5 Multipolar Governance in the Palm Oil Value Chain 105
6 Toward Place-Based Sustainability? 137
7 Conclusion 165

Notes 185
References 191
Index 247

Series Foreword

Humans now influence all biological and physical systems of the planet. Almost no species, land area, or part of the oceans has remained unaffected by the expansion of the human species. Recent scientific findings suggest that the entire earth system now operates outside the normal state exhibited over at least the past 500,000 years. Yet at the same time, it is apparent that the institutions, organizations, and mechanisms by which humans govern their relationship with the natural environment and global biogeochemical systems are utterly insufficient—and poorly understood. More fundamental and applied research is needed.

Such research is no easy undertaking. It must span the entire globe because only integrated global solutions can ensure a sustainable coevolution of biophysical and socioeconomic systems. But it must also draw on local experiences and insights. Research on earth system governance must be about places in all their diversity, yet seek to integrate place-based research within a global understanding of the myriad human interactions with the earth system. Eventually, the task is to develop integrated systems of governance, from the local to the global level, that ensure the sustainable development of the coupled socioecological system that the Earth has become.

The series Earth System Governance is designed to address this research challenge. Books in this series will pursue this challenge from a variety of disciplinary perspectives, at different levels of governance, and with a range of methods. Yet all will further one common aim: analyzing current systems of earth system governance with a view to increased understanding and possible improvements and reform. Books in this series will be of interest to the academic community but will also inform practitioners and at times contribute to policy debates.

This series is related to the long-term international research program "Earth System Governance Project."

Frank Biermann, Copernicus Institute of Sustainable Development, Utrecht University

Oran R. Young, Bren School, University of California, Santa Barbara
Earth System Governance Series Editors

Acknowledgments

This book is the product of a long journey. The research and writing process was full of joyful and insightful moments, but also moments of doubt and exhaustion. Finding the focus to finish this project during a global pandemic, which left my wife and me locked down in a small Amsterdam flat with our newborn son, was not easy. Luckily, I had the amazing support of my family, mentors, and a terrific community of scholars. Without them, this book would not have been possible, and I feel infinite gratitude for all the encouragement, motivation, and advice I received. There is a long list of people and organizations that deserve to be acknowledged for contributing directly and indirectly to this book.

Let me begin by expressing my gratitude to Robert Falkner, my PhD supervisor at the London School of Economics. Robert has been a fantastic supervisor, mentor, and role model to me over the years. He has helped me become the scholar I am today and he in many ways contributed to the academic and intellectual foundations of this book. I am also grateful to the Department of International Relations and the Grantham Research Institute on Climate Change and the Environment at the LSE. They provided a stimulating environment for my PhD studies and important sections of this book were written during two visiting fellowships at the Grantham Research Institute. I also would like to express my gratitude to Andrea Liese, who mentored me very early in my academic career. Moreover, I would like to thank Frank Biermann and Oran Young, the academic editors of the MIT Earth System Governance series. Following our conversation at the Earth System Governance conference in 2017, they invited me to develop a book proposal, and they tirelessly supported the project on its long journey from idea to manuscript. Throughout the process, Beth Clevenger and Anthony Zannino from

MIT Press were very supportive and helped me navigate all kinds of practical challenges during the drafting stage and production process of this book. I am also grateful to the three anonymous reviewers for their praise, criticism, and constructive feedback. Their excellent comments helped me immensely in making this a more compact and compelling manuscript.

At the University of Amsterdam, which has been my professional home since 2016, I had wonderful support from the Department of Political Science and the members of the Political Economy and Transnational Governance program group. Particularly, I would like to thank Jonathan Zeitlin, Luc Fransen, and Daniel Mügge for commenting on draft chapters and for all their advice, encouragement, and support over the years. I am also grateful for the financial support I received from the Political Economy and Transnational Governance program group, the Amsterdam Institute for Social Science Research, and the Amsterdam Centre for European Studies for this project. Moreover, the development of the research agenda that culminated in this book has benefited from a Jean Monnet Fellowship at the European University Institute under the mentorship of Bernard Hoekman. It was during my fellowship at the EUI's Robert Schuman Centre of Advanced Studies, where I started to engage more systematically with questions of global market shifts in the world food economy. This led to a first publication on sustainability certification in India's palm oil supply chain in *Global Environmental Politics*, which informed the framing and approach of this book. My research agenda in this area was also shaped by collaborations and conversations with many friends and colleagues over the years. I am very lucky to be part of a vibrant research community on transnational governance. Particularly, I would like to thank Michael Bloomfield, Yixian Sun, Graeme Auld, Peter Dauvergne, Hamish van der Ven, Janina Grabs, Maja Tampe, Greetje Schouten, Benjamin Cashore, Kate MacDonald, Genevieve LeBaron, Stefan Renckens, Axel Marx, Stefano Ponte, Joana Setzer, Matteo Fiorini, Clara Brandi, Rupal Verma, Nilmawati, Michael Mason, and Karen Bäckstrand.

I also wish to express my deep gratitude to all the individuals who agreed to be interviewed for this project, as well as to the many individuals and organizations in Asia, Europe, and South America that supported my research work in various ways. Particularly, I would like to thank Arya Hadi Dharmawan, Bayu Eka Yulian, and Dyah Ita Mardiyaningsih from Institut Pertanian Bogor for warmly welcoming and hosting me during a research stay in Indonesia. Moreover, I would like to express special thanks to Greenpeace Indonesia,

Acknowledgments

SPKS, the Gecko Project, Sawit Watch, CIFOR, and the United Nations Forum on Sustainability Standards.

Finally, I am indefinitely grateful for being blessed with such a loving and caring family. My parents, my brother, and my sister have always supported me in all my endeavors, giving me stability, strength, and confidence. Last but certainly not least, there is my wife Simone, the love of my life, and my son Oskar, the joy of my life. I dedicate this book to you. This journey would have been impossible without you.

London, April 2022

List of Abbreviations

ABIOVE	Brazilian Association of Vegetable Oils
APRSOJA	Brazilian Association of Soy Producers
BRICS	Brazil, Russia, India, China, South Africa
CGF	Consumer Goods Forum
EU	European Union
FAO	Food and Agriculture Organization
FCI	Forest Conversion Initiative
GCF Task Force	Governors' Climate and Forest Task Force
GAPKI	Indonesian Palm Oil Association
GVC	global value chain
IDH	Sustainable Trade Initiative
ISPO	Indonesia Sustainable Palm Oil
ISPOC	India Sustainable Palm Oil Coalition
NGO	nongovernmental organization
PCI Strategy	Produce, Conserve, Include Strategy
REDD+	Program on Reducing Emissions from Deforestation and Forest Degradation
RSPO	Roundtable on Sustainable Palm Oil
RTRS	Roundtable on Responsible Soy
WTO	World Trade Organization
WWF	World Wide Fund for Nature

1 Introduction: A Failed Market Transformation

"We've got to wake up to the fact that this is a finite planet." In July 2010, Jason Clay, executive director of the Markets Institute at the World Wide Fund for Nature (WWF), gave a TED Talk at Oxford University titled "How Big Brands Can Help Save Biodiversity" (Clay 2010). In this talk, Clay shares an alarming analysis that shows how the unprecedented rate of tropical forest loss around the world has destroyed the habitats of millions of animal and plant species. Without transformative change, he warns, the crisis will escalate. Moreover, the global population is expected to reach nine billion people in the next half-century, which will require the production of more food, feed, and fiber than in the last 8,000 years.

Despite the enormity of the challenge, Clay argues that a global market transformation is possible, if we can learn from past mistakes. In a personal example, he describes a collaboration with Ben Cohen from Ben & Jerry's in the late 1980s, which resulted in Rainforest Crunch, the world's first ice-cream made of sustainably harvested Brazil nuts. This partnership marked the beginning of a commercially successful rainforest marketing campaign that generated over US$100 million in annual sales. Despite the initial optimism, however, the campaign eventually failed because, according to Clay, "the people who made money from Brazil nuts were not the people who made money from cutting the forest" (Clay 2010). In other words, the campaign failed because it provided market incentives for Brazil nut farmers to behave sustainably but ignored even higher profits being generated by other actors. To understand this failure, one must thus identify these other actors and their motivations.

The 1980s also marked the beginning of what environmental economists later dubbed the "Tropical Oil Crop Revolution," a process of historically unprecedented agricultural expansion in the global tropics during which large swaths of forestland, grassland, and peatland were cleared for industrial oil palm plantations and soybean fields in South America and southeastern Asia. Between 1991 and 2013, the land devoted to these crops grew by over sixty-six million hectares (Byerlee, Falcon, and Naylor 2016, 7), or the size of France and its overseas territories. Moreover, the expansion of oil crops has driven indirect land-use changes in these regions. For example, in the Brazilian Amazon, expanding soybean farms have displaced cattle pastures further into the forest frontier (Song et al. 2021). These industrial agricultural processes now represent the largest threat to tropical forests on the planet (Trase 2018), much larger than illegal logging, which had long been the focus of conservation groups and policymakers.

Learning from its mistakes, the WWF was one of the first major environmental nongovernmental organizations (NGOs) to focus on industrial agriculture in its forest conservation strategy (former director of the Forest Conversion Initiative, phone interview, May 2013). In 2001, it launched a global program called the Forest Conversion Initiative (FCI), the aim of which was to identify the commodities responsible for the most deforestation on the planet. To transform these industries, the WWF implemented a new theory of change, which it had previously pioneered in the forestry sector. Specifically, it sought to build on a powerful mechanism to leverage global supply chains in the absence of government regulation (WWF 2012). The governance model underlying the initiative rests on the market power of big-brand companies. Incentivized through reputational and regulatory pressures, as well as through the prospect of tapping markets of virtue, these corporations are meant to function as "key leverage points for change" (WWF 2004, 3).

Initially focusing on the soy and palm oil industries in Brazil and Indonesia and the most powerful companies in these supply chains, the FCI identified about one hundred companies that control 25 percent of the global trade in these commodities. As Clay (2010) explains in his TED talk, "if these companies demand sustainable products, they'll pull 40 to 50 percent of production. . . . If Cargill makes a decision, the entire palm oil industry moves." To harness the market power of these companies, the WWF intensely lobbied them to join commodity-specific roundtables. Unlike fair-trade and organic certifications, which focus on premium markets, the FCI aimed to create mainstream sustainability platforms to transform the entire agriculture sector and its supply chains. To this end, the WWF launched the Roundtable on Sustainable Palm Oil and Roundtable on Responsible Soy in 2004 and 2006, respectively. Additional roundtables for sugarcane, cotton, biofuels, beef, and other commodities have since been established (WWF 2017).

When Clay gave his TED talk, I had just started a PhD program at the London School of Economics. Through my affiliation with the Grantham Research Institute on Climate Change and the Environment, I had had many discussions with my colleagues about tropical deforestation. I had also read a lot about the oil palm boom in Indonesia and how plantation agriculture threatened the rainforests in Kalimantan and Sumatra. As a student of transnational governance, I was intrigued by the FCI and its supply chain-driven approach. When I started my PhD studies, the members of the Consumer Goods Forum (CGF), a network of 400 leading global retailers and consumer goods manufacturers, had just pledged to eliminate deforestation from their supply chains by 2020. Thereafter, hundreds of big-brand companies made zero-deforestation commitments, and many joined the commodity roundtables of the WWF (Donofrio, Leonard, and Rothrock 2017; Lister and Dauvergne 2014). As the political momentum behind zero-deforestation increased, I wondered if these transnational actors could help address one of the world's most pressing environmental problems.

Up to that point, governments had made little progress in reducing commodity-driven deforestation. Multilateral institutions for governing deforestation linked to international trade remain underdeveloped to this day. Thus, support from some of the world's most powerful corporations created a sense of optimism at the 2010 Cancun summit (former director of WWF International, phone interview, November 2011). However, ten years later, that optimism had turned to disappointment. The 2010s have been called "tropical forests' lost decade" (Butler 2019). Commodity-driven deforestation remains a major problem around the world (Global Forest Watch 2020), and the zero-deforestation supply chain movement missed its 2020 targets by a very large margin. The original targets may have been ambitious but the slow change has disappointed many analysts (Chagas et al. 2018; Climate Focus 2016; Taylor and Streck 2018). Even the people at the heart of the movement, such as Marco Albani, then director of the Tropical Forest Alliance, an organization established to support companies' transitions to deforestation-free supply chains, acknowledged the lack of progress. Already in 2017, he warned that "the pace of change that is happening is not making us confident that we will meet the 2020 goal."[1]

To increase the effectiveness of zero-deforestation commitments, analysts demand that more companies adopt zero-deforestation targets with immediate implementation deadlines and that clear sanction-based implementation mechanisms are needed (Garrett et al., 2019). The importance of these factors notwithstanding, this research tends to neglect the broader historical, political, and economic contexts from which transnational regulatory authority emerges and in which it is exercised. My contention in this book is that in a time of major structural change in the world economy, such contexts require close investigation. Therefore, I take this failed market transformation as a starting point to launch an investigation into global shifts in markets, power, and authority, and how these shape the politics and governance of sustainability in the current phase of globalization. This situates the analysis of this book at the intersection of broader themes in earth system governance research on power and transformations and their implications for actors and governance architectures (Earth System Governance Project 2018).

Governing Agriculture and Forests in an Era of Globalization

To provide empirical and conceptual context to the analysis, this section revisits the rise of transnational governance for forests and agriculture in the late twentieth century. During this period, economic globalization ushered in an era of "governance without government," which allowed nonstate actors, such as NGOs and firms, to participate more in global politics (Rosenau and Czempiel 1992). In their landmark study *Private Authority in International Affairs*, Cutler, Haufler, and Porter (1999a, 16) observed that "private actors are increasingly engaged in authoritative rule-making that was previously the prerogative of sovereign states." This diffusion of private authority permeated the world economy (see Bieler, Higgott, and Underhill 2000; Hall and Biersteker 2002; Strange 1996), particularly the field of global environmental politics (Auld 2014; European Environment Agency 2011; Green 2014; Pattberg 2007). Scholars describe these dramatic changes in the institutional landscape as a "Cambrian explosion" (Abbott 2012b, 571). Whereas the growth of formal intergovernmental organizations dedicated to global environmental issues has mostly stopped, private governance organizations have increased almost exponentially (Abbott, Green, and Keohane 2016; Green 2014).

Robert Falkner, my PhD supervisor at the London School of Economics, was among the first to elaborate on the concept of private environmental governance and to explore its links to theories of international relations. From a regime theoretical perspective, he defined such governance as "the interactions among private actors, or between private actors on the one hand and civil society and state actors on the other [, that] give rise to institutional arrangements that structure and direct actors' behavior in an issue-specific area" (Falkner 2003, 72–73). Many of these arrangements seek to harness market forces to instigate change in global production networks. In their trailblazing book on the authority of forestry certification, Cashore, Auld, and Newsom (2004, 4) refer to these arrangements as a form of "nonstate market-driven governance." Others have coined the term "transnational business governance" to describe the multiplicity of schemes that apply nonstate authority to govern business conduct across borders (Eberlein et al. 2014). This also is the main conceptual label used in this book. However, as we see later in this chapter, it can be misleading to treat private and public governance realms as distinct and static (Cashore et al. 2021; Renckens 2020).

In the agriculture sector, the empirical focus of this book, private sustainability schemes have proliferated in the sector's globalizing supply chains (see figure 1.1). Initially lagging behind other industries in the development of such mechanisms (World Bank 2004, 17–25), the sector has evolved into one of the most dynamic sites of transnational business governance (Fuchs and Kalfagianni 2010; Gibbon, Ponte, and Lazaro 2010). The rise of sustainability standards and certification mechanisms in this area can be traced back to the organic and fair-trade movements (Bennett 2013; Lockeretz 2007). At the beginning of the twentieth century, organic farmers' associations emerged in several countries. Early examples include Demeter in Germany (1928) and the British Soil Association in the United Kingdom (1946). These organizations developed standards for organic agriculture and sought ways to distinguish themselves from conventional food production. Reportedly, the British Soil Association developed the world's first organic certification scheme in 1973. In addition, in the 1980s, fair-trade NGOs started to experiment with certification and on-product labelling. Fair-trade certification was initiated in the coffee sector in 1988 by Dutch development NGO Solidaridad, which created the Max Havelaar label. Similar initiatives, such as Transfair and Fairtrade Mark, soon emerged in other European countries and in North America. Today, many of these programs

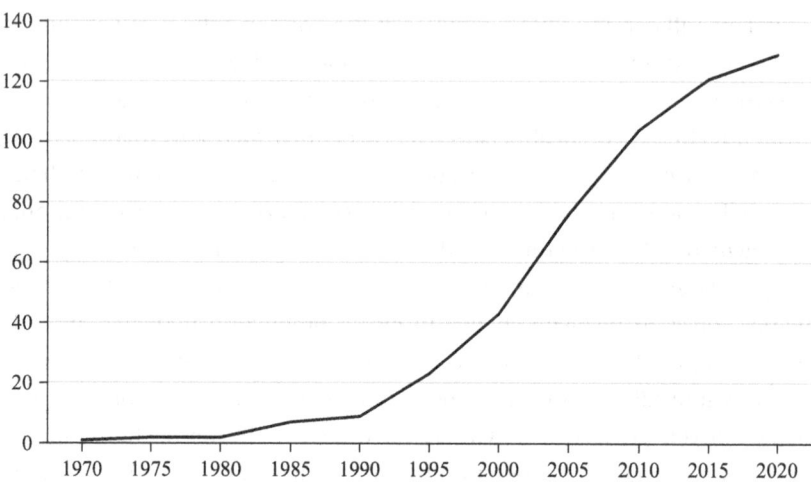

Figure 1.1
Proliferation of private sustainability standards in the agriculture sector
Source: Analysis of data from the International Trade Centre's Sustainability Map, available at https://www.sustainabilitymap.org/standards

are organized under the umbrella of Fairtrade International. These early efforts in organic and fair-trade agriculture aimed to create premium markets and thus they set the stage for NGOs and firms to become important providers of standards and regulation in global agrifood governance.

Mainstreaming certification as a mode of transnational business governance began in the forestry sector in the early 1990s. Throughout the 1980s, environmental groups led powerful advocacy campaigns against unsustainable practices in the trade of tropical timber. These groups initiated consumer boycotts and directly targeted do-it-yourself retailers like B&Q in the United Kingdom and Home Depot in the United States (Schwartzman and Kingston 1997). Research shows that under certain conditions NGO advocacy can have high influence on environmental outcomes (Pacheco-Vega and Murdie 2021). Over time, however, dissatisfaction with the effectiveness of the tropical timber campaign increased. When states failed to agree on an intergovernmental mechanism to regulate trade in tropical timber, some environmental groups shifted their strategy from "boycotts to partnerships" (Domask 2003, 157). In the early 1990s, the Forest Stewardship Council was formed, with the aim of transforming mainstream production via a multi-stakeholder process and certification scheme with global reach.[2] NGOs like the WWF then "carried" the certification model to other commodity sectors, including the palm oil and soy industries (Auld et al. 2007, 2).

According to the Standards Map of the International Trade Centre, a database of standard-based sustainability initiatives,[3] 129 private schemes were active in the agriculture sector as of October 2020, as shown in figure 1.1. Developed by industry actors, NGOs, and multistakeholder initiatives, these schemes contain "requirements that producers, traders, manufacturers, retailers or service providers may be asked to meet, relating to a wide range of sustainability metrics, including respect for basic human rights, worker health and safety, the environmental impacts of production, community relations, land use planning and others" (UNFSS 2013, 3). As shown in figure 1.1 and starting with the sector's rapid globalization in the 1990s, the number of private sustainability schemes increased sharply, particularly in the early 2000s, which can be interpreted as a rough indicator of nonstate actors' increasing rule-making power in global agrifood governance during this period (see Fuchs 2005, 785–789).

Figure 1.2 depicts the total land area that is certified by twelve leading certification organizations for select agricultural commodities.[4] As shown,

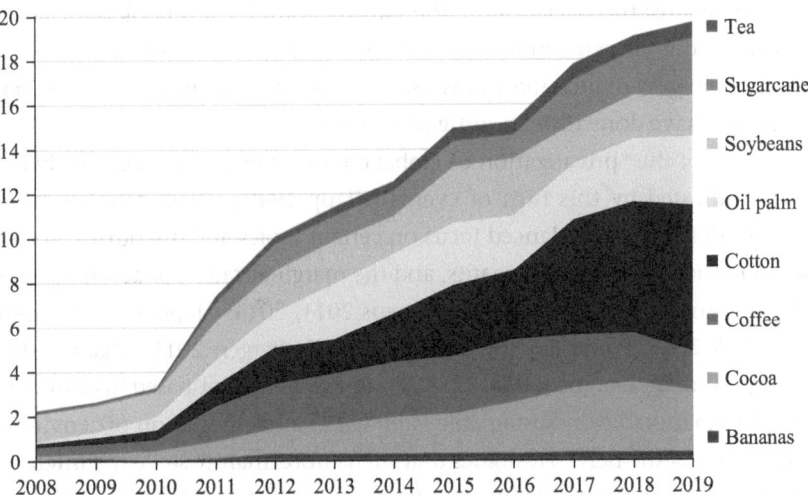

Figure 1.2
Agricultural commodity land use certified by leading certification organizations, in millions of hectares
Source: Data from https://www.sustainabilitymap.org/trends

the total size of "sustainable markets" has grown substantially over the past decade, increasing from two million hectares in 2008 to almost twenty million hectares in 2019 (ITC 2021).[5] According to the International Trade Centre and its partners, these figures demonstrate that "sustainability standards are no longer a novelty serving niche markets. Over the past decade, they have increasingly found their way into mainstream markets" (Willer et al. 2019, xi). One example is the palm oil industry, one of the focal sectors of this book. Here, the Roundtable on Sustainable Palm Oil was able to expand the amount of land certified under its scheme from 0.6 million hectares in 2010 to over three million hectares in 2019 (ITC 2021). For illustration, this amounts to more than 4.2 million soccer fields of certified land.

More Governance without Environmental Benefits?

The point of departure for a critical analysis is the apparent incongruity of a worsening ecological crisis despite unprecedented degrees of environmental governance. The objective is to identify instances where environmental degradation coincides with governance failure and to investigate their historical, political, and economic origins (Kütting 2014; Newell 2012, 34–60). Against this background, the starting point for this book is the crisis of commodity-driven deforestation and mounting evidence that proliferating private governance mechanisms, for long the dominant global policy response, have done little to mitigate the crisis.

Critics of the "privatization of global environmental governance" likely feel vindicated by this turn of events (Clapp 1998). These scholars have long criticized an unbalanced focus on certain topics and discourses, power asymmetries between participants, and the marginalization of actors such as those from developing countries (Cheyns 2011, 2014; Clapp 1998; Fransen and Kolk 2007; Ponte 2008; Schouten and Glasbergen 2011). Against this background, Dauvergne (2016, 127–139) describes market-based instruments like the Roundtable on Sustainable Palm Oil as a manifestation of "environmentalism of the rich." He argues that such efforts mainly serve the interests of powerful corporations by helping them build green reputations, while failing to address the root causes of environmental harm in these industries, such as extractivism and overconsumption. In a similar vein, Ponte (2019, 212) argues that transnational business governance works for "green capital" but does not address "brown environments." Hence, from this perspective, a "big brand takeover of sustainability" would hinder, not help, the greening of the global economy (Dauvergne and Lister 2013).

The idea of governing through markets nevertheless has many proponents. When nonstate, market-driven schemes first emerged, many scholars viewed them favorably. Multistakeholder initiatives like the Forest Stewardship Council were praised as "startling institutional designs" (Cashore, Auld, and Newsom 2004, 298), a "good governance model" (Gulbrandsen 2008), and "sites of meaningful deliberation" (Dingwerth 2007, 9). Although questions of legitimacy were central to the early debate on these "new modes of governance" (Bäckstrand et al. 2010), the issue of their effectiveness has since become more prominent (Carlson et al. 2017; Garrett et al. 2016; Grabs 2020b; Kalfagianni and Pattberg 2013; Marx and Cuypers 2010). In the debate on gridlock in global governance, which is concerned with political stalemate in important intergovernmental forums, transnational private governance is often discussed as a pathway to overcome the failure of multilateralism (Abbott and Faude 2020; Hale and Held 2017; Partzsch 2020). In the field of global agrifood governance, proponents of market-based instruments often highlight the "potential additionality," or added environmental benefit, of private sustainability standards. This is the additional environmental benefit that a large-scale adoption of these programs would bring, when compared to a business-as-usual scenario (see Carlson et al. 2017; Garrett et al. 2016; Smith et al. 2019). In this regard, Smith et al. (2019) argue that if adopted widely enough, private sustainability standards could significantly reduce the detrimental impact of global agriculture. For the case of Bonsucro, a private sustainability standard for sugarcane production, they estimate that global compliance with the program would, among other impacts, reduce greenhouse gas emissions from global sugarcane cultivation by 51 percent.

From this perspective, the expansion of previously described sustainable markets is a positive development. The wider literature on transnational business governance also points to several conditions that should work in favor of these instruments. First, many agricultural commodities have a high export rate, which theoretically enables lead firms in these supply chains to influence and control smaller producers, such as those in developing countries. Large global buyers can pressure their suppliers to adhere to company or third-party standards. Everything else being equal, these commodity chains are thus fertile ground for big-brand sustainability

(Cashore, Auld, and Newsom 2004, 41; Gereffi, Humphrey, and Sturgeon 2005, 92–94). Second, corporate concentration in the global agrifood system has increased strongly since the 1960s, when a wave of corporate mergers and acquisitions transformed the retail industries in Europe and North America. Today, the annual revenue of Walmart, the world's largest retail corporation, exceeds the GDP of entire countries (Bloomfield 2017); the top ten food and beverage companies (e.g., PepsiCo, Unilever, Nestlé, etc.) control over a quarter of the global market for packaged food products; and four corporations (ADM, Bunge, Cargill, and Louis Dreyfus) dominate the world's trade in grains and oil seeds (Clapp 2020, 90–125). As van der Ven (2018) shows, these "gatekeeper" companies can be powerful drivers behind the adoption of private sustainability standards. Third, there is a high level of public controversy surrounding issues of tropical deforestation and biodiversity loss (Greenpeace 2006; WWF 2021a). In the past, NGOs have linked industrial agriculture to these and other problems by targeting lead firms in transnational advocacy campaigns (e.g., Greenpeace 2006; Schlesinger 2010). Finally, with the commodity roundtables of the WWF, the sector is home to several well-established private governance mechanisms.

Together, these factors should create a favorable environment for the large-scale adoption of transnational business governance in the sector. The apparent failure of these programs to realize their hypothesized potential more fully is perplexing. A closer look at the case of commodity-driven deforestation illustrates this further. Although powerful business actors and their civil society and government partners have made unprecedented efforts to promote private sustainability standards in forest-risk supply chains, it is increasingly clear that these initiatives and their theory of change have come nowhere near the global market transformation envisioned by Clay and others. Worse yet, as the following section illustrates, the prioritization of private market-based mechanisms has gone hand in hand with a worsening deforestation crisis in the agriculture sector.

The Case of Commodity-Driven Deforestation

Until a few decades ago, the island of Borneo in southeastern Asia's Malay Archipelago was almost fully covered by pristine rainforests (Gaveau et al. 2014). As a biodiversity hotspot, the island is home to millions of animal, insect, and plant species, among them many endangered species such as the orangutan, clouded leopard, and Irrawaddy river dolphin. Borneo's rich flora and fauna are key components of indigenous life on the island. For centuries, the Dayak people, referring to hundreds of forest-dwelling and riverine ethnic groups, have used the island's natural riches in a sustainable way, foraging and practicing small-scale subsistence agriculture (Crevello 2004). Today, however, Borneo's rainforests, biodiversity, and indigenous lifestyles are at risk. The Atlas of Deforestation of the Centre for International Forestry Research shows that, since the 1970s, the island has lost half of its tropical forest cover. These land-use changes have multiple causes, the most prominent of which is the expansion of industrial agriculture (Austin et al. 2017; CIFOR 2022).

Agricultural expansion drives tropical deforestation in many parts of the world. Studies estimate that in the second half of the twentieth century, over 50 percent of new agricultural land in the tropics came from clearing intact forests (Gibbs et al. 2010). The vast majority of forest conversion can be traced to the "big four" forest-risk commodities (oil palm, timber and pulp, soy, and cattle), which have accounted for about two-thirds of total tropical deforestation in recent decades (Trase 2018). Oil palm and to a lesser extent timber are the fastest expanding commodities in southeastern Asia, and cattle pastures and soybean monocultures drive large-scale land-use changes and forest conversion in South America. Whereas cattle are mainly raised for domestic consumption, timber and particularly oil palm and soybeans, the two commodities focused on in this book, are largely export-driven (Climate Focus 2016, 13). This should make the two sectors fertile ground for transnational business governance and its theory of change, but global demand has also fueled their expansion. As previously mentioned, economists dubbed the massive land-use change linked to oil palm and soy cultivation the Tropical Oil Crop Revolution. Between 1991 and 2013, the area of land planted with the two crops grew by over sixty million hectares (Byerlee, Falcon, and Naylor 2016, 7). Given the scale of forest loss involved in these processes, commodity-driven deforestation is one of the largest sources of global greenhouse gas emissions. According to the World Resource Institute, if tropical deforestation were a country, it would rank third in the world behind China and the United States in terms of its greenhouse gas emissions (Gibbs, Harris, and Seymour 2018).

The FCI and its agricultural roundtables were created to address issues related to commodity-driven deforestation. Today, they are part of a zero-deforestation supply chain movement involving many of the world's most powerful agrifood companies. Nestlé was the first big-brand company to make a public zero-deforestation commitment for its supply chain, in response to a Greenpeace campaign targeting its trademark KitKat brand. Under mounting activist pressure, other industry leaders followed suit. At the Cancun Climate Summit in 2010, the CGF pledged to achieve zero net deforestation by 2020 (Consumer Goods Forum 2010).[6] In 2014, this pledge was incorporated into the United Nations New York Declaration on Forests, a joint declaration of governments, companies, NGOs, and indigenous people's organizations aiming to stop the loss of natural forests and to restore millions of hectares of degraded land. The second goal of this declaration endorses the private sector's target of eliminating deforestation from the production of agricultural commodities by no later than 2020 (Forest Declaration 2017).

In response to these efforts, hundreds of retailers, consumer goods companies, and traders around the world made zero-deforestation commitments for their supply chains. By 2017, the advocacy network Forest Trends reported over 760 such commitments from 447 companies (Donofrio, Leonard, and Rothrock 2017). With many powerful agrifood companies developing no-deforestation policies and joining certification organizations like the Roundtable on Sustainable Palm Oil and Roundtable on Responsible Soy, global market transformation finally gained momentum. At the 2010 Cancun Climate Summit, WWF's director of the Market Institutes welcomed the development: "The scale, geographical presence and purchasing power of [these] companies could transform these commodity markets and help put an end to tropical deforestation in countries like Brazil and Indonesia" (Consumer Goods Forum 2010).

Unfortunately, beyond statements about their potential additionality (Carlson et al. 2018, 125), there is little evidence that these supply chain initiatives reduced tropical deforestation in any significant way. As shown in figure 1.3, since the launch of the FCI in 2001, the rate of commodity-driven deforestation has remained stubbornly high. Although the data presented here serve only as a rough indicator of a complex phenomenon and changes in assessment methodologies over time complicate the description of deforestation trends,[7] many analysts agree that the zero-deforestation movement missed its 2020 targets by a large margin. Some even call its impact "elusive" (Taylor and Streck 2018, 1; also see Chagas et al. 2018; Climate Focus 2016).

After the 2020 deforestation targets were missed, many businesses and NGOs linked to the zero-deforestation movement made new commitments

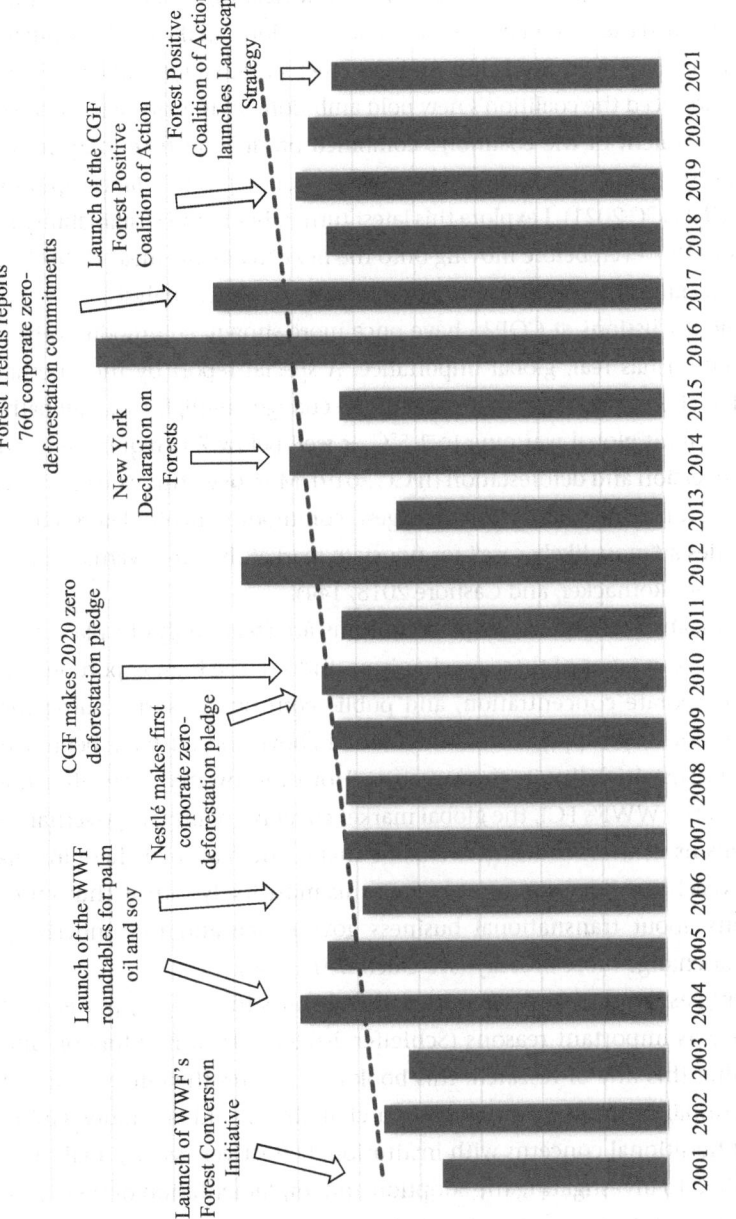

Figure 1.3
Global annual tree cover loss linked to commodity-driven deforestation, in millions of hectares
Source: Data from https://www.globalforestwatch.org/dashboards/global/

and launched new initiatives. The CGF deleted the weblink to its 2020 deforestation resolution and twenty-one of the world's leading retailers and manufactures formed the Forest Positive Coalition of Action.[8] At the COP26 Climate Summit in Glasgow in 2021, Jim Andrew, chief sustainability officer at PepsiCo, announced the coalition's new bold ambition "to transform landscapes to the equivalent of the coalition's combined production base footprint of palm oil, soy, paper packaging and beef into forest positive landscapes by 2030" (UNFCCC 2021). I explore this latest turn in big-brand sustainability in chapter 6. However, before moving onto the next "really big idea" (UNFCCC 2021), this failed market transformation requires a deeper analysis.

As the discussions at COP26 have once more shown, commodity-driven deforestation has real, global importance. A special report by the International Panel on Climate Change on land-use change highlights that all pathways that limit global warming to 1.5°C or well below 2°C require reduced land conversion and deforestation (IPCC 2019). Moreover, this case has theoretical relevance. As some scholars suggest, commodity-driven deforestation exemplifies a "most-likely case" for nonstate market-driven governance (see van der Ven, Rothacker, and Cashore 2018, 144).

This means that several scope conditions are (seemingly) in place that should work in favor of these mechanisms. Indeed, the high export dependency, corporate concentration, and public controversy surrounding the palm oil and soy supply chains mentioned above should have benefited big-brand sustainability in these sectors. However, twenty years after the launch of the WWF's FCI, the global market coverage of private governance mechanisms in these industries remains small. The failure of these instruments to achieve large-scale coverage in this most-likely setting thus raises questions about transnational business governance and the underlying theory of change more broadly (see Odell 2003, 166).

In my past work, I have identified global shifts in markets, power, and authority as important reasons (Schleifer 2016b, 2017). Building on and expanding this line of research, this book investigates the effectiveness of transnational business governance in a changing world economy. Going beyond traditional concerns with institutional effectiveness, my analysis is not limited to investigating the adoption and implementation of these programs. Instead, in the tradition of political economy research (Dauvergne and Clapp 2016), my ambition is to explore the broader environmental and institutional consequences of contemporary globalization in the agriculture sector. The following section synthesizes the book's argument and approach.

The Argument in Brief

In this book I argue that processes of contemporary globalization are changing the politics and governance of sustainability in major ways. My objective is to explore the environmental and institutional consequences of these processes in the case of commodity-driven deforestation. I do so with a focus on the palm oil and soy sectors, where transnational actors have become important providers of sustainability governance over the past two decades. Transnational business governance to address environmental and social problems in global supply chains emerged in the late twentieth century, a period during which the international economic system was dominated by North-South trade and the global economic predominance of the West. Countries in the Global South contained the factories, farms, and mines of the world. These industries supplied the raw materials and cheap goods for mass consumption and prosperity in the Global North. In an era of neoliberal globalization, these international economic relations were made possible by free trade policies, financialization, and innovations in transport and communication.

In the twenty-first century, this North-South division of labor in the world economy is ending due to an "irresistible shift in global power" (Mahbubani 2008). Accelerated by the world economic crisis of 2008, major political and economic forces are changing the international economic order as markets and supply chains shift toward rising countries in the Global South (Staritz, Gereffi, and Cattaneo 2011). In natural resource industries, these shifts in the global economic order were accompanied by a commodity supercycle, which, driven by demand from fast-growing emerging economies (Coxhead and Jayasuriya 2010), led to a massive increase in the volume of South-South trade in tropical commodities. To study these developments and their implications for the environment and the effectiveness of transnational business governance in the agriculture sector, this book broadens the scope of the analysis. I change the focus of inquiry from questions of institutional design and a narrow view on private regulation's environmental benefits to the shifting global political economy structures and processes in which cross-border sustainability governance takes place. I share this broader perspective with other scholars, such as those of the Rising Powers and Global Standards research network. However, while those scholars are mainly concerned with labor and social standards (Nadvi 2017), this book puts the focus on standards for environmental sustainability.

But to be clear, my point is not that institutional design does not matter. Rather, by drawing on research on international environmental regimes (Underdal 2008; Young 1999, 2002), scholars of transnational business governance have shown how the design of membership rules and enforcement mechanisms are important determinants of their effectiveness. These studies show theoretically and empirically how the sponsors of private governance schemes confront difficult trade-offs and design dilemmas that condition the outcomes and impacts of these programs (see Darnall, Ji, and Potoski 2017; Grabs 2020b; Kalfagianni and Pattberg 2011; Potoski and Prakash 2009; Prakash and Potoski 2006).

I also do not question the usefulness of impact research. To the contrary, geographers, economists, and rural sociologists assess on-the-ground impacts of certification schemes and companies' zero-deforestation commitments with increasing accuracy (e.g., Blackman, Goff, and Rivera Planter 2018; Carlson et al. 2017; Cattau, Marlier, and DeFries 2016; Heilmayr and Lambin 2016). Using geospatial analysis, farm-level surveys, and other research methods, they are making important progress in measuring the effects of these programs on various sustainability metrics, including conservation and livelihood effects (Garrett et al. 2021). In this way, these studies fill a gap in political science research, which has long struggled to measure on-the-ground-impacts (Gulbrandsen 2010, 180).

These literatures advance our understanding of transnational business governance in major ways. However, they tend to neglect the role played by broader political, economic, and historical forces in shaping regulatory institutions (Prakash and Potoski 2009, 286). More generally, the institutionalist perspective has long been criticized for overemphasizing the static and underemphasizing the dynamic elements of change in the world economy (Strange 1982). A similar criticism can be brought against the body of impact research, which so far has paid little attention to global political economy structures and processes. Conversely, scholars of political economy have long noted the importance of the macro political economic context in influencing the logic and operations of regulatory systems (Büthe and Mattli 2011). Therefore, my contention is that in a time of major structural change in the world economy, greater attention must be paid to newly powerful countries and actors, and to how their actions have environmental and institutional consequences (see Clapp and Helleiner 2012, 494–497).

But it is important to clarify that this does not imply that Global South actors are mainly responsible for the environmental externalities of agricultural trade. Historically, the system of industrial agriculture emerged in Europe and North America, and the modern world food system has deep roots in the colonial period (Clapp 2020, 29–66). For example, in the palm oil sector, it was Western companies, administrators, and scientists that drove the expansion of export-oriented clusters in the tropics (Giacomin 2018). It also is important to note that Global North countries and their demand for agricultural commodities continue to drive large-scale environmental destruction around the world. A recent study estimates that the European Union is still responsible for 16 percent of globally traded deforestation (Trase 2021). Mindful of these historical and present-day dynamics, my contention, nevertheless, is that in the current phase of globalization, newly powerful countries and actors and their role in the politics and governance of agricultural supply chains merit closer attention.

Ontologically, a political economy approach is best positioned to achieve this goal. Such an approach does not apply institutional boundaries as the defining parameters of the analysis of governance effectiveness. Likewise, the approach is not limited to the investigation of narrowly defined environmental benefits while ignoring history and political context. Instead, a political economy approach broadens the scope of the analysis by seeking to uncover the root causes of environmental degradation and assessing the dominant actors and modes of governance in light of these processes (Kütting 2005; Newell 2012, 34–60). Another important contribution of political economy scholarship to the study of global governance is the insight that actors' authority and power to govern are inextricably linked to the material and ideational structures that surround them (Phillips and Payne 2014).

Transnational business governance has been studied from different political economy perspectives, including those of international political economy (e.g., Clapp 2005; Fuchs and Kalfagianni 2010; Newell 2012), comparative political economy (e.g., Bartley 2018a; Cashore, Auld, and Newsom 2004; Espach 2009; Schleifer and Sun 2018), and global value chain analysis (e.g., De Marchi, Di Maria, and Micelli 2013; Ponte 2019; Poulsen, Ponte, and Lister 2016). Scholars also note the potential for these literatures to complement each other in important ways. Particularly in a time of major political and economic transformation, it would be helpful to revisit the structural foundations of transnational regulatory authority in the world economy, to comparatively study different sectoral and domestic political economies, and to map and analyze the reorganization and relocation of the industrial networks through which sustainability governance disseminates. However, as others note, it is a curious characteristic of political economy debates around this and other issues that the different branches in the field remain too disconnected (see Graz and Nölke 2008; Phillips 2005).

By bridging these divides, this book leverages the full spectrum of political economy analysis to interrogate the worsening ecological crisis in global agriculture despite unprecedented levels of transnational regulation. In doing so, it reveals a complex and evolving picture of both risks and opportunities for sustainability. Through the varied lenses of international political economy, comparative political economy, and global value chain scholarship, the empirical chapters of this book provide rich analyses of the politics and governance of agricultural supply chains in a changing world economy. In the remainder of this section, I synthesize the book's main findings.

At the level of environmental consequences, I show that the link between globalization and environmental degradation (see Christoff and Eckersley 2013; Newell 2012) remains strong in twenty-first-century agricultural trade. Since industrial agriculture began in Europe and North America, demand from rich countries has driven the expansion of export-oriented agriculture sectors in the global tropics. Recently, that demand has increasingly emanated from different places in the world economy (Kharas 2010). Fast-growing emerging economies fuel domestic consumption and the South-South trade of natural resources. In the agriculture sector, Global South markets increasingly replace Global North markets as the main consumers of major forest-risk commodities. The rise of South-South trade can offer opportunities for sustainable development (Bloomfield 2020; Jepson 2020), but it also entails risks for environmental and social conditions in the producing countries (Adolph, Quince, and Prakash 2017; Hochstetler 2012). In the sectors that are the focus of this book (palm oil and soy), the deforestation contained in the South-South trade of these commodities has increased substantially in recent years. There is mounting evidence that global market shifts result in additional demand for land, which is now a key driver of agricultural expansion and deforestation in countries like Brazil and Indonesia (Fearnside and Figueiredo 2015; Greenpeace 2012; Trase 2020b).

At the level of institutional consequences, I show how the existing system of transnational business governance is ill equipped to deal with the evolving crisis of commodity-driven deforestation. In the age of advanced globalization, private market-based governance is undermined by a growing incongruity between the location of "sustainable markets" (Meier et al. 2020) and the "new geography of trade" (UNCTAD 2004, 2). As we shall see, the regime complex for deforestation is evolving quickly as new governance actors enter the regulatory space. However, it has long been dominated by actors from the Global North, with a strong role for private governance. This can be traced back to the politics of late-twentieth-century globalization and reflects the efforts of entrepreneurial NGOs and companies in rich countries to re-embed agricultural supply chains in a regulatory framework (see Bartley 2007). The outsourcing of governance to nonstate actors in this period also was a conscious choice by public authorities to govern sustainability in a "global value chain world" (Mayer and Phillips 2017; see also Larsen et al. 2018). The regime complex for commodity-driven deforestation reflects these processes and decisions. In a globalized agrifood system, it is based on a pragmatic political settlement between Western governments, companies, and civil society organizations unable or unwilling to achieve more fundamental reforms (see McCarthy 2012). However, in the current context of advanced globalization, the regime's enduring focus on Global North markets undermines its regulatory effectiveness. Comparing the market uptake of two mature private governance schemes in the palm oil and soy sectors, I show how the political economy context of these programs has become less favorable over time, hindering their large-scale adoption. As the resulting gap in coverage persists, the environmental benefits of these programs will remain limited.

However, global economic shifts do not only affect existing institutions, they also empower Southern actors to create new ones. This has increased the degree of institutional fragmentation in the regime complex for commodity-driven deforestation, raising critical questions about the nature of interactions between Northern-led and Southern-led sustainability initiatives (see Eberlein et al. 2014). While Northern actors continue to dominate the agenda on sustainability in twenty-first-century agricultural trade, I find that Southern actors are increasingly powerful players in the "regulatory standards bargaining game" (Abbott and Snidal 2009, 70). In the age of advanced globalization, sustainability governance takes place in a context of polycentric trade, characterized by intersecting networks of North-South, South-South, and domestic supply chains (Horner and Nadvi 2018). Through exploring the politics of environmental upgrading in these multipolar production networks, I describe the formation of powerful regulatory coalitions on the supply side of forest-risk supply chains. Responding to transnational actors and their sustainability agendas, government and industry actors in major commodity producing countries, such as Brazil and Indonesia, have launched campaigns to renationalize regulation through the creation of national standards and certification regimes (Hospes 2014; Schouten and Bitzer 2015). In the palm oil and soy industries, these measures have taken place in a political climate characterized by increasing antagonism between domestic and transnational actors. However, the experience in other commodity sectors (e.g., tea and timber) shows that more complementary transnational interactions are possible (Langford 2019; Zeitlin and Overdevest 2021).

New regulatory coalitions for sustainable agricultural supply chains also are forming in Asia's fast-growing emerging economies. In China's state-led capitalist system, new policies on green supply chains are driven by parts of the political and bureaucratic elite. At the center of these efforts is the "Ecological Civilization" policy framework (Hanson 2019), which includes proposals for sustainable trade at the regional and global levels through the development of standards, procurement policies, and other arrangements for green supply chains. In India, progress has been slower but is not absent. Over the past decade, the Delhi-based Centre for Responsible Business has emerged as an important platform for policy dialogue and advocacy on issues of sustainable trade and supply chains in the country. There also is cooperation between Western and Chinese and Indian actors in the context of newly created emerging market-centered sustainability initiatives, such as the India Sustainable Palm Oil Coalition and the China-focused Sustainable Soy Trade Platform. While these are promising developments, regulatory coalitions that are powerful enough to steer these vast markets and their supply chains toward sustainable sourcing have yet to emerge.

As processes of contemporary globalization shape the politics and governance of agricultural production, trade, and consumption, what pathways are available to advance a sector-wide sustainability transformation? In the case of commodity-driven deforestation, the mainstream debate focuses on the creation of "smart policy mixes," which combine public and private, and demand- and supply-side measures (Lambin et al. 2018; Tropical Forest Alliance 2020). These include the development of new place-based governance programs in commodity-producing countries (Earth Innovation Institute 2018; Hovani et al. 2018). In developing a forward-looking research agenda, I explore the opportunities and challenges of these "jurisdictional programs," as they emerge in Brazil and Indonesia.

A new mode of Southern-led sustainability governance, jurisdictional programs broadly refer to place-based multistakeholder initiatives with jurisdiction-wide sustainable development goals (Hovani et al. 2018, 1). Moving beyond a narrow focus on zero-deforestation supply chains, jurisdictional programs pursue "sustainability at scale" (Earth Innovation Institute 2018). They aim to achieve this through a strong involvement of local government actors, the creation of public-private complementarities, and the integration of environmental with economic development and social inclusion objectives. Through strengthening governance systems in the producer countries, the approach has potential to advance sustainability objectives in a world of polycentric trade, in which regional and domestic markets are of growing importance. However, there are signs that transnational actors and local elites are compromising on a conservative version of the approach, in which marginalized groups remain excluded from decision making and economic concerns take precedence over environmental ones. Moreover, the private market-based governance instruments studied in this book are increasingly central to the jurisdictional approach, as practitioners try to deliver "global value propositions" to local stakeholders through mechanisms of "jurisdictional sourcing" and "jurisdictional certification" (Boshoven et al. 2021; RSPO 2021). If this trend prevails, the jurisdictional approach risks reifying their flawed theory of change.

A Note on Data and Methods

This book is based on research spanning the past decade. I started working on transnational business governance, agricultural supply chains, and commodity-driven deforestation in the context of a PhD thesis at the London School of Economics (2010–2014). The study of global market shifts and their implications for sustainability then became an important focus during a Jean Monnet Fellowship at the European University Institute. I have continued this line of research in my current position at the University of Amsterdam. Over this period, I have engaged in more than one hundred interviews and personal communications with key stakeholders in global agrifood governance, including firms along the supply chain, farmers, NGOs, trade unions, government agencies, international organizations, certification programs, and research organizations. Among those, forty-three interviews were conducted with stakeholders in the palm oil sector. Interviews were conducted in various formats (in-person, videocall, phone) and various locations, including during fieldwork in Indonesia (the world's leading exporter of palm oil) in 2018 and in India (the world's leading importer of palm oil) in 2015. A total of thirty-seven interviews targeted actors in the soy sector. With a focus on the stakeholders of the Roundtable on Responsible Soy, an initial round of interviews was carried out between 2012 and 2014. Additional interviews were conducted in 2019. The book also draws on insights from my research in the biofuel industry, which uses palm oil and soybean oil as important feedstocks. For this, a total of twenty-eight interviews were carried out between 2011 and 2014. The interviews were organized in a semistructured way and targeted key informants with first-hand knowledge of the themes researched in this book. Most interviews were recorded, transcribed, and analyzed with NVivo, qualitative data analysis software. The field research was carried out according to the guidelines of the Ethics Advisory Board of the University of Amsterdam to guarantee the highest standards in protecting vulnerable groups and the rights of the study participants. In addition to interview data, the book draws on field notes compiled during my attendance at numerous practitioner events over the years. This includes conferences and workshops organized by Greenpeace Indonesia, the Center for International Forestry Research, Bogor Agricultural University, the Roundtable on Sustainable Palm Oil, the Roundtable on Responsible Soy, ISEAL Alliance, Fern, Centre for Responsible Business in Delhi, the Trade for Sustainability Forum of the International Trade Centre, the United Nations Forum on Sustainability Standards, the European Commission, and the World Trade Forum. Moreover, webinars, such as those organized by the Jurisdictional Approaches Resource Hub of the Tropical Forest Alliance, have been a source of information.[9] In this book, I draw on this expertise, as well as archival material including hundreds of documents (e.g., meeting minutes and other organizational records), media reports, policy documents, as well as trade statistics and supply chain data.

In the empirical-analytical chapters, I examine and draw conclusions from this rich body of data. My analytical approach is best described as exploratory. Many aspects of contemporary globalization and its environmental and institutional consequences in global agriculture are not well explained by extant theories. This requires making induction an important element of the underlying research strategy (see George and Bennett 2005, 74). I combine this exploratory approach with deductive analysis in areas where theories of transnational business governance are sufficiently developed to define ex ante propositions. For example, in chapter 4 I study comparatively the uptake of private sustainability governance. To conduct the analysis in this and the other empirical chapters, I employ multiple methods, each linked to a different perspective of political economy analysis, which provide the theoretical framework for this book. In the tradition of international political economy scholarship, I use historical and structural analysis to examine the ways in which global political economy processes shape environmental and institutional outcomes. In addition, I employ a comparative political economy analysis to gain a more granular understanding of the ways in which market and nonmarket conditions, and changes therein over time, affect the uptake of private sustainability governance. Finally, informed by research on global value chains and global production networks, I trace sustainability governance within and through the palm oil value chain. To this end, I employ value chain mapping and analysis to study the geography, strategies, and interactions between governance actors in this production network.

Organization of the Book

This book is organized in three main parts. The first part, which includes this chapter, introduces the subject and develops the theoretical framework. Chapter 2 reviews the extant scholarship on the effectiveness of transnational business governance and shows how the dominant approaches neglect the ways in which global political economy structures and processes shape environmental and institutional outcomes. Notably, in this literature there has been little explicit theorizing of the role played by processes of contemporary globalization. Although political economists are attuned to these types of questions, the extant research does too little to integrate the different perspectives. To overcome this divide, chapter 2 describes how the international political economy, comparative political economy, and global value chain perspectives complement one another in important ways. By integrating them, the chapter develops a framework for analyzing political economy structures and processes at multiple levels.

The second part of the book consists of three empirical chapters that put this framework to work. Chapter 3 applies the lens of international political economy. Using a historical-structural approach, it explores the link between globalization and environmental degradation in the modern world food economy. Focusing on the problem of commodity-driven deforestation, it shows how this link remains strong in the early twenty-first century. By exploring the implications of contemporary globalization for sustainability governance, the chapter makes two main observations. First, the existing regime complex for forest-risk commodities has struggled to adapt to the new global context, as many of its established elements remain anchored in the world of late-twentieth-century trade. Second, global power shifts have contributed to further regime fragmentation, which undermines regulatory capacity. Switching the focus of analysis from the regime to the program level, chapter 4 examines the political economies of two mature private governance programs in the palm oil and soy sectors. It compares the political economy of each industry and analyzes how key demand-side and supply-side factors and variations in these conditions promote and hinder private governance uptake. Chapter 5 then investigates the dissemination of sustainability standards at the value chain level. It describes how agricultural commodity chains are becoming increasingly polycentric in their structure and multipolar in their governance. Tracing the main governance actors and their strategies and interactions along the Indonesian palm oil value chain, the chapter uncovers the reasons why governance actors are still struggling to implement sustainability standards in this production network.

The third part of the book develops a forward-looking research agenda. In response to calls for public-private policy mixes to reduce tropical deforestation (Lambin and Thorlakson 2018), chapter 6 considers new place-based governance approaches in the producer countries, which have received little attention in the scholarly literature thus far. From a political economy perspective, the chapter explores the opportunities and challenges of these jurisdictional programs, as they emerge in Brazil and Indonesia. The concluding chapter reviews the book's main findings, considers implications for practice, and identifies avenues for future research.

2 Varieties of Political Economy Analysis: A Framework

In the late twentieth century, there was a diffusion of transnational private regulatory authority in the world economy, as scholars observed (Cutler, Haufler, and Porter 1999a; Higgott, Underhill, and Bieler 2000; Strange 1996). Globalization, liberal environmentalism, and the political and economic predominance of the West provided a background against which firms and NGOs became central to the regulation of sustainability in global production. In the governance of forest-risk commodities, which is the empirical focus of this book, corporate self-regulation, civil society initiatives, and multistakeholder partnerships are cornerstones of an emerging transnational regime complex (Ludwig 2018).

In the early twenty-first century, the world economy is once again undergoing major structural changes. Globalization has entered a new phase, and the market power of the West is in relative decline (Mahbubani 2008; Pieterse 2012). These developments have many political and economic implications, which, with the system of global governance as a whole increasingly in flux, also raises crucial questions about the future of transnational actors in environmental governance (Hale 2020, 214–215). Surprisingly, however, until recently, little attention has been paid to the ways in which global power shifts affect the exercise of transnational business governance (Nadvi 2014).

This book aims to address this gap in two ways. First, on a theoretical level, it develops a framework centered on the changing global political economy context. This analytical focus is crucial to understanding the politics of sustainable trade in a time of global transformation and how it affects the ability of transnational actors to gain regulatory authority and to achieve environmental outcomes. Second, it examines these processes in a crucial case setting, commodity-driven deforestation. As described in chapter 1, the case of tropical deforestation is highly relevant to academic and societal debates about the role of corporate power and transnational actors in helping to overcome pressing global environmental problems.

In this chapter, I develop the book's theoretical contribution, beginning with an outline of what I take from the literature to be the two dominant lines of research on transnational business governance and its effectiveness. The first is institutionalist, which is rooted in the international relations and public policy literatures on environmental regimes and voluntary environmental programs. A main contribution of this literature is its exploration of the complex relationships that link institutional design to behavioral outcomes. The second perspective, which I call impact evaluation, consists of contributions from geographers, rural sociologists, economists, and development scholars. This literature examines the environmental benefits of private regulatory programs, such as certification schemes and corporate zero-deforestation commitments. This fast-growing body of literature has made important progress in quantifying the potential additionality and on-the-ground impacts of these programs. Both perspectives have greatly advanced understanding of questions of private governance effectiveness. However, I argue that both tend to neglect the broader processes that reshape the politics of sustainability governance in the current phase of globalization. Beyond traditional concerns with institutional effectiveness, this requires placing global political, economic, and historical structures and processes at the center of the analysis.

In this chapter, I show how a political economy approach is well positioned to address this gap. Going beyond traditional concerns with institutional effectiveness, scholars of international political economy and the environment study how large structural trends shape ecological problems and the institutions designed to govern them (Clapp and Fuchs 2009; Newell 2012). Scholars working with a comparative political economy methodology examine how different country and industry contexts shape private regulatory authority, as they promote or hinder the uptake and implementation of transnational business governance (Bartley 2018a; Cashore, Auld, and Newsom 2004; Espach 2009; Schleifer and Sun 2018). In addition, value chain scholars trace sustainability standards and environmental upgrading processes within global, regional, and local production networks (De Marchi, Di Maria, and Micelli 2013; Ponte 2019). I discuss how each of these strands offers important insights into the question at hand and how they

Varieties of Political Economy Analysis

must be combined to unlock the full potential of political economy analysis. To that end, this chapter integrates them into an overarching framework for analysis to guide the empirical research in subsequent chapters.

Beyond Traditional Concerns with Institutional Effectiveness

Early scholarship on transnational business governance focused on emergence and institutionalization (e.g., Auld 2014; Dashwood 2012; Green 2014; Hale and Held 2011; Pattberg 2005). Scholars of international relations also examine the democratic qualities of private governance institutions. In particular, the legitimacy, accountability, and transparency of multistakeholder initiatives has been researched in much detail (e.g., Bäckstrand 2006; Dingwerth 2007; Mena and Palazzo 2015; Schleifer 2019; Schleifer, Fiorini, and Auld 2019). Now that these once "new modes of governance" have become a fixture in global environmental politics, questions about their effectiveness have moved to the foreground of the academic debate. In the field of agrifood governance, a fast-growing multidisciplinary literature has focused on governance effectiveness (e.g., Carlson et al. 2017; Fuchs and Kalfaggiani 2012; Grabs 2020b; Lambin et al. 2018). My objective in this section is not to provide a systematic review of this literature. Instead, I outline what I identify to be the two dominant lines of research: the institutionalist perspective, which has roots in international relations and public policy, and the impact evaluation perspective, which involves contributions from geographers, sociologists, economists, and development scholars. After discussing their contributions and limitations, I turn my attention to political economy scholarship, which provides a perspective that goes beyond traditional concerns with institutional effectiveness.

The Institutionalist Perspective

In the 1990s and early 2000s, researchers in the field of international relations investigated the effectiveness of environmental regimes (e.g., Breitmeier, Young, and Zürn 2006; Miles et al. 2002; Mitchell 1994; Young 1999). This research focused on the "implicit or explicit principles, norms, rules, and decision-making procedures around which actors' expectations converge" in the area of environmental governance, such as formal multilateral environmental agreements (Krasner 1983, 2). Since then, there has been little new empirical research in this area, which Andresen (2013, 304) links, among other things, to a loss of momentum in multilateral environmental diplomacy.

This tapering of growth in the intergovernmental arena is in stark contrast to the proliferation of private and hybrid modes of governance (see Abbott, Green, and Keohane 2016; Reinsberg and Westerwinter 2019). In particular, private sustainability standards and certification schemes and public-private partnerships for sustainable development have grown substantially since the early 2000s (Pattberg et al. 2012; Schleifer, Fiorini, and Fransen 2019). In addition to research into the emergence and legitimacy of these arrangements, scholarship on their effectiveness has thrived (e.g., Auld 2010; Beisheim and Liese 2014; Dietz, Grabs, and Chong 2019; Gulbrandsen 2010; Marx and Cuypers 2010; Pattberg and Widerberg 2016; van der Ven, Rothacker, and Cashore 2018). Unsurprisingly, much of the work by international relations scholars draws (explicitly or implicitly) on the conceptual toolkit of the environmental regime literature.

A widely used conceptualization in the regime "effectiveness community" draws on Easton's (1965) theory of political systems and distinguishes between three dimensions of institutional effectiveness: output, outcome, and impact (Andresen 2013, 335). In this context, output relates to a regime's institutional design and capacity (e.g., the stringency of standards and enforcement procedures); outcome measures behavioral changes that can be attributed to a regime's activities; and impact concerns the extent to which a regime can solve the problem it was set up to deal with (e.g., a reduction in deforestation). Analytically, regime theorists treat output, outcome, and impact as distinct, consecutive steps in a causal chain of events, with each serving as a starting point for analyzing the subsequent step (Miles et al. 2002, 6).

Scholars of international relations study the effectiveness of new modes of governance using this and related conceptualizations (Fuchs and Kalfaggiani 2012; Pattberg and Widerberg 2016). In empirical studies, particular attention has been paid to arguments about institutional design and capacity (see Miles et al. 2002; Mitchell 1994), and multiple studies have identified the degree of institutionalization as an important determinant of effectiveness (see Beisheim and Campe 2012; Beisheim et al. 2014; Szulecki, Pattberg, and Biermann 2011). More elaborate analytical frameworks have sought to explain the outcomes and impacts of private governance organizations through the interplay of institutional design variables, institutional contexts, and problem structures (Kalfagianni and Pattberg 2011, 16; also see Pattberg and Widerberg 2016).

However, none of these frameworks in empirical research has been applied to the study of on-the-ground impacts (see Kalfagianni and Pattberg 2013, 125). This gap in the research reflects a broader shortcoming in the international regimes literature, which has long viewed impact indicators as "so demanding in terms of methodology that they are difficult to apply in empirical studies" (Andresen 2013, 310; also see Gulbrandsen 2010, 180). However, promising efforts aim to address this gap. For example, a recent study by Grabs (2020b) attempts to broaden the institutionalist perspective by including operational-level implementation practices in a rigorous quantitative analysis. In addition, as explained later in this chapter, advances in impact evaluation research may offer more precise assessments of on-the-ground environmental impacts of certification programs and other supply chain initiatives.

The public policy literature on voluntary environmental programs also subscribes to an institutionalist perspective (Prakash and Potoski 2006, 34–81). Voluntary programs, such as the certification programs studied in this book, induce firms to produce environmental benefits beyond legal requirements (Prakash and Potoski 2012, 3). More precisely, drawing on club theory (Coase 1960), Prakash and Potoski (2006) conceptualize voluntary programs as "green clubs" that firms join to gain reputational benefits. A central assumption of club theory is that the branding benefits from voluntary participation depend on the stringency of the program's standards and enforcement rules. External audiences (e.g., consumers, civil society actors, and regulators) use those standards as a proxy signal to determine the level of environmental benefit that is associated with program membership (Prakash and Potoski 2007, 7).

By modeling program design as an exogenous driver of program efficacy, club theory has greatly refined understanding of the links between institutional design choices and expected behavioral outcomes. In particular, this literature has identified important institutional design trade-offs and collective action dilemmas (also see Grabs 2020b, 58–70). For example, Prakash and Potoski (2006, 63) illustrate these trade-offs in a theoretical typology comprising four types of green clubs. First, "greenwashes" have lenient standards and weak enforcement rules but high membership levels due to low entry barriers; these clubs suffer from noncompliance. Second, "country clubs" have stringent standards but weak enforcement rules; these clubs have low membership levels due to high entry barriers, as well as problems with noncompliance. Third, "mandarins" have stringent standards and credible enforcement rules; these clubs have no problems with noncompliance but high entry barriers lead to adverse selection, as only high-performing firms will participate (see Lenox and Nash 2003). Finally, "bootcamps" are identified as the most promising program design. Over time, their lenient standards but credible enforcement rules are hypothesized to produce the highest level of aggregate behavioral change and thus environmental benefit.

More recently, voluntary program theorists have sought to explain variation in program design by studying different sponsorship arrangements, such as independent, government, and industry sponsors (Darnall, Ji, and Potoski 2017). However, a major criticism of the club theory approach is its tendency to treat program design as given and thus as exogenous to the analysis. Such simplifying assumptions have greatly advanced understanding of the causal relationships between institutional design features and expected behavioral outcomes. However, the downside is that the club theory approach leaves the ways in which private governance programs are shaped by their context and the political processes that led to their creation largely unexamined (see Auld 2014). As acknowledged by Prakash and Potoski (2009, 286), this critique applies to the institutionalist research program more broadly.

The Impact Evaluation Perspective

Beyond the fields of international relations and public policy, a fast-growing literature on impact evaluation unites contributions from geographers, rural sociologists, economists, and development scholars who use a wide range of research techniques (e.g., GIS data analysis, farm-level surveys, focus group discussions) to study on-the-ground impacts of transnational business governance. To date, the bulk of this work has focused on the livelihood effects of fair trade, organic, and generic sustainability certification schemes. In particular, many studies focus on the cocoa and coffee sectors (e.g., Akoyi and Maertens 2018; Barham et al. 2011; COSA 2013; Elder, Zerriffi, and Le Billon 2012; Schleifer and Sun 2020), two industries with the most mature certification programs. Two recent systematic reviews of this literature point to a positive, albeit weak and highly context-dependent, relationship between certification and farmers' livelihoods (DeFries et al.

2017; Oya, Schaefer, and Skalidou 2018). In addition to the assessment of livelihood effects, impact evaluation research is thriving in other areas, and there is a sizeable literature on conservation effects (Blackman and Naranjo 2012; Tscharntke et al. 2015).

Of particular relevance to this book is a flurry of recent studies seeking to assess the role of supply chain initiatives (including sectoral-level certification programs and company-level commitments) in reducing agricultural deforestation (Garrett et al. 2021; Lambin et al. 2018). The stated ambition of these scholars is to rigorously conceptualize, measure, and assess the effectiveness of zero-deforestation supply chain initiatives. The burgeoning literature in this area includes many ex ante theoretical and quantitative analyses of the potential additionality of supply chain initiatives, that is, the added environmental benefit of a program beyond a business-as-usual scenario (e.g., Garrett et al. 2016; Smith et al. 2019). Over the past decade, advances in remote-sensing technology and geospatial analysis have also enabled impact researchers to conduct ex post assessments of the biophysical effects of supply chain initiatives, including impact metrics on forest fire incidents, biodiversity loss, agricultural expansion, and deforestation rates. The most rigorous studies use carefully constructed counterfactuals, that is a comparison to a group or scenario in which the supply chain intervention was not present (e.g., Alix-Garcia and Gibbs 2017; Carlson et al. 2018; Gibbs et al. 2015).

However, the environmental impact evaluation literature has not yet produced conclusive results. Several studies find evidence of a positive environmental benefit, such as those that model potential additionality of mainstream certification programs. For example, as described in chapter 1, Smith et al. (2019) estimate that global compliance with the Bonsucro Production Standard, a certification scheme for sugarcane production, would reduce the greenhouse gas emissions of sugarcane cultivation by 51 percent, compared to a business-as-usual scenario. Other studies present evidence for on-the-ground biophysical impacts (Carlson et al. 2018; Cattau, Marlier, and DeFries 2016; Heilmayr and Lambin 2016). For instance, in a widely referenced study, Carlson et al. (2018) report that certification by the Roundtable on Sustainable Palm Oil (RSPO) reduced deforestation in Indonesia by 33 percent, relative to noncertified plantations. Based on their findings, Carlson et al. attest that the program has "great potential to influence tropical land cover change" (2018, 5). Another often cited success case is the Amazon Soy Moratorium, a buyer-driven regional moratorium on the trade of deforestation-linked soy. Studying the program's environmental impact, Gibbs et al. (2015) find that between 2004 and 2014, it reduced soy-related deforestation in the Amazon from 30 percent to about 1 percent.

In contrast, other scholars find no or only very limited evidence for the environmental benefits of supply chain initiatives (Anderson, Asner, and Lambin 2019; Blackman, Goff, and Rivera Planter 2018; Morgans et al. 2018; Panlasigui et al. 2018). Morgans et al. (2018) also assess the effectiveness of RSPO in Indonesia, and unlike Carlson et al. (2018), they find no significant difference between certified and noncertified plantations across a wide range of sustainability metrics. Likewise, in the case of the Amazon Soy Moratorium, West et al. (2020) estimate that the amount of total deforestation attributed to soy production is much higher than that reported by Gibbs et al. (2015).

These inconsistencies reflect the state of impact evaluation literature, which so far has produced mixed and inconclusive results (Oya, Schaefer, and Skalidou 2018). Differences in research design and methodology between studies contribute to this inconsistency, which is why leading scholars in the field call for more rigorous analysis, standardized criteria, and independent evaluations to counter these problems (DeFries et al. 2017). Responding to this call, scholars studying the effectiveness of corporate zero-deforestation commitments have been at the forefront of efforts to establish rigorous criteria for assessing the effectiveness of these programs (Garrett et al. 2019).

In sum, the literature on impact evaluation addresses a major shortcoming of the institutionalist perspective by addressing the methodological challenges of assessing on-the-ground impacts. It also offers important insight into the measures of environmental benefits of supply chain initiatives, and more rigorous analysis and better data will generate more robust results. However, the drive for high-quality data and analytical rigor may lead to a narrow focus. Conservation effects are estimated with increasing precision, but leading private governance programs have largely failed to realize their potential additionality, as the case of commodity-driven deforestation shows. The insights of impact evaluation point to institutional design flaws, insufficient adoption, and spillover effects as limiting factors (Garrett et al. 2019). Indeed, these are important proximate causes that undermine the effectiveness of supply chain initiatives to reduce tropical deforestation. However, such analysis falls short of assessing the deeper causes of environmental crisis and governance failure in the agri-food sector.

Toward a Multi-level Political Economy Analysis

Scholars of political economy and the environment have long sought to expose the deeper causes of ecological crisis, including economic globalization (Christoff and Eckersley 2013; Newell 2012), overconsumption (Dauvergne 2008), financialization (Baines and Hager 2021; Fairbairn 2015), contentious technologies (Falkner 2009; Neville 2021), and corporate power (Clapp and Fuchs 2009; Higgins and Lawrence 2005). In the tradition of this research, this book sets out to explore the consequences of major structural shifts in the world food economy. In the current phase of globalization, global economic shifts are transforming systems of production, trade, and consumption. This has far-reaching implications for global environmental change and global environmental governance. In the agrifood sector, these processes challenge deeply entrenched assumptions about North-South divisions in international trade, the structure and governance of supply chains, and the role of Southern actors in sustainability regulation. In the remainder of this chapter, I show how a multilevel political economy analysis can offer important insights into these processes and how this requires the overcoming of existing divides within this literature. Specifically, I discuss three varieties of political economy analysis (i.e., international political economy, comparative political economy, and global value chain analysis), with particular attention on writings on environmental sustainability and transnational business governance in the agrifood sector. Each strand offers important insights into the question at hand, and together they unlock the full potential of political economy analysis.

International Political Economy

The literature on international political economy and the environment addresses questions of ecological change, sustainable development, and governance in the context of globalization (Ramos 2020). Its analytical focus is on global political economy structures and processes and their underlying power relationships. Moving beyond regime theory's concentration on institutions, international political economists put global change processes at the center (Strange 1982, 1996). Such research has also studied the diffusion of private power in the world economy, uncovering its material and ideational foundations (Higgott, Underhill, and Bieler 2000). Moreover, scholars have used this perspective to study the environmental consequences of global change processes (Clapp and Helleiner 2012). In the following, I elaborate on how this line of research can help us answer the questions raised in this book.

International political economy research on private authority in global governance has a long lineage. In the late 1990s, Strange (1996, 44–65) argued that processes of globalization, financialization, and technological change had shifted the balance of power from public to private actors in the world economy, with transnational corporations increasing their influence in disproportionate ways. Since Strange's (1982, 1988, 1996) analysis, other scholars have examined these processes in relation to the role of nonstate actors in global governance. In the early days of the globalization debate, scholars asked whether "footloose corporations" would trigger a "race to the bottom" of social and environmental standards (Hart and Prakash 2000). Though dire predictions of an "eclipse of the state" (Evans 1997) or "corporations ruling the world" (Korton 1995) have not materialized, research has documented the pervasiveness of private authority in the global economy (Biersteker and Hall 2002; Cutler, Haufler, and Porter 1999a; Higgott, Underhill, and Bieler 2000). Over time, a complex picture has emerged. Instead of opposing global environmental governance per se, transnational corporations have supported certain policies and arrangements, and have increasingly acted as providers of environmental governance (Bartley 2018b; Meckling 2015). They have overcome past antagonisms and formed strategic partnerships with international organizations and civil society actors in the context of multistakeholder initiatives (Pattberg 2005; Utting and Zammit 2008).

Drawing on the works of Strange (1996) and Lukes (1974), Fuchs (2005, 785–789) links the diffusion of private authority in global governance to transnational corporations' increased structural power, a power that she argues is rooted in both material and ideational structures. More specifically, in the field of agrifood governance, Fuchs and Kalfagianni (2010) describe how transnational corporations' control over global supply chains grants them the power to impose their rules and norms on developing country suppliers. In a similar vein, van der Ven (2018) shows how retailers possess significant "gatekeeper power," which allows them to control the degree to which transnational sustainability standards gain market uptake in their production networks (also see Dauvergne and Lister 2010). Moreover, scholars see corporations' legitimacy to govern as constituted through dominant normative structures, such as liberal market norms, norms of consumer protection, and through perceptions of business actors as providers of technical expertise.

International political economy analysis has shown how, beyond institutional design considerations, these structures have become foundational to the effectiveness of private governance in global production (Fuchs 2007).

However, according to Fuchs (2005, 799), the "commanding heights" to which business has climbed in the world economy have unstable foundations. She describes how corporations' legitimacy to govern is constantly contested by countervailing societal forces and other factors, such as business conflict (see Falkner 2008). She also hypothesizes that shifts in global norms away from neoliberalism eventually could undermine private regulatory authority (Fuchs 2005, 796). Though much debated in the decade that followed the global financial crisis, such normative change has not materialized. If anything, transnational corporations have expanded their role as providers of global environmental governance (Bartley 2018b; Dauvergne and Lister 2012). The case of commodity-driven deforestation illustrates this well. As described in chapter 1, in the 2010s, there was a major push to leverage the power of global supply chain actors in this issue area. More generally, despite a major backlash against what Rodrik (2011) called hyperglobalization after the 2008 crisis, liberal market norms have proven to be astonishingly resilient (Schmidt and Thatcher 2013). Moreover, gridlock in many intergovernmental forums, particularly those pertaining to environmental issues, has led to more, not less, involvement by private actors in global governance (Hale and Held 2017). The normative foundations of private authority seem thus largely intact, though its material foundations are far more uncertain.

In the early twenty-first century, globalization has entered a new phase of development (Pieterse 2012). This has been accompanied by major economic shifts, including growth of consumption in middle-income countries (Guarín and Knorringa 2014), expansion of South-South trade (Shirotori and Molina 2009), and the growth of multinational corporations from emerging markets (Nölke 2014). These shifts have important implications for the location, organization, and governance of global industries. As shown in the empirical chapters of this book, in the agriculture sector, countries like China and India account for a rapidly growing proportion of the international trade in forest-risk commodities. Domestic consumption in the producer countries has also increased substantially. It is not difficult to see how this can exacerbate environmental problems and undermine existing modes of governance. Yet, as the above literature discussion has shown, these processes have been sidelined in research on the institutional effectiveness of transnational business governance. Surprisingly, they are also sidelined in the policy debate on commodity-driven deforestation. For example, at the Forest, Agriculture, and Commodity Trade Dialogue to Tackle Deforestation at the COP26 Climate Summit in 2021 in Glasgow, the role of South-South trade as a critical driver of tropical deforestation was hardly mentioned (United Nations Framework Convention on Climate Change 2021). By showing us the "big picture," international political economy analysis can add significantly to our understanding of global change processes and their broader environmental and institutional consequences (Clapp and Helleiner 2012). At the same time, this research lens alone is too broad to capture the politics of these processes with any precision. This requires closer analysis of the political economy contexts and industrial networks in which transnational business governance takes place.

Comparative Political Economy

A comparative political economy methodology can be used to analyze the country or sectoral contexts in which private governance programs operate (Bartley 2018a; Cashore, Auld, and Newsom 2004; Espach 2009; Schleifer and Sun 2018). The starting point for such an analysis is the observation that these programs do not exist in an institutional vacuum; rather, they operate in "crowded spaces" (Bartley 2018a, 45–47) full of institutions, actors, and political agendas. As a transborder phenomenon, this involves transnational as well as domestic spaces. Consequently, comparativists explore how variation in these contexts can hinder, promote, or distort the adoption and implementation of transnational business governance.

An important focus in this literature is how certain "scope conditions" influence the ways in which private governance programs gain, maintain, or lose regulatory authority in a given country or industry sector (Bloomfield and Schleifer 2017, 130). Regulatory authority is thereby understood as a program's legitimate decision-making power, which is granted or denied by its primary audiences (Cutler, Haufler, and Porter 1999b, 5). In the case of sustainability certification in the forestry sector, Cashore (2002) identifies as primary audiences a range of economic demand-side and supply-side actors, environmental groups, and government actors. He theorizes that a program's ability to gain rule-making authority in a sector depends crucially on the support of these actors. Studies examining these questions empirically focus on economic actors, using market uptake (e.g., the proportion of production that is certified to a sustainability standard) as an important indicator of economic actors' level of support (Bartley 2010; Cashore, Auld, and Newsom 2004; Espach 2005; Schleifer and Sun 2018). Market uptake is also considered to be a necessary, although not a sufficient, condition for the effectiveness of these programs. The logic here is that market-driven programs require broad market coverage to achieve sector-wide behavioral change, or what regime scholars refer to as "outcome effectiveness."[1] In this regard, impact evaluation scholars call for the large-scale adoption of voluntary sustainability standards and corporate zero-deforestation commitments to enhance their effectiveness (Carlson et al. 2018; Garrett et al. 2019; Smith et al. 2019). However, this literature fails to consider the political economy of these processes. It is here that the comparative perspective adds significant value to the analysis.

To explain the adoption of private governance programs, the literature has stressed important transnational factors, such as export dependency, transnational regulatory pressure, and social movement pressure. In their pioneering work on the rule-making authority of the Forest Stewardship Council, Cashore, Auld, and Newsom (2004, 41) were among the first to theorize the link between cross-regional variation in market uptake and differences in export dependency between timber-producing regions. The effect of export dependency on private governance uptake has been found to be strongest in its interaction with transnational regulatory pressure and social movement pressure. Regarding the former, my past work has shown how the uptake of the Bonsucro production standard in the Brazilian sugarcane industry was helped by sustainability regulation on biofuels in the European Union (EU) (Schleifer 2017, 13). Regarding the latter, Bartley (2007, 2009), among others, describes how social movements play key roles in getting firms to support private regulation. He argues that social movement pressure is a catalyzing force that can hardly be overstated (Bartley 2009, 130).

In the age of advanced globalization, some of the common wisdom of the early literature on transnational business governance needs to be revisited, however. Instead of strengthening support for transnational business governance, increased export dependency on low-standard jurisdictions could undermine incentives for producers to adopt sustainability standards (Adolph, Quince, and Prakash 2017). Relatedly, as the global market power of developed economies continues to decline, the strength of transnational regulatory pressures from these jurisdictions also is likely to decline. The reason is that developing countries become less dependent on these markets for their exports. This could reduce the effectiveness of using trade policy and supply chain regulation to influence environmental and social conditions in commodity-producing countries (see Schilling-Vacaflor and Lenschow 2021). Finally, transnational advocacy campaigns could lose efficacy as state-owned multinational corporations from emerging economies are less responsive to reputational pressures (Whelan and Muthuri 2015). Studies also show that civil society actors are generally less likely to target firms from remote and unfamiliar locations (Hatte and Koenig 2018).

In addition to transnational factors, research shows that transnational sustainability standards are "filtered, renegotiated, or compromised as they enter particular political economies" (Bartley 2018a, 27; also see Malets 2015). Important factors that can influence the local adoption of transnational standards are the regime type, domestic policy environment, and design and capacity of domestic institutions. In addition, studies show that it matters a great deal whether powerful domestic actors (e.g., government agencies, peak industry associations) are passive, supportive, or actively opposed to transnational business governance (Dermawan and Hospes 2018; Espach 2005; Marques and Eberlein 2020; Schleifer 2017). Drawing inductively on field research in China and Indonesia, Bartley (2018a, 61) hypothesizes that when transnational private governance and domestic governance clash, the latter will usually retain primacy.

This "grounding" of transnational business governance in domestic political economies has emerged as an important research theme in recent years (Graz 2021; Marques and Eberlein 2020; Sun 2022). However, a gap persists in the understanding of how structural shifts at the global level filter through and influence political dynamics at the domestic level. As countries and industries in the Global South become less dependent on consumer markets in the Global North, the political-strategic calculus of Southern actors vis-à-vis transnational business governance is likely to change. A comparative political economy approach allows examination of these dynamics and the political-institutional contexts that shape private regulatory authority across industries, countries, and time.

Global Value Chain Analysis

Scholars of transnational business governance often link its effectiveness to the ways in which sustainability standards disseminate through global value chains (GVCs). As previously mentioned, Fuchs and Kalfagianni (2010) describe how transnational corporations' control over global supply chains grants them the power to impose their rules and norms on their suppliers (also see Bartley 2018a, 47–52). Surprisingly, however, there has been little explicit theorizing in these writings about the supply chain "as a conduit for influencing the social and environmental conditions of production and consumption" (Bush et al. 2015, 13). Conversely, scholars of GVCs (Gereffi, Humphrey, and Sturgeon 2005) and global production networks (Henderson et al. 2002) have long neglected questions of environmental sustainability and the governance actors outside these networks. Realizing the potential for mutual learning and cross-fertilization, scholars from both sides have started to engage each other's work more systematically (Macdonald 2014; Partzsch 2020; Ponte 2019; Schleifer 2016b; van der Ven 2018). In this book, I continue this dialogue by integrating insights from transnational business governance and GVC research. To further understand how supply chains function as conduits of sustainability standards, and how the structure and governance of these networks is changing in the age of advanced globalization, I draw on recent advancements in the GVC literature on environmental upgrading (de Marchi et al. 2019), polycentric trade (Horner and Nadvi 2018), and multipolar governance (Ponte 2014; Ponte and Sturgeon 2014).

The term GVC describes "the full range of activities that firms and workers perform to bring a product from its conception to end use and beyond" (Gereffi and Fernandez-Stark 2016, 7). These activities include input provision, production, trade, processing, and retail, which are performed not by a single company but by networks of companies around the world (e.g., retailers, consumer goods manufacturers, traders, and suppliers). Providing an alternative to state-centered accounts of economic globalization, the GVC framework offers a distinct firm-centered perspective (Gibbon, Bair, and Ponte 2008, 317–319). In the 1990s, massive outsourcing of labor-intensive manufacturing to developing countries began to restructure entire industries, and sociologists and geographers began to study the changing organization and governance of these sectors,[2] specifically the role of (Northern) lead firms in governing GVCs and the resulting economic implications for developing country suppliers (Gereffi 1994).

Lead firms are particularly powerful companies with control over functionally important segments of a value chain. In his initial conceptualization, Gereffi (1994, 96–100) distinguished between two governance structures in value chains: buyer-driven and producer-driven. In the globalization debate, in particular buyer-driven value chains have received much scholarly attention. These are value chains in which large retailers or brand manufactures play pivotal roles in creating and governing decentralized production networks in a variety of exporting countries, typically located in the developing world. In contrast, producer-driven chains are dominated by powerful manufacturers. The automotive industry is a classic example of a producer-driven chain (Gereffi and Memedovic 2003). Later, Gereffi, Humphrey, and Sturgeon (2005) developed a more comprehensive framework comprising five principal modes of value chain governance: market, modular, relational, captive, and hierarchy. These ideal types differ in the degree of coordination and power asymmetry between lead firms and their suppliers. For example, in market value chains, suppliers have the capacity to make products with little input from lead firms, and transactions between suppliers and buyers occur through horizontal market exchanges. In contrast, captive value chains are characterized by explicit coordination and power asymmetries between lead firms and suppliers. Lead firms in these sectors exert a great deal of control as suppliers depend on their buying decisions. Gereffi, Humphrey, and Sturgeon (2005, 92–94) describe how agricultural value chains have moved from market coordination to explicit coordination through the power of large retail companies such as Tesco, Asda, and Sainsbury's.

Value chain research has been particularly concerned with the distributional and developmental implications of value chain structure and governance. At the center of this research is the concept of economic upgrading, which describes the multiple pathways through which suppliers in developing countries can "move up the value chain" to increase their economic gains (Ponte and Ewert 2009, 1638; also see Dolan and Humphrey 2000; Gereffi 1999). Over time, the research agenda on value chain upgrading has broadened to include processes of social upgrading, that is, improvements in the rights and entitlements of workers (Barrientos, Gereffi, and Rossi 2011; Riisgaard 2009).

More recently, this literature has also begun to consider environmental issues (De Marchi, Di Maria, and Micelli 2013; Khattak et al. 2015; Krishnan 2017; Ponte 2019; Poulsen, Ponte, and Lister 2016; Poulsen, Ponte, and Sornn-Friese 2018). In this regard, environmental upgrading refers to the "process by which economic actors move towards a production system that avoids or reduces environmental damage" (De Marchi, Di Maria, and Micelli 2013, 65). Environmental upgrading can take place through process improvements (e.g., making production more eco-efficient), product improvements (e.g., creating environmentally friendly product lines), and organizational improvements (e.g., enhancing organizational behavior through standards) (De Marchi et al. 2019, 313). Environmental upgrading research, initially focused on the role of powerful buyers as primary drivers of these processes (Jeppesen and Hansen 2004; Khattak and Stringer 2017; Poulsen, Ponte, and Lister 2016). For example, Poulsen, Ponte, and Lister (2016) link the effectiveness of "buyer-driven greening" to the structure of the value chain in an industry. They argue that environmental upgrading is more likely to occur in unipolar value chains where lead firms dominate the chain, especially if those firms are consumer-facing companies who face reputational risks.

However, the role of lead firms in greening global supply chains requires a critical reexamination for several reasons. One is that powerful lead firms have been shown to abuse their control over strategically important supply chain segments by shifting the costs of sustainability to producers while capitalizing on their green reputations. Ponte (2019, 16) calls this the "sustainability-driven supplier squeeze." Another reason is that the evolutionary dynamics of global capitalism are reconfiguring the structure and governance of value chains around the world, thus challenging the role of (Northern) lead firms as the only drivers of these processes.

In what Gereffi (2014) dubs the "post-Washington Consensus world," trade flows and value chain structures have become polycentric. Whereas trade in the late twentieth century was dominated by North-South value chains, in the early twenty-first century, global, regional, and domestic South-South value chains have gained importance (Horner 2016; Horner and Nadvi 2018; Langford 2021). This restructuring of supply chains around the world has also accelerated the evolution of value chain governance from unipolar to multipolar modes of governance. In contrast to unipolar value chains, multipolar value chains, as the term implies, are governed by multiple actors inside and outside these networks (Ponte 2014; Ponte and Sturgeon 2014). In addition to lead firms, these include government actors and NGOs. In the age of advanced globalization, they also include new governance actors from the Global South. Given the central role of the state in coordinating in many developing country economies, government actors in particular have assumed important roles in the governance of South-South value chain (Langford, Nadvi, Braun-Munzinger 2022). It is easy to see how these changes in the structure and governance of value chains influence processes of standard setting and standard-driven environmental upgrading within them. Value chain mapping and analysis offer insight into these processes and the evolving regulatory coalitions linked to different positions in global, regional, and local production networks. This is critical for understanding how the supply chain functions as a conduit for influencing the environmental conditions of production in the modern world economy.

A Framework for Analysis

The previous sections review relevant scholarship in the fields of international political economy, comparative political economy, and global value chain analysis, which can advance research on the politics and governance of sustainable trade in a changing world economy. However, as noted above, this research often emerges independently with too little exchange or cross-fertilization between scholars working in these fields. To advance and synthesize research in this area, this section combines these theoretical lenses in an overarching framework to guide the analysis. Based on multiple strands of political economy scholarship, this framework is purposively broad in scope. The goal is not to develop a middle-range theory to explain a narrowly defined set of output, outcome, or impact indicators (see Andresen 2013, 335). While political economy analysis can be used to fill gaps in the regime effectiveness and impact evaluation literatures by, for example, identifying the contextual conditions that drive private governance adoption, the ambition of this book is greater. In the tradition of critical political economy scholarship (Dauvergne and Clapp 2016), the goal is to develop a deeper understanding of contemporary globalization processes and their consequences for deforestation and the effectiveness of transnational governance in the world food economy.

To advance this research agenda, I integrate the three political economy perspectives reviewed above into a multilevel framework. In the empirical chapters of this book, this framework is used in a layered analysis, which focuses on relevant political economy structures and processes at the global, sector, and value chain level. Conducting the analysis in such a layered way, from the macro to the meso levels, provides a more comprehensive window into the environmental and institutional consequences of contemporary globalization in the agriculture sector than seen in previous studies.

To guide the investigation, the framework identifies salient research themes at these levels of analysis. These themes are formulated as questions, not hypotheses, which reflects the explorative nature of the research. However, this does not preclude the use of a more deductive approach in parts of the analysis where theory is sufficiently developed to formulate ex ante propositions (e.g., chapter 4). I summarize the three layers of the framework below (also see table 2.1). Grounded in the research methodologies of international political economy, comparative political economy, and value chain analysis, the framework also provides tools for the actual analysis.

At the *global level*, the framework explores the link between globalization and environmental degradation. It puts these processes into historical perspective and examines how the crisis of commodity-driven deforestation has deepened in the current phase of globalization. As explained above, the global shift in economic power is also believed to have major implications for governance, including the exercise of private regulatory authority. As

Table 2.1
A multilevel political economy analysis

	International political economy	Comparative political economy	Global value chain analysis
Level of analysis	Global	Sector	Value chain
Focus of analysis	Global economic shifts and their environmental and institutional consequences in the agrifood sector	The authority of transnational business governance across forest-risk commodity sectors and time	The evolving structure and governance of forest-risk supply chains and the implications for environmental upgrading
Guiding questions	What is the link between contemporary globalization and commodity-driven deforestation? How is the transnational regulatory regime adapting to global economic shifts? How is the regime's institutional fragmentation shaped by global power shifts?	What is the state of sustainable markets across agriculture sectors? How does the political economy context in forest-risk commodity sectors shape adoption rates? How have the scope conditions of transnational business governance evolved in the current phase of globalization?	How have global economic shifts shaped the structure of forest-risk supply chains? What are the main governance drivers? What are the implications for environmental upgrading in twenty-first-century supply chains?
Method	Structural-historical analysis	Comparative political economy analysis	Value chain mapping and value chain analysis

global markets for forest-risk commodities shift from North to South, how is the system of transnational business governance adapting? Relatedly, how are newly powerful actors from emerging economies reshaping the regime complex for forest-risk commodities? Through a structural-historical analysis the framework enables us tackle these "big picture" questions.

At the *sector level*, the framework allows for a closer analysis of the contextual conditions that shape the adoption of transnational business governance. As explained above, in the age of advanced globalization, global market shifts are likely to influence the ways in which export dependency, social movements pressure, transnational regulatory pressures, and other scope conditions shape the uptake of private governance programs in an industry. The lens of comparative political economy brings these factors into focus. It compares how the scope conditions of private market-driven governance have evolved across forest-risk commodity sectors and over time.

At the *value chain level*, the framework directs attention to the supply chain as the conduit through which environmental and social standards disseminate in global production. In the past, Northern lead firms used to be the main governance drivers of these processes. However, in the current phase of globalization, which is characterized by the rise of polycentric trade, a more complex picture is emerging. Against the background of global economic shifts, the framework uses value chain mapping and value chain analysis to explore in more depth the evolving structure and governance of forest-risk supply chains. This allows for a more comprehensive understanding of environmental upgrading processes in twenty-first-century supply chains and the politics and power relationships that underly these processes.

Conclusion

The modern world economy is undergoing major structural changes with far-reaching implications for power, governance, and environmental issues. In the agrifood sector, these shifts are transforming entire industries as these processes exert pressure on natural ecosystems and raise critical questions about systems of governance. Over the past decades, transnational business governance has become central to the regulation of sustainability in agriculture supply chains. However, in an age of advanced globalization, global power shifts and changes in production, trade, and consumption could erode the very foundations on which private regulatory authority is based.

These processes are also beginning to reshape the politics and governance of sustainability in more fundamental ways. Surprisingly, these dynamics have received little attention from the dominant lines of research, which tend to neglect the historical, political, and economic contexts from which transnational regulatory authority emerges and in which it is exercised. In this time of global transformation, such contexts require close investigation. To advance research in this area, this chapter develops a framework for analysis that integrates contributions from scholars of international political economy, comparative political economy, and global value analysis. Starting with the first layer, the global level, the next chapter puts this framework to work.

3 Global Shifts and the Zero-Deforestation Regime Complex

This chapter uses the lens of international political economy to examine how global shifts in markets and power are transforming the world food system and its governance. It shows how, in the age of advanced globalization, the "Tropical Oil Crop Revolution" (Byerlee, Falcon, and Naylor 2016) has entered a new phase of development. What are the consequences for agricultural expansion and deforestation in the global tropics? How is the emerging regime complex for commodity-driven deforestation adapting to the new geography of trade and consumption? Are rising power actors contesting its norms, rules, and procedures? To answer these questions, I proceed in three steps. First, I provide historical context on agricultural transformations, including exploring the link between globalization and environmental degradation, particularly as it relates to the rise of South-South trade and its role in tropical deforestation. Second, I shift the focus of analysis from environmental consequences to institutional consequences. With a focus on the palm oil and soy sectors, I map the emerging regime complex for commodity-driven deforestation and examine its coverage of Global South markets. Finally, I investigate how the regime's institutional fragmentation is shaped by contemporary globalization and the underlying power shift.

Transformations in Global Agriculture

Throughout history the agrifood system has undergone major transformations. Driven by technological, political, and economic changes, these processes often had wide-ranging societal and ecological consequences. In the nineteenth century, the technological progress ushered in by the industrial revolution made it possible to work the land much more effectively. The invention of the steel plow and consequent industrial-scale production allowed farmers in the American Great Plains to bring millions of hectares of new agricultural land into productive use. The resulting increase in food production played an important role in the economic development of the still young nation. However, there were unintended consequences. The massive expansion of plow agriculture led to large-scale soil erosion in the Great Plains area. In the 1930s, during a period of extended drought, the loose topsoil was turned into dust. The result was gigantic dust storms, so-called black blizzards, which buried entire towns and destroyed the livelihoods of hundreds of thousands of people (Worster 2004). Famously described in John Steinbeck's classic novel *The Grapes of Wrath*, the "American Dust Bowl" was one of the great manmade ecological disasters in North America.

In the twentieth century, the "Green Revolution" fundamentally transformed agricultural production—this time in the developing world. Beginning in the 1960s, Western governments established large-scale agricultural support programs to supply farmers in Asia, Latin America, and Africa with high-yield seed varieties, fertilizers, and agrochemicals. The political objective was to reduce developing countries' dependency on food imports and thus curb the global influence of the Soviet Union. According to William Gaud, former director of the US Agency for International Development, the peaceful Green Revolution aimed to end the violent Red Revolution (Gaud 1968). The result was a period of unprecedented growth in global agriculture. From 1965 to 1985, the size of wheat fields and rice paddies in South America and South Asia (the two main regions and crops targeted) increased by 16 million hectares and 8.5 million hectares, respectively (analysis of data from FAOSTAT). Historically, the scale of this land use change was unprecedented. In terms of stimulating output, the Green Revolution was a great success; however, these gains came at significant environmental and social costs. Analyzing the Green Revolution in India, Shiva (2016) describes decreasing groundwater levels and large-scale soil erosion due to monocropping, irrigation, and widespread use of pesticides. In addition, the replacement of traditional farming systems with industrial agriculture led to rising inequalities and social conflict in the Punjab and other regions. In many ways, the Green Revolution was neither peaceful nor successful.

As described in chapter 1, in the late twentieth century, global agriculture underwent yet another major transformation, the Tropical Oil Crop Revolution. According to Byerlee, Falcon, and Naylor (2016, 7), between

1991 and 2013, the total land area for soybeans in South America and oil palm in southeastern Asia increased by 54 million hectares and 12 million hectares, respectively. The environmental consequences of this expansion are severe. Modern industrial agriculture is the single most important driver of tropical deforestation and biodiversity loss on the planet (Curtis et al. 2018). Between 1980 and 2000, over 50 percent of new agricultural land in the tropics came from clearing intact forests (Gibbs et al. 2010). To understand the Tropical Oil Crop Revolution, we must consider the economic context, because, unlike in the Green Revolution, a new factor played a key role in driving this transformation: economic globalization.

International trade in agricultural commodities has always been restricted. Many countries continue to shield their markets from foreign competition through tariffs, quotas, subsidies, and other trade barriers. Until the rise of neoliberalism in the 1980s, which liberalized trade in the sector, agricultural commodities were largely exempted from free trade rules. Developed countries with highly subsidized agriculture sectors resisted pressure to include agriculture in the Uruguay Round of the General Agreement on Tariffs and Trade (1986–1994). Nevertheless, pressure mounted. In the mid-1980s, the Cairns Group of Fair Trading Nations, an Australia-led coalition of countries with large export-oriented agricultural sectors, spearheaded an effort to include agriculture in the negotiations.[1] The result was the inclusion of an Agreement on Agriculture in the treaties of the newly formed World Trade Organization (WTO). Though criticized for its unevenness, the agreement helped to liberalize international agricultural trade (Clapp 2020, 57–90).

These global-level measures were accompanied by measures at the national level. In the 1980s and 1990s, many countries slashed their import and export taxes for agricultural products, especially tropical commodities (Byerlee, Falcon, and Naylor 2016, 8). The reduced trade barriers helped globalize these sectors further by allowing retailers and consumer goods companies to massively expand their global supply chains and to source their agricultural raw materials more cheaply from foreign producers. The liberalization of the agriculture sector was accompanied by a commodity supercycle in the 2000s (Coxhead and Jayasuriya 2010). Driven by rising demand from emerging economies, this led to a strong increase in international agricultural trade. WTO statistics reveal that between 1990 and 2020 trade in the sector more than tripled in export value from US$442 billion to US$1.492 trillion (analysis of data from FAOSTAT). As we shall see later in the chapter, with high export ratios, tropical commodities like palm oil and soy accounted for a significant proportion of this increase.

In addition to trade liberalization, a range of other factors contributed to the Tropical Oil Crop Revolution. In the producer countries, technological innovation and government policy favoring agricultural expansion and export-led growth were important factors. New crop varieties, farming methods, agrochemicals, and genetically modified organisms greatly increased productivity. Government policy in Brazil and other commodity-producing countries favored the formation of large industrial conglomerates and provided agribusiness companies with cheap public land for expansion (Schnepf, Dohlman, and Bolling 2001). In an analysis of the state's role in the formation of the palm oil industry in southeastern Asia, Cramb and McCarthy (2016b, 27–77) describe how a coalition of political, bureaucratic, and business elites in Indonesia and Malaysia drove the transformation of traditional farming systems into export-oriented industries. This export-driven development strategy was supported by loans from the World Bank and other international donors.

In the consumer countries, again facilitated by trade liberalization, the expansion of markets for tropical oil crops was an important factor. For a long time, this demand was concentrated in Europe and North America. For example, biofuel consumption in the Global North contributed to agricultural expansion in the Global South. This consumption accelerated in the early 2000s, when the EU launched the ambitious Renewable Energy Directive, including a 10 percent biofuel target for its transport sector (EU Commission 2006, 2007; European Union 2009).[2] Due to shortages in the local supply, there was high demand for so-called energy crops from foreign producers. Imports contributed to European biofuel production from the beginning. It is estimated that over 50 percent of the imported palm oil from southeastern Asia is for biofuel (Transport and Environment 2020). Only recently has the EU taken steps to end this practice and phase out the use of palm oil–based biofuels (Bloomberg 2019b). Policymakers also have called for reductions in Europe's consumption of other forest-risk commodities, including soy. If implemented, these policies could help address Europe's "imported deforestation problem" (Duboua-Lorsch 2020). At the same time, these measures likely will accelerate the growing importance of Global South markets in the trade in forest-risk commodities.

South-South Trade and the Tropical Commodity Boom

Scholars argue that twenty-first-century globalization is markedly different from twentieth-century globalization (Pieterse 2012). A defining characteristic of the contemporary period is what the United Nations Conference on Trade and Development calls the "new geography of trade" (UNCTAD 2004). In a close look at the phenomenon, Horner and Nadvi (2018) argue that the previous dominance of North-South trade has been replaced by polycentric trade characterized by strong South-South interactions as trade flows between developing countries have gained size and significance. They further identify three major interrelated trends: (1) increased global exports from the Global South; (2) rapidly growing consumption in emerging economies; and (3) a shifting of trade flows from South-North to South-South as goods flow increasingly polycentrically within global, regional, and domestic channels. These global economic shifts have important ramifications for the distribution of power, authority, and sustainability in the world economy. They have overall effects, but different sectors are affected differently, often with significant variation even within the same sector.

The United States and the EU have long dominated international agricultural trade, and they remain the world's largest exporters and importers of agricultural products today. However, trade statistics show that their market power in the world food economy has declined. On the supply side, the developing country members of the Cairns Group, plus China and India, have significantly expanded their export-oriented agricultural sectors since the creation of the WTO.[3] From 1995 to 2020, the combined value of their exports grew from US$89 billion to US$390 billion. Today, a quarter (26 percent in 2020) of global agricultural exports (in value terms) originate from these countries (analysis of data from FAOSTAT). Projections of the UN Food and Agriculture Organization (FAO) suggest that this trend will continue. To feed the rapidly growing populations in the Global South, the FAO estimates that world cereal production will have to grow by 904 million tons (46 percent) and meat production by almost 200 million tons (76 percent) by 2050. Developing countries are projected to produce about 90 percent of this increase in global agricultural output, raising their collective share of global production to 74 percent by 2050 (Alexandratos and Bruinsma 2012, 95–96). A similar trend can be observed on the demand side. In particular, Brazil, Russia, India, China, and South Africa, known as the BRICS economies (see O'Neil 2001), have increased their imports of agricultural raw materials. Whereas these economies accounted for only 11 percent (US$52 billion in value terms) of global agricultural imports in 1995, this figure rose to 17 percent (US$258 billion in value terms) in 2020. In the same period, the combined share of US and EU global agricultural imports (exclusive of intra-EU trade) fell from 22 percent to 18 percent (analysis of data from FAOSTAT).

As part of a broader change process in the world economy, these figures reveal a steady shift in agricultural trade flows from North-North and North-South to South-South. However, in interpreting these trends, it is important to note that these data are highly aggregated, stemming from trade in all agricultural products. This aggregation obscures significant shifts in individual agricultural sectors. For example, developed economies are still the largest importers of cocoa and coffee, but trade flows have shifted dramatically in other commodity sectors. Since the turn of the millennium, particularly, the forest-risk commodities of palm oil and soy have seen a strong increase in the volume of South-South trade (see figure 3.1). This suggests that in the age of advanced globalization, the Tropical Oil Crop Revolution has entered a new phase, in which Global South markets are increasingly replacing Global North markets as the main drivers of further growth and expansion.

As examined in more detail in chapter 4, China and India in particular have massively expanded their consumption of these commodities. With an import volume of 100 million tons in 2020 (58 percent of total global imports), China is by far the largest buyer of internationally traded soy, and Brazil is its largest individual supplier. The speed of this global market shift is remarkable. The Brazil-China soy trade had a volume of only 6.2 million tons in 2003, which rose to 61 million tons in 2020 (+884 percent). In the palm oil sector, India now tops the list of the world's largest international buyers. In 2019, it imported 20 percent (9.7 million tons) of the globally traded palm oil. The Indonesia-India palm oil trade accounts for most of it. Between 2001 and 2019 it grew from 1.3 million tons to 4.9 million tons (+277 percent). China also has high demand for palm oil, importing 7.6 million tons in 2019 (analysis of data from International Trade Centre [ITC] n.d.). Often overlooked by analysts, domestic markets are another important source of consumption. In Brazil, 27 percent of soybean production is consumed domestically (Chain Reaction Research 2018a). In Indonesia, the introduction of a new government-mandated biofuel blend in 2019 increased domestic palm oil consumption to one-third of total production (Trase 2019).

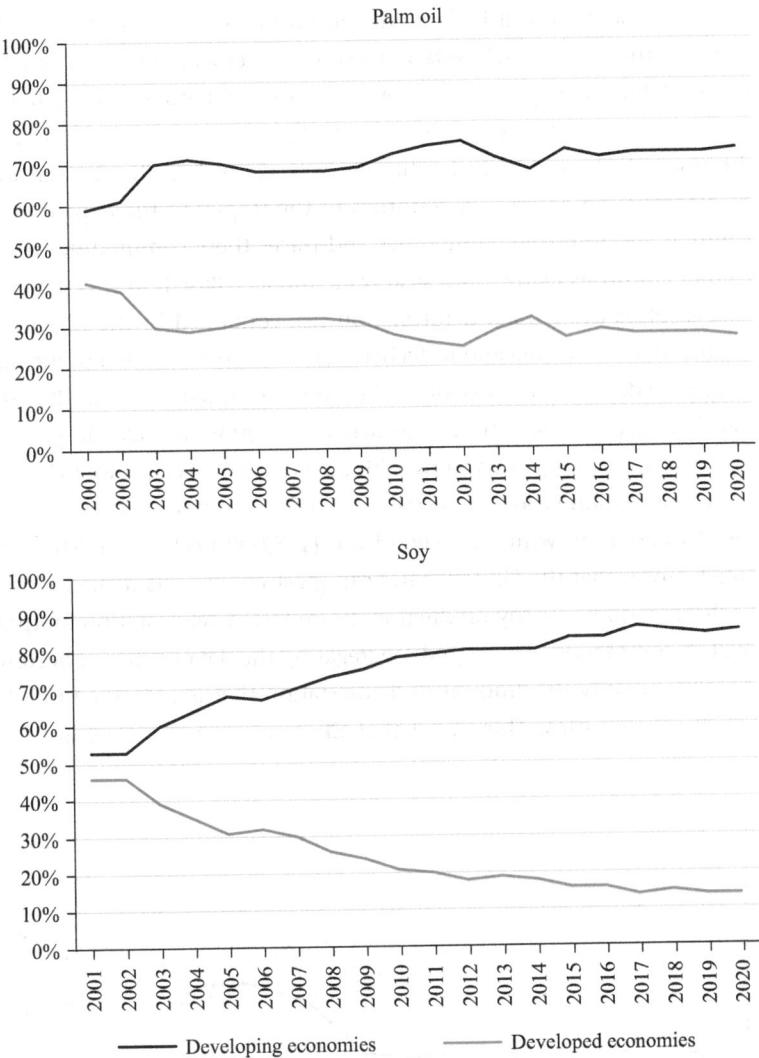

Figure 3.1
Share of global imports (in value terms)
Source: Analysis of data from ITC International Trade Statistics, https://www.intracen.org/itc/market-info-tools/trade-statistics/

A new dataset by Pendrill, Persson, and Kastner (2020) makes it possible to quantify the tropical deforestation risk that is embodied in the trade of agricultural and forestry commodities, including palm oil and soy. Analysis of this data reveals how the above-described global market shift has major environmental consequences in the producer countries. The dataset attributes deforestation across 135 countries in the tropics to the expansion of agricultural and forestry commodities and traces these commodities to the consumer countries using a physical trade model.[4] Based on this data, figure 3.2 displays the annual deforestation risk contained in the imports of palm oil and soy by China and India between 2005 and 2017. It also includes the imported deforestation risk of the EU and the United States for the same period. The figure shows how, in the 2010s, deforestation linked to palm oil and soy was increasingly driven by Chinese (174,000 hectares in 2017) and Indian consumption (106,000 hectares in 2017). Conversely, the rate of EU-driven deforestation, while still significant (118,000 hectares in 2017), has declined. Given that the United States can meet much of its demand for oil crops through domestic soy production, its imported deforestation footprint is small in comparison. Through disaggregating the data further, it becomes possible to quantify the amount of deforestation that is contained in bilateral trade relationships. This shows that Chinese soy imports are linked to

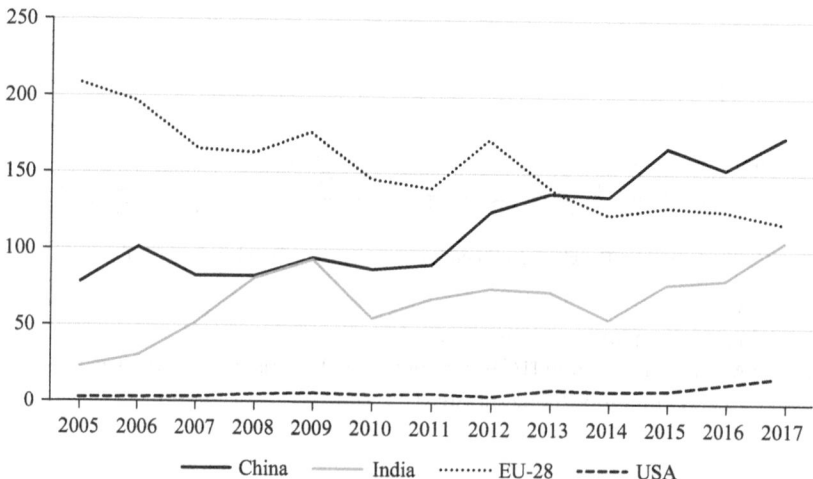

Figure 3.2
Tropical deforestation linked to imports of palm oil and soy (thousand hectares)
Source: Analysis of data from Pendrill, Persson, and Kastner (2020)

837,000 hectares of deforestation in Brazil in the period between 2005 and 2017. For the same period, Chinese and Indian consumption of palm oil is associated with 496,000 hectares and 786,000 hectares of deforestation in Indonesia, respectively. Together, this amounts to 2.1 million hectares of China- and India-driven deforestation in Brazil and Indonesia.

For the problem of tropical deforestation, these data show that the link between globalization and environmental degradation (see Christoff and Eckersley 2013; Newell 2012), remains strong in the twenty-first century, with markets in developing countries increasingly replacing those in developed countries as the main drivers of these processes. To study the implications of these developments for transnational business governance and the wider tropical deforestation regime, the next sections shift the focus of analysis from environmental to institutional consequences.

The Zero-Deforestation Regime Complex

Initially lagging behind other industries in the development of sustainability standards and implementation mechanisms (see World Bank 2004), the agriculture sector has emerged as one of the most dynamic sites of transnational business governance in recent years. As described in chapter 1, particularly, the problem of commodity-driven deforestation has led to substantial action by business and civil-society actors to regulate deforestation risks in agricultural supply chains. In the absence of a focal intergovernmental institution, however, the emerging global governance landscape is fragmented, and scholars are only beginning to explore the evolving institutional complexity in this policy domain (see Brandi 2021; Ludwig 2018; Overdevest and Zeitlin 2014; Pacheco et al. 2018; Rodríguez Fernández-Blanco, Burns, and Giessen 2019).

Transnational governance research examines institutional complexity using various conceptual lenses and at multiple levels of analysis (Eberlein et al. 2014). Areas of research include interactions between actors within transnational schemes (e.g., Boström and Hallström 2010; Schleifer 2016a), the nature of interorganizational ties (e.g., Fransen, Schalk, and Auld 2016), and the properties of organizational populations (e.g., Schleifer, Fiorini, and Fransen 2019). Moreover, at the macro level of analysis, so-called architectural approaches examine "the overall institutional setting in which distinct institutions exist and interact" (Biermann et al. 2009, 17). Scholarship on regime complexes (Keohane and Victor 2011; Mera-Gomez, Morin, and

Van de Graaf 2020; Orsini 2013), global governance architectures (Biermann et al. 2009; Zelli and van Asselt 2013), polycentric governance (Jordan et al. 2018), and experimentalist governance (Overdevest and Zeitlin 2014; Zeitlin and Overdevest 2021) falls into this category.[5] With a focus on the macro level, this chapter uses the concept of a "transnational regime complex" (Abbott 2012b) to map the loosely coupled set of public and private regulatory institutions that aim to reduce deforestation within agricultural supply chains. The concept of a transnational regime complex derives from regime complex theory (Keohane and Victor 2011; Mera-Gomez, Morin, and Van de Graaf 2020; Orsini, Morin, and Young 2013; Raustiala and Victor 2004) and has been used to emphasize the increasing importance of private authority in this context (Green and Auld 2017).

The Mapping

To map the emerging regime complex for forest-risk commodities, a simple two-dimensional framework is used. Borrowing from Abbott and Snidal's (2009) famous "governance triangle," the first dimension distinguishes between different sponsorship arrangements (i.e., state-led, hybrid, and private-led). This categorization helps establish the relative importance of public and private modes of governance in the overall regime. Departing from Abbott and Snidal's framework, the second dimension accounts for governance actors linked to different positions in global commodity chains by distinguishing between schemes that are primarily demand-side driven, such as by buyers, NGOs, or government actors from consumer countries, and those that are primarily supply-side driven, such as by producers, NGOs, or governments from producer countries. This separation allows for a systematic assessment of the evolving interactions between Northern and Southern regulatory schemes. In addition, a category for collaborative or multilateral schemes includes both demand-side and supply-side actors.

The scope of the mapping is delineated as follows. First, the mapping focuses on the collective of governance arrangements that aim to address problems of deforestation in agricultural supply chains, such as voluntary and mandatory regulatory programs, high-level commitments, principles, and frameworks, as well as instruments and forums for policy coordination. Second, the mapping focuses on the transnational level—that is, its focus is on governance arrangements aimed at moving actors' behavior toward a shared goal in at least two countries (see Roger and Dauvergne

2016, 416). Legislation by consumer or producer countries is included here only if it has a transnational scope.[6] Due to their large number, corporations' zero-deforestation commitments are not included individually but as a group. Third, in terms of the sectoral and geographic scope, the mapping focuses on the palm oil and soy sectors (the analytical focus of this book) and the major producers and consumers of these commodities. Fourth, to capture the proliferation of governance schemes over time, three time periods are selected for the descriptive analysis: pre-2010, 2010–2020, and post-2020 (the 2010 zero-deforestation pledge of the Consumer Goods Forum and its 2020 target mark important moment in the regime's development). Finally, to conduct the mapping, data from different sources are used, including information sourced from public databases, such as the Sustainability Map of the International Trade Centre.[7] Additional information is obtained through a review of policy reports, academic research, communications with practitioners, and extended internet searches.

As shown in table 3.1, the mapping identified a total of fifty-three sustainability governance schemes and groups of schemes active in the palm oil and soy sectors. Whereas the pre-2010 regime consisted of only fifteen schemes, this number increased to forty-eight schemes or groups of schemes by 2020. This includes 339 and 104 corporate zero-deforestation commitments for palm oil and soy, respectively (Supply Change 2020b). Between 2020 and (April) 2022, another five new governance initiatives were established, bringing the known universe of schemes to fifty-three. The results show that the emerging governance architecture in these sectors closely fits the concept of a transnational regime complex (see Abbott 2012a; Green and Auld 2017). There is no integrated intergovernmental institution; instead, the regulatory space is populated by a multitude of loosely coupled public and private governance arrangements.

The Transnational Regulatory Space

When considering the two dimensions of the framework (sponsorship and position in global commodity chains), three features of the emerging regime stand out. First, privately sponsored schemes from the Global North dominate. Second, the overall regime is strongly demand-side driven, but supply-side actors from the Global South have become more active providers of sustainability governance in recent years. Third, while multilateral institutions remain weak, unilateral government-led regulation has

Table 3.1
List of governance schemes mapped

Zone	Abbreviation	Name	Founding Year
1	ADP	Amsterdam Declarations Partnership	2015
	EU-RED	EU Renewable Energy Directive	2009
	EU-SCRRD	EU Supply Chain Regulation to Reduce Deforestation	2024 (expected)
	GSCA	German Supply Chain Act	2023 (expected)
	UK EA	UK Environment Act	2021
	SNDI	French National Strategy against Imported Deforestation	2018
2	GCF	Governors Climate and Forest Task Force	2008
	GLDFL	Glasgow Leaders Declaration on Forests and Land Use	2021
	REDD+	Reducing Emissions from Deforestation and Forest Degradation	2009
	UNSDG 15.2	UN Sustainable Development Goal 15.2	2015
3	CPOCP	Council of Palm Oil Producing Countries	2015
	ISPO	Indonesian Sustainable Palm Oil	2011
	LTKL	Indonesia Sustainable Districts Platform	2017
4	IDH-VSAs	IDH Verified Sourcing Areas (multiple)	since 2018
	TFA	Tropical Forest Alliance	2012
5	EU-BR PSS	EU-Brazil Partnership for Sustainable Soy	2017
	GGP	Good Growth Partnership	2017
	NYDF	New York Declaration on Forests	2014
	SPOI	Sustainable Palm Oil Initiative	2012
6	JPs	Jurisdictional programs (25–39 programs)[a]	since 2009
	MSPO	Malaysian Sustainable Palm Oil	2014
7	AFI	Accountability Framework Initiative	2019
	BCRSP	Basel Criteria for Responsible Soy Production	2004
	CGF-ZDP	Consumer Goods Forum Zero Net Deforestation Pledge	2010
	CSPOA	China Sustainable Palm Oil Alliance	2018
	EPOA	European Palm Oil Alliance	2016
	FEFAC-SSG	European Feed Manufacturers Soy Sourcing Guidelines	2015
	FPCA	Forest Positive Coalition of Action	2019
	ISPOC	India Sustainable Palm Oil Coalition	2018
	IPOP	Indonesia Sustainable Palm Oil Pledge	2015 (dissolved)
	ISCC	International Sustainability and Carbon Certification	2007
	PF	Proterra Foundation	2006
	POIG	Palm Oil Innovation Group	2013
	RA	Rainforest Alliance	1987
	RC	Rimba Collective	2021
	RSB	Roundtable on Sustainable Biomaterial	2008
	RSG	Retail Soy Group	2013
	RSPO	Roundtable on Sustainable Palm Oil	2004
	RTRS	Roundtable on Responsible Soy	2006
	SCC	Soft Commodities Compact	2014
	SCF	Soft Commodities Forum	2019
	SSTP	Sustainable Soy Trade Platform	2015
	TSC	The Sustainability Consortium	2009
	UK-RSSP	UK Roundtable on Sourcing Sustainable Palm Oil	2012

Table 3.1
(continued)

Zone	Abbreviation	Name	Founding Year
	WWF-FCI	WWF Forest Conversion Initiative	2001
	ZDCs	Zero Deforestation Commitments (338 in palm oil, 104 in soy)[b]	since 2010
8	ASM	Amazon Soy Moratorium	2006
	CM	Cerrado Manifesto	2017
	SASPO	Singapore Alliance for Sustainable Palm Oil	2016
9	ISPOF	India Sustainable Palm Oil Framework	2017
	SPB	Soy Platform Brazil	2004
	SPOM	Sustainable Palm Oil Manifesto	2014
	SPP	Soja Plus Program	2011

[a] See von Essen and Lambin (2021) and Stickler et al. (2018).
[b] See Supply Change (2020b).

increased recently on both the demand and supply sides. Below, I describe the emerging regime and its salient features in more detail, and follow that by inquiring into its adaptation to global market shifts. Figures 3.3 and 3.4 in this section illustrate these patterns and trends.

Originating in the politics of late-twentieth-century globalization, transnational business governance flourished under the Western-led liberal international order. Beginning in the early 1990s, firms and NGOs from the Global North began to construct transnational, often private, modes of governance to re-embed globalizing industries in a regulatory framework (see Bartley 2007). Driven by the neoliberal zeitgeist, governments actively pursued the outsourcing of sustainability governance to regulate the "global value chain world" (see Mayer and Phillips 2017; Ponte 2019). The regime complex for forest-risk commodities reflects these processes and decisions. In an increasingly globalized agrifood system, this regime is the outcome of a pragmatic political settlement between governments, companies, and a civil society unwilling or unable to achieve more fundamental reforms (see McCarthy 2012).

As shown in figure 3.3, zone 7 (demand side-driven private governance) is the most densely populated. Most of the schemes in zone 7 were created by loose coalitions of Northern NGOs, buyers, and banks, often directly and indirectly supported by Western governments and international organizations. The WWF, the world's largest environmental NGO, participates in more than a dozen of the private schemes mapped above, many of which it helped to create. Examples are the Accountability Framework Initiative, the

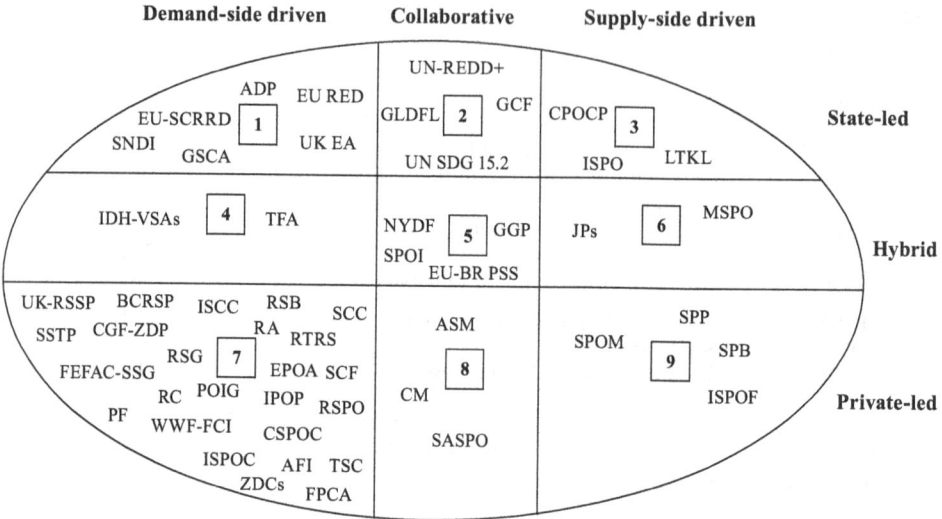

Figure 3.3
The regime complex for forest-risk commodities (palm oil and soy)

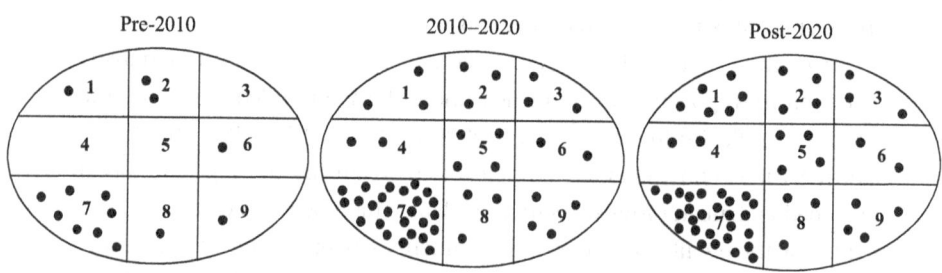

Figure 3.4
Proliferation of governance schemes over time

Basel Criteria for Responsible Soy Production, the Roundtable on Responsible Soy, the Roundtable on Sustainable Biomaterials, and the Roundtable on Sustainable Palm Oil. Other organizations involved in multiple schemes include the World Resource Institute, the Sustainable Trade Initiative, Solidaridad, Rainforest Alliance, Unilever, Mars, Nestlé, Rabobank, and HSBC. Policy analysts refer to this loose coalition of transnational actors as the "zero-deforestation supply chain movement" (see Climate Focus 2018).

The first generation of private governance schemes to tackle problems of commodity-driven deforestation were created in the early 2000s. As described in chapter 1, transnational NGOs and corporations created a series of industry roundtables and certification programs in key agricultural commodity sectors. An important first initiative was the Forest Conversion Initiative of the WWF. Launched in 2001, it served as an incubator for the Roundtable on Sustainable Palm Oil (RSPO) and the Roundtable on Responsible Soy (RTRS) and various other certification programs in key natural resource sectors (see WWF 2010). In the 2010s, these certification-based mechanisms were complemented by a second generation of private governance instruments.

Following a high-level pledge by the Consumer Goods Forum, a network of 400 globally leading retailers and consumer goods manufacturers, to eliminate deforestation from global supply chains, transnational corporations developed hundreds of no-deforestation commitments (Lister and Dauvergne 2014). As of 2017, the NGO Supply Change has tracked 760 commitments linked to major forest-risk commodities (Donofrio, Leonard, and Rothrock 2017). This wave of firm-level commitments was accompanied by another wave of industry-level initiatives, such as the Retail Soy Group in 2013, the European Palm Oil Alliance in 2016, the Soft Commodities Forum in 2019, and the Forest Positive Coalition of Action in 2019. There have also been various attempts to create meta-governance mechanisms to coordinate the increasing number of supply chain initiatives in this domain, such as the civil society–led Accountability Framework Initiative and the Tropical Forest Alliance, a public-private partnership initiated by the Consumer Goods Forum in collaboration with the US government.

The "Cambrian explosion" of transnational governance schemes (Abbott 2012b, 571) in this issue area has given rise to a regime complex that is driven by demand-side actors from the Global North. Out of the fifty-three schemes mapped in figure 3.4, thirty-three (62 percent) are sponsored by demand-side actors, of which private governance schemes make up the largest share. As of April 2021, there were twenty-five schemes active in zone 7, and this number would be many times higher if it included firm-level commitments, such as Nestlé's no-deforestation commitment. In addition, many collaborative schemes in zones 2, 5, and 8 were created on the initiative of Global North actors. For example, the Amazon Soy Moratorium, a regional moratorium on the trade of deforestation-linked soy from the Amazon biome, took shape after a Greenpeace campaign successfully targeted the sector's major buyers (Nepstad et al. 2019, 2). Similarly, the Singapore Sustainable Palm Oil Alliance was initiated by the WWF.

Demand-side actors from the Global North clearly dominate the present regime, but Global South actors are no longer passive bystanders. Particularly in recent years, government and industry actors from major commodity-producing countries, including Brazil and Indonesia, have sought to regain their regulatory sovereignty in the sustainability field. They have created domestic standards and certification regimes, some of which are now mandated by national law. The governance schemes in zones 3, 6, and 9 include important examples of this transition from rule takers to rule makers (see Sun and van der Ven 2020), such as the government-led Indonesia Sustainable Palm Oil and the Malaysia Sustainable Palm Oil programs. Another example is Brazil's Soja Plus Program, created by the country's peak soy industry associations. As we shall see later in this chapter, these "Southern standards" often compete with the Northern-backed sustainability schemes over authority in the transnational regulatory space.

Another feature of the regime complex for forest-risk commodities concerns the role of the state. Until recently, state actors have played a background role in the governance of forest-risk supply chains. Multilateral institutions (state-led and hybrid) remain underdeveloped (zones 2 and 5), despite several high-level declarations. This includes the United Nations New York Declaration on Forests, whose global platform has been endorsed by over 190 public and private entities, including central governments, subnational governments, multinational corporations, NGOs, and organizations representing indigenous communities (NYDF Global Platform 2019). More recently, at the COP26 Climate Summit in Glasgow in 2021, 141 heads of state, representing 91 percent of the world's forest cover, endorsed the Glasgow Leaders Declaration to halt and reverse forest loss and land degradation by 2030. This is a clear signal that the issue of commodity-driven deforestation has risen on the international policy agenda. However, it remains to be seen whether high-level government declarations will translate into meaningful multilateral action. The wider domain of global forest governance also hosts several well-established intergovernmental programs, such as the International Tropical Timber Organization of 1986 and the United Nations Program on Reducing Emissions from Deforestation and Forest Degradation of 2009. However, neither of these programs directly addresses problems with commodity-driven deforestation.

While multilateral institutions to govern forestry-risk supply chains remain weak, government actors in both consumer and producer countries have become more active in providing regulation in recent years. On the demand side, governments in the Global North have resorted to unilateral action (zone 1), including country-level commitments and regulations to eliminate deforestation from their supply chains (e.g., the Amsterdam Declaration on Deforestation,[8] France's National Strategy against Imported Deforestation, the German Supply Chain Act, and the UK's new Environment Act). The regulatory agenda on forest-risk supply chains is most advanced in the timber sector. In particular, the EU has been instrumental in assembling a transnational legality verification regime to stop trade in illegally logged timber. In the form of the EU Timber Regulation of 2013, the regime combines demand-side supply chain regulation in the EU with so-called voluntary partnership agreements to build national legality verification systems in major timber-producing countries, such as Indonesia and Ghana (Overdevest and Zeitlin 2014, 2018). To minimize EU-driven deforestation, the EU Commission has recently taken steps to broaden its regulatory agenda on forest-risk supply chains beyond the timber sector. In November 2021, the commission tabled a proposal for a new regulation, covering the forest-risk commodities of beef, cocoa, coffee, palm oil, soy, and timber (EU Commission 2021). To ensure that only deforestation-free products enter the European market, the regulation will establish mandatory due diligence requirements for companies importing these commodities and products containing them. While this is widely praised as a pathbreaking regulation, analysts are concerned that weaknesses in its design (e.g., weak state monitoring, limited stakeholder involvement, and difficulties in establishing legal liabilities) could undermine its effectiveness (Schilling-Vacaflor and Lenschow 2021). Beyond concerns with institutional design, the remainder of this chapter explores how global shifts in markets and power could challenge regime effectiveness in this issue area.

Regime Complexity in a Changing World Economy

The regime complex for forest-risk commodities is taking shape at a time when the international economic order and the system of global governance as a whole are increasingly in flux (Hale 2020, 214–215). To explore these global processes and their implications for regime effectiveness, two questions are particularly relevant. First, how is the regime adapting to the new context of polycentric trade in terms of coverage? In this regard, I explore the ability of the regime's most established governance schemes to diffuse their standards into the growing South-South trade, as well as the formation of new schemes focused on China's and India's fast-growing palm oil and soy supply chains. Second, how do processes of contemporary globalization and the underlying power shifts shape the regime's overarching governance architecture in terms of institutional fragmentation? As I explain in more detail below, for regime theorists, institutional fragmentation is a key variable linked to questions of governance effectiveness (see Biermann et al. 2009; Zelli and van Asselt 2013).

Adapting to Polycentric Trade

As described in the first part of the chapter, an increasing proportion of the global trade in forest-risk commodities flows through South-South supply chains (also see Zu Ermgassen et al. 2020). From a regime effectiveness perspective, this raises the question of how existing regulatory institutions adapt to the new world of polycentric trade. This section begins to explore this question by combining insights from the previous mapping analysis with data about sustainability certification and corporate zero-deforestation commitments. I show that many established transnational schemes remain anchored in the "world of late twentieth century trade" (Horner and Nadvi 2018, 229), whereas actors from emerging economies have been slow to engage with the zero-deforestation agenda. The result is a growing incongruence between the regime's coverage and the changing geography of globalization. If these gaps in coverage persist, they will limit the regime's reach and ability to achieve sustainability outcomes on a large enough scale.

As the mapping analysis shows, the production and trade of forest-risk commodities is increasingly regulated, with private market-driven governance playing an important role. Historically, societal, economic, and political pressures for the transnational regulation of environmental and social concerns have been strongest in the developed economies of the Global North. In the agriculture sector, this has allowed private sustainability standards to significantly expand their global market coverage over the past decade. As shown in chapter 1, the standard-compliant area of export-oriented tropical commodities grew from two million hectares in 2008 to almost twenty million hectares in 2019, an increase of 900 percent (ITC 2021).[9] In several tropical commodity sectors, the global market coverage of private sustainability standards has now reached double-digit figures, including the forest-risk commodities of palm oil (10.9 percent), cocoa (22.7 percent), and coffee (16.1 percent). Also, the volume of standard-compliant soy production has increased, however, with 1.5 percent of global production certified, it remains relatively small (ITC 2021). Much of this growth is concentrated in North-South supply chains. For example, for the palm oil sector, the European Palm Oil Alliance reports that in 2019 the Roundtable on Sustainable Palm Oil certified 86 percent of European imports under its various supply chain traceability systems (IDH and EPOA, 2020). For the same year, the European Soy Monitor estimates that 42 percent of the EU's soy imports were compliant with a private sustainability standard, although only 25 percent are estimated to be deforestation free (IDH 2021b). In addition to the uptake of third-party certification programs, like the Roundtable on Sustainable Palm Oil and the Roundtables on Responsible Soy, many of Europe's lead firms have developed firm-level zero-deforestation policies for their supply chains. Among lead firms with headquarters in Europe, the NGO Supply Change has tracked 160 and 68 zero-deforestation commitments in the palm oil and soy supply chains, respectively (Supply Change 2020b). In the short-term, new EU regulation of trade in forest-risk commodities could also lead to a "hardening" of corporate accountability in Europe's supply chains, as mandatory due diligence requirements and the risk of legal liability coerce companies into complying with public no-deforestation commitments (Schilling-Vacaflor and Lenschow 2021).

While the data presented above suggests a steady growth in the size of "sustainable markets" in the Global North (Meier et al. 2020), the no-deforestation regime complex appears to have very limited coverage in the major emerging economies. Unfortunately, there is little systematic information about the share of standard-compliant products in these markets. However, information from the leading certification programs suggests that uptake is very low. In the Chinese and Indian palm oil markets the uptake of the Roundtable on Sustainable Palm Oil is estimated to be 4–7 percent and 2–3 percent (values for 2019), respectively (WWF 2021b). For the Chinese soy market, the Roundtable on Responsible Soy even reports to have had no uptake in 2020 at all (RTRS 2021b). Similarly, multinational corporations from emerging economies have been slow to develop zero-deforestation commitments. According to Forest 500, a ranking of major companies' no-deforestation policies, none of the big Indian palm oil buyers has currently a strong commitment in place. In China, only COFCO, a state-owned food processor, manufacturer, and trader, has a commitment of medium strength for its palm oil and soy operations (Forest 500 2021). The mapping analysis conducted above also identified several new sustainability schemes targeting emerging markets, including the

China-focused Sustainable Soy Trade Platform, the China Sustainable Palm Oil Alliance, the India Sustainable Palm Oil Coalition, and the Singapore Alliance for Sustainable Palm Oil (see zone 8 and 9). Although focused on China and India, Northern companies, and civil society actors (e.g., Unilever, WWF, and Rainforest Alliance) were instrumental in initiating and financing these programs. As described in more detail in chapter 5, at the time of writing, participation from emerging market companies in these schemes was marginal.

In sum, the analysis suggests that significant gaps in coverage persist. Overall, the zero-deforestation regime complex has been slow to adapt to the changing global economic context. The growing volume of South-South trade in forest-risk commodities remains largely excluded from the regime, and established transnational schemes struggle to diffuse their standards into these supply chains. It is too early to tell whether the commitments by emerging market companies and the creation of new China- and India-centered schemes will translate into tangible transnational regulatory action. It is clear, though, that such action must happen soon to prevent irredeemable environmental damage from a growing demand for forest-risk commodities from emerging economies.

Global Power Shifts and Regime Fragmentation

Turning from the question of regime coverage and adaptation to the ways in which the overarching governance architecture is shaped by contemporary globalization and the underlying power shift, this section explores the implications for institutional fragmentation. The point of departure for the analysis is the above-described rise of Southern standards in agrifood governance.[10] Recalling figure 3.3, major Southern-led schemes in the zero-deforestation regime complex include the Indonesia Sustainable Palm Oil program, the Malaysia Sustainable Palm Oil program, and Brazil's Soja Plus program. The emergence of these programs is believed to have multiple, interrelated root causes, such as a lack of local legitimacy of established transnational schemes and motivations among government actors in the producer countries to regain regulatory sovereignty in the sustainability field. These domestic factors are considered to be important immediate causes behind the rise of these programs (see Giessen et al. 2016; Hospes 2014; Hospes, van der Valk, and Mheen-Sluijer 2012; Schouten and Bitzer 2015). However, in a changing world economy, a deeper understanding of the phenomenon requires close consideration of the global political economy context as well. In the current phase of globalization, actors from rising powers are increasingly involved in shaping "the rules of the game" that govern international economic relations, including the setting of environmental and social standards in supply chains (Nadvi 2014).

One way to theorize the link between global power shifts and the emergence of Southern standards in agrifood governance is to invoke Abbott and Snidal's (2009, 70–83) governance triangle and their metaphor of a "regulatory standards bargaining game." They conceive of the transnational regulatory space as a site of complex bargaining over the creation and design of regulatory standard-setting schemes. To explain the form and distribution of schemes in the governance triangle of states, firms, and civil society, they theorize that actors' competencies in the regulatory process (i.e., what they can bring or deny to any potential regulatory scheme) translate into power resources. In this context, an actor's level of "go it alone" power (i.e., its ability to establish a scheme that meets some or all of its objectives) is of particular importance in determining institutional outcomes (Abbott and Snidal 2009, 72).

The governance triangle has been widely used to describe and explain processes of institutional change in global governance (see Newell, Pattberg, and Schroeder 2012; Vogel 2009; Zelli et al. 2020). However, reflecting the debate on transnational business governance from over a decade ago, the framework pays little attention to the interactions between actors in different positions in the global economy. Its focus on the regulatory process also fails to acknowledge the role of large structural trends in the world economy and how they shape actors' power resources in negotiating institutional settlements. When revisiting the framework in a time of major transformation, the inclusion of such structural factors creates direct links between the global political economy context, actors' bargaining power, and processes of institutional change and interaction. Put differently, global economic shifts increase Southern actors' go-it-alone power in the regulatory bargaining game. Of course, Southern standards, such as the Indonesia Sustainable Palm Oil program, currently do not fulfill all or even most of their sponsors' objectives. In fact, many of them continue to suffer from major shortcomings, including a lack of global market acceptance (Hidayat, Offermans, and Glasbergen 2018). Nonetheless, in the current phase of globalization, Southern actors have gained significant power and leverage, and they increasingly use this power to insert themselves more forcefully into the regulatory standards bargaining game.

For the zero-deforestation regime complex, this raises the question how Southern actors' increased structural power affects the nature of governance interactions in this transnational regulatory space. It is clear that the influx of new governance actors from the Global South has further increased institutional complexity. However, it is an open research question whether this will result in cooperative or conflictive fragmentation between Northern-backed and Southern-backed schemes (see Biermann et al. 2009, 19). In regime theory, cooperative fragmentation describes a collaboration of loosely coupled institutions with enough integration of the governance architecture to prevent open conflict. In contrast, conflictive fragmentation refers to multiple competing institutions with conflicting sets of principles, norms, and rules, and a lack of integration in the overall governance architecture.[11] Commonly, regime theorists associate conflictive fragmentation with low regulatory capacity, whereas cooperative fragmentation is viewed more positively (see Alter and Raustiala 2018; Biermann et al. 2009; De Búrca, Keohane, and Sabel 2014; Keohane and Victor 2011).

Scholars of international politics have begun to analyze how long-term power shifts toward emerging countries in the Global South affect the fragmentation of global governance regimes (e.g., Paris 2015). In particular, in the literature on transnational sustainability governance, the question of whether Southern-led standards complement or conflict with established transnational schemes has emerged as an important research theme (see Brandi 2021; Dermawan and Hospes 2018; Giessen et al. 2016; Hospes 2014; Pacheco et al. 2018; Pickles, Barrientos, and Knorringa 2016; Schouten and Hospes 2018; van der Ven and Barmes 2019). This literature has produced important insights into the nature of these interactions in different countries and industry sectors. However, most of these studies focus on interscheme interactions, whereas the effects on the regime as a whole are less well understood.[12] Also, these works have paid little attention to the implications of global power shifts. To address this gap, the remainder of this section synthesizes the empirical insights from these studies. I show how the distribution of global market power is an important background condition that shapes transnational governance interactions in a sector.

In the palm oil sector, domestic and transnational governance actors have a history of conflict and cooperation. In Indonesia and Malaysia, the world's largest producers of palm oil, national governments and peak industry associations initially avoided interfering with sustainability standards set by transnational actors and even collaborated closely with them (Schouten and Hospes 2018, 4–7). However, as these schemes grew in market significance, powerful political, bureaucratic, and industry actors began to exert more authority, such as the previously described efforts by domestic governments and peak industry associations to create national competitor programs (Hospes 2014; Schouten and Bitzer 2015; Wijaya and Glasbergen 2016). Governments in these markets also tried to curb the influence of transnational actors in their jurisdictions. For example, in 2016, the Indonesian government dissolved the Indonesia Palm Oil Pledge, a consortium of global palm oil traders and internationally oriented producers working toward zero deforestation (Dermawan and Hospes 2018). The academic debate remains inconclusive about the trajectory of these interactions. Some scholars argue that an increased focus on national sovereignty has intensified conflicts between domestic and transnational governance actors (Schouten and Hospes 2018). Others see a trend toward increased collaboration, pointing to market and regulatory pressures from the EU as an important driver (Brandi 2021; also see van der Ven and Barmes 2019). However, as the volume of South-South trade in the palm oil sector continues to grow, these drivers are likely to become less powerful over time.

A somewhat similar dynamic characterizes the Brazilian soy sector, which experienced parallel development of multiple sustainability initiatives centered on the supply chain in the early 2000s (Hospes, van der Valk, and Mheen-Sluijer 2012). Interactions between domestic and transnational actors became conflictive when Brazilian producers clashed with international buyers and NGOs over the standards and authority of the transnational Roundtable on Responsible Soy (Schleifer 2017, 5–6). After years of conflict, the leading Brazilian producer associations finally left the Eurocentric initiative and created the industry-led Soja Plus program instead. As detailed in chapter 4, these interactions cannot be understood without placing them in the global market context, which experienced a massive shift in Brazil's soy exports from Europe to China in the 2000s. Under the populist Bolsonaro administration, the position of transnational sustainability schemes in Brazil has been further weakened. There has been growing opposition to the buyer-driven Amazon Soy Moratorium, a regional moratorium on the sourcing of deforestation-linked soy production from the Amazon biome (Samora 2019a, 2019b).

For comparison, the dynamics in the palm oil and soy sectors differ from those in the timber sector. Government authorities in timber-producing countries have also sought to reclaim regulatory authority from transnational governance actors. The Indonesian Ecolabelling Program was an early attempt to develop an independent national certification system. Backed by the Ministry of Forestry, the program became operational in the early 2000s and competed directly with the transnational Forest Stewardship Council. In the late 2000s, the Indonesian Ministry of Forestry again attempted to restore its sovereignty over national forests by creating a national Timber Legality Assurance System (Giessen et al. 2016). However, the subsequent integration of the Indonesian system in the EU's Forest Law Enforcement, Governance, and Trade framework resulted in a more collaborative pattern of interactions (see Overdevest and Zeitlin 2014, 2018; Zeitlin and Overdevest 2021). No doubt this was aided by the fact that the EU and United States continue to be the world's largest end markets for internationally traded wood products. This includes direct exports from tropical timber producing countries as well as reexports from third-party countries such as China (see Zeitlin and Overdevest 2021, 15). In the case of the EU-led transnational legality regime, Europe's central position in the global timber economy, combined with a regulatory penalty default to sanction for noncompliance (the EU Timber Regulation of 2013 prohibits operators from placing illegally harvested wood on the European market), have been powerful incentives for cooperation.

In sum, this section shows that the onset of twenty-first-century globalization has been accompanied by conflict and cooperation in the broader regime complex for forest-risk commodities. In palm oil and soy sectors, it has bred conflictive fragmentation (Dermawan and Hospes 2018; Hospes, van der Valk, and Mheen-Sluijer 2012; Schouten and Hospes 2018), whereas cooperative fragmentation dominates in the timber sector (Overdevest and Zeitlin 2014; Zeitlin and Overdevest 2021). Revisiting Abbott and Snidal's (2009, 72) "regulatory standards bargaining game" helps to make sense of these patterns. It shows how the type of interaction (cooperative or conflictive) correlates with the distribution of global market power in these industries. It needs to be understood as an important background condition that shapes actors' (structural) power resources. However, there is no determinism in this relationship. As we shall see later in this book, there are multiple examples suggesting that new forms of North-South (Langford 2019) and South-South (Bloomfield 2020) cooperation for sustainable development are possible in the context of contemporary globalization.

Conclusion

With a focus on the big picture questions, this chapter introduces the in-depth analyses provided in subsequent chapters. Following a historical reflection on agricultural transformations, the chapter examines the link between globalization and tropical deforestation. A strong increase in the volume of South-South trade in forest-risk commodities indicates that this link will remain strong in the twenty-first century. As the Tropical Oil Crop Revolution enters a new phase of development, global, regional, and local South-South supply chains account for a growing proportion of the world's traded deforestation. Through their imports of palm oil and soy, particularly China and India drive deforestation in countries like Brazil and Indonesia.

Shifting the focus of analysis from environmental to institutional implications, this chapter also examines how the emerging regime complex for forest-risk commodities adapts to and is shaped by processes of contemporary globalization. The politics of "old" globalization forged the current regime, which is dominated by private governance actors from the Global North. Consequently, the incongruity between the regime's coverage and the new geography of agricultural trade threatens to undermine its effectiveness. It remains to be seen whether the creation of emerging market-centered schemes and stronger state-led governance on both the demand and supply sides of global commodity chains will help to close this gap. This chapter also discusses how contemporary globalization is increasingly fragmenting the regime's overarching governance architecture. A wave of governance actors from the Global South has entered the transnational regulatory space, which has further increased the institutional complexity in this domain. Closer attention must be paid to structural factors to make sense of the resulting patterns of interaction. In a changing world economy, shifts in global economic power is an important background condition that shapes the politics around transnational sustainability governance.

In sum, this chapter identifies important trends and challenges. However, the perspective of international political economy is too broad to capture the new politics of sustainability with any precision. A closer analysis of the sectoral contexts in which these processes unfold is needed. As a next step, chapter 4 shifts the focus from the macro to the meso level by conducting a comparative analysis of the political economy of private governance uptake in two forest-risk commodities sectors. Its emphasis is on the Roundtable on Sustainable Palm Oil and Roundtable on Responsible Soy, two of the regime's most established transnational schemes.

4 The Comparative Politics of Sustainable Markets

In 2010, the Consumer Goods Forum pledged to achieve zero net deforestation by the end of the decade. This has accelerated the diffusion of sustainability standards and commitments in global agricultural supply chains. However, as described in the previous chapter, the emerging regime complex for forest-risk commodities faces multiple challenges, including a growing incongruence between the regime's coverage and the "new geography of trade" (UNCTAD 2004, 2). The objective of this chapter is to gain deeper understanding of the political economy conditions that promote or frustrate uptake of transnational business governance and how these conditions are interacting and evolving in the age of advanced globalization.

My aims in this chapter are twofold. First, I provide a more detailed analysis of the state of "sustainable markets" in major forest-risk commodity sectors, including palm oil and soy.[1] Linked to questions about the authority and effectiveness of transnational business governance, the study of market adoption has been an important focus in the political science and impact evaluation literatures on sustainability certification and corporate zero-deforestation commitments (Cashore 2002; Cashore, Auld, and Newsom 2004; Espach 2009; Garrett et al. 2016; Marx and Cuypers 2010; Prakash and Potoski 2006). To advance understanding of patterns related to this important outcome variable, this chapter reviews new data sources that allow for a more nuanced examination.

My second objective is explanatory. Building on the description of adoption patterns in the first part of the chapter, I conduct a comparative political economy analysis of two mature private governance programs: the Roundtable on Sustainable Palm Oil (RSPO) in the palm oil sector and the Roundtable on Roundtable on Responsible Soy (RTRS) in the soy sector. Although very similar in their institutional design, these two programs display significant variation in their global market uptake. At the same time, the two cases reveal a common overall trend: the adoption of private sustainability standards has stagnated in recent years. Studying the political economy of sustainable markets in the palm oil and soy industries, this chapter reviews the arguments and integrates them in a comparative framework. By focusing on demand-side and supply-side drivers of private governance uptake, the framework offers a structured and focused comparison of these two commodity sectors, with particular attention paid to Brazil and Indonesia as the main producer countries.

The State of Sustainable Markets

Market uptake or adoption is an important dependent and independent variable in the research literature on transnational business governance (Cashore 2002; Cashore, Auld, and Newsom 2004; Cashore et al. 2007; Espach 2009; Marx and Cuypers 2010; Schleifer and Sun 2018). As discussed in chapter 2, large-scale adoption is a necessary, although not a sufficient condition for the effectiveness of market-driven sustainability governance, such as certification schemes and zero-deforestation commitments. Likewise, the impact evaluation literature views large-scale adoption as a precondition for these programs to generate "additionality" beyond business-as-usual practices (Garrett et al. 2016). Against this background, some scholars argue that large-scale adoption of voluntary sustainability standards could significantly reduce the environmental impact of global agriculture (Smith et al. 2019). However, caution is advisable. Evidence suggests that even in sectors with high adoption rates, private standards have not successfully overcome sustainability challenges. A notable example is the coffee sector, in which more than 50 percent of global production is grown according to some sustainability standard (Grabs 2020b; Ponte 2019, 71–83). Moreover, recommendations to increase adoption of private standards are of little use if the political economy conditions that drive these processes remain poorly understood.

To advance our understanding of the issue, this section begins with a descriptive analysis of the state of sustainable markets in the major forest-risk commodity sectors (i.e., palm oil, timber and pulp, soy, and cattle). In recent years, new data sources have become available for a deeper and more nuanced analysis. Using this new information, this chapter triangulates information from the Global Canopy Program's Forest 500 Index,[2] Forest Trends'

Supply Change Initiative,[3] and International Trade Centre's Sustainability Map.[4] The analysis focuses on the adoption of firm-level sustainability and no-deforestation commitments and third-party certification programs.

The Global Canopy Program's Forest 500 Index is the "world's first rainforest rating agency" (Forest 500 2017, 1). It identifies the most influential companies with exposure to the production of palm oil, timber and pulp, soy, and beef and leather and assesses the quality of their sustainability commitments.[5] Forest 500's selection methodology is based on corporate concentration and uses a combination of qualitative and quantitative indicators to identify 350 "corporate powerbrokers" with the highest market shares along forest-risk commodity chains.[6] Forest 500's 2019 Assessment Report highlights that 140 (40 percent) of these powerbrokers do not have a deforestation commitment, and seventy-five (21 percent) have a commitment for one of the commodities they source but not the others (Forest 500 2019a, 3). A closer look at the sectoral distribution of companies' no-deforestation commitments reveals significant variation across commodity sectors. With considerable margin, adoption is highest in the palm oil sector, where 73 percent of exposed companies adopted a sustainability commitment, followed by 58 percent in the timber and pulp industry, and just 37 percent and 28 percent, respectively, in the soy and cattle sectors (analysis of data from Forest 500).

Data published by the Supply Change Initiative reveal a similar pattern. Introduced by Forest Trends, a Washington-based nonprofit organization, the platform aims to cover the "global universe of companies" whose supply chains depend on palm oil, timber and pulp, soy, or cattle (Donofrio, Leonard, and Rothrock 2017, 4). With 718 companies profiled in 2017, the Supply Change Initiative works with a larger sample than the Forest 500 Index. However, similar to the Forest 500 Index, it omits small- and medium-sized companies (Supply Change 2020a), which is problematic because collectively these companies have a major deforestation footprint with low uptake of sustainability commitments (Taylor and Streck 2018, 9). Figure 4.1 depicts the uptake of deforestation-related commodity commitments by companies across the major forest-risk commodity sectors.

The International Trade Centre's Sustainability Map includes information about the uptake of third-party certification programs. Table 4.1 summarizes the leading schemes in the four major forest-risk commodity sectors. The data reveal a close correlation between the number of corporate commitments in a sector and the adoption of certification programs. There

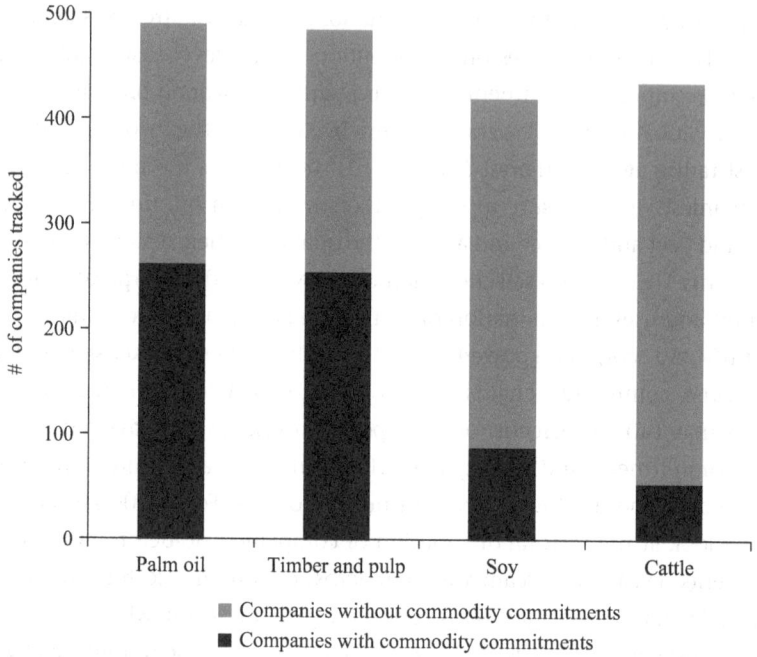

Figure 4.1
Companies' sustainability commitments by commodity, in values for 2017 (number of companies tracked)
Source: Analysis of data from Supply Change, available from https://www.supply-change.org

are several reasons for this. First, in sectors with well-established third-party sustainability standards, companies can base their deforestation commitments on existing standards. Second, certification programs often provide off-the-shelf implementation mechanisms. In this regard, analysts find that progress reporting by companies is much more frequent for certification-based commitments than it is for non-certification-based commitments (Donofrio, Leonard, and Rothrock 2017, 12). However, as observed in sectors with mature private sustainability governance (e.g., coffee), global buyers may abandon third-party certification programs over time in favor of firm-level programs, which offer more direct control over standard development and implementation (see Grabs 2017).

The data collected by Forest 500, Supply Change, and Sustainability Map have various limitations, including incomplete samples and selection bias. However, triangulating the data can help identify general adoption patterns

Table 4.1
Market uptake of leading certification programs by commodity

Leading certification programs	Commodity	Total certified area, as of 2019 (hectares)	Percent of global production area, as of 2019
Roundtable on Sustainable Palm Oil (RSPO), Rainforest Alliance	Palm oil	3.1 million	11
Forest Stewardship Council (FSC), Program for the Endorsement of Forest Certification (PEFC)	Timber and pulp	528 million	13
Roundtable on Sustainable Soy (RTRS), ProTerra Foundation	Soy	1.8 million	1.5
Global Roundtable for Sustainable Beef (GRSB), Brazilian Roundtable for Sustainable Livestock (GTPS), Rainforest Alliance	Cattle*	Very small (no precise estimate available)	< 1

Source: Analysis of data from the International Trade Centre's Sustainability Map, available at https://www.sustainabilitymap.org
* For the cattle sector, which is excluded from the Sustainability Map, a manual review of the leading certification programs in the sector was conducted.

and trends. First, a clear divergence occurs in adoption rates across commodity sectors. Notably, the sectors with the highest deforestation footprint, namely soy and cattle, have the lowest uptake of corporate zero-deforestation commitments and third-party certification systems.[7] This finding indicates that the size of sustainable markets has no apparent correlation with the severity of environmental degradation in a sector. The emerging distribution of private governance is thus suboptimal from a problem-solving perspective. Second, the overall adoption rate remains far below expectations (Climate Focus 2016). Since the declaration of the Consumer Goods Forum in 2010, the number of corporate no-deforestation commitments has grown year by year (see Slavin 2018). However, many companies in these sectors have not adopted such policies, and some firms have reneged on their earlier commitments or stopped reporting progress (Forest 500 2019a, 4). Analysts estimate that some 20 percent of all company commitments are currently "dormant," meaning they are past their target date (Donofrio, Leonard, and Rothrock 2017, 7). The uptake of third-party certification schemes reveals a similar picture. According to the theory of change put forward by WWF, sectorwide sustainability transformations require a market share between 40 and 50 percent of total production being certified (former director of the Forest Conversion Initiative, phone interview, May 2013). As shown in table 4.1, none of the leading schemes has gained transformative market share. Instead, as we shall see later in the chapter, market share of some leading schemes has stagnated or declined in recent years.

Explaining Market Uptake

Using data from Forest 500, Supply Change, and Sustainability Map, the preceding section sought to increase understanding of the state of sustainable markets in the major forest-risk commodity sectors. Some of the previously described patterns are easily explained. For instance, low uptake of transnational sustainability standards in the cattle sector is due to the dominance of local supply chains and local consumption in that sector. For example, in Brazil, some 80 percent of beef production is consumed domestically (Chain Reaction Research 2018a). Thus, a key condition for the adoption of nonstate market-driven governance, high export dependency (Cashore, Auld, and Newsom 2004, 43), is absent in this commodity sector. Conversely, the relatively high adoption rate in the timber and pulp industry can at least partially be attributed to the fact that sustainability certification is most advanced in this sector. Two of the world's first global certification programs, the Forest Stewardship Council and the Program for the Endorsement of Forest Certification, date from the early 1990s. Many studies have examined the institutionalization and adoption of these programs in this sector (e.g., Auld 2014; Cashore et al. 2007; Cashore, Auld, and Newsom 2004; Gulbrandsen 2010; Marx and Cuypers 2010; Pattberg 2007).

Some of the other patterns identified are less well understood, however. In particular, the observed variation in the adoption of private sustainability governance in the palm oil and soy sectors raises questions. At first glance, the two cases have many commonalities. Both are highly traded commodities. Indonesia, the world's largest palm oil producer, exports about 70 percent of its production, and Brazil exports approximately 65 percent of its soy (analysis of data from FAOSTAT; ITC n.d.). Both sectors also attract public controversy regarding the environmental impact of commodity production. NGOs and the media have publicly linked palm oil and soy production to tropical deforestation, biodiversity loss, and other environmental and social problems, and firms linked to these commodity chains have been targeted by transnational advocacy networks (see Dauvergne 2017; Greenpeace 2006). These sectors also have nearly identical "twin initiatives" for third-party certification (RSPO and RTRS) (former director of the Forest Conversion Initiative, phone interview, May 2013), both of which began with the WWF's Forest Conversion Initiative in the early 2000s. Finally, these two sectors also appear to be connected by stagnating or decreased market share of leading third-party certification schemes. The RTRS has struggled to capture a significant market share of the global soy trade from the beginning, and though more successful in that regard, RSPO also has largely stagnated in its certification growth in recent years.

A Comparative Political Economy Analysis

In preparation for the empirical analysis, this section reviews the literature on the adoption of transnational business governance, identifies the conditions for market uptake, and integrates them into a comparative political economy framework. At a general level, two types of conditions can be distinguished: institutional and contextual. Institutional conditions are linked to the design and operations of private governance programs (e.g., stringency of standards, robustness of monitoring and enforcement procedures). Scholars have studied these institutional design features as key drivers of program efficacy (see Potoski and Prakash 2009; Prakash and Potoski 2006, 2007). In the present chapter, these factors are largely held constant because the analysis focuses on two private governance schemes (the RSPO and RTRS) with very similar institutional designs. Contextual conditions are linked to the political economy setting of private governance. Building on the discussion in chapter 2, I systematically review these factors and integrate them into a common analytical framework that draws on my past work (Schleifer 2016b, 2017; Schleifer and Sun 2018).

In developing the framework further, I add two new features. First, I include a geographical dimension by distinguishing between demand-side and supply-side conditions. This dimension represents a parsimonious view of the organization of global commodity chains, which in reality have many more segments (see Gereffi and Fernandez-Stark 2016, 8–10). However, this serves the important analytical function of distinguishing between conditions that are linked to different positions in these commodity chains, while maintaining parsimony in the overall framework. Second, I add a temporal dimension to the analysis. A criticism of the literature on the adoption of private governance is its static analysis (Bloomfield and Schleifer 2017, 130). A longitudinal approach allows examination of the politics of transnational sustainability governance over an extended period of time. Covering the decade following the launch of the RSPO and RTRS in the mid-2000s, I investigate how the political economy of sustainable markets in the palm oil and soy sectors has evolved during a period of major structural change in the world economy.

Demand-Side Conditions

In developing the framework, I identify four demand-side conditions. The first condition is the *location of end markets* in a sector. In their pioneering study on the drivers of forest certification, Cashore, Auld, and Newsom (2004) show how export dependency was a key factor in determining the level of business support for the Forest Stewardship Council in different geographical regions. Subsequently, the link between a sector's export dependency and its adoption of transnational private governance has been investigated in a wide range of studies and contexts (e.g., Bartley 2010; Cashore et al. 2007; Overdevest 2010). More recently, scholars have started to examine how shifts in the location of end markets from the Global North to the Global South can undermine support for environmental and social standards in the global economy (Adolph, Quince, and Prakash 2017; Kaplinsky, Terheggen, and Tijaja 2011; Schleifer 2016b; Schleifer and Sun 2018). I therefore hypothesize that the size of Southern end markets in a sector will limit the global uptake of transnational sustainability standards.

Related to the discussion on export dependency, the second condition, *support from lead firms*, is a key factor (Mayer and Gereffi 2010, 8). So-called buyer-driven global value chains are characterized by significant power asymmetries between upstream buyers and downstream suppliers (Gereffi 1994; Gereffi, Humphrey, and Sturgeon 2005). Private governance programs seek to harness these power differentials between supply chain actors to push their standards upstream in globally dispersed production networks. However, as research on global value chains has shown, the degree of "drivenness" in supply chains is not constant but varies across industries (see Gibbon, Bair, and Ponte 2008; Ponte 2019, 3). Returning to the discussion on global market shifts, buyers from emerging economies may also not be attuned to sustainability issues in the same way as their developed country counterparts (Forest 500 2019a, 8).

Third, *transnational advocacy pressure* is an important condition that is stressed throughout the academic literature (Bartley 2009; Bloomfield 2017, 2014; Haufler 2009). According to Bartley (2009), this pressure is a strong catalyst for action, but the strength of transnational advocacy networks varies (see Risse 2013, 432–439). Depending on industry concentration, product characteristics, and proximity to consumers, firms' "vulnerability" to transnational advocacy campaigns can vary too (Mayer and Gereffi 2010, 10). Moreover, these campaigns could become less effective as trade flows shift from North-South to South-South. For example, national pressures might cause state-owned emerging market enterprises to be less responsive to transnational advocacy campaigns (Whelan and Muthuri 2015). Research shows that advocacy NGOs are generally less likely to target firms from remote and unfamiliar locations (Hatte and Koenig 2018). Finally, evidence suggests that transnational advocacy networks face increasing regulatory restrictions in emerging economies that limit their activities (Fransen et al. 2021).

The final demand-side condition is *support from external state actors*. In recent years, governments in major consumer countries have taken steps to regulate transnational business conduct (LeBaron and Rühmkorf 2017; Overdevest and Zeitlin 2014). These regulatory pressures are transmitted through global supply chains as lead firms in consumer countries engage in mandatory due diligence reporting of their social and environmental practices. Weak institutions in producer countries can further intensify regulatory pressures if they induce policy makers to demand additional assurance through private governance (Berliner and Prakash 2014). The literature on orchestration shows how, in addition to enforcing hard regulatory pressures, public actors can generate support for private governance through various soft measures, such as endorsement, financial assistance, and coordination (Abbott et al. 2015). However, as with some of the other factors discussed, global power shifts might limit the strength of transnational regulatory pressures from Northern government actors.

Supply-Side Conditions

Moving to the supply side, I identify four further conditions. First, the *domestic industry structure* condition draws on arguments from transaction cost economics hypothesizing that large producers can generate economies of scale when they adopt sustainability standards, which means they face proportionally lower adoption costs than smaller producers (see Cashore, Auld, and Newsom 2004, 45). By that same logic, auditing and implementation costs can be prohibitively high for small- and medium-sized enterprises, depending on factors such as prior preparedness (see Hidayat, Offermans, and Glasbergen 2016). In addition to high costs, small-scale producers often lack the necessary organizational capacity and access to technology to comply with transnational sustainability standards (Brandi et al. 2015). Hence, all else being equal, concentrated industries provide more favorable conditions for private governance programs than fragmented ones.

The second supply side factor is *support from producer groups* for transnational business governance. A highly concentrated production segment has more bargaining power in the global supply chain (see Locke, Amengual, and Mangla 2009, 325). The extant research literature also suggests that peak producer associations can be powerful forums through which domestic industry actors organize collective action. Just as support from an influential industry association can increase uptake of a private governance scheme, opposition can limit uptake (see Andonova 2004; Auld et al. 2007; Overdevest and Zeitlin 2014).

The third condition is *support from domestic state actors*. The literature on the political economy of natural resource production in the Global South indicates that these industries are often controlled by powerful state-industrial complexes consisting of tightly knit elite networks and interplay between government agencies and major firms (see Cramb and McCarthy 2016b; Kaup 2015). Successful private governance through external actors requires support from dominant bureaucratic and political coalitions. The literature finds that host governments' attitudes toward transnational business governance vary from supportive to indifferent and even hostile (Espach 2009, 43–44; also see Marques and Eberlein 2020). However, as hypothesized by Bartley (2018a, 61), when transnational standards and domestic governance clash, the latter usually retains primacy. As foreshadowed in chapter 3, global power shifts could increase the likelihood of such clashes. If their "go it alone" power increases (see Abbott and Snidal 2009, 72), actors in producer countries are likely to insert themselves more forcefully into the "regulatory standards bargaining game."

Finally, *support from local civil society* can be an important factor. Domestic civil society actors campaign for sustainability by partnering with international NGOs in transnational networks to support the adoption of private governance and to encourage participation, capacity building, and local advocacy (see Cheyns 2014; Keck and Sikkink 1998; Nikkhah and Redzuan 2010). A strong local civil society can encourage adoption of transnational sustainably standards, but evidence also points to an inverse relationship. For example, Bartley (2018a, 59–61) finds that (at least initially), the Forest Stewardship Council's market uptake increased quickly in authoritarian China as the scheme's auditors, in the absence of pressure from a local civil society, were more likely to accept minimalistic definitions of compliance.

The demand-side and supply-side conditions identified above will guide the empirical analysis of the RSPO in the palm oil sector and the RTRS in the soy sector. The objective is not to examine the individual conditions as competing hypotheses. Instead, the framework aids in investigating the configuration of relevant political economy factors in the two cases and how they relate to the adoption of the two schemes. This analysis requires a structured, focused comparison that accounts for changes in demand-side and supply-side conditions over time.

Despite the notable interaction effects between the above-described conditions, a refined theory of such interactions has not yet been proposed. Therefore, my working assumption at the start of the analysis is that the different conditions are complementary: all else being equal, a more favorable political economy context is associated with a higher uptake of transnational business governance in a sector (see table 4.2). Although similar to a qualitative comparative analysis (Ragin 2008), this configurational approach is less formal, and the small number of cases ($N=2$) allows for a more in-depth analysis. I also include induction as an important element of the research strategy (George and Bennett 2005, 23). To this end, I use the case material to inductively learn about the relationships between the

Table 4.2
Hypothesized outcomes for private governance uptake

		Supply-side conditions		
		Favorable	Moderately favorable	Unfavorable
Demand-side conditions	Favorable	Very high	High	Moderate
	Moderately favorable	High	Moderate	Low
	Unfavorable	Moderate	Low	Very low

different factors. In light of major structural changes in the world economy, I am particularly interested in the favorability of the global political economy context in the two sectors and how it has changed over time.

The Roundtable on Sustainable Palm Oil

Palm oil is a highly versatile edible vegetable oil. It is mainly used as a cooking oil and as an ingredient in a large variety of food, cosmetic, and chemical products. A significant proportion of global production is also processed into biodiesel. Because of palm oil's cost-effectiveness, global demand for the commodity is booming. The environmental impact of palm oil expansion is amplified by the fact that almost 90 percent of global production is concentrated in just two countries, Indonesia and Malaysia. Against this background, the comparatively high adoption rate of transnational sustainability standards in the industry can be interpreted as a positive development. And analysts have identified the RSPO as an important driver behind the relative success of the zero-deforestation supply chain movement in this sector (Climate Focus 2016; Donofrio, Leonard, and Rothrock 2017). A closer look at certification data shows that the RSPO had indeed been able to gain a significant global market share in a relatively short time (see figure 4.2).

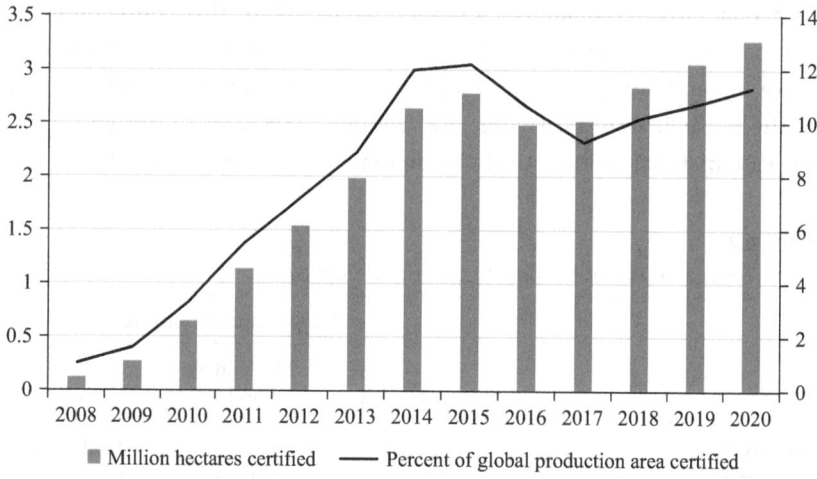

Figure 4.2
Global adoption of the RSPO
Source: Analysis of data from FAOSTAT and RSPO (2021a)

As shown in figure 4.2, today, the RSPO certifies approximately 11 percent of the global oil palm production area, making it one of the most certified commodities in the world. Moreover, the RSPO is one of the largest certification programs in terms of membership, with 2,045 full members as of February 2022 (RSPO 2022). However, the RSPO market uptake data also show that most of its growth occurred prior to 2014 and that progress has stagnated since. To explain the observed patterns in the palm oil certification market, I employ the framework developed in this chapter to investigate the political economy context in this sector and how it has evolved over time.

Demand-Side Conditions
Location of end markets. Palm oil has one of the highest export rates of all agricultural commodities. In 2018, approximately 70 percent of palm oil from Indonesia (valued at US$18 billion), the world's largest producer, shipped to overseas markets (analysis of data from ITC n.d.). High export dependency is a key scope condition for the uptake of transnational sustainability standards (Cashore, Auld, and Newsom 2004, 40–43). However, as hypothesized, a change in the direction of trade from North-South to South-South could offset the effect. Indeed, today, most of Indonesia's palm oil is destined for Global South markets. Unlike some other industries with high volumes of South-South trade, where a significant proportion of raw material imports is used in reexports to developed countries (Zeitlin and Overdevest 2019, 31), almost all palm oil imported by developing countries is for domestic consumption. In an interview, an Indonesian official at the Council of Palm Oil Producing Countries shared his assessment of the changing market environment: "It [Europe] is significant but it is not as significant as in the past. In 1990 most palm oil exports were to Europe. Now it's much less. Now it's mostly India, China, Bangladesh, and other developing countries. And the direction is clear. And then there is also our own domestic market. We had production last year of 37 million tons and we consume almost 10 million tons" (Indonesian official at the Council of Palm Oil Producing Countries, interview, Jakarta, April 2018). Trade statistics confirm that palm oil consumption within the Global South has increased strongly over the past decade, but also Europe continues to be a major importer of the commodity. Since the launch of the RSPO, the EU's share of Indonesian exports has declined only moderately from 19 percent in 2004 to about 14 percent in 2019. In comparison, in 2019, China's and India's share of Indonesian palm oil exports was 19 percent and 18 percent,

respectively (analysis of data from ITC n.d.). These data suggest that this scope condition remains moderately favorable for the RSPO.

Nonetheless, the changing global market environment poses a challenge to the large-scale global adoption of the program. Indeed, in a study investigating the uptake of certified palm oil in the Chinese and Indian end markets, Yixian Sun and I find that unfavorable market and nonmarket conditions limit RSPO adoption in these two countries, although conditions are somewhat better in China (Schleifer and Sun 2018). At the same time, an Indonesian official of the Council of Palm Oil Producing Countries pointed out to me that it is "not only about the size of the market. Of course, [Europe's] market size is decreasing but it is also about signals and agenda. Europe is still an important setter of standards for the industry" (interview, Jakarta, April 2018).

This suggest that Europe continues to have significant agenda-setting power in the palm oil sector. However, recent developments could further undermine its position. In 2017, the European Parliament passed a resolution to phase out the use of palm oil–based biofuels by 2030, which would reduce Europe's palm oil imports. Countries producing palm oil have fiercely criticized the move, calling it a form of "crop apartheid" (Reuters 2018) and filing a complaint with the WTO's Dispute Settlement Body (WTO 2019). The EU's decision has also motivated Indonesia to further intensify its trade relationships with China and India and to shore up domestic consumption of palm oil (Coca 2020). The Indonesian government's new biofuel mandate, which is believed to pose a major deforestation risk (Jong 2020b), must be seen in this context. If these dynamics continue, experts at the Centre for International Forestry Research in Bogor, Indonesia, warn that international sustainability standards, such as the RSPO, could be further weakened (Robinson and Purnomo 2019).

Support from lead firms. In the palm oil sector, support from lead firms for the zero-deforestation agenda has increased significantly over time. As shown in the data from Forest 500 and Supply Change, a comparatively large number of firms in the palm oil sector have formulated sustainability and no-deforestation commitments, and many joined the RSPO. As of February 2022, the organization had 983 buyers (retailers and consumer goods manufacturers) as full members. This suggests growing support for the RSPO from lead firms in the industry. Hence, this scope condition can be said to have improved from moderately favorable to favorable. However, two caveats must be noted. Most member firms are from the Global North, mainly Europe, with only fourteen and eight buyers participating in the RSPO from China and India, respectively (analysis of data from RSPO 2022). At a conference of the Centre for Responsible Business in Delhi, the employee of a large Indian consumer goods manufacturer shared his assessment of the situation: "there are some globally oriented brands that have taken to [palm oil] certification, but companies in the domestic market have little incentives" (personal communication, Delhi, November 2015). The second caveat concerns the high level of fragmentation of the palm oil supply chain's downstream segment. As explored in more detail in chapter 5, palm oil is used in a wide range of industries, including foodstuffs, cosmetics, pharmaceuticals, and biofuels. This limits the possibility of buyer-driven sustainability in the sector.

Transnational advocacy pressure. The literature on transnational advocacy suggests that civil society actors are most successful in promoting norm changes if they form strong networks in which domestic and international NGOs coordinate activities and exercise pressure from below and above (Keck and Sikkink 1998; Risse, Roop, and Sikkink 1999). For more than a decade, companies in the palm oil sector have been targeted by a powerful advocacy network focused on deforestation, biodiversity, land rights, and climate change (see Friends of the Earth 2013; Greenpeace 2008). The transnational palm oil campaign network has successfully pushed these topics up the media agenda through "information politics" (Keck and Sikkink 1999, 95). A study of media coverage of commodity-driven deforestation analyzed thirty-four media outlets from six major forest-risk countries, as well as a selection of international media outlets, during the period 2013–2017 (Chagas et al. 2018, 9–10).[8] The results show that media coverage on deforestation increased significantly during this period, from fewer than 500 media mentions in 2013 to over 1,600 in 2017. They also show that the palm oil sector dominates in the domestic and international media, accounting for approximately 50 percent of total coverage on commodity-driven deforestation.[9]

Evidence also suggests increasing awareness of sustainable consumption in China and India (Tropical Forest Alliance 2018, 15), but transnational advocacy targeting palm oil firms in these countries remains weak. In authoritarian China, the movements of international and local NGOs are strongly restricted. "Naming and shaming campaigns" against companies are uncommon (Schleifer and Sun 2018, 12). In India, Greenpeace launched a campaign focused on the country's growing consumption of palm oil as a driver of deforestation (Greenpeace 2012). However, the campaign had weak links with domestic civil society groups (policy officer, Centre for Responsible Business, personal communication, New Delhi, November 2015). Other concerns include the increasingly restrictive policy environment for international NGOs in India. In 2015, the Indian government froze Greenpeace India's assets and suspended its license to receive foreign donations. A spokesman for the group described it as "yet another attempt to silence campaigns for a more sustainable future" (Singh 2015). This suggests that advocacy groups may not function as a "catalyst" for the RSPO in emerging economies in the same way they did in the Global North (see Bartley 2009). Overall, however, it can be said that the organization has benefited from a favorable environment on this dimension of the framework.

Role of external state actors. Environmental and social standards have long been excluded from the WTO, which views process standards as a nontariff barrier. To bypass gridlock in the multilateral trade regime, policymakers in the European Union have actively supported the use of private standards to achieve its sustainability objectives in global production (see Schleifer 2013). In recent years, particularly, the issue of commodity-driven deforestation has risen on the EU's external action agenda. Following the New York Declaration on Forests in 2014, European regulators have taken various measures at the EU and national levels to address problems with "imported deforestation." Many of these efforts have focused on the palm oil supply chain, and the use of private governance mechanisms has long been central to the overall approach. In the context of the 2015 Paris Agreement on Climate Change, seven European countries (Denmark, France, Germany, Italy, the Netherlands, Norway, and the United Kingdom) signed the Amsterdam Palm Oil Declaration, committed to 100 percent sustainable sourcing and trade by no later than 2020 (Amsterdam Declarations Partnership 2015). In 2016, the newly formed Amsterdam Declarations Partnerships adopted an implementation strategy delineating concrete steps to achieve its sustainable sourcing objectives. The strategy mentions the RSPO as a baseline sustainability standard for the industry (Amsterdam Declarations Partnership 2016). More recently, the EU Commission has proposed a new regulation for deforestation-free supply chains, including the palm oil supply chain (EU Commission 2021). Although the proposal does not formally allow certification schemes to provide companies with a "green lane" into the EU market (Lawson 2021), it is likely to increase the adoption of established private sustainability standards, as companies make efforts to comply with the EU's mandatory due diligence requirements (Europe director at RSPO, phone interview, May 2022).

In recent years, Chinese government actors have also become more supportive of private standards and certification systems to promote sustainability in the palm oil supply chain. Despite its being a "foreign standard," this effort has benefited the RSPO in this important demand-side market (Schleifer and Sun 2018, 12–13). This optimism is tempered by a cautionary tale from the Chinese forestry sector, however. Since its entry in China around the turn of the millennium, the Forest Stewardship Council experienced strong growth until the mid-2010s, but faltered after the Chinese state withdrew its support in favor of a government-controlled and less stringent China Forest Certification Council (Bartley 2018a, 119–163). Nonetheless, the developments described above suggest a moderately favorable transnational regulatory context for the RSPO.

Supply-Side Conditions
Domestic industry structure. In Indonesia, privately owned plantation companies account for about 50 percent of the country's total oil palm area. The five largest groups control about 20 percent of the concessions (Trase 2020a). When applying for sustainability certification, large companies benefit from economies of scale, which lower their cost to adopt and comply with the standards of the RSPO. This is not the case for the growing number oil palm smallholders, however. Since the mid-1980s, smallholders' share of national production grew from 10 percent to almost 40 percent by 2015. Today, Indonesia has about two million small-scale oil palm farmers with less than 25 hectares of land (Jelsma and Schoneveld 2016, 2). The Palm Oil Agribusiness Strategic Policy Institute estimates that the share of smallholder farms could reach 60 percent by 2030 (Saragih 2017). Advancing sustainability certification in the smallholder sector is a major challenge for the RSPO, as these farmers typically lack the organizational capacity and access to finance and technology necessary to adopt and implement transnational standards (Brandi et al. 2015). In an interview, a union representative highlighted the problems faced by independent smallholders in the sector, that is, smallholder farmers who are not associated with and managed by an oil palm estate: "Our experience is where the smallholder farmers got RSPO certification like in Jambi in Riau in South Sumatra, they

are all managed farmers. Off the concession there is no chance to get RSPO certification. All the smallholders that got certification are on the concession" (interview, Bogor, April 2018). In sum, this suggests that the structure of Indonesia's palm oil industry has become less favorable for sustainability certification over time.

Support from producer groups. In Indonesia, the leading producer association is the Indonesian Palm Oil Association (GAPKI). GAPKI has about 700 members, which collectively account for over 25 percent of the country's total oil palm acreage (IPOC 2018). The RSPO initially enjoyed the support of this important industry association, and the director of GAPKI sat on its founding board. However, as explored in more detail in chapter 5, stakeholder relations in the RSPO became more conflictual over time, and GAPKI clashed with Northern NGOs and buyers over the strengthening of the RSPO's rules and certification regime. These issues have intensified producers' concerns over the cost of RSPO certification: "The costs are born by the producers. RSPO gives incentives through a premium for certified sustainable palm oil. Although declining, declining now, there are still incentives, but they don't match the costs for certification. For RSPO, we are talking about US$30 per hectare, which is a lot" (industry representative, interview, Jakarta, April 2018). In 2011, these problems led GAPKI to leave RSPO and to join the government-controlled Indonesian Sustainable Palm Oil program instead. Although many major Indonesian palm oil producers continued their membership in the RSPO, GAPKI's withdrawal was a major setback for the organization in the country (NGO member of RSPO, personal communication, Paris, June 2018). This points to an increasingly unfavorable context for the RSPO on this dimension of the framework.

Support from domestic government actors. GAPKI's decision to leave the RSPO must be understood in the national policy context, which has also become less favorable over time (see Schouten and Hospes 2018). The RSPO was conceived as a private governance mechanism without formal government involvement (former director of the Forest Conversion Initiative, phone interview, May 2013). However, in many producer countries, industry and state actors have close ties. In Indonesia, the influence of the state became clear when the government shifted from initially supporting the RSPO to opposing it, when politicians and bureaucrats began to perceive it as intruding in Indonesia's domestic affairs. The Ministry of Agriculture responded by launching its own national palm oil certification program in 2011. A few years later, the Indonesian government dealt another blow to transnational sustainability governance in the sector. Following the New York Declaration on Forests in 2014, a group of leading international palm oil buyers launched the Indonesian Palm Oil Pledge to coordinate implementation of their zero-deforestation commitments in the country. The government, suspicious of this pledge from the start, ordered its dissolution in July 2016 (Vit 2016). As shown by Dermawan and Hospes (2018), these decisions were driven by domestic considerations of sovereignty and legitimacy. However, they also need to be seen in the global context, how global market changes influence the strategies of actors in the producer countries. In this regard, the Indonesian official at the Council for Palm Oil Producing Countries, cited above, explained: "We see different markets with very different demands on price and sustainability. For sustainability you will have two different markets. It is already happening, and we respond to that" (interview, Jakarta, April 2018).

Support from local civil society. Following the fall of the Suharto regime in the late 1990s, civil society organizations became important catalysts of political change in Indonesia (Nyman 2006). In the palm oil industry, in addition to the local affiliates of large transnational NGOs, these organizations include mostly small-scale environmental, labor rights, and indigenous people's rights groups. As of February 2022, nine Indonesian NGOs participated in the RSPO (RSPO 2022). One of the most active organizations in the palm oil sector is Sawit Watch ("Oil Palm Watch" in Bahasa). Founded in 1998, Sawit Watch is a network of over fifty local advocacy groups from across the archipelago (Sawit Watch 2020). The organization has been a member of the RSPO since 2004. A campaigner at Sawit Watch described its position vis-à-vis the RSPO: "RSPO is an important mechanism for us but there are many problems and troubles inside the system. [The palm oil companies] have a lot of power inside and can steer the RSPO. That is the problem but as X said we still need RSPO. At least, we can use this system to improve production. Because besides RSPO there is no alternative" (interview, Bogor, April 2018). This and further communications with representatives from civil society organizations in Indonesia, including Greenpeace Indonesia, Inobu, and Solidaridad Indonesia, indicate a moderately favorable local civil society context for the RSPO in Indonesia.

The Roundtable on Responsible Soy

The soybean is often referred to as the "king the beans" (Clay 2004, 174). The dry seed contains 38 percent protein, more than any other food crop and twice as much as pork. About 85 percent of global production is processed into meal and oil. Due to its cost-effectiveness and high protein content, approximately 98 percent of soybean meal is processed as a raw material for industrial livestock feed (Clay 2004, 173–202). Soybean oil contributes to about 15 percent of the world's biodiesel (Kim, Hanifzadeh, and Kumar 2018, 9). To satisfy rapidly growing global demand for vegetable oil and protein, Brazil has converted millions of hectares of land into soybean fields, which has contributed directly and indirectly to deforestation in the country (Arima et al. 2011; Henders, Persson, and Kastner 2015).

The WWF's Forest Conversion Initiative has targeted both palm oil and soy commodities (WWF 2005). However, unlike the RSPO with palm oil, the RTRS never successfully captured a significant share of global soy production. As shown in figure 4.3, the RTRS scheme remains significantly behind the RSPO in terms of global market uptake. With some 200 firms participating, the RTRS also has a much smaller membership (RTRS 2020). To explain this lack of market uptake, I use the analytical framework developed above to examine the demand-side and supply-side conditions in this industry.

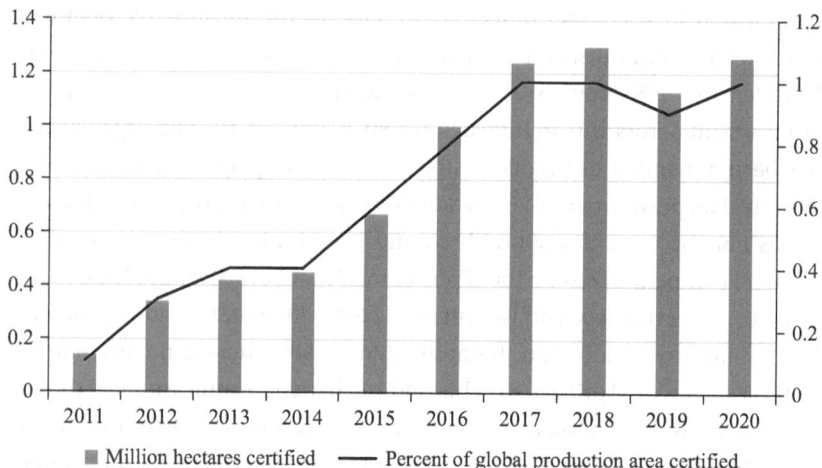

Figure 4.3
Global adoption of the RTRS
Source: Analysis of data from FAOSTAT and RTRS (2021a)

Demand-Side Conditions

Location of end markets. Brazil is the world's largest exporter of soybeans. In 2018, the value of its exports was US$33 billion, with 65 percent of this production being shipped overseas (analysis of data from ITC n.d.). The EU has long been the world's largest importer of Brazilian soy. European soy imports increased strongly after the "mad cow disease" in the UK and a ban throughout the EU on feeding animal protein to ruminants in 1994. According to theories of nonstate market-driven governance (see Cashore, Auld, and Newsom 2004, 40–43), European demand for Brazilian soy should have made the sector a favorable environment for transnational sustainability certification. Indeed, when the WWF's FCI was launched in 2001, its founders recognized an opportunity for European supply chains to function as a "powerful driver of change" in the industry. As explained by its former director, "we did stakeholder analysis, we mapped the trade flows and got into the details how this industry operates and who the key players are" (phone interview, May 2013). However, the global soy economy has shifted dramatically since the FCI conducted its mapping analysis in the early 2000s (see figure 4.4.). The EU's share of Brazilian soy exports dropped sharply, whereas China's skyrocketed. To a large extent, this shift in the global trade in soy was driven by changing diets in China. Growing meat consumption in China, particularly pork, in combination with limited domestic supply of animal feed, drove large-scale soy imports from Brazil

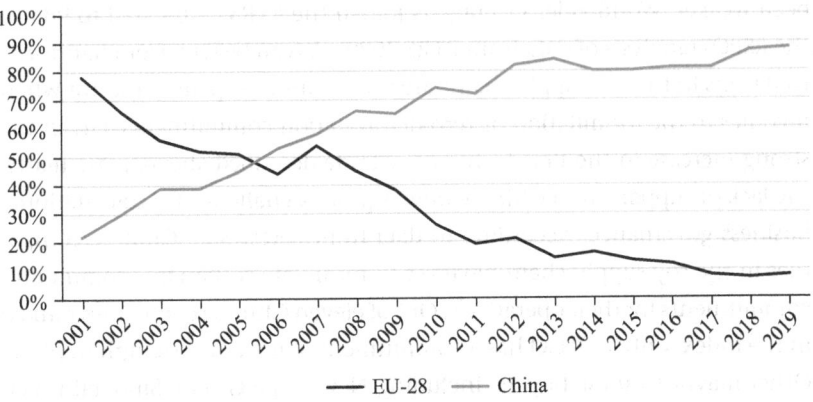

Figure 4.4
Share of Brazilian soybean and soymeal exports (in value terms)
Source: Analysis of data from ITC International Trade Statistics, https://www.intracen.org/itc/market-info-tools/trade-statistics/

and the United States for the country's growing livestock industry (Brown-Lima, Cooney, and Cleary 2009). More recently, the trade conflict between China and the United States has increased China's reliance on Brazil even further. In 2018, in response to US tariffs, the Chinese government imposed import duties of 25 percent on select US goods, including soybeans. As a result, Chinese imports of soybeans from the United States dropped sharply by 50 percent in 2018. Analysts expect that the US-Chinese trade conflict risks causing further agricultural expansion and deforestation in Brazil and other soybean-producing countries (Fuchs et al. 2019).

Responding to the changing global context, the RTRS and its partners have made several attempts to gain traction in the Chinese soy supply chain. In 2013, the organization held its annual conference in Beijing to better understand the Chinese market and to develop partnerships with buyers in this market. However, as noted by a member of the RTRS secretariat, Chinese companies have yet to embrace sustainability as a priority. In China, "it's mainly about food safety. Food safety and food security. Sustainability in the soy supply chain is not a big issue yet" (member of RTRS secretariat, phone interview, June 2013). In sum, for this condition, the analysis reveals a shift from a favorable to an unfavorable context for the RTRS.

Role of lead firms. Since the launch of the RTRS in the mid-2000s, lead firms in the soy supply chain have increased their support for transnational sustainability standards and the zero-deforestation agenda in the sector. However, in comparison to the palm oil sector, support from lead firms has been weaker. Worldwide, 113 buyers joined the RTRS (compared to 983 in the RSPO) (analysis of data from RTRS 2020). As can be seen from figure 4.1, lead firms in the soy supply chains are also behind the palm oil sector when it comes to the formulation of zero-deforestation commitments. Given the strong increase in the Brazil-China soy trade described above, particularly, the lack of support from Chinese buyers poses a challenge for transnational business governance. According to data from Forest 500, Chinese companies in the soy supply chain have yet to formulate sustainable commodity commitments for their operations. Out of eleven Chinese companies ranked in the index, only COFCO has a commitment of medium strength in place. Other mayor Chinese buyers, including New Hope Group, Sinograin, Beidahuang Group, and East Hope Group, have made no commitments (Forest 500 2021). Moreover, none of these companies has endorsed the New York Declaration on Forests, and the RTRS does not have a single buyer from

China among its members (NYDF Global Platform 2019; RTRS 2020). While several of the major trading companies supplying soybeans to China (e.g., Bunge, Cargill, and ADM) have commitments in place, their willingness and ability to implement their standards remain in question (see chapter 5). Overall, the analysis suggests that this condition has improved, from unfavorably to moderately favorably. However, in comparison to the palm oil sector, support from lead firms is weaker.

Transnational advocacy pressure. In the early 2000s, a Greenpeace campaign targeting McDonalds, Cargill, and other major players in the soy supply chain was instrumental in putting pressure on these companies to engage with the problem of commodity-driven deforestation (e.g., Greenpeace 2006). Ever since, the soy industry's link to deforestation has been the focus of transnational activism, particularly among civil society groups in Europe. However, this campaign did not have the same strength as the similar campaign in the palm oil sector. One indicator for this is the previously cited media analysis by Chagas et al. (2018, 10). It shows that soy is less frequently mentioned as a driver of tropical deforestation than palm oil. According to a campaigner at an NGO based in Brussels, one reason for this is that soy is mainly used as animal feed, which is even more "hidden" from consumers than palm oil (personal communication, Brussels, July 2018). Another challenge is the widespread use of genetically modified organisms (GMOs) in the industry. About 80 percent of global soy production is genetically modified (European Biotechnology 2017). The widespread use of GMOs in the sector and the RTRS decision to certify genetically modified soy as "responsible" resulted in activist groups in Europe and the producer countries opposing the RTRS (campaigner at GM Watch, interview, London, July 2013). In sum, the RTRS has benefited from international campaigns on soy-driven deforestation. However, the international campaign has been less powerful than in the palm oil sector, and concerns about GMOs have led to resistance from civil society groups in Europe. The result is a moderately favorable context for the RTRS.

Support from external state actors. As in the palm oil sector, private governance in the soy sector has benefited from the support of European governments and institutions, though arguably to a somewhat lesser degree. Due to the importance of the port of Rotterdam in the Netherlands for Europe's soy trade, the Dutch government in particular has taken a proactive stance on the issue. In the past, the Dutch state had directly supported the RTRS with financial contributions and was a main driver behind the Amsterdam Declaration on Deforestation, which included soy as one of the focus commodities (policy officer, Dutch Ministry of Economic Affairs, personal communication, Amsterdam, December 2017). Another European-led initiative is the EU-Brazil Sustainable Soy Partnership. Launched in 2017, it includes a memorandum of understanding between leading Brazilian producers and European feed manufacturers to advance sustainability in the soy supply chain. To reach its objectives, the partnership relies on existing sustainability standards. Interestingly, however, this partnership did not benefit the RTRS. Instead, it used the Soja Plus Program, sponsored by the Brazilian soy industry, as a benchmark (policy analyst at ITC, personal communication, Geneva, October 2017). The WWF criticized the partnership, arguing that it would strengthen the industry-controlled Soja Plus program over the more stringent and inclusive RTRS (see Byrne 2017). More recently, soy was also included in the above-mentioned EU regulation for deforestation-free supply chains (EU Commission 2021). When it comes into force, the regulation will intensify transnational regulatory pressures on companies in the soy supply chain to address problems of deforestation. As in the case of palm oil, these developments suggest a more favorable transnational regulatory context for the RTRS.

At the same time, intensifying regulatory pressures from Europe are likely to be tempered by the EU's strongly decreased share of Brazilian soy exports. As shown in figure 4.4, in 2019, the EU accounted for only 8 percent of Brazil's exports, whereas China absorbed 88 percent. According to analysts, this puts the Chinese government in a strong position to provide sustainability regulation for the industry. "If the Chinese government starts to advocate, regulate and develop guidelines for sustainable agricultural supply chains, and starts to ask financial institutions to incorporate deforestation considerations into their financial decisions, that would provide a strong driving force for both companies and financial institutions to implement changes in line with the government" (director of CDP China, as cited in China Dialogue 2019, 46). Recently, representatives of the Chinese Ministry of Commerce have signaled their support for the efforts of Solidaridad, a Dutch NGO, to draft sustainable soy guidelines for China (Solidaridad 2019). However, at this point in time, there is no indication of the formation of a broader regulatory coalition on the issue in China.

Supply-Side Conditions

Domestic industry structure. Supported by government programs, large-scale soybean cultivation started in the 1960s in southern Brazil, and then expanded to the tropical savannas of the Cerrado in the midwestern part of the country. In 2018, 216,000 farms produced 122 million megatons of soybeans on 36 million hectares of land, accounting for approximately 36 percent of global production (Cattelan and Dall'Agnol 2018; FAOSTAT). Brazil's major soy-producing states are Mato Grosso (nicknamed "Soylandia"), followed by Paraná and Rio Grande do Sul (USDA 2020). In terms of production modes, the sector is divided along geographical lines. Large-scale, highly mechanized farms dominate in the midwest and small-scale farms in the south. In the industrial midwest, where the majority of production takes place, Byerlee and Deiniger (2010) estimate that the average farm size is over 1,000 hectares, with many megafarms planting more than 100,000 hectares of cropland. For example, the Mato Grosso–based Amaggi Group owns nineteen farms on 200,000 hectares (Barbosa 2015, 69). In contrast, the average farm in southern Brazil is about 35 hectares (Cattelan and Dall'Agnol 2018, 4). For certification schemes, this means that conditions are favorable in some parts of the country but unfavorable in others, pointing to a moderately favorable environment for certification programs like the RTRS in Brazil.

Support from producer groups. Brazilian soy farmers and processing companies are organized in two powerful industry associations, the Brazilian Association of Soy Producers (Aprosoja), founded in 1990, and the Brazilian Association of Vegetable Oils (ABIOVE), founded in 1981. Aprosoja represents approximately 90 percent of Brazil's soybean cultivation, and ABIOVE accounts for approximately 70 percent of the country's soy-processing volume (Zanon, Saes, and Macchione 2010). Similar to the dynamics observed in the palm oil sector, the two industry associations initially supported the RTRS, but the relationships with Northern NGOs and buyers was conflictual. In particular, the RTRS's policy on agricultural expansion and deforestation became a major source of disagreement between Brazilian producer groups and Northern NGOs and buyers. Aprosoja and ABIOVE both strongly opposed a criterion that prohibited the clearing of new land for soybean production after a certain cut-off date (manager at soy producing company, phone interview, July 2013). As one of their representatives stated in a meeting of the RTRS executive board: "Producers are legally entitled to deforest because their level of compliance goes beyond the quota required by law. RTRS should not forbid something that is permitted by Brazilian law" (RTRS 2009, 3). Eventually, these disagreements between producers, NGOs, and downstream companies could not be resolved, and the two industry associations left the RTRS in 2010 (member of the RTRS executive board, phone interview, May 2013). Shortly after, ABIOVE, Aprosoja, and other major Brazilian industry actors created the Soja Plus program, "as an alternative to the imposing and removed-from-reality character of some certification programs, such as the Roundtable on Responsible Soy" (ABIOVE, as cited in Schouten and Bitzer 2015, 180). A policy officer of the Amazon Environmental Research Institute described the Soja Plus Program as more "flexible" and "easy" for producers to implement, questioning its effectiveness on the ground. He also expressed concerns about the competition that Soja Plus posed for the RTRS, worrying that the loss of support from the two industry associations would undermine the RTRS in Brazil (phone interview, July 2013). As in the palm oil sector, this condition changed from moderately favorable to unfavorable over time.

Support from domestic government actors. The Amazon Soy Moratorium of 2006, a regional moratorium on the sourcing of deforestation-linked soy production from the Amazon biome, is often cited as a successful example of supply chain interventions and domestic policies reinforcing one another. In this case, public policy initiatives complemented the buyer-driven moratorium by improving land-use management, forest protection, and government monitoring in the Amazon. The result was a significant reduction in deforestation in the Amazon toward the end of the 2000s (Boucher, Roquemore, and Fitzhugh 2013; Hansen et al. 2013; Nepstad et al. 2014). The example of the Amazon Soy Moratorium shows that supportive government policies are of key importance for the effectiveness of supply chain initiatives to reduce tropical deforestation. Unfortunately, Brazil's domestic policy context has changed dramatically in recent years. Emboldened by President Bolsonaro's antienvironmentalist agenda, the country's powerful agribusiness lobby has further increased its influence and environmental institutions and regulations have been weakened (Branford and Borges 2019). This weakening includes growing opposition against the Amazon Soy Moratorium and the broader zero-deforestation agenda (Samora 2019b). According to the director of agriculture at the Nature Conservancy, "under Bolsonaro, soy farm associations have been emboldened. . . . [Bolsonaro] whipped a populist support against interfering NGOs [while billing] zero deforestation as a neo-imperialistic manoeuvre" (as cited in Hillson 2020).

However, even before Bolsonaro's rise to power, the local policy context had become increasingly unfavorable for the RTRS. The country's central legislation to protect forests, the National Forest Code of 1965, which became a de facto environmental law in the 1990s, requires landowners to conserve parts of the natural vegetation on their property. The law also creates Areas of Permanent Preservation across the country to protect valuable ecosystems. Under pressure from the agriculture lobby, which used declining deforestation rates in the Amazon to make its case, the government reformed the Forest Code in 2012 (researcher at the Amazon Environmental Research Institute, phone interview, July 2013). The revisions made significant reductions in the size of preservation areas and granted amnesty for past illegal deforestation (Soares-Filho et al. 2014). The decision of Brazil's producer associations to withdraw their support from the RTRS, as described above, occurred in the context of these policy changes. The standards of the RTRS were increasingly at odds with domestic legislation at a time when Brazilian producers were becoming less dependent on Europe as an end market (see also Schleifer 2017, 7–8).

Support from local civil society. Like Indonesia, Brazil has a vibrant civil society sphere, with many domestic groups focused directly or indirectly on the agriculture sector as part of their work on rainforest protection, rural development, and indigenous peoples' rights. Local civil society groups played an important role in the Amazon Soy Moratorium (see Boucher, Roquemore, and Fitzhugh 2013). However, attempts by the RTRS to create a sectorwide certification scheme were met with skepticism and outright opposition from a coalition of transnational and local civil society actors. Only two Brazilian NGOs (Aliança da Terra and Associação Amigos da Terra) joined the RTRS (RTRS 2020). A campaigner from Amigos da Terra described fierce opposition to RTRS from local groups in Brazil and other South American countries (phone interview, December 2012). The roundtable's first conference in Foz do Iguaçu in 2005 became a highly politicized event when Via Campensina, Grupo de Reflexión Rural, and other local groups protested against its close ties with big agribusiness and the RTRS's acceptance of genetically modified and monoculture soybeans (Grupo de Reflexión Rural 2005). Criticism of the RTRS spread to other producer countries and international NGOs, and more protests were held at the second and third roundtable conferences in Paraguay and Argentina (campaigner at Friends of the Earth, phone interview, December 2012). The intense criticism faced by the RTRS from civil society actors in the producer countries points to an unfavorable context.

Comparative Findings

The comparative analysis reveals differences and similarities between the political economy context of the RSPO and RTRS as well as changes over time (see table 4.3). Since the launch of the WWF's FCI in the early 2000s, global markets for tropical commodities have shifted. These shifts are changing the geography of trade in both the palm oil and soy industries, but to different degrees. In the soy sector, the shifting of supply chains from North-South to South-South was dramatic. In the decade following the launch of the RTRS, Europe's share of Brazilian soy exports dropped from over 50 percent to less than 10 percent (see figure 4.4). More recently, the trade conflict between the United States and China has accelerated this trend, with Chinese buyers shifting even more orders to Brazil to avoid costly tariffs (Bloomberg 2019a). The international trade in palm oil also experienced global market shifts, including growing domestic consumption and demand for imported vegetable oil in China and India. However, unlike the soy sector, the EU has retained more of its share of the global palm oil market.

Market size is not the only factor that matters though. In the palm oil sector, European actors retained substantial agenda-setting power in this industry due to the interplay of several market and nonmarket conditions, which reinforced one another. In particular, the RSPO benefited from a high level of support from European buyers and a powerful transnational

Table 4.3
The scope conditions for the RSPO and RTRS

Position	Condition	Type	Palm oil	Soy
Demand-side	Location of end markets	Market	+	++→−
	Support from lead firms		−→++	−→+
	Transnational advocacy pressure	Nonmarket	++	+
	Support from external state actors		−→+	−→+
Supply-side	Domestic industry structure	Market	+→−	+
	Support from producer groups		+→−	+→−
	Support from domestic state actors	Nonmarket	+→−	+→−
	Support from local civil society		+	−

++ favorable, + moderately favorable, − unfavorable, → change over time advocacy network, as well as from direct endorsement and support from EU state actors. In comparison, in the soy sector, the RTRS had less support from lead firms and relations with civil society actors were more antagonistic. Together, these differences help explain the observed variation in market uptake between the two schemes and why the RSPO was at least moderately successful, but the RTRS was not.

At the same time, these cases have important similarities that can help explain why even the initially successful RSPO has stalled in its mission to transform global markets and to "make sustainable palm oil the norm" beyond European supply chains (RSPO 2014). One important reason is the previously described bifurcation of global commodity markets and the apparent inability of established transnational schemes to gain traction among emerging market buyers. Many of the described scope conditions are absent in these end markets (Schleifer and Sun 2018), though some promising developments are noted. For example, major emerging market players, such as China's COFCO, have announced efforts to increase action on commodity-driven deforestation and other sustainability issues (World Economic Forum 2019). Also, there is growing awareness among state actors in emerging economies about the importance of sustainable sourcing guidelines and standards for their industries. However, as examined in more depth in chapter 5, it is unclear whether and how this will translate into transnational regulatory action.

In addition to challenges at the global level, the RSPO and RTRS confronted a deterioration of the domestic political economy context in the producer countries. Indeed, the supply-side conditions experienced negative trends in both sectors. Over the period of investigation, producer groups and state actors in Indonesia and Brazil changed their positions from initially supporting these programs to opposing them. These attempts by Southern actors to reclaim the regulatory space have multiple causes, including bureaucratic politics, the transnational scheme's lack of local legitimacy, and changing discourses about national sovereignty (see Giessen et al. 2016; Schouten and Bitzer 2015; Schouten and Hospes 2018). However, these developments also need to be understood in the global context. As markets for agricultural commodities shift to the Global South, actors in producer countries will become empowered to transition from rule takers to rule makers. These dynamics are indeed observed in the soy and palm oil industries. Figure 4.5 illustrates the findings from the comparative analysis. Based on the empirical assessment of demand-side and

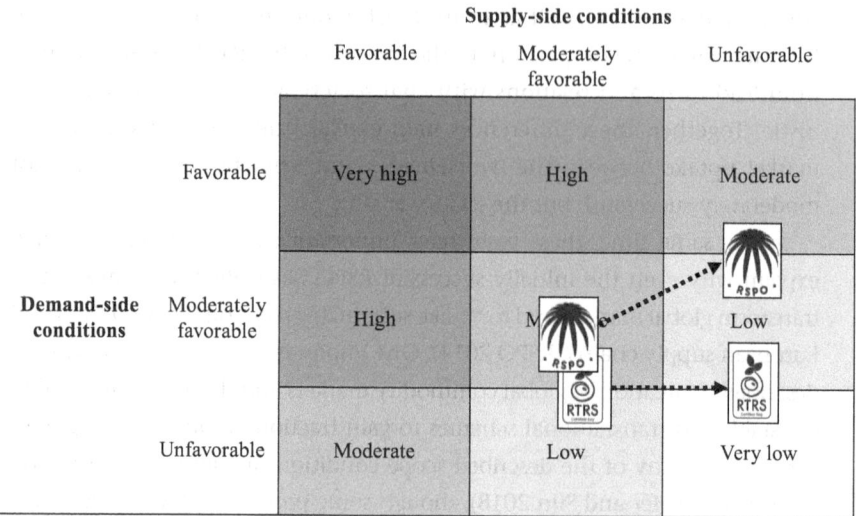

Figure 4.5
Potential for private governance adoption in the palm oil and soy sectors

supply-side conditions, it shows how the potential for private governance uptake in the two sectors has evolved.

Conclusion

This chapter explores two questions linked to the uptake of private sustainability standards in the agrifood sector. First, what is the state of sustainable markets in the major forest-risk commodity sectors? Second, how do differences and common trends emerge in the palm oil and soy sectors during times of major structural change in the world economy? Below, I revisit these questions in light of the chapter's main empirical findings.

Regarding the first question, the triangulation of data from Forest 500, Supply Change, and Sustainability Map allows for a detailed description of the state of private governance in global markets for forest-risk commodities. The emerging patterns and trends confirm past criticisms regarding insufficient progress in meeting international policy targets. Although certification coverage and corporate commitments have increased significantly since the New York Declaration on Forests, overall policy uptake has fallen far short of expectations (NYDF Assessment Partners 2019). Moreover, the analysis reveals a highly uneven distribution of company commitments and adoption of third-party certification schemes across commodity sectors. In particular, low adoption rates in the beef and soy supply chains are problematic, as these commodities have the highest deforestation impact. Another observation is that policy uptake has slowed overall, with some companies even backtracking on their earlier commitments.

To explain the observed variations and commonalities, the second part of the chapter focused on two mature transnational sustainability schemes: the RSPO in the palm oil sector and the RTRS in the soy sector. Using a comparative political economy framework, relevant demand-side and supply-side conditions were systematically compared across the two cases. The results help explain why the RSPO remains at least moderately successful, as the interplay of several demand-side factors enabled the scheme to gain significant uptake in the North-South setting of the Indonesia-EU palm oil trade. In contrast, with less support from European firms, civil society, and state actors, the almost identical RTRS failed to achieve the same level of success in the soy sector.

Some important commonalities between the two cases are worth mentioning. Confronted with global market shifts, a lack of support from emerging market buyers, and growing antagonism from powerful state and industry actors in the producer countries, both schemes have struggled to adapt to the new geography of polycentric trade. As a consequence, their uptake in emerging market and domestic supply chains remains low. As the volume of South-South trade in forest-risk commodities continues to grow—and there are good reasons to believe that it will (Chain Reaction Research 2020a)—challenges to the effectiveness of transnational private governance in these sectors will become even more salient. To further deepen this analysis, the next chapter shifts the focus from questions of market uptake to the ways in which sustainability governance disseminates through global, regional, and domestic production networks. Therefore, chapter 5 uses the lens of global value chain analysis to examine the politics and governance of environmental upgrading in Indonesia's palm oil supply chain.

5 Multipolar Governance in the Palm Oil Value Chain

Political scientists have linked the causes and consequences of transnational regulatory authority to the power of lead firms in global supply chains (Bartley 2018a; Cashore, Auld, and Newsom 2004; Clapp and Fuchs 2009; Dauvergne and Lister 2010; Fuchs and Kalfagianni 2010). However, the structure and governance of these production networks remain surprisingly neglected in this literature. Only recently have scholars begun to systematically combine insights from supply chain research with the political science literature on transnational business governance (Macdonald 2014; Partzsch 2020; Ponte 2019; Schleifer 2016b; van der Ven 2018). This chapter advances research in this area by exploring the politics of sustainability in the supply chains of the "post-Washington Consensus world" (Gereffi 2014).

My focus in this chapter is on the value chain for palm oil, which is one of the world's most highly traded agricultural commodities, with an export value of US$32 billion in 2020 (analysis of data from FAOSTAT). Among the major forest-risk commodities, the palm oil value chain also has the highest uptake of transnational sustainability standards, which makes it a most-likely case for standard-driven environmental upgrading, or the "process[es] by which economic actors move towards a production system that avoids or reduces environmental damage" (De Marchi, Di Maria, and Micelli 2013, 65). In this chapter, however, I am not so much interested in the technical side of environmental upgrading, nor do I attempt to systematically measure it. Instead, my aim is to advance understanding of how evolving regulatory coalitions in the sector's global, regional, and local production networks shape the politics and governance of environmental upgrading in this industry. Guided by the analytical framework developed in chapter 2, I focus on the following questions: What is the structure of the palm oil value chain in the age of advanced globalization? What are the main modes of sustainability governance in its global, regional, and domestic production networks? What are the implications for the governance of standard-driven environmental upgrading in this industry?

This chapter proceeds in three main steps: First, I give a brief overview of the palm oil industry to provide important historical context for understanding its present-day political dynamics. Second, I unpack the Indonesian palm oil value chain, which I describe as polycentric in its structure (i.e., it has intersecting trade networks of North-South, South-South, and domestic supply chains) and multipolar in its governance (i.e., multiple actors internal and external to the chain coordinate and govern the industry). Finally, I draw on interviews, organizational records, and other primary and secondary sources to analyze the politics and governance of environmental upgrading in the palm oil value chain.

A Brief History of the Palm Oil Industry

The palm oil industry has its origins in colonial Africa and Asia. In 1911, the Lever Brother's Company (Unilever after 1929) obtained a concession from colonial authorities to develop 750,000 hectares of land for oil palm cultivation in the Belgian Congo. Unilever's Congo-based operation was one of the industry's first export-oriented plantation developments. For the most part, however, African palm oil production remained based on smallholder agriculture and the farming of semiwild trees and was soon outcompeted by a fast-growing Southeast Asian industrial cluster, organized on estate lines inherited from the cultivation of rubber (Giacomin 2018). When European colonial rule ended, many African countries also became locked in cycles of political crisis and conflict. This political instability adversely affected the development of the African palm oil industry (Berger and Martin 2000), although "big palm oil" has made a comeback on the continent in recent years (Cannon 2016).

With an ideal climate and more favorable political economic context, Southeast Asia emerged as the center of the modern palm oil industry. In the mid-1900s, Dutch colonialists planted the first oil palm trees in the botanical gardens of Bogor (Buitenzorg) on Java Island in the Dutch East Indies, now known as Indonesia. Western businessmen and scientists also introduced modern planting and processing techniques to the region, and by the 1940s, Indonesia had some 110,000 hectares of land under oil palm cultivation, with most of the product destined for Europe, where it was used in soap and margarines. New high-yield plant varieties, improved oil refineries, and innovations in the consumer goods industries in Europe led to rapid expansion of the industry in the second half of the twentieth century (Berger and Martin 2000; Byerlee, Falcon, and Naylor 2016).

Cramb and McCarthy (2016b) describe how this growth is inextricably linked to state-led development policies after World War II. They describe how a government-industrial complex, consisting of political, bureaucratic, and corporate elites, drove the expansion of the industry in the region. The close ties between industry and government persist to this day, with important implications for contemporary regulatory politics, as discussed later in this chapter. The development of the modern industry first took shape in Malaysia in the 1960s. Responding to declining rubber prices and supported by loans from the World Bank, the Malaysian government diversified its agriculture sector and invested heavily in the expansion of its palm oil sector as part of an export-oriented development strategy (Byerlee, Falcon, and Naylor 2016, 13). However, as land in Malaysia became scarcer and wages increased, the industry eventually sought alternative locations.

Palm oil boomed in the late twentieth century, mostly in areas of Southeastern Asia with abundant land and cheap labor. In the 1980s, the promotion of an export-oriented plantation sector became a key government policy of Indonesian President Suharto's New Order Regime. The government offered large swaths of state forests and native land to attract foreign investments in this sector (Cramb and McCarthy 2016a). Policymakers also implemented a countrywide transmigration regime (*transmigrasi*), which had started under Dutch colonial rule and which resettled millions of families from the overcrowded island of Java to the much less populated outer islands, such as Sumatra, Kalimantan, and West Papua. These transmigrants were an important source of cheap labor and a key driver of industry expansion (Li 2016). The abundant availability of land, labor, and capital, along with rapidly growing global demand for cheap vegetable oil, initiated unprecedented agricultural expansion in Indonesia. Between 1990 and 2019, oil palm cultivation in the country increased from less than one million to more than fourteen million hectares (see figure 5.1).

Driven by the global commodity boom of the 2000s, the sector has become one of Indonesia's main foreign currency earners, with a total export value of US$17 billion in 2020 (analysis of data from FAOSTAT). As

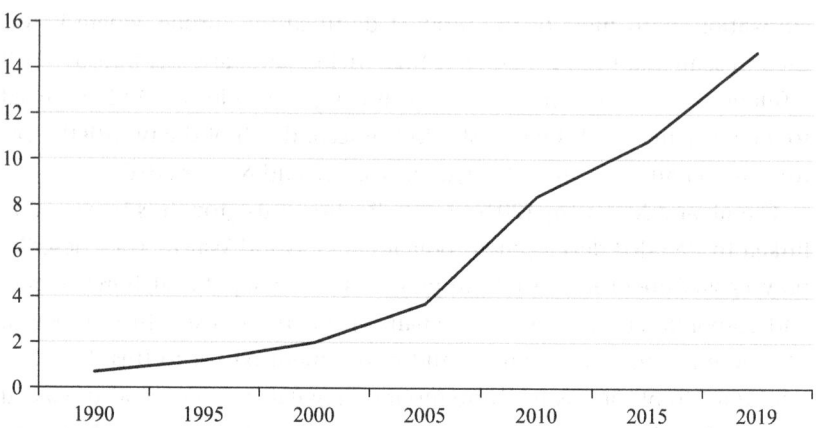

Figure 5.1
Oil palm cultivation area in Indonesia (million hectares)
Source: Analysis of data from FAOSTAT

detailed in chapter 1, this rapid expansion came at significant environmental and human costs, though. Since 2000, Indonesia has lost over six million hectares of primary forests, mostly due to large-scale land use changes and forest fires. The palm oil industry has been a major driver of these processes (Margono et al. 2014; Wicke et al. 2011). The industry is linked to deforestation and biodiversity loss; poor labor conditions on the plantations; and conflicts over land rights between native communities, transmigrants, and palm oil companies (Abram et al. 2017; Li 2016).

The Indonesian Palm Oil Value Chain

The modern palm oil value chain can be divided into three main segments: an upstream segment (growers, processors, and refiners), a midstream segment (exporters and importers), and a downstream segment (ingredient manufacturers, consumer goods companies, retailers, and other industrial users). Figure 5.2 illustrates this chain.

These segments are common to many primary commodity sectors and production networks. However, the palm oil value chain does not closely resemble the typical supply chain identified in the global value chain (GVC) literature (see Gereffi 1994, 1999; Gereffi, Humphrey, and Sturgeon 2005). I therefore take a close look at this value chain and its evolving features.

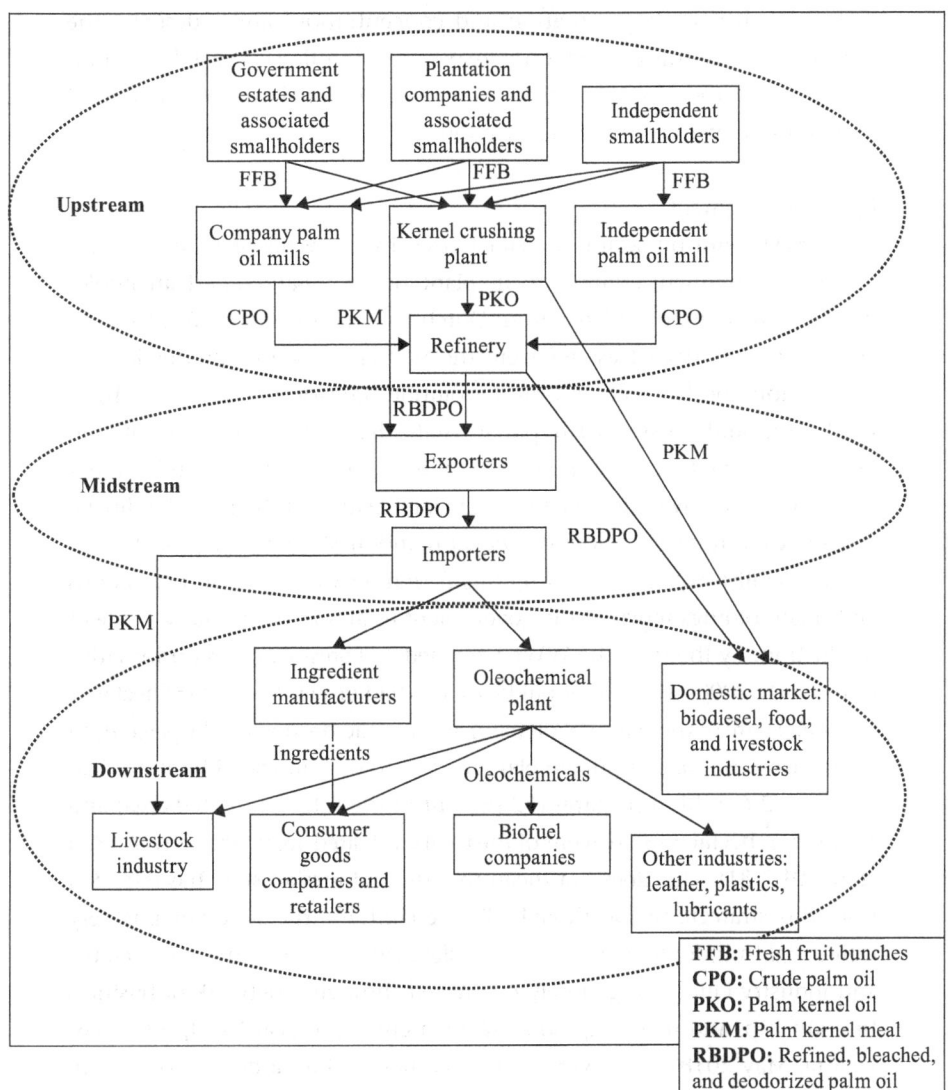

Figure 5.2
The Indonesian palm oil value chain (simplified)

I identify areas of fragmentation and concentration, and I describe the polycentricity of this production network. This is followed by a description of the main governance drivers in the industry's global, regional, and local production networks in the next section.

Upstream Segment

Indonesia's palm oil sector is characterized by three major modes of production: government estates, private plantation companies, and smallholdings. Following independence from Dutch colonial rule after World War II, government-controlled estates were the primary mode of production. In 1980, before the Tropical Oil Crop Revolution transformed the sector (Byerlee, Falcon, and Naylor 2016), public estates had 200,000 hectares of land under oil palm (68 percent of the total cultivated area). After the end of President Suharto's New Order Regime in the late 1990s and the period of liberal economic reforms that followed (*reformasi*), Indonesia experienced a phase of rapid capitalist expansion. During this period, privately owned plantations and smallholdings replaced the government estates as the primary mode of production. By the time the WWF launched its Forest Conversion Initiative in the early 2000s, the size of public estates had grown to 560,000 hectares, but their share of the national oil palm acreage had dropped to 11 percent. In comparison, the size of private plantations and oil palm smallholdings had grown to 2.6 million hectares (52 percent of the total cultivated area) and 1.8 million hectares (37 percent of the total cultivated area), respectively (Zen et al. 2016, 81). This does not mean that the Indonesian state has retreated from this strategic sector, though. To the contrary, the state remains very influential in Indonesia's oil palm complex, with government, bureaucratic, and industry elites being closely connected through a network of business ties, kinship, and revolving doors (campaigner at a local NGO, interview, Jakarta, May 2018). However, when it comes to the mode of production, private companies and smallholders clearly dominate the modern industry.

In the upstream segment of the palm oil value chain, corporate concentration is highest at the refining stage, in which the five largest groups (PTPN III, Sinar Mas, Sime Darby, Astra Agro Lesarti, and Wilmar) control about two-thirds of the refining capacity. Otherwise, the production segment lacks vertical integration. Refiners source from a large number of palm oil mills (there are approximately 1,100 mills in Indonesia), which are controlled by 178 industrial groups (Trase 2020a, 2). In addition, there is a growing number of independent mills (Jelsma and Schoneveld 2016, 4). The production stage of the palm oil value chain is even more fragmented, with approximately 38,000 oil palm concessions owned by 1,739 companies that are part of 187 larger industrial groups. Taken together, the five large groups mentioned above control approximately 20 percent of these concessions (Trase 2020a, 2–5).

In addition to government estates and privately owned groups, smallholder agriculture is an important mode of production in Indonesia. As previously described in chapter 4, over two million smallholders account for approximately 40 percent of national production and over half of the country's total oil palm acreage (Jelsma and Schoneveld 2016, 2). The group of oil palm smallholders is highly diverse. It includes so-called scheme or plasma smallholders, who are linked to a private or government-owned estate. Scheme smallholders sell their produce to these estates, from which they also receive seedlings, fertilizer, and training.[1] The independent smallholder sector (not connected to a public or private estate) in Indonesia also is growing rapidly (Jelsma et al. 2017). Many smallholders are subsistence farmers who sell their produce via middlemen to independent mills. This segment of the palm oil supply chain is highly complex. Precise information about the number, location, and production of these independent oil palm smallholders is lacking.

Midstream Segment

The palm oil chain does not fit into the buyer-driven versus producer-driven dichotomy (Gereffi 1994). Instead, like other primary commodity sectors, it is best described as a trader-driven chain (Gibbon 2001). Trading companies represent a crucial link connecting upstream producers to downstream buyers. Operating on very small profit margins, the business model of grain and oilseed traders has historically been based on bulk and economies of scale (Clapp 2020, 24–57). As size is such an important factor for these companies, this segment of the palm oil value chain is highly concentrated. In the case of Indonesia, over 40 percent of the country's palm oil exports are handled by just four companies and their subsidiaries: Apical,[2] Golden Agri-Resources, Musim Mas, and Wilmar. Taken together, the top ten companies in this supply chain segment have a combined market share of approximately 60 percent (analysis of data from FAOSTAT; Trase n.d.). Some of these companies are vertically integrated conglomerates that own plantations, mills, and refineries at the upstream end of the supply chain, in addition to their trading operations. As discussed later in this chapter, these companies are very powerful players in the palm oil industry.

Downstream Segment

The downstream segment of the modern palm oil value chain has two salient features, high fragmentation and fast-growing end markets in the Global South. Palm oil is used in a wide range of consumer goods and industrial products (e.g., processed foods, body care and cosmetics products, detergents, and pharmaceuticals). Oleochemicals also are used in many industrial products and processes (e.g., plastics, lubricants, and leather). The downstream segment thus is more fragmented than that of other primary commodity sectors. For example, whereas the coffee value chain is dominated by a relatively small number of large lead firms mostly from the Global North, palm oil has many corporate consumers. Unilever, the world's largest palm oil buyer, accounts for only 4 percent of global demand (Pacheco et al. 2017, 13), whereas Nestlé controls over 20 percent of the global coffee retail market (Grabs 2020a, 10).

In addition to this fragmentation, the palm oil value chain is characterized by polycentric trade and growing end markets in the Global South (see figure 5.3). As described in chapter 3, both the volume of South-South trade (China and India) and domestic consumption have increased considerably in recent years. A closer look at the structure of the industry's Southern supply chains provides important context for the analysis in this chapter. India is the world's largest importer of palm oil, using 90–95 percent of its imported oil for food-based downstream activities, mostly cooking, and about 5–10 percent for products other than food, such as biodiesel, cosmetics, and detergents (Centre for Responsible Business 2018, 24). India's edible-oils market has a branded and an unbranded product market. However, unlike Northern consumer markets, the share of branded products in India is relatively small: about 11 percent of palm oil is sold as a branded product, compared to 89 percent sold as unbranded cooking oil to lower-end consumers. Both types are supplied by thirty to forty companies that control about 70–80 percent of the market (Centre for Responsible Business 2014, 20–24; 2018). They process the palm oil and sell it to local wholesalers and retailers. However, unlike Northern consumer markets, the retail end of the Indian palm oil supply chain is highly fragmented. Organized retail accounts for less than 10 percent of total sales; most consumers in India shop in street markets and small family-owned stores (Singh 2014).

Multipolar Governance in the Palm Oil Value Chain

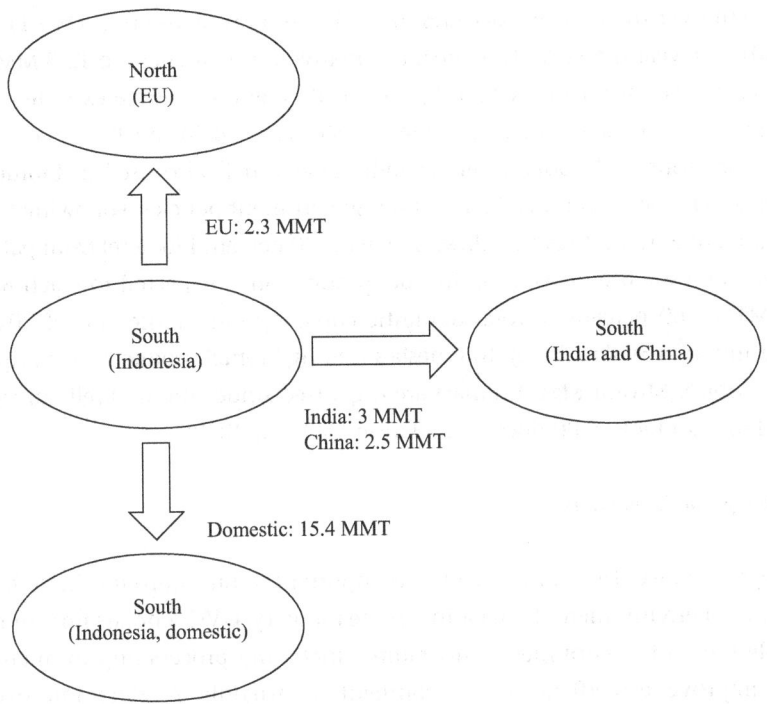

Figure 5.3
Indonesia's polycentric palm oil value chain; quantities in million metric tons (MMT) for 2020
Source: Adapted from Horner and Nadvi (2018), trade data from ITC, Index Mundi

Compared to India, the Chinese end market is more concentrated and developed. In China, 80 percent of palm oil products are for human consumption and 20 percent for industrial processes. Palm oil is mainly used as an ingredient in branded consumer goods (e.g., instant noodles, confections, personal care products, and detergents) from major companies such as Bright Food Company, Nice Group, and Liby. Unlike India, China has a large and increasingly concentrated food retail sector; for example, the Sun Art Retail Group, Vanguard Group, and Yonghui Group together account for about 20 percent of total retail sales in the country (*China Daily* 2018).

Often overlooked by analysts of transnational business governance, the fastest growing end markets of the Indonesia palm oil value chain is the domestic market. Domestic consumption has experienced very strong growth over the past two decades, from 3.4 million metric tons (MMT) in 2001 (the year the WWF Conversion Initiative was launched) to 15.3 MMT in 2020 (data from Index Mundi). This is double the volume exported to China, the EU, and India combined. Historically, palm oil has been the primary source of cooking oil for Indonesians. It is also used in biofuel, which has been promoted in ambitious government policies. Following the launch of a new B30 blend (diesel fuel with 30 percent biodiesel from palm oil), domestic use of palm oil for fuel production is expected to reach 8.3 MMT, or 60 percent of total domestic consumption by the end of 2020 (Yasmin and Syukra 2020). Indonesia's leading biofuel producers (e.g., Apical Group, Musim Mas, Wilmar) are organized under the umbrella of the Indonesian Biofuel Producer Association (APROBI 2020).

Multipolar Governance

The structure of the palm oil GVC has important implications for the governance of environmental upgrading in the industry. GVC scholars note multiple types of environmental upgrading, including process improvements to improve eco-efficiency, environmentally friendly product improvements, and organizational improvements through standards and certification (De Marchi et al. 2019, 313). As shown in chapter 1, in agricultural supply chains, particularly, standard-driven environmental upgrading has come to play an important role. Focused on behavioral change, standard-driven upgrading aligns with what political scientists refer to as outcome effectiveness (Fuchs and Kalfaggiani 2012). It also is a focus of the present analysis. However, I am not so much interested in systemically measuring such outcomes. Instead, my aim is to advance understanding of the politics around these processes. A first step in this endeavor is to identify the main drivers of environmental upgrading in the palm oil industry's global, regional, and domestic production networks.

The GVC literature has long focused on the role of powerful lead firms as main drivers of upgrading processes (Jeppesen and Hansen 2004; Khattak and Stringer 2017; Poulsen, Ponte, and Lister 2016). For example, in their analysis of the global shipping industry, Poulsen, Ponte, and Lister (2016) find that environmental upgrading is more likely to occur when GVCs are characterized by unipolar governance and led by consumer-facing lead firms. However, as previously explained, twenty-first-century globalization has led to increasingly polycentric trade flows and supply chains. In response to these and other evolutionary dynamics, many value chains have evolved from "unipolar" to "multipolar" modes of governance (Ponte 2014; Ponte and Sturgeon 2014). Yet scant empirical research in the field of environmental sustainability has examined the political dynamics of multipolar governance in polycentric trade networks. I therefore draw on the mapping analysis conducted in chapter 3 to identify the main drivers of environmental upgrading in the Indonesian palm oil value chain, which I analyze in more depth in this chapter. The scope of the analysis includes governance actors that are private and public, internal and external, and linked to different positions in the chain.

The principal Northern drivers are the RSPO and the sustainability commitments and programs of the major buyers and traders supplying the EU and other markets in developed countries. In the Indonesia-EU palm oil supply chain, the RSPO has emerged as the primary instrument of standard-driven upgrading. The organization's seven principles cover multiple aspects of sustainability, including economic, social, and environmental dimensions. Principle 7 focuses on the protection, conservation, and enhancement of ecosystems and the environment, including a criterion on the protection of high conservation value areas, such as primary forest and peatlands (RSPO 2018a, 62). Private mechanisms have dominated the governance of sustainability in this chain, though the EU and other Northern demand-side jurisdictions are developing mandatory due diligence legislation for forest-risk supply chains. At the time of this writing, these regulations had not yet come into effect and thus do not feature prominently in the present analysis. However, they are already beginning to reshape the regulatory politics of the palm oil value chain and that of other forest-risk commodities and should be the subject of future research (Partiti 2020; Schilling-Vacaflor and Lenschow 2021).

In the palm oil industry's largest Southern end markets (India and China), government actors play central roles in the coordination of the economy, especially in strategic sectors such as agriculture. Southern lead firms also are important providers of governance and coordination in the value chains supplying these markets. They select suppliers and negotiate contracts, and they use their market power to set standards. However, these companies are only beginning to formulate standards for sustainable sourcing. In addition, the mapping analysis conducted in chapter 3 identifies several newly created emerging-market-centered sustainability schemes, such as the India Sustainable Palm Oil Coalition (ISPOC).

For the purpose of this analysis, the category of domestic drivers includes governance actors linked to the supply side of the palm oil value chain. The advantage of supply-side governance is that it covers but is not limited to domestic supply chains. Instead, stronger supply-side governance can benefit product flows regardless of their final destination. The main supply-side drivers in the palm oil value chain are Indonesian government actors and major producers in the Indonesia Sustainable Palm Oil (ISPO) program. In addition, the analysis considers emerging jurisdictional and landscape programs as a new institutional form to govern sustainability in the palm oil sector. Figure 5.4 illustrates the nature of multipolar governance in the palm oil sector.

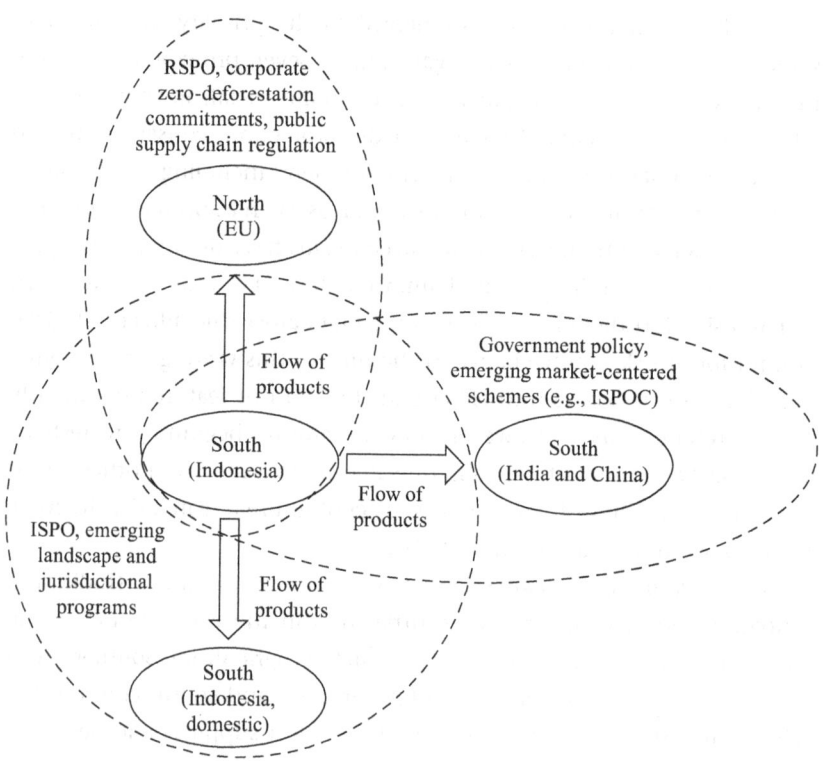

Figure 5.4
Multipolar governance of Indonesia's palm oil value chain

Global North Drivers: Market Transformation with Loopholes

The RSPO's stated goal is "to transform markets to make sustainable palm oil the norm" (RSPO 2018a). As shown in chapter 4, at least in the Indonesia-EU palm oil value chain, the large-scale adoption of sustainability standards is becoming a reality. In 2019, the RSPO certified 86 percent of European imports under its various supply chain traceability systems (IDH and EPOA 2020). This makes the Indonesia-EU palm oil value chain a forerunner in the global no-deforestation movement. At the same time, market transformation through certification does not equal sustainability. To gain a better understanding of the loopholes that continue to undermine environmental upgrading in this North-South value chain, this section explores the recent history of the RSPO to probe more deeply into the politics of these processes. I begin by exploring the role of commodity traders as a "missing link" (Serdijn, Kolk, and Fransen 2020) in the palm oil value chain and its sustainability transformation. I then trace the flow of deforestation-linked palm oil through the industry's complex production networks, and use the case of IOI Group, a powerful producer conglomerate, to investigate the politics of accountability in the sector. Finally, I show how the RSPO's strategy of standard-driven environmental upgrading reaches its limits in Indonesia's "silent expansion" (Yulian et al. 2020).

Traders: Sustainability Champions or Reluctant Giants?

As mentioned, the palm oil value chain's downstream segment is highly fragmented, which limits the potential of traditional buyer-driven environmental upgrading in this chain (see Poulsen, Ponte, and Lister 2016). In search of alternative drivers, scholars and practitioners have turned their attention to trading companies as actors in sustainability governance (Grabs and Carodenuto 2021; Greenpeace 2017). Given their market power, commodity traders also play an important role as "points of leverage" in the RSPO's market transformation strategy (WWF 2012). According to the executive director of the Markets Institute at the World Wide Fund for Nature: "if these companies demand sustainable products, they'll pull 40 to 50 percent of production. . . . If Cargill makes a decision, the entire palm oil industry moves" (Clay 2010).

Major trading companies have publicly formulated sustainable commodity commitments and joined third-party certification programs in recent years. In 2013, Wilmar, the world's largest palm oil trader, was the first major commodity trader to make a zero-deforestation commitment for its supply chain (Wilmar 2013). Today, all four major palm oil traders (Apical Group, Golden Agri-Resources, Musim Mas, and Wilmar) have zero-deforestation commitments (see Forest 500 2021). Yet, ample evidence suggests that major traders continue to source from producers that are implicated in large-scale, often illegal, forest clearing (Chain Reaction Research 2020b). To explore these loopholes, I take a closer look at the big commodity traders and how they implement their commitments in their supply chains.

Apical Group, Golden Agri-Resources, Musim Mas, and Wilmar are long-standing members of the RSPO. As part of their membership requirements, each company must submit an Annual Communication of Progress report.[3] An analysis of these reports reveals that all four traders made commitments to source 100 percent of RSPO-certified palm oil by 2030, but progress has been slow. The justifications given by these companies provide clues about their self-perceived role in the transformation of the palm oil value chain. For example, Apical's trading arm, AAA Oils & Fats Pte, qualifies that its "target is subject to market demand for RSPO certified oil" (RSPO 2017a). Musim Mas similarly states that it is "mindful of the current level of supply and demand (which varies significantly between markets)" and "dependent on availability of supply and to a great extent demand from customers" (RSPO 2017c). These statements suggest that these trading companies see themselves primarily as intermediaries responding to demand and supply of certified palm oil and with limited ambitions to pursue active sustainable sourcing strategies of their own. As a senior sustainability manager at one of the big trading companies suggests, there is a sense among traders that the no-deforestation agenda is imposed upon them and that "many of these commitments were created by end users looking at the world in a very different way."[4]

When asked about the role of palm traders in sustainability governance, a forest campaigner from Greenpeace Indonesia explained to me that "they are still dragging their feet and not driving the process" (interview, Jakarta, April 2018). The hesitancy among major traders to source third-party certified palm oil is supported by evidence. The global marketplace offers an abundance of RSPO-certified palm oil, and millions of tons go unsold every year (RSPO 2020a). However, Golden Agri-Resources reports having traded only 0.43 MMT of RSPO-certified palm oil in 2016, which is less than 10 percent of its trading volume that year (RSPO 2017b; analysis of data from

Trase n.d.). Apical and Musim Mas did not trade any certified palm oil in 2016 (RSPO 2017a, 2017c).

So far, most progress has been made by Wilmar. The company has traded 1.05 million MMT of certified palm oil, or approximately 30 percent of its total trading volume (analysis of data from RSPO 2017d; Trase n.d.). Wilmar also has taken more ambitious steps outside the RSPO system. In 2018, it announced a new action plan to increase the effectiveness of its zero-deforestation policy, which even Greenpeace celebrated as a "breakthrough" for the industry (Greenpeace 2018; Wilmar 2018). The action plan included an ambitions timeline to create an externally verified reporting and monitoring program for Wilmar's palm oil supply chain. An important element of the plan was the creation of an independent monitoring program based on precise concession maps of suppliers and a near real-time satellite remote sensing system.

Greenpeace Indonesia initially supported Wilmar in this endeavor, but the collaboration struggled to find common ground on issues of governance and monitoring. In addition, Greenpeace raised concerns about the one-sidedness of Wilmar's action plan, which focused almost exclusively on monitoring and included no measures to build the capacity of small-scale producers on the ground (forest campaigner at Greenpeace Indonesia, interview, Jakarta, April 2018). Ultimately, the main stumbling block for the collaboration was lack of agreement on the definition of a third-party supplier and whether these suppliers should be included in Wilmar's supply chain mapping. Unable to overcome these divisions, Greenpeace withdrew its support from the project (Greenpeace 2019). Wilmar renewed its commitment to "delink our supply chain from deforestation, peatland conversion and social conflicts" (Wilmar 2020). However, in 2020, Wilmar's management surprised the community of sustainability practitioners by announcing its exit from the High Carbon Stock Approach, a widely recognized multistakeholder mechanism to identify and protect forested areas in the concession areas of plantation companies (Jong 2020c). The company's role as a sustainability champion thus is in question.

Tracing Compliance

To verify compliance with its standards, the RSPO uses third-party, independently accredited auditors who control documentation and conduct onsite audits of the supply chain.[5] In the palm oil value chain, the mill plays a key role as the first node in the chain that is certified. Located in the upstream segment of the value chain, the mill is where growers deliver the oil palm fruit (known as fresh fruit bunches) to be processed into crude palm oil (see figure 5.2). Auditors attempt to trace the produce from here back to the growers and onto the next stages of the production process. However, as shown in the value chain mapping, corporate concentration in this segment is fairly low. The vast majority of oil palm acreage and mills are not directly controlled by the big industrial conglomerates that dominate exports and refining capacity. In this part of the chain, ownership structures are complex and opaque, which limits traceability through certification bodies like the RSPO.

To be RSPO certified, palm oil mills must provide documentation about their supply base and submit to audits. Palm oil mills have a catchment area with a radius of approximately 50–100 km (Pacheco et al. 2017, 15). Typically, this involves dozens of suppliers, and documentation is often incomplete and lacks critical information, such as order volume. In the fast-growing independent smallholder sector, which supplies produce to many independent mills, matters are further complicated by dubious land titles and a lack of information on numbers and locations of smallholdings. Moreover, many company-owned mills receive deliveries from undocumented third-party suppliers in addition to their official supply base. These deliveries involve several tiers of brokers and middlemen who collect the fresh fruit bunches from various unknown sources, including illegal oil palm plantings in protected areas (interview with an auditor, Jakarta, April 2018).

Given the lack of transparency at the upstream end of the palm oil value chain, there is great uncertainty about these product flows, and some environmental groups note significant problems. To investigate these issues, the NGO Eyes on the Forest conducted supply chain investigations in which it used GPS devices to follow trucks carrying fresh fruit bunches from illegal plantations in two high conservation value areas in central Sumatra to twenty-two local mills. Its findings confirm that Indonesia's leading palm oil conglomerates, many of them RSPO certified, have repeatedly sourced deforestation-linked palm oil from these mills. It is also likely that this illegally sourced material enters the supply chains of global brands, such as Unilever and Nestlé (Eyes on the Forest 2018). This is only one of several well-documented cases (Chain Reaction Research 2020b; EIA 2015; Eyes on the Forest 2016; RAN 2016a). In a personal communication, a researcher at the Oil Palm Adaptive Landscape project at Bogor Agricultural University confirmed that "there is often little visibility beyond the mill, and that this leaves the door wide open for deforestation to leak into global supply chains" (personal communication, Bogor, May 2018). Despite the high degree of certification coverage, loopholes in the RSPO's traceability systems continue to hinder standard-driven environmental upgrading in the Indonesia-EU palm oil supply chain. As shown in the next section, it also remains a significant challenge to hold powerful corporations accountable in the case of noncompliance.

IOI Group and the Politics of Accountability

IOI Group is one of Southeastern Asia's leading plantation companies. The group and its subsidiaries have close to 180,000 hectares devoted to oil palm, including large plantations on the Indonesian archipelago (IOI Group 2021). Like some of the other plantation conglomerates, IOI has been embroiled in controversy, including allegations of illegal deforestation and land grabbing. However, what makes IOI a crucial case for the RSPO and the idea of big-brand sustainability (Dauvergne and Lister 2012) is that it is a key supplier to many of the world's leading consumer goods brands, all of which have made no-deforestation commitments for their supply chains. The company also is a certified member of the RSPO and even occupied a seat on the organization's executive board.

The controversy surrounding IOI Group started in 2008, when the RSPO began rolling out its certification program in Indonesia. Environmental NGOs accused several of IOI's subsidiaries of involvement in illegal forest clearing and peatland conversion in Central Kalimantan province and other places (Greenpeace 2008). IOI dismissed the allegations in a public statement: "We strictly avoid encroaching forested or peat land and/or develop new plantation estates that will result in deforestation" (IOI Group 2009). However, criticism from environmental groups only intensified. In 2010, a coalition of eleven NGOs filed a formal complaint against IOI Group under the RSPO dispute settlement system (see Friends of the Earth 2010). As an RSPO member, the company had to take the complaint seriously, so it commissioned Société Générale de Surveillance, a leading international auditing firm, to investigate allegations against an IOI subsidiary, PT SNA. Although the 2011 audit report indicated no evidence of violations, the NGO coalition rejected it on the grounds that it was biased and omitted incriminating information. The incident sparked a contentious debate within the RSPO about the role of paid auditors and their conflicts of interest (Environmental Investigation Agency 2015). The RSPO grievance panel, however, largely sided with IOI, concluding that there was "insufficient evidence to prove that HCV [high conservation value] areas were deliberately cleared by IOI" (RSPO 2012).

New allegations against IOI Group surfaced in April 2015 when the NGO Aidenvironment resubmitted the complaint, providing new evidence that IOI majority-owned subsidiaries were continuing to violate the RSPO's principles and criteria in Central Kalimantan. Specifically, the complaint cited construction of a drainage canal through a high conservation value forest and the continued clearance of forest and deep peat even after IOI had been informed about the wrongdoings (Greenpeace 2016). During a lengthy RSPO complaint procedure,[6] IOI again commissioned external auditors to investigate the issue, which triggered new allegations regarding conflicts of interest (Environmental Investigation Agency 2015, 15). An informant closely involved in this process told me that the coalition of NGOs became increasingly frustrated with the bureaucracy and perceived bias of the RSPO. The palm oil companies seemed to wield too much influence, making RSPO leadership unwilling to confront them even in the face of well-documented violations. The frustration intensified when a "pro-NGO" complaint manager was forced to resign (campaigner at a local NGO, interview, Bogor, May 2018).

The RSPO's response in the case of IOI was slow and bureaucratic, but an external event introduced a new dynamic to the process. In August 2015, extremely dry weather led to widespread fires in the forests and peatlands of Sumatra and Kalimantan. The fires burned for months, triggering a regional environmental and public health crisis known as the 2015 South East Asian Haze. The root causes of Indonesia's perennial forest fires remain unclear, but the palm oil industry is widely believed to have directly and indirectly contributed to the problem (Purnomo et al. 2017). The disaster also focused international attention on the country, intensifying the debate about "sustainable" palm oil and putting the RSPO and its members under close public scrutiny.

Under growing political pressure, the RSPO and big-brand buyers finally took a tougher stance on IOI. In early 2016, the RSPO suspended the company, stripping it of its certification. Subsequently, Unilever, Mars, Kellogg's, and Nestlé all dropped IOI as a supplier. The company reacted by filing a lawsuit in Switzerland against the RSPO for lost business. However, when pressure mounted, IOI dropped the lawsuit and started to work with its subsidiaries to address the allegations. In August 2016, the RSPO lifted the suspension, and many buyers resumed their business relationships with IOI (Cuff 2016; Mathiesen 2016). NGOs inside and outside the RSPO wrote a public letter urging global brands and traders to boycott IOI until a strict set of requirements was met (NGO Coalition 2016). Rainforest Action Network accused the RSPO of being "willing to certify companies that are operating in open breach of its own standards" (RAN 2016b). Aidenvironment ultimately reached a settlement with IOI over the forest clearing incidents in Central Kalimantan, but several other NGOs involved in the initial complaint left the RSPO (Borneo Post 2016; POI 2018).

Certifying the "Silent" Oil Palm Expansion
When the RSPO launched in the early 2000s, its strategy was to focus on the "key leverage points for change" in the agricultural supply chain (WWF 2004). However, as the RSPO rolled out its certification system in producer countries, its founders realized that a standards-driven approach was ill-suited for certain modes of production in the industry (former director of the Forest Conversion Initiative, phone interview, May 2013). In particular, Indonesia's expanding smallholder sector posed a challenge to the organization's certification regime. In this section, I explore the RSPO's efforts to adapt its system so that smallholders could be eligible for sustainability certification.

As previously described, the complexity and opaqueness of the smallholder mode of production makes traceability difficult in this part of the supply chain. Other challenges include the contested legality of land titles, which poses fundamental problems for certification schemes that take compliance with national law as a starting point (Bartley 2010, 18). Smallholders also have a limited organizational capacity and ability to implement transnational sustainability standards (Brandi et al. 2015). These challenges notwithstanding, integrating smallholders in sustainability governance is crucial. From a developmental perspective, these producers are highly vulnerable as their livelihoods depend on the economic, social, and environmental sustainability of their farming activities. Moreover, as previously described, oil palm smallholder agriculture is expanding. According to some estimates, smallholders in Indonesia will account for 60 percent of total national palm oil production by 2030 (Saragih 2017). This "silent expansion" of the sector is associated with significant deforestation and other socioecological challenges (World Resource Institute 2017; Yulian et al. 2020).

Responding to these challenges, the RSPO formed a Smallholder Working Group in 2012 and published a Smallholder Strategy in 2017 (RSPO 2017e, 2018b). The strategy aims to create a smallholder support fund, to deliver training to smallholders on the ground, and to adapt the certification process to smallholders' needs (e.g., adding group certification). The RSPO invested significant organizational resources in these activities (senior manager at RSPO Indonesia, interview, Jakarta, April 2018). According to its own data, by May 2020, the implementation of the Smallholder Strategy resulted in the certification of 160,000 smallholders cultivating 450,000 hectares of oil palm worldwide (RSPO 2020b). These numbers illustrate progress. However, RSPO certification remains limited to a very small fraction of the smallholder sector. In Indonesia alone, two million smallholders plant five million hectares of oil palm, with independent smallholders accounting for the largest share (Jelsma and Schoneveld 2016, 2). A closer look also reveals that 95 percent of RSPO smallholder certificates are given to scheme smallholders associated with a plantation company or government estate. At the time of the analysis, only 7,800 independent smallholders worldwide were RSPO certified (RSPO 2020b). A member of RSPO Indonesia's senior management team described the difficulties of certification in the smallholder sector, including legal and organizational challenges, a lack of support and training for independent smallholders, and a lack of incentives for these smallholders to recertify (interview, Jakarta, April 2018). Other studies confirm the uncertain economic benefits of certification for smallholders (DeFries et al. 2017). In the case of the RSPO, market premiums for certified palm oil have been consistently low. The average market premium paid for a ton of certified palm oil was US$2.87 in 2017, or 0.04 percent of the average price of US$715 for a ton of palm oil (analysis of data from RSPO 2020a). There also is a large supply-demand gap, which means that more certified palm oil is produced than bought. Since the launch of the RSPO's certification scheme in 2008, the supply-demand gap has varied between 40 and 50 percent (analysis of data from RSPO 2020a). One reason for this is the low demand for certified palm oil in Asia's fast-growing regional supply chains (senior manager at RSPO Indonesia, interview, Jakarta, April 2018). The next section will explore these markets in more detail.

Global South Drivers: Still Waiting for Progress

How has sustainability governance evolved in the industry's major South-South value chains? In an article on emerging markets and private governance, Yixian Sun and I explored this question via a comparative analysis of Chinese and Indian end markets for palm oil (Schleifer and Sun 2018). At the time, we observed that the political economies of these markets were not (yet) favorable for transnational business governance. For example, in both markets, consumer demand for certified palm oil was practically nonexistent. Moreover, in the Chinese context, advocacy pressure on business actors to adopt sustainability standards for their supply chains was largely absent, whereas in India the uptake of certification was hampered by the high volume of unbranded products in this market. However, we also found that the scope conditions for transnational business governance in emerging markets evolve quickly, with market and nonmarket conditions becoming more favorable, particularly in China.[7] This section revisits our analysis. I begin by describing several new developments in the two end markets since the publication of our study. I focus on the role of the state, which, in the absence of social movement pressure, is central to shaping sustainability governance in both China and India. I then analyze ISPOC, which belongs to a group of newly created initiatives centered on emerging markets. Comparisons are made to the Trustea program, which forged a regulatory coalition of public and private and transnational and domestic actors to govern sustainability in India's fast-growing domestic tea market (Langford 2019). The section concludes by identifying several roadblocks that continue to hamper progress on sustainability in the palm oil industry's largest South-South value chains.

New Developments in China and India

A global survey of 30,000 consumers revealed that 44 percent of Chinese and 50 percent of Indian consumers "actively look for information on product sustainability" (Tropical Forest Alliance 2018). This and other surveys indicate changing attitudes among emerging market consumers. However, a disconnect between consumer preferences and buying behavior persists as price considerations often seem to override sustainability concerns (Guarín and Knorringa 2014). Surveys about consumer attitudes toward palm oil also show that emerging market consumers remain largely unaware of the commodity and sustainability issues in the industry (Samuel 2021), though consumers are rarely the primary drivers of supply chain sustainability (Gulbrandsen 2006). Consumers are likely to have even less influence in emerging economies where the state is central to regulating all aspects of economic activity, particularly in strategic sectors such as agriculture and food.

In China's state-led capitalist system, the government dominates all phases of the regulatory process (Huseh 2011). Against this background, the rise of sustainability issues on China's domestic but also external policy agenda can be interpreted as a promising sign. A sign of a shifting policy environment in this area is the Communist Party's Five-Year Plan (2016–2020), which includes three times as many sustainability-related terms as the previous one (Tropical Forest Alliance 2018). In 2018, the Communist Party also adopted a new policy framework to transform the country into an "Ecological Civilization" (Hanson 2019). This framework aims to promote sustainable trade at the regional and global levels through the development of standards, procurement policies, and other arrangements for green supply chains. In this context, the newly launched Alliance of Consumption and Green Supply Chains serves as a platform for knowledge exchange and policy dialogue. Sponsored by the government-led China Environmental United Certification Center, this alliance unites over one hundred government, business, and academic representatives (Commission on Environmental Cooperation 2017). Another new initiative focused on sustainability in China's agricultural supply chains is a policy study, "Greening China's Soft Commodity Value Chains," launched by the China Council for International Cooperation on Environment and Development (CCICED), a high-level advisory body to the Chinese government. Published in 2020, the study findings include detailed recommendations for developing a national green supply chain strategy and adopting new laws and due diligence requirements for soft commodities on the Chinese market (CCICED 2020). As shown later in this section, there is evidence that major companies in China's palm oil value chain are beginning to respond to the changing policy environment.

In India, the public policy context is less supportive but not without progress. In 2019, in an effort to align its objectives under the Sustainable Development Goals and the United Nations Guiding Principles on Business and Human Rights, the Ministry of Corporate Affairs upgraded the National Guidelines on Responsible Business Conduct, which it first released in 2009. It contains nine principles urging companies to conduct business responsibly and sustainably, and to encourage and support their suppliers in adopting the guidelines (CII and Sedex 2020, 25–27). Based on the updated guidelines, the Securities and Exchange Board of India also extended its mandatory Business Responsibility and Sustainability Report framework to the top 1,000 listed companies (by market capitalization). These companies must disclose nonfinancial information on business responsibility and sustainability indicators (Ministry of Corporate Affairs 2020). The Ministry of Corporate Affairs also is developing a National Action Plan on Business and Human Rights, a draft version of which was published in February 2019 (Ministry of Corporate Affairs 2019). These developments illustrate that the issue of sustainable business conduct has gained salience in Indian policy making in recent years. At the same time, most of these measures remain voluntary. Mandatory measures are limited to reporting only. These policies also are mainly directed at businesses operating in India, with little discussion among policy makers about extraterritorial impacts of Indian consumption and supply chains. In recent years, civil society actors have sought to promote this agenda. The Delhi-based Centre for Responsible Business has emerged as an important platform for policy dialogue and advocacy around these issues. Among other activities, it organizes an international conference on sustainability standards and has entered into a strategic partnership with the RSPO and other transnational and domestic actors to promote the uptake of sustainable palm oil in the world's largest consumer market. In 2018, this resulted in the creation of ISPOC.

The India Sustainable Palm Oil Coalition
ISPOC is part of a group of newly created schemes centered on emerging markets that aim to promote sustainability in fast-growing South-South commodity chains (see chapter 3). Other initiatives belonging to this group include the China Sustainable Palm Oil Alliance, the Singapore Alliance for Sustainable Palm Oil, and the China-focused Sustainable Soy Trade Platform. There are several parallels between these initiatives and the Trustea program, which was launched several years earlier in the Indian tea sector, but there are also important differences.

Initiated in 2013, Trustea develops sustainability standards and operates a certification scheme for India's vast domestic tea market. Branded as a "Southern sustainability initiative," Trustea in reality involves actors from multiple geographical origins and links domestic and global production networks (Langford 2019). Despite being criticized for a lack of inclusiveness (Bitzer and Marazzi 2021), the program has made significant inroads into the Indian tea market. For 2020, it reportedly verified 56 percent of Indian tea production and reached over 600,000 plantation workers and 65,000 smallholders (Trustea 2020, 9). A look at the structure and configuration of political and commercial interests and power in this tea value chain helps to explain why Trustea was able to gain significant market uptake in India in a short period of time. In the sector, Unilever, Tata, and their affiliates control 16 percent of the global market and over 50 percent of the branded tea market in India. Unilever was one of the first companies to develop a sustainable sourcing strategy for its entire supply chain network. Following the acquisition of the UK-based Tetley Group, sustainability became also central to Tata's efforts to build a global tea brand. In the process leading up to the creation of Trustea, these powerful commercial interests aligned with transnational NGOs. There also was support from the Indian government, which saw Trustea as an opportunity to promote sustainable livelihoods in the country's fast-expanding smallholder sector (Langford 2019).

ISPOC attempts to build on the success of Trustea in India (policy officer, environmental NGO, personal communication, Amsterdam, January 2020), with differences between the two initiatives. Unlike Trustea, ISPOC does not develop standards or operate a certification system. Instead, its main activities are advocacy work, knowledge sharing, and capacity building (ISPOC 2021c). Moreover, whereas Trustea focuses on India's domestic supply chain and market, ISPOC targets the regional palm oil supply chain that connects India to Indonesia and other producer countries. However, there are many interlinkages between the coalition of actors that govern the two programs and there are similarities in the strategies used to garner local support. For example, the Sustainable Trade Initiative, Hindustan Unilever, and Rainforest Alliance played key roles in the formation of Trustea, and all serve as members of ISPOC's steering committee (ISPOC 2021b). As in the case of Trustea, ISPOC founders also sought to partner with home-grown Indian companies, although less successfully (policy officer, environmental NGO, personal communication, Amsterdam, January 2020); ISPOC's member list confirms the program's marginal position in the Indian palm oil market. At the time of writing, the organization had approximately a dozen companies as members, many of which are Northern brands operating in India (e.g., Colgate-Palmolive, L'Oréal, Procter & Gamble) or joint ventures of Northern brands and Indian companies (e.g., Hindustan Unilever, AKK Kamani) (ISPOC 2021a). ISPOC launched in 2018, so it is too early to assess its performance. However, it is possible to identify several roadblocks that continue to undermine transnational sustainability governance in the South-South palm oil value chain.

Roadblocks

One persistent roadblock is linked to the structure of this value chain. As previously described, the downstream segment of the palm oil supply chain is highly fragmented, particularly in India, where palm oil is predominantly sold in unbranded and unpackaged form to lower-end consumers who are extremely price sensitive and mostly unaware of sustainability issues (Centre for Responsible Business 2018, 20–28). These constraints severely limit the scope of buyer-driven environmental upgrading in this chain.

Another major roadblock in the Indian context is the lack of supportive public policy. Palm oil is the country's primary edible oil, accounting for approximately 68 percent of total consumption (Financial Express 2020). Given the importance of palm oil for domestic food security, there has been a strong focus on security of supply, including efforts to expand domestic palm oil production (Ministry of Agriculture and Farmers Welfare 2018). The Indian government supports the creation of a national framework for sustainable palm oil production, led by the Solvent Extractor Association of India (IPOS 2021). However, under any conceivable scenario, India will remain heavily dependent on palm oil imports for the foreseeable future and, so far, the government has shown little interest in promoting sustainability in the industry in a transnational context.

As previously described, China's public policy environment is overall more favorable, as it includes an evolving regulatory agenda on imported deforestation and shows signs that Chinese agribusiness companies are responding to these developments. At the 2019 World Economic Forum in Davos, the chief executive officer of COFCO, one of China's leading importers of palm oil and soy, surprised the world with a strong public commitment to no-deforestation in its supply chains (World Economic Forum 2019). However, COFCO remains the exception, not the norm. Data from Forest 500, an environmental NGO that tracks the sustainability commitments of companies linked to forest-risk supply chains, reveal that in 2019, 80 percent of major Chinese buyers of forest-risk commodities did not have a deforestation commitment (Forest 500 2019a, 8). Similarly, the China Sustainable Palm Oil Alliance, a partnership between the RSPO and China's Chamber of Commerce for Foodstuffs, launched in 2018, has not yet garnered substantial support from Chinese companies. As in the case of ISPOC, mostly Western multinationals and their affiliates have joined the alliance, whereas participation from Chinese companies remains very limited. According to analysts of the Chinese market, certified palm oil has failed to take off at scale, as Chinese firms would get certification only when this is needed for export orders (Yifan 2021). Industry experts attribute this lack of progress to two main, interrelated reasons. First, Chinese authorities and businesses are "unlikely to do all they can" to promote a foreign standard, such as the RSPO (Head of China's South-North Institute for Sustainable Development, as quoted in Yifan 2021). Yet an equivalent national standard would take several years to develop and implement. Second, no single government authority regulates the palm oil supply chain. Palm oil is used in different industries (e.g., foodstuffs, cosmetics, and chemicals) with various environmental impacts and issues and regulatory competencies involving multiple ministries (e.g., Ministry of Agriculture, Ministry of Industry and Information Technology, and Ministry of Ecology and Environment). Making progress on the issue requires broad consensus on sustainable palm oil. According to a senior adviser of the Greening China's Soft Commodity Value Chains policy study, such consensus has yet to occur and would require a great deal of coordination (Yifan 2021).

Domestic Drivers: Between Conflict and Cooperation

Studying the prospects and limits of private regulation in GVCs, Mayer and Gereffi (2010, 20) hypothesize that "as globalization progresses, particularly as the larger developing country economies mature, it is both likely and desirable that some significant part of the private governance innovations be institutionalized with the national governments of those countries. In the longer run, this would provide more effective, stable, and representative governance for the global economy." In line with their hypothesis, national sustainability standards and certification schemes in Indonesia and other large commodity-producing countries have emerged (Schouten and Bitzer 2015; Sun and van der Ven 2020). However, contradicting their optimistic predictions of a desirable incorporation of private rules through national authorities, these initiatives, like the Indonesia Sustainable Palm

Oil (ISPO) program, often compete with established transnational schemes (see chapter 3). These and other domestic governance initiatives are important rising trends, but relatively little is known about their implementation and ability to mitigate sustainability challenges.

Renationalizing Sustainability Governance

As previously described, the state is a central participant in the development of Indonesia's modern palm oil industry. Until the 1990s, the Indonesian government controlled most of the country's oil palm cultivation (Zen et al. 2016, 81). The *reformasi* that came about at the end of the Suharto era initiated a wave of privatization in the sector. However, given the importance of the plantation sector to the Indonesian economy, the government remains closely involved in all aspects of its development. Against this background, it is not surprising that Indonesia's "oil palm complex" (Cramb and McCarthy 2016b) sought to regain control over sustainability regulation in the sector when transnational actors began to dominate the agenda. This section examines these national actors and the domestic politics surrounding the renationalization of sustainability standard setting in the sector. It reveals how Indonesian government and industry actors pursued their interests forcefully and strategically, not at all conforming to the image of dependent developing country suppliers, as portrayed in the early GVC literature (Humphrey 2018).

In October 2011, GAPKI announced its retreat from the RSPO and joined the newly created government-led ISPO program. Founded in 1981, GAPKI is Indonesia's powerful national palm oil industry association, with close ties to the Ministry of Agriculture and other relevant ministries. GAPKI's participation in the RSPO had been conflictual throughout. In an interview, an industry representative cited imbalanced decision-making in the organization favoring demand-side country interests over the interests of producer countries. The representative also criticized the unfair distribution of costs of sustainability certification (interview, Jakarta, April 2018). In the period leading up to GAPKI's withdrawal from the RSPO, two issues in particular sparked intense conflict between Indonesian palm oil companies and global buyers and NGOs in the organization.

The first issue was the plan by the RSPO to tighten its rules for developing new oil palm plantations, the so-called New Planting Procedure (see RSPO 2021b). Additional plans included a new criterion in the RSPO's Principles and Criteria to minimize greenhouse gas emissions due to new plantings, which further limited future expansion. Unsurprisingly, these measures were vehemently opposed by palm oil growers in the RSPO, who criticized them as trade barriers in disguise (industry representative, interview, Jakarta, April 2018). The second divisive issue was the revision of the RSPO's rules for certifying companies in a group. The corporate structures of the large palm oil conglomerates are often highly complex, and it was common practice for these groups to certify only parts of their associated companies and subsidiaries. In some instances, groups also made use of "shadow companies" to hide ownership of controversial assets (Chain Reaction Research 2018b). As one of my interviewees put it, "they all have a clean and a dirty hand" to serve the needs of different buyers and markets while allowing the parent company to cultivate a green image (researcher at the Center for International Forestry Research, Bogor, April 2018). This loophole in the certification regime had long been criticized by NGOs in the RSPO, who demanded stricter rules and deadlines requiring parent companies to certify all their subsidiaries (RSPO 2011b).

At a 2011 meeting of the RSPO executive board in London, conflicts over the New Planting Procedure and stricter group certification rules escalated. A GAPKI representative requested veto rights for his organization in the RSPO and the immediate cancellation of the New Plantings Procedure. As expected, the group of NGOs and Northern buyers on the board rejected these requests (RSPO 2011a). Participants at the meeting suspected that the conflict over the New Plantings Procedure was a pretext for leaving the RSPO, which had become increasingly controversial in Indonesian industry and government circles (manager at a large consumer goods manufacturer, phone interview, June 2013). Indeed, shortly after GAPKI declared its departure from the RSPO, it announced that it would join a newly created government-led program (*Jakarta Post* 2011).

Like GAPKI, Indonesian state actors initially collaborated with the RSPO. However, the government's position vis-à-vis the transnational scheme changed when it started to implement its standards on Indonesian territory (Schouten and Hospes 2018). When the RSPO became a focal sustainability regulator for the industry, the domestic discussion in Indonesia became more critical. As a high-ranking government official in the Coordinating Ministry of Economic Affairs explained to me, "We think that Indonesian industry should be regulated here by us in Indonesia" (interview, Jakarta, April 2018). In 2009, the Ministry of Agriculture made concrete efforts to renationalize sustainability regulation in the sector by forming an interministerial commission and issuing a decree on the Guidelines for Plantation Business Assessment, which bundled existing environmental regulations. The decree forms the basis of the ISPO program, which was officially launched in 2011.

Indonesian government actors have been determined to build ISPO as the primary sustainability regulator in the industry (government official, Coordinating Ministry of Economic Affairs, interview, Jakarta, April 2018). They also have shown their resolve in taking action against perceived competition, such as the Indonesian Palm Oil Pledge. This pledge, launched at the United Nations Climate Change Summit in New York in 2014, was an initiative of major palm oil traders and internationally oriented producers to coordinate implementation of no-deforestation policies in the country (Vit 2016). The initiative came under attack when it established a secretariat in Jakarta. Critics accused it of violating Indonesian law and threatening the livelihoods of smallholders. In 2016, the government ordered its dissolution. Antagonisms continue to define the relationship between ISPO and RSPO, although some scholars see evidence for more collaborative interactions (Brandi 2021). However, it is clear that the Indonesian state has reinserted itself into the palm oil GVC (Dermawan and Hospes 2018), and it remains an open question whether this will help or hinder sustainability in the sector.

Implementing Indonesia Sustainable Palm Oil

As a domestic scheme, ISPO can strengthen governance on the supply side of the palm oil value chain. However, in its current form, the program suffers from multiple problems, including weak standards and a lack of regulatory authority and organizational capacity. In designing ISPO, the Ministry of Agriculture borrowed heavily from the RSPO and its standards. In line with the argument presented by Mayer and Gereffi (2010, 20), this could be interpreted as a desirable institutionalization of private governance through national authorities. However, ISPO policies are significantly weaker than transnational sustainability standards as several comparative assessments have shown (McInnes 2017; Wijaya and Glasbergen 2016; Yaap and Paoli 2014), especially in defining high conservation value areas, designing environmental and social safeguards, and recognizing customary land rights. Unsurprisingly, these issues have generated international criticism of ISPO.

Indonesian policy makers defend ISPO on the grounds that it corresponds more closely to the Indonesian context and that, unlike the RSPO, it is based on national law and in compliance with mandatory standards for all Indonesian producers (government official, Coordinating Ministry of Economic Affairs, interview, Jakarta, April 2018). At least in theory, a sustainability program with less stringent standards but mandatory (and therefore large) membership could generate higher environmental benefits at an aggregate level than a program with more stringent standards but a smaller membership (see Prakash and Potoski 2006, 63). Below, I examine this claim in more detail in the case of ISPO.

Initially, the ISPO Commission set an ambitious timeline for mandatory certification for all companies operating in Indonesia in 2014, with a five-year transition period for smallholders. It extended this timeline multiple times due to implementation problems (member of the ISPO Commission, personal communication, May 2018). As described by Hidayat et al. (2018), a major challenge for the implementation of ISPO is a lack of direct authority and limited enforcement power. To be effective, a mandatory program requires a credible sanctioning mechanism. For example, the government could issue fines to noncompliant companies or withdraw plantation licenses. However, ISPO does not hold this authority. For the enforcement of its standard, it depends on horizontal and vertical cooperation from multiple ministries and subnational governments. ISPO is based on ministerial regulations, but the authority to enforce these regulations has not been transferred to the program and remains vested in the individual ministries. This lack of authority complicates implementation in a polity characterized by complex bureaucratic politics with conflicting regulatory agendas (Giessen et al. 2016). In addition to horizontal cooperation between ministries, implementation of ISPO also depends on vertical coordination between different levels of government. In Indonesia's highly decentralized political system, local governments have significant autonomy in natural resource governance, including the authority to issue and withdraw plantation licenses. As with conflicts between ministries, the policy objectives between national and local levels of governments are often not aligned, particularly on issues as contentious as sustainability.

Another challenge is ISPO's limited organizational capacity. To perform supply chain audits for the whole country, the ISPO Secretariat has only four staff members and only 800 auditors, many of whom work for multiple certification organizations (Hidayat, Offermans, and Glasbergen 2018, 228). This staffing is insufficient to monitor the sector's approximately 1,500 companies. Moreover, ISPO is mandatory not only for companies but also for the country's two million smallholders. Under the initial timeline of the ISPO Commission, all smallholders in Indonesia would have had to be certified by 2020. From the outset, smallholder representatives have criticized the feasibility of this timeline (union representative, interview, Bogor, April 2018). Particularly, independent smallholders require significant capacity building to meet any type of sustainability standard. ISPO has conducted several small-scale smallholder projects (Jelsma 2019, 6; Pradipta 2018). However, as in the case of the RSPO, the overall number of ISPO-certified smallholders remains small. To date, only about 12,200 hectares of oil palm smallholdings, or 0.2 percent of the total oil palm area under smallholder agriculture, are certified (Jong 2020a).

Weak standards, lack of direct authority, and low organizational capacity limit the ability of ISPO to drive environmental upgrading in the Indonesian palm oil value chain. However, a reform of the ISPO program is under way that could strengthen its implementation. After a long process, in March 2020, President Jokowi signed Presidential Regulation Number 44 to strengthen the ISPO certification system. In Indonesian politics, the upgrade from a ministerial to a presidential regulation is a strong sign of political support from the president, and it will increase ISPO's authority. The directive also contains provisions to strengthen the organization behind ISPO, including new sanctioning powers and increased financing for certification of smallholders (Fahamsyah 2020). In addition to the prospect of a stronger ISPO, new approaches at the subnational level aim to enhance complementarities between domestic and transnational governance instruments in the palm oil sector.

Toward Place-Based Sustainability?

Recent years have seen a "jurisdictional turn" in tropical forest governance, and Indonesia and Brazil have emerged as important policy laboratories for the jurisdictional approach (Milhorance and Bursztyn 2018; Seymour, Aurora, and Arif 2020). Jurisdictional programs are place-based multi-stakeholder initiatives that develop broad sustainability agendas for entire jurisdictions (e.g., a district or province). These programs seek to combine domestic and transnational governance interventions in innovative ways. As such, they aim for a high level of local government involvement and create transnational linkages with supply chain initiatives and other international instruments (Nepstad et al. 2013). The jurisdictional approach also aims to be closely attuned to social justice concerns and to promote the inclusion of marginalized stakeholders, such as smallholders and indigenous people. Its proponents promote the approach as a new pathway to advance sustainability transitions in tropical forest countries (Hovani et al. 2018). In the next chapter, I explore this jurisdictional approach in tropical forest governance in more depth.

Conclusion

This chapter sought to shed light on the politics and governance of environmental upgrading in the palm oil value chain. Tracing the sector's origins back to the colonial period, it shows how the modern industry is characterized by a polycentric network of North-South, South-South, and domestic value chains. The chapter maps the structure and main actors in these production networks and probes the processes of their multipolar governance. It shows how standard-driven environmental upgrading is reaching a point of market transformation in the industry's North-South value chain. However, market uptake does not equal sustainability. Powerful supply chain actors have exploited loopholes and resisted compliance with standards, problems with traceability and accountability have persisted, and standard-driven upgrading has not aligned well with changing local production systems. Though certified palm oil is becoming the norm in Europe, the industry's South-South value chains remain largely without sustainability standards. New public policies on green supply chains in China and the creation of new schemes centered on emerging markets are promising developments. However, regulatory coalitions that are powerful enough to steer China's and India's vast markets toward more sustainable sourcing practices in the palm oil sector have yet to arise. Conversely, powerful coalitions have formed on the supply side of the industry. Responding to transnational actors and their activities, Indonesia's "oil palm complex" (Cramb and McCarthy 2016b) has taken steps to renationalize sustainability governance. For the most part, these measures have occurred in a political climate characterized by controversy and antagonism between domestic and transnational actors. Against this background, the jurisdictional approach may help resolve such antagonisms (Pacheco et al. 2018). In the next chapter, I examine this approach in more detail.

6 Toward Place-Based Sustainability?

In 2017, a group of sustainability practitioners from around the world met in Brasilia, the Brazilian capital, for a workshop to exchange knowledge about new approaches in tropical forest governance. At the center of the workshop was the so-called jurisdictional approach, which has become a buzzword among practitioners. "It's the new game in town" a forest campaigner explained at a workshop in Brussels, describing a shift from approaches centered on the supply chain to those centered on entire production landscapes or jurisdictions (policy officer, environmental NGO, personal communication, Brussels, April 2018).

In further conversations with practitioners in Brussels, Paris, and Jakarta, I learned more about this "jurisdictional turn" in tropical forest governance. When global buyers missed their no-deforestation targets, there were demands that more companies should adopt such commitments with immediate deadlines and clear sanction-based implementation mechanisms (Garrett et al. 2019). However, other analysts have noted that even if big-brand companies from the Global North were to clean up their supply chains, they would create only "islands of green in a sea of deforestation" (Gaworecki 2015). According to my interviewees, a place-based jurisdictional or landscape approach was needed to achieve "sustainability at scale" (policy officer, environmental NGO, Jakarta, May 2018).

Moving beyond a narrow focus on deforestation-free supply chains, jurisdictional programs pursue broad and integrated sustainable development agendas at the scale of entire jurisdictions. They aim to achieve this through a strong involvement of local government actors, the creation of complementarities between domestic regulation and supply chain initiatives, and the integration of environmental with economic development and social inclusion objectives. If successful, jurisdictional programs would strengthen governance systems in the producer countries. This is essential for governing sustainability in the modern world food economy, in which emerging markets, including domestic markets, are growing rapidly (see Kharas 2010).

As part of a forward-looking research agenda, this chapter advances understanding of the jurisdictional turn in tropical forest governance. These programs are still in their infancy and apart from gray literature publications and specialized literature on tropical land use governance, they have received little attention from scholars of politics and regulation. To address this gap, I situate the jurisdictional approach in the broader sustainability governance literature. This is followed by a brief description of its conceptual foundations and institutional antecedents and a discussion of its emerging features. I then trace the development of advanced jurisdictional programs in Brazil and Indonesia in two illustrative case studies. Finally, I reflect on the opportunities and challenges of the jurisdictional approach from a political economy perspective and identify avenues for future research in this area.

The Jurisdictional Approach in the Sustainability Governance Debate

Recent decades have seen waves of institutional innovation in transnational business governance, many of them private and market-based (Hale 2020). However, despite unprecedented degrees of private regulation, global supply chains continue to cause widespread ecological and social harm around the world. Against this background, scholars of private business governance have long called for "bringing the state back in" (Mayer and Gereffi 2010, 18). In the trade in agricultural and forest commodities, the return of the state in sustainability governance is now well under way. Important state-led interventions include public orchestration of private sustainability standards in the biofuel industry through governments and international organizations (Ponte 2019, 175–211; Schleifer 2013); the assembling of a transnational legality verification regime to govern the tropical timber trade (Overdevest and Zeitlin 2014; Zeitlin and Overdevest 2021); and plans for mandatory due-diligence regulation for forest-risk supply chains in the EU, United Kingdom, and United States (Global Resource Initiative 2020; Mukpo 2020; Partiti 2020).

In recent years, also state actors linked to the supply side of global commodity chains have "brought themselves back in" (Dermawan and Hospes 2018). As described in chapter 5, the rise of these Southern sustainability standards has often sparked conflictive interactions between domestic and transnational actors (Schouten and Hospes 2018). Against this background, the jurisdictional approach is seen as a way to overcome such antagonisms (Pacheco et al. 2018). These programs are a new type of Southern-led sustainability governance (see Sun and van der Ven 2020), conceived as experimental arenas in which domestic, transnational, and intergovernmental instruments interact in complementary ways (Nepstad et al. 2013). Instead of seeking to bypass the state in the producer countries (Bartley 2018a, 258–284), the jurisdictional approach aims to achieve a high level of local government (Earth Innovation Institute 2018). The proponents of the approach also highlight social justice and equity concerns and inclusion of marginalized stakeholders as important governance objectives (DiGiano, Stickler, and David 2020; Hovani et al. 2018).

The emerging features of the jurisdictional approach, described in detail in this chapter, situate these programs at the intersection of major debates in the sustainability governance literature. Specifically, these programs resonate with recent calls by academics for a recentering of the state in sustainability governance (Bartley 2018a), the creation of public-private complementarities (Cashore et al. 2021; Pacheco et al. 2018), and the need to prioritize the poor in earth system governance (Kashwan et al. 2020). In the age of advanced globalization, in which consumption and trade shift to the Global South (Horner and Nadvi 2018), the jurisdictional approach also promises a strengthening of governance systems at the supply side of global, regional, and local supply chains. These and other features make the jurisdictional turn an intriguing trend in sustainability governance, a trend that calls for further conceptual and empirical exploration.

Conceptual and Institutional Antecedents

Conceptually, jurisdictional programs belong to a broader class of integrated landscape approaches with roots in the biodiversity conservation literature of the 1980s (Noss 1983). Although biodiversity conservation has been practiced in a landscape context for decades, this new generation of integrated programs has a broader sustainable development agenda that evolved in response to international policy agendas, such as the United Nations Sustainable Development Goals (Reed et al. 2016). In more recent conceptualizations, the integrated landscape approach broadly refers to governance initiatives that engage multiple stakeholders in efforts to integrate environmental, developmental, and societal policy objectives at the landscape scale (Reed et al. 2020). Against this background, the jurisdictional approach can be understood as a subset of this new class of sustainable and development-oriented landscape initiatives. However, rather than being defined by ecologically defined boundaries, it is defined by policy-relevant boundaries.

An important institutional antecedent of jurisdictional programs aiming to reducing tropical deforestation is the Program on Reducing Emissions from Deforestation and Forest Degradation, or REDD+ (Lederer and Höhne 2021; Seymour, Aurora, and Arif 2020, 4–5). Established in 2008 under the United Nations Framework Convention on Climate Change (UNFCCC), REDD+ assists developing countries in building governance capacities and providing results-based payments for forest protection. Initially focused on the project level, REDD+ has evolved to include capacity building and finance mechanisms for jurisdiction-wide initiatives. One of the best-established REDD+ jurisdictional programs is in the Brazilian state of Acre, which was the first subnational jurisdiction in the world to receive funding from the REDD+ Early Movers program. Another jurisdictional-scale REDD+ initiative was launched in Indonesia in 2009. This initiative arose from a collaboration between the local government of Berau District in East Kalimantan and the Nature Conservancy, an environmental NGO, to develop a multistakeholder institutional framework and action plan to reduce deforestation in the district (Anandi et al. 2014). Other Indonesian provinces have since received funding under REDD+, but political enthusiasm for the REDD+ agenda declined both nationally and internationally in the 2010s. Nevertheless, in Indonesia and elsewhere, REDD+ has sponsored initiatives that helped develop policy networks, knowledge, and institutional infrastructures to further develop the jurisdictional approach (Seymour, Aurora, and Arif 2020).

Emerging Features

At this early stage of development, the jurisdictional approach continues to evolve. However, through scenario building, information gathering, and lesson drawing, several key features, practices, and viewpoints are beginning to converge (see Fishman, Oliveira, and Gamble 2017; Paoli et al. 2016). In this chapter, I draw on interviews with practitioners, gray literature, and

Table 6.1
Comparing supply chain initiatives to the jurisdictional approach

	Supply chain initiatives	Jurisdictional approach
Governance	Private governance: NGO-led, firm-led, or multistakeholder; transnational private actors dominate; no government involvement	Hybrid governance: multistakeholder; strong involvement of domestic government actors; transnational actors in supporting role
Scale	Transnational: supply chain focused; vertical logic dominates	(Sub)national: jurisdictional scale with transnational interlinkages; horizontal logic dominates
Scope	Narrow scope: individual sectors and land uses; farm-level focus; short-term to medium-term perspective	Broad scope: integrates multiple sectors and land uses; jurisdictional scale; long-term perspective

specialized literature on sustainable land use governance to delineate and describe these features. The discussion is organized around the governance, scale, and scope of these initiatives. Table 6.1 summarizes the emerging features of jurisdictional programs and compares them with traditional supply chain-centered initiatives.

Governance

The multistakeholder model is widely used in sustainability governance and beyond (Scholte 2020). In the agriculture sector and elsewhere, it has become the "gold standard" to organize transnational governance processes (Schleifer 2019). Jurisdictional programs also use a form of multistakeholderism. However, unlike the first wave of multistakeholder initiatives for sustainable agriculture, which focused on collaborations between business and civil society actors, jurisdictional programs focus on local actors and governments. As a policy officer at an environmental NGO explained to me, "The essence of the approach is that there needs to be a stronger role for local governments. The traditional certification model is focused on interactions between civil society and the private sector. Governments are missing from that picture" (interview, Jakarta, May 2018).

The literature highlights this aspect of jurisdictional programs. For example, Seymour, Aurora, and Arif (2020, 1–2) define jurisdictional programs as government-led multistakeholder processes. Along similar lines, von Essen and Lambin (2021, 3) describe them as a "formalized collaboration between government entities and actors from civil society and/or the private sector," noting that the degree of government involvement in jurisdictional programs can vary. However, in their conceptualization, initiatives with very high or very low levels of government involvement fall outside of the jurisdictional approach parameters (also see Paoli et al. 2016). In this way, jurisdictional programs are a hybrid mode of governance.

Scale

In addition to the central role of government actors, jurisdictional programs quite literally take the multistakeholder model to another level. Transcending the vertical logic of supply chain initiatives, jurisdictional programs are place-based and defined by relevant political boundaries. The scale of the jurisdictional approach depends on the country context, including factors such as the distribution of political authority to make land-use decisions across levels of government and the existence of institutional capacity (van Houten and de Koning 2018, 7). Therefore, broader definitions of the approach include both national and subnational jurisdictional scales (von Essen and Lambin 2021, 3). However, the current commodity-focused jurisdictional programs are mostly situated at the subnational scale, typically the second or third administrative level in a country (LTKL and Tropical Forest Alliance 2020). These midsize scales represent a "sweet spot" wherein programs can be adapted to local contexts but are large enough to contribute to systemwide transformations (Boyd et al. 2018, 2; von Essen and Lambin 2021, 7).

Although grounded in the subnational, jurisdictional programs are not a purely local mode of governance, however. Transnational actors and linkages play important roles in the theory of change of these programs. Transnational actors support program development through activities within jurisdictions and through external incentives (Seymour, Aurora, and Arif 2020, 7–15). Activities within jurisdictions include supporting articulation of jurisdictional-scale visions, convening multistakeholder forums, and developing monitoring systems (Hovani et al. 2018). External incentives include mobilizing international climate finance and private green investment. In addition, transnational actors have sought to interlink the jurisdictional approach with supply chain initiatives through developing systems of "jurisdictional certification" and "jurisdictional sourcing" (Boshoven et al. 2021; Nepstad et al. 2013; van Houten and de Koning 2018).

Scope

Another salient feature of the jurisdictional approach is a broad definition of sustainability, which acknowledges the interdependences of human and natural systems and seeks to integrate environmental, economic, and social policy objectives. In particular, the approach seeks to include the concerns of smallholders and indigenous communities in these processes (members of the Climate and Land Use Alliance, personal communication, Jakarta, April 2018), which are often excluded from transnational sustainability governance (Brandi 2017). Beyond overly simplistic "win-win" narratives, the jurisdictional approach attempts to acknowledge the trade-offs and histories of conflict between groups so that they can be identified, negotiated, and settled (Reed et al. 2020, 2). Against this background, customary rights, human rights, and the settlement of land-use conflicts have emerged as salient issues for the jurisdictional approach community of practice (Colchester et al. 2020; DiGiano, Stickler, and David 2020).

However, this does not mean that all programs have the same design and thematic scope. Two recent studies describe the existing variation among jurisdictional programs aimed at sustainable resource use (LTKL and Tropical Forest Alliance 2020; von Essen and Lambin 2021). Over time, some of this variation may disappear as the "organizational field" of jurisdictional programs becomes more institutionalized (see Dingwerth and Pattberg 2009). However, local problems and political economies often vary widely and thus require contextualized solutions. The adaptability of jurisdictional approaches thus is their key strength (policy officer at an environmental NGO, interview, Jakarta, April 2018). At the same time, this integration and contextualization have resulted in highly complex programs with long-term perspectives (Fishman, Oliveira, and Gamble 2017).

Exploring the Jurisdictional Approach in Brazil and Indonesia

In recent years, the jurisdictional approach has gained significant momentum in tropical forest governance. In Brazil, Indonesia, and other tropical forest countries, numerous subnational governments have taken steps to develop policies and implementation mechanisms to advance jurisdiction-wide sustainable development agendas. Depending on the definition used, there are between twenty-five and thirty-nine deforestation-focused jurisdictional programs in development in the global tropics (Stickler et al. 2018;

von Essen and Lambin 2021). Moving "beyond certification," jurisdictional and landscape programs have also become central to the post-2020 forest conservation strategies of many NGOs. The Nature Conservancy, the Earth Innovation Institute, the Sustainable Trade Initiative (IDH), and other NGOs have served as "backbone organizations" for many of these processes. In this role, they provide important coordination and management function to support and steer the networks of actors working toward jurisdictional sustainability (discussion with practitioners at a meeting at the Climate and Land Use Alliance, Jakarta, April 2018). While global buyers have long been reluctant to accept responsibility beyond their supply chains, this is beginning to change. After failing to meet their 2020 zero-deforestation target, members of the Consumer Goods Forum's (CGF) newly formed Forest Positive Coalition of Action announced at the COP26 Climate Summit in Glasgow their ambition "to transform landscapes to the equivalent of the coalitions combined production base footprint of palm oil, soy, paper packaging and beef into forest positive landscapes by 2030" (UNFCCC 2021).

This section explores the institutionalization of the jurisdictional approach, with a focus on two advanced commodity-centered jurisdictional programs in Brazil (Mato Grosso) and in Indonesia (Central Kalimantan). The analysis is based on a review of gray literature, internet research, and interviews with practitioners. Information from existing studies on the jurisdictional approach in Brazil and Indonesia was also included (e.g., LTKL and Tropical Forest Alliance 2020; Milhorance and Bursztyn 2018; Seymour, Aurora, and Arif 2020; von Essen and Lambin 2021).

Mato Grosso's Produce, Conserve, and Include Strategy

Following the end of military rule in the mid-1980s, Brazil's new constitution devolved significant powers to subnational governments, creating a federal system. In this process of democratic transition, the country's twenty-six states (the first level of local government) acquired wide-ranging executive, legislative, judicial, and fiscal powers, making states and their governors influential players in Brazilian politics (Samuels and Abrucio 2000). Governed by elected mayors, the second level of local government in Brazil is the municipality. Brazil's twenty-six states together comprise 5,570 municipalities, which vary greatly in size and population. Also, municipalities in Brazil possess important executive and legislative competencies, including authority over local land use planning (OECD 2016).

Toward Place-Based Sustainability? 145

It is not surprising that jurisdictional programs to govern commodity-driven deforestation first emerged in the Brazilian context (policy officer at an environmental NGO, phone interview, April 2018). The country's federalist polity and devolution of important regulatory competencies to subnational governments make it fertile ground for the jurisdictional approach. Brazil also has a history of progressive environmental legislation and executive action by subnational governments and cities (Lederer et al. 2020; Setzer 2017), including the previously described experimentation with initiatives related to REDD+. Though the political momentum behind REDD+ has waned in Brazil, activities to develop jurisdictional programs for sustainability transitions have continued.

Today, numerous states and municipalities in Brazil have taken steps to develop visons, targets, and implementation mechanisms for jurisdictional sustainability. Nine Brazilian states (Acre, Amapá, Amazonas, Maranhão, Mato Grosso, Pará, Rondônia, Roraima, and Tocantins) have joined the Governors' Climate and Forest (GCF) Task Force, a transnational network of subnational governments committed to forest protection and low emissions rural development (see figure 6.1). All nine states have developed strategies and investment plans for jurisdictional sustainability, which can be reviewed in the GCF Task Force Knowledge Database.[1] One example of an advanced initiative is the Municipal Pact to End Illegal Deforestation of São Félix do Xingu, a municipality in the state of Pará. When São Félix do Xingu was placed on the federal government's deforestation blacklist in 2008, the municipal government responded by creating a rural environmental registry, accompanied by a multistakeholder agreement to end illegal deforestation and foster economic development and social inclusion. The Nature Conservancy facilitated the process and helped develop a low-carbon agricultural strategy and build a local system for licensing and monitoring land use in the municipality. The strategies developed in São Félix do Xingu have spilled over to neighboring municipalities, and the governor of Pará has taken steps to scale the model for use in the state's 2030 sustainable development plan (Varns et al. 2018). However, the most advanced jurisdictional program to reduce tropical deforestation in the Brazilian context is the Produce, Conserve, and Include (PCI) strategy of the state of Mato Grosso (Milhorance and Bursztyn 2018). Launched at the Paris Climate Conference in 2015, it attempts to integrate the state's REDD+ program, global supply chain initiatives, and municipal-level climate actions into a statewide governance

Figure 6.1
Brazilian states with membership of the Governors' Climate and Forest Task Force
Source: Map by author with Natural Earth data

structure and agenda for low-emission rural development. The remainder of this section explores this program in more depth.

Located in the Amazon and Cerrado biomes, Mato Grosso is Brazil's agricultural powerhouse. The state is a major producer of beef, corn, and soy. Soybean agricultural in Mato Grosso covers over nine million hectares of land, contributing about a third to total national soy exports. Since the 1990s, the expansion of industrial agricultural and cattle pastures drove large-scale conversion of tropical forests and biodiverse grasslands in the state. By the mid-2000s, the annual forest loss exceeded 10,000 km^2 (GCFTF 2021), making Mato Grosso one of the "fastest deforesting places in the world" (policy officer development NGO, phone interview, May 2012). In 2005, Blairo Maggi, Mato Grosso's then governor, was awarded the Golden Chainsaw award by Greenpeace as the Brazilian person who most contributed to Amazon forest destruction (Environmental News Network 2005). However, the high deforestation rate in combination with increasing pressures from environmental NGOs, foreign governments, and global market actors initiated a process of institutional change in the state. Over the next

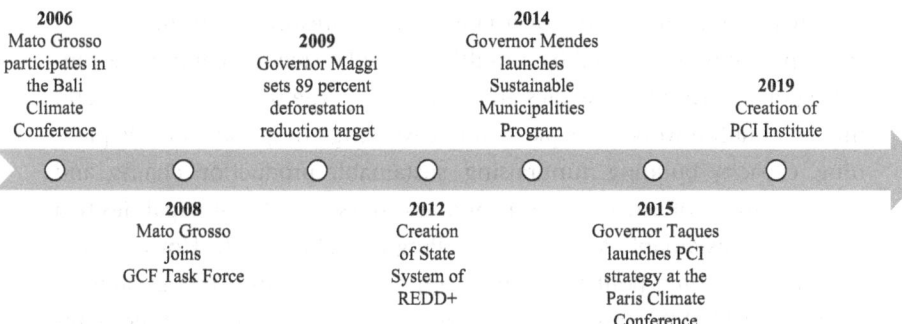

Figure 6.2
Milestones of Mato Grosso's jurisdictional approach

decade and a half, a stepwise institutionalization of a statewide jurisdictional program for sustainable agriculture and development has occurred in Mato Grosso (see figure 6.2).

This process began in 2006, when Governor Blair Maggi participated in the United Nations Climate Conference in Bali, where commitment to low-carbon rural development was emphasized. Mato Grosso became a founding member of the GCF Task Force in 2008. These activities in the international climate policy arena were accompanied by domestic legislative action. In 2009, Governor Maggi launched the Action Plan for Prevention and Control of Deforestation and Burning. The action plan established a policy framework for cross-agency cooperation and coordination with civil society and the private sector in Mato Grosso. It included a goal to eliminate illegal deforestation and reduce statewide deforestation by 89 percent (from a baseline deforestation rate of 5,510 km^2) by 2020 (GCFTF 2021). To implement its ambitious agenda, Mato Grosso turned to REDD+ and the newly created REDD+ Early Movers Program for funding. In 2013, state law No. 9878 established Mato Grosso's State System of REDD+, which created a formal legal framework for the program. The objective was to receive results-based payments for reductions in deforestation. In the following years, Mato Grosso successfully secured US$5 million in funding through the Early Movers program, with payouts conditional on the state keeping its annual deforestation rate below 1,788 km^2 (Funbio 2017).

Another building block of Mato Grosso's jurisdictional program is the Sustainable Municipalities Program. Initiated by Governor Mendes in 2014, the program pursues three main objectives: strengthening local economies, improving municipal-level governance, and addressing environment and social problems. Governed by a multistakeholder steering committee consisting of government agencies and civil society, the program's policy and implementation work takes place in five working groups on strategic planning, capacity building, fundraising, sustainable production chains, and land reform. As of 2019, sixty-one of Mato Grosso's 143 municipalities had joined the Sustainable Municipalities Program (SMP 2019). However, the program lost some political momentum after Governor Mendes stepped down in 2015 (Milhorance and Bursztyn 2018, 15). Recently, there have been renewed efforts to reinvigorate the program and promote it as an instrument to connect sustainability initiatives in Mato Grosso, both horizontally across municipalities and vertically across levels of government (director of Mato Grosso's PCI Institute, phone interview, April 2019).

A major push for Mato Grosso's jurisdictional approach happened under the Taques administration (2015–2019). Taques, a university professor and public attorney who became famous for his role in high-profile environmental defense cases, made advancement of a progressive sustainability agenda a political priority. After his election in 2015, he set out to integrate the existing sustainability initiatives into an overarching strategy and vision to achieve low-carbon agricultural development in Mato Grosso by 2030. A coalition of transnational and national NGOs, including the Earth Innovation Institute, the Environmental Research Institute, and the Life Centre Institute (Instituto Life), played important roles in this process, helping draft the strategy and convening a workshop where the final version of the strategy was eventually approved. The NGOs also organized a side event at the United Nations Climate Conference in Paris in 2015, where Governor Taques officially launched the PCI strategy (Milhorance and Bursztyn 2018, 13). The international launch generated international visibility, but there is criticism that the strategy was drafted before many stakeholders were brought on board (Fishman, Oliveira, and Gamble 2017, 8). Local communities and producers were not sufficiently involved in the design process, which undermined their trust in and support for its policy objectives.

As implied by its name, the PCI strategy rests on three main pillars: economic growth (produce), environmental conservation (conserve), and social policy objectives (include), as shown in table 6.2. These pillars and the objectives they contain are linked to different stakeholder groups and their positions in Mato Grosso's political landscape, such as agribusiness,

Table 6.2
Objectives of the PCI strategy

Produce	Conserve	Include
Expansion and increased efficiency of agricultural, livestock, and forest production	Conservation of native vegetation and recovery of liabilities	Socio-economic inclusion of family farming and traditional populations
Beef cattle • Recover 2.5 million ha of pasture areas of low productivity by 2030 • Raise productivity from 50 to 95 kg/ha/year by 2030 Agriculture • Expand areas of grains in areas of degraded pasture from 9.5 to 12.5 million ha by 2030. • Increase production of grains from 50 to 92 MMT by 2030 Native forests • Expand area under sustainable forest management from 2.8 to 6 million ha by 2030 Planted forests • Raise timber production from 4.9 to 11.75 m³ by 2030	Deforestation • Maintain 60 percent of native vegetal coverage • Reduce deforestation in the forest by 90 percent from a baseline of 5,714 km² in 2001–2010 to 571 km²/year by 2030 • Reduce 95 percent of the deforestation in the Cerrado from a baseline of 3,016 km² to 150 km²/year by 2030 • Eradicate illegal deforestation • Conserve 1 million ha of those areas likely to be legally deforested Environmental regulation • Register 90 percent of the rural properties by 2016 • Validate 100 percent of declared rural properties by 2018 • Recompose 1 million ha (100 percent) of degraded permanent preservation areas by 2030 • Regulate 5.8 million ha (100 percent) of Legal Reserve and 1.9 million ha by reconstitution by 2030	Production and inclusion in the market • Expand technical assistance coverage and rural extension of family farming from 30 percent to 100 percent of families by 2030 • Raise participation of family farming in the regional market from 20 to 70 percent by 2030 • Expand participation of family farming products in all institutional markets from 15 to 30 percent by 2030 Land regularization • Perform land regularization of 70 percent of family farming plots by 2030

Source: Adapted from PCI strategy, http://pci.mt.gov.br

environmental NGOs, and smallholder farmers. The PCI strategy aims to integrate these frequently conflicting positions by recognizing the underlying trade-offs (director of Mato Grosso's PCI Institute, phone interview, April 2019). As previously mentioned, the strategy also attempts to integrate governance instruments (e.g., National Forest Code, Mato Grosso's State System of REDD+, and Sustainable Municipalities Program at the national, state, and municipal level, and supply chain commitments and certification programs in the private sector) into an overarching policy agenda and institutional platform for sustainable agricultural development.

In 2016, State Decree 468/2016 turned the PCI strategy into a formal instrument for public policy planning, creating a multistakeholder governance structure. Coordinated by the Strategic Affairs Office of Mato Grosso, the governance structure comprised four constituency groups: public-sector agencies, civil society organizations, private-sector organizations, and farmers' associations. Though local stakeholders dominate the PCI governance structure, transnational actors also participate, including international NGOs such as Earth Innovation Institute and IDH, and multinational corporations such as Carrefour (PCI 2019). In 2019, this governance structure was integrated into the newly created PCI Institute, an independent not-for-profit association. Government actors serve on its board, but it is not controlled by government. This separation is meant to protect the PCI Institute from political turnover, a problem that, as shown in this chapter, has hindered jurisdictional programs in other municipalities. The main functions of the PCI Institute include multistakeholder coordination, policy advice, fundraising, and implementation and monitoring of Mato Grosso's sustainable development agenda (director of PCI Institute, phone interview, April 2019).

Most jurisdictional programs in Brazil are in the early stages of institutional development (von Essen and Lambin 2021). Mato Grosso's PCI strategy is one of the few programs that has taken measures for statewide implementation. The PCI Institute plays a central role in these activities. It developed a jurisdiction-wide plan for implementation, a system for monitoring and oversight, and a strategy to launch and coordinate multiple implementation partnerships. The implementation plan divides Mato Grosso into seven macro regions and defines indicators and timebound targets (PCI Monitor 2021).

Three municipalities (Sorriso, Juruena, and Cotriguaçu) are the furthest along in their implementations (head of markets at IDH, interview, March 2022). In 2018, Sorriso entered into a regional PCI compact with IDH. The agreement connects the state-level PCI strategy to implementation efforts at the municipal level, including jurisdictional certification by the RTRS and plans to transform Sorriso into a "verified sourcing area" that connects global buyers of agricultural commodities to coalitions of progressive stakeholders in production areas. Numerous global buyers, including China's largest grain trading company (COFCO), are signatories to Sorriso's PCI compact. Similar regional compacts were signed in Juruena and Cotriguaçu.

There are also plans to transform the entire state of Mato Grosso into a verified sourcing area by 2030 (director of Global Landscapes at IDH, personal communication, April 2018). However, as these and other projects throughout the state progress, statewide implementation of the PCI strategy remains limited. An internal evaluation of the strategy's first four years (2015–2019) reveals that progress on its core policy objectives has been slow and insufficient (PCI Monitoring Committee 2019). In an interview, the director of the PCI Institute explained that lack of funding, unclear incentives for producers, conflict between stakeholder groups, and problems with data quality and monitoring constrain the implementation efforts (phone interview, April 2019).

Central Kalimantan's Roadmap to Low-Deforestation Rural Development

Indonesia has also emerged as an important policy laboratory for the jurisdictional approach (Seymour, Aurora, and Arif 2020). After the fall of Suharto's New Order Regime in the late 1990s, Indonesia underwent a democratic transformation and decentralization, transferring substantial executive, legislative, and judicial authority from the national to the subnational level. Local governors gained significant powers, making them an influential force in Indonesian politics (Vickers 2013). Administratively, the country is divided into thirty-four provinces comprising 416 regencies and ninety-six cities. Following decentralization, regencies and cities became key administrative units with direct authority over a wide range of policy areas, including land-use decisions. While Indonesia's decentralization has brought challenges, it also created opportunities for policies and regulations to be more attuned to local conditions and contexts. As in the case of Brazil, Indonesia's decentralized polity provided an entry point for the jurisdictional approach (policy officer, environmental NGO, interview, Jakarta, April 2018).

An early pioneer in the development of a jurisdiction-wide sustainability initiative in Indonesia was Berau regency in East Kalimantan. In 2008, the governor of Berau and the Nature Conservancy began a dialogue about a low-emissions economic development strategy for the district. Under the leadership of the local governor, a multistakeholder working group was formed to develop an institutional framework and action plan for deforestation reduction. In 2009, the Berau Forest Carbon Program was launched and began implementing pilot projects throughout the district (Anandi et al. 2014). Initially focused on the pulp and paper industry, the program soon broadened its scope to include palm oil production, the main driver of deforestation in the province (CIFOR 2019; Mafria, Rakhmadi, and Novianti 2018). Supported by the Nature Conservancy, the German International Cooperation Agency, and the Climate Policy Alliance, Berau regency launched a jurisdiction-wide sustainable palm oil program in 2015. Still in its infancy, the program seeks to increase transparency in oil palm licensing, improve the district's system for social and environmental impact assessment, and strengthen smallholder inclusion and productivity. Considered a pioneer in Indonesia's emerging jurisdictional movement, the Berau Carbon Forest Program has served as an important point of reference for other jurisdictions (Paoli et al. 2016).

Today, seven Indonesian provinces (Aceh, North Kalimantan, West Kalimantan, East Kalimantan, Central Kalimantan, West Papua, Papua) are members of the Governors' Climate and Forest Task Force formulating province-wide visions and roadmaps for low-emission rural development (see figure 6.3).

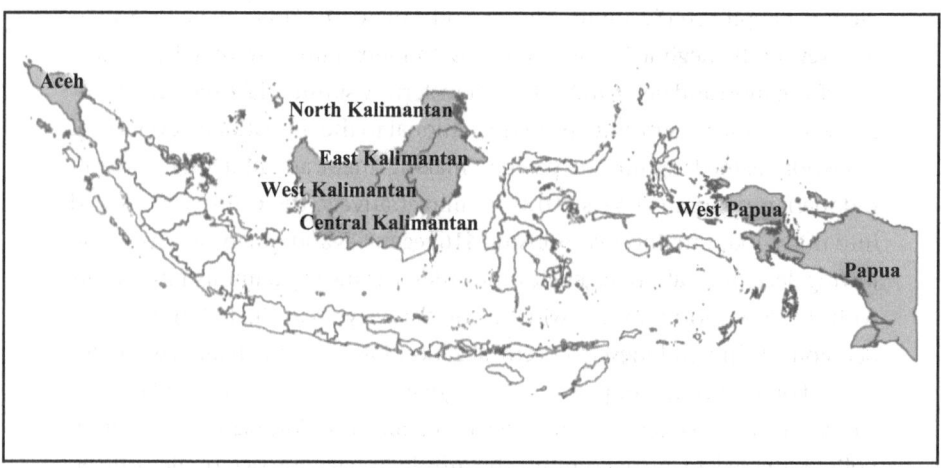

Figure 6.3
Indonesian provinces with membership in the Governors' Climate and Forest Task Force
Source: Map by author with Natural Earth data

In addition, several regencies (the second level of local government) launched jurisdictional programs, and nine regencies currently participate in the Lingkar Temu Kabupaten Lestari (Sustainable Districts Platform, LTKL) (LTKL 2021). Facilitated by the Indonesian branch of the World Resource Institute, the Sustainable Districts Platform evolved out of an informal collaboration between local heads of government (head of secretariat, LTKL, interview, Jakarta, May 2018). Like the GCF Task Force at the global level the Sustainable District Platform is a network of subnational districts in Indonesia. It has eight members, with a combined forest area of 5.5 million hectares.[2] While many of these initiatives are at an early stage of development (Paoli et al. 2016), this illustrates that the jurisdictional approach is gaining ground in Indonesia. To gain a better understanding of these programs and how they evolve, the remainder of this section explores Central Kalimantan's Roadmap to Low-Deforestation Rural Development, which belongs to the most advanced jurisdictional programs in Indonesia.

Central Kalimantan is one of Indonesia's primary palm oil producing provinces. The plantation sector is a key pillar of the local economy, supporting 165,000 jobs and accounting for a third of the province's gross domestic product (Plantation Office Central Kalimantan 2013). However, as elsewhere on the archipelago, the rapid expansion of industrial plantations in Central Kalimantan has caused widespread environmental degradation. Since the 1970s, the province has lost about a third (30,000 km^2) of its forest cover (about the size of Massachusetts). As part of Indonesia's Green Revolution, Central Kalimantan's Mega Rice Project cleared over a million hectares of peat swamp forest in the 1990s (GCFTF 2019). In the 2000s, oil palm plantations replaced rice agricultural and timber and pulp wood plantations as the main drivers of land use change in the province. The total oil palm area in Central Kalimantan reached 2.5 million hectares in 2015, and is estimated to exceed 3.5 million hectares by 2025 if left unchecked (researcher at the Forestry Department of Palangka Raya University, personal communication, May 2018). To develop a more sustainable plantation sector, the government of Central Kalimantan, with support from international NGOs, has taken steps to develop a province-wide agenda and policy framework for low-emissions rural development. Figure 6.4 depicts the milestones of this process.

As in the case of Mato Grosso, the United Nations REDD+ program provided an entry point for the development of a jurisdictional program for sustainable land use in Central Kalimantan. As one of four REDD+ pilot

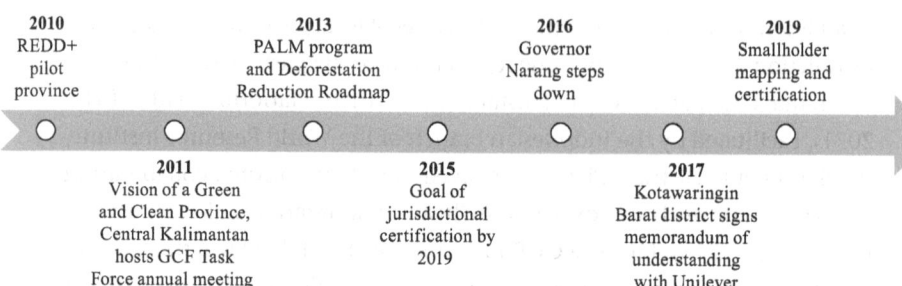

Figure 6.4
Milestones of Central Kalimantan's jurisdictional approach

projects in Indonesia, the Kalimantan Forests and Climate Partnership was launched in 2010. Funded by the government of Australia with approximately US$30 million, the partnership's goal was to reduce carbon emissions due to peatland degradation. Conservation efforts focused on the environmental impact of the Mega Rice Project and the conversion of peatlands in the rapidly expanding palm oil sector. However, a poor information strategy, disputes over the right approach, and a lack of demonstrable progress attracted criticism in both Indonesia and Australia, and the program officially ended in 2014 (Atmadja et al. 2014). Despite its mixed record, the Kalimantan Forests and Climate Partnership created an initial infrastructure and policy network for further collective action to advance the jurisdictional approach in Central Kalimantan (policy officer at Climate and Land use Alliance, interview, Jakarta, April 2018).

An important supporter of a progressive environmental agenda in the province was Governor Teras Narang. In 2011, his administration announced a vision of Central Kalimantan as a "green and clean province" and several accompanying policies and regulations (Government Central Kalimantan 2015), including development of a "sustainable plantation sector" and a two-year moratorium on new permits for primary forests and peatlands. Provincial regulation (*perda*) 5/2011 provided the legal foundation for the moratorium. The governor also issued a decree 36/2012 to reduce greenhouse gas emissions in the agriculture sector. Another milestone was hosting the annual meeting of the GCF Task Force, which Central Kalimantan joined shortly after the network's inception in 2008 (GCFTF 2019).

Further steps toward jurisdictional sustainability were taken in subsequent years. In 2013, the provincial government of Central Kalimantan, in partnership with the Climate Policy Institute and the University of Palangka Raya, launched the Production and Protection Approach to Landscape Management (PALM) program. In two districts (Kotawaringin Timur and Katingan), pilot projects were established to develop strategies for a district-wide approach to sustainable oil palm development (researcher at the Forestry Department of Palangka Raya University, personal communication, May 2018). These activities on the ground were supported by development of an overall strategy and roadmap for the province. Launched in 2013, Central Kalimantan's Roadmap to Low-Deforestation Rural Development defines immediate and medium-term actions and targets for deforestation reduction, institutional development, and smallholder inclusion (see table 6.3). The provincial government also expressed its intent to have the entire province acquire jurisdictional certification from the Roundtable on Sustainable Palm Oil and Indonesia Sustainable Palm Oil program (Plantation Office Central Kalimantan 2013).

In 2015, several measures were taken to advance jurisdictional certification in Central Kalimantan. Governor Narang issued Decree No. 188.44/435/2015, which reiterated the commitment to zero deforestation in the palm oil sector for the entire province. It also included the objective to have all oil palm plantations certified by 2019 (Watts and Irawan 2018). To advance this agenda, a Jurisdictional Certification Working Group was formed and held its first meeting in Jakarta in May 2015. Chaired by the head of Central Kalimantan's Plantation Office and facilitated by Inobu, the Indonesian sister organization of the Earth Innovation Institute, the working group united a broad coalition of stakeholders, including government officials, palm oil companies, indigenous people's organizations, and local and international NGOs (Plantation Office Central Kalimantan 2015). The working group identified the mapping of the fast-expanding independent smallholder sector as a priority. In cooperation with Inobu and the RSPO, jurisdictional certification pilot projects were established in three districts: Gunnung Mas, Kotawaringin Barat, and Seruyan (member of the secretariat of the RSPO Indonesia, interview, Jakarta, April 2018).

Until 2015, Central Kalimantan had made good progress with its jurisdictional program. As described above, REDD+ provided an entry point, and the agenda was driven by a coalition of actors including the provincial government, several district governments, and transnational NGOs. However, political turnover at the province level slowed collective action for

Table 6.3

The Central Kalimantan Roadmap to Low-Deforestation Rural Development

Immediate goals and actions	Medium-term goals and actions
Agreement on land classification and forest cover • Creation of a working group consisting of the Ministry of Agriculture of Central Kalimantan and other relevant stakeholder New plantation permits only for degraded land • Based on provincial regulation 5/2011 • Pilot projects in Kotawaringin Barat and Barito Selatan Registration and monitoring system • Designing an online permit, registration, and monitoring system • Building capacity and installing necessary equipment • Institutionalizing civil society involvement in the processes of registration and monitoring processes, including the Dayak Council Primary forests and peatlands in nonforest areas • Preserve remaining primary forest and peatlands in areas classified as "nonforest" Promotion of smallholder plantations and increasing their productivity levels • Increase the role of smallholders, particularly Dayak farmers, as proportion of total production • Analysis of profile of smallholder farmers in Central Kalimantan	2020 Goals • Province-wide deforestation declines to 20 percent of 2006–2009 level • Zero deforestation in the palm oil sector • Smallholder palm oil production reaches 20 percent of total Impacts • 1.2 million hectares of deforestation avoided • 0.6 billion tons CO_2 emissions avoided • Reduced poverty among Dayak community Support needed to achieve goals • Commitment from buyers to buy sustainable palm oil • Collaboration to help overcome bureaucratic obstacles • Financing to build institutional capacity of provincial and district governments • Financing and technical support for smallholders and Dayak communities to participate in palm oil supply chain

Source: Adapted from Plantation Office Central Kalimantan (2013)

sustainability in Central Kalimantan. After ten years in office, Teras Narang stepped down as governor in 2016, resulting in a critical loss of political momentum as the new governor was less supportive of the low-carbon rural development roadmap. Several district governments continued to develop their sustainability initiatives, but progress was slower and even partly reversed (Boyd et al. 2018, 5–6).

An exception is Seruyan regency, which is a major palm oil–producing district in midwestern Central Kalimantan. In 2016, a multistakeholder steering group for jurisdiction-wide certification was established under the chairmanship of the district governor (Seruyan Regency 2016). The working group initiated a process to identify and protect high conservation value and high carbon stock areas in Seruyan (van Houten and de Koning 2018, 31). It also began mapping and certifying the district's oil palm smallholders. In 2017, coordinated by Inobu, Seruyan began implementing SPIKEBUN, a digital tool for mapping smallholders. Over the next year, 2,560 smallholders were mapped and catalogued through SPIKEBUN (Fitri 2016). These mappings were complemented with measures to prepare smallholders for certification. The district government of Seruyan and Inobu, with support from the United Nations Environmental Program, also established a new agricultural facility for training and technical assistance (Pro Sampit 2019).

Bordering Seruyan, Kotawaringin Barat district also has made progress toward jurisdictional certification. In 2017, the district signed the first jurisdictional sourcing agreement with an international buyer. Following a memorandum of understanding between the district government and Unilever, the company committed to source palm oil from 600 certified smallholders from the village of Pangkalan Tiga (Unilever 2017). Since then, Inobu and its partners have continued to conduct smallholder mappings and prepare for certification in Kotawaringin Barat, Seruyan, and Gunnung Mas districts. By 2019, thousands of smallholders had been mapped under these programs. However, four years after Central Kalimantan announced its jurisdictional certification goal, progress stalled. Certification of the entire province and its palm oil sector remains a distant goal. One reason for this delay has been a lack of clear commitments from global buyers to engage in jurisdictional sourcing (policy officer at an environmental NGO, interview, Jakarta, April 2018). Moreover, in light of deep-seated problems with corruption, land disputes, and complex histories of conflict over land rights in the district, observers have raised critical questions about jurisdictional sustainability in places like Seruyan (Gecko Project 2017).

The Opportunities and Challenges of the Jurisdictional Approach

The previous sections explored two case studies illustrating the evolution and emerging features of the jurisdictional approach, focusing on two advanced programs in Brazil and Indonesia. The remainder of this chapter discusses the potential and limits of the approach to contribute to large-scale sustainability transitions in tropical forest countries. However, beyond traditional concerns with institutional effectiveness, the focus of the discussion is not on measures and measurements of "jurisdictional sustainability" (see Stickler et al. 2018). Instead, drawing on the political economy perspective developed in chapter 2, I reflect on the opportunities and challenges of these programs to recenter the state, create public-private complementarities, and prioritize marginalized actors in tropical forest governance. In doing so, the discussion draws analytical attention to the political, economic, and historical dimensions of jurisdictional transitions. The reflections presented here aim to stimulate future research in these areas.

Opportunities

Recentering the State   One of the most promising features of the jurisdictional approach it its attempt to recenter domestic government actors in sustainability governance. This is a response to the perceived limits of transnational private regulation, which has long been criticized for bypassing the state in the producer countries (Bartley 2018a, 258–284). This lack of domestic government involvement in the agenda setting, negotiation, implementation, monitoring, and enforcement stages of sustainability governance has undermined the effectiveness and legitimacy of these arrangements. Jurisdictional programs are designed to overcome these limitations. Their theory of change aims to harness the convening and regulatory powers of domestic government actors to galvanize support and to scale sustainability across entire jurisdictions, as opposed to individual supply chains. For this theory to work, participating government actors need to possess the willingness and authority (e.g., authority over land-use decisions) to enact jurisdiction-wide regulatory reforms (see RSPO 2021c, 14). Therefore, depending on the distribution of regulatory authority in a country, the level of jurisdictional programs can vary. As previously described, in most countries, including Brazil and Indonesia, it is the second or third administrative level. If successful, this recentering of domestic state actors at these levels has potential to create more legitimate and effective regulatory systems on the supply side of global, regional, and local supply chains. This is of key importance in a changing world food economy, in which domestic and regional consumption increasingly drive agricultural expansion and environmental change.

Creating Public-Private Complementarities Conceived as arenas in which REDD+, global supply chain initiatives, and domestic policies interact (Nepstad et al. 2013), jurisdictional programs are thought to enhance public-private complementarities in sustainability governance (Pacheco et al. 2018). However, despite high initial expectations, REDD+ finance has turned out to be "too low, too slow, and too constrained as aid" (Seymour and Busch 2016, 359). The "pay for performance" approach of REDD+, which makes payments conditional on achieving timebound carbon emission reduction targets, limits its usefulness to support long-term oriented sustainability transitions. In particular, the governance structures and nonenvironmental policy objectives of jurisdictional programs (e.g., economic development and social inclusion) are difficult to finance through REDD+. Searching for alternatives, sustainability practitioners have increasingly focused their attention on linking jurisdictional programs to global supply chain initiatives. The declared goal is to generate "global value propositions" for local stakeholders through mechanisms of "jurisdictional sourcing" (Boshoven et al. 2021; van Houten and de Koning 2018). While global lead firms have long been reluctant to accept responsibilities beyond their supply chains, the failure to meet their 2020 zero-deforestation targets has created pressures for a broader engagement in production landscapes. This has led the CGF's Forest Positive Coalition of Action to embrace jurisdictional and landscape programs as a key element of its post-2020 forest conservation strategy. As part of the strategy, the coalition has developed plans to scale up twenty-two jurisdictional and landscape initiatives in Brazil, Chile, Indonesia, Malaysia, Mexico, and Russia (CGF Forest Positive Coalition of Action 2021). NGOs and certification organization, including the ISEAL Alliance, the RSPO, and IDH, have also intensified their efforts to develop the infrastructure of standards, verification systems, and platforms necessary to enable large-scale jurisdictional sourcing. As observed in the case studies, Mato Grosso plans to become a "verified sourcing area," and Central Kalimantan and several of its districts have formulated plans to achieve jurisdiction-wide certification. By creating linkages with global supply chain initiatives, practitioners hope to give a major push to the development of jurisdictional programs in tropical forest countries.

Including Marginalized Stakeholders The multistakeholder model has attracted much criticism in recent years. Scholars cite an imbalanced focus on certain discourses, power asymmetries between participants, and exclusion of marginalized actors (Cheyns 2011, 2014; Fransen and Kolk 2007; MSI Integrity 2020; Ponte 2008; Schouten, Leroy, and Glasbergen 2012). More broadly, scholars are concerned about a lack of inclusion and accountability in the design phase of environmental governance institutions (Park and Kramarz 2019). Against this background, the jurisdictional approach resonates with recent calls for more participation from, social justice for, and prioritization of the poor in sustainability governance (Kashwan et al. 2020). Particularly, local communities, smallholders, and indigenous people are often excluded from systems of socioeconomic and environmental governance. Consequently, their traditions, values, and customary rights are poorly reflected in these institutions. At least in theory, the jurisdictional approach offers more access points to these stakeholders and is more attuned to their concerns. Sustainability practitioners highlight that participation from all affected segments of society in all phases of a jurisdictional program is essential to the approach (Fishman, Oliveira, and Gamble 2017, 8; Hovani et al. 2018, 31–33). As illustrated in the case studies, these concerns also figure prominently in the visons and roadmaps of jurisdictional programs, at least on paper. For example, the "I" (Include) in Mato Grosso's PCI strategy sets ambitious goals for economic inclusion and regularization of small-scale farmers. Smallholder and indigenous rights also feature prominently in Central Kalimantan's Low-Deforestation Rural Developmental Strategy. The jurisdictional approach thus creates opportunities to better advance the livelihood and justice concerns of local communities. Including these traditionally marginalized actors also increases the likelihood that they will accept and lend their support to low-carbon rural development agendas.

Challenges

Succumbing to "Dreams of Domestication" There is growing consensus that transnational private regulation cannot replace or transcend the state in the producer countries and that domestic political economy contexts matter greatly for the adoption and implementation of sustainability governance (Bartley 2018a; Distelhorst et al. 2015). There are thus good reasons to welcome the jurisdictional approach and its efforts to recenter domestic state actors in sustainability governance. At the same time, it is important to remember that transnational private regulation developed in response to the perceived weakness of systems of environmental and social governance in the producer countries in the Global South. Of course, these institutional weaknesses have not disappeared, creating a risk that the proponents of the jurisdictional approach succumb to "dreams of domestication" by creating expectations and agendas that are far too ambitious for local authorities, regulatory institutions, and the realities on the ground (see Quack 2020). In Indonesia and other tropical countries, governments often have weak managerial and enforcement capacity, problems with collusion and corruption are widespread, and longstanding conflicts over land rights undermine public trust in the state and its institutions (Aspinall and Berenschot 2019; Gecko Project 2017). Closely tying the success of jurisdictional programs to the support of local heads of government may also compromise the longevity of these programs. As illustrated in the case of Central Kalimantan and its jurisdictional approach, political turnover after elections can quickly undo years of progress and reverse past achievements (Boyd et al. 2018). Another risk is that that local elites use these programs to "greenwash" past environmental destruction for global market actors demanding sustainably produced commodities. Indeed, there is evidence to suggest that many jurisdictions with high-profile sustainability agendas have historical deforestation rates that far exceed the global average for the tropics (von Essen and Lambin 2021, 5).

Limits to Big-Brand Sustainability As the world's leading retailers and consumer goods manufactures pledge to support jurisdictional and landscape programs to meet their global climate and deforestation commitments, the limits of big-brand sustainability should not be forgotten. Students of political economy have long pointed out that the environmental benefits of big brands' sustainability strategies are undermined by their business models, which, based on perpetual economic growth, drive overexploitation and overconsumption in the global economy (Dauvergne and Lister 2012). As argued throughout this book, the declining market power of Northern lead firms in a world of "polycentric trade" (Horner and Nadvi 2018), in which forest-risk commodities are increasingly traded within South-South supply chains, is another limitation. As yet, no retailer or consumer goods manufacturer from China or India—the largest importers of forest-risk commodities—has joined the CGF's Forest Positive Coalition of Action. If corporate engagement in jurisdictional and landscape programs remains limited to only a small group of big brand companies from the Global North, so will the power of "jurisdictional sourcing" (Boshoven et al. 2021) to incentivize local business and government actors to support jurisdictional transformations. But also, the commitments of the small group of leading companies organized in the Forest Positive Coalition of Action need to be treated with care. As the experience with the CGF's 2020 zero-deforestation agenda shows, ambitions targets have been set and missed before. Against this background, the coalition's newly formulated Strategy for Collective Action in Production Landscapes lack of detail (e.g., no indication of the land area that is to be transformed, no clear financial commitments, little information about the ways in which the coalition plans to engage in jurisdictional/landscape programs) is not a promising sign. Another reason for concern is the strategy's highly ambitious timeline. After a short start-up and learning phase (until 2023), an implementation and scaling-up phase (2023–2025) is supposed to lead to "steady phase" (from 2025 onward), in which programs are "scaled up and deliver landscape/jurisdictional level forest positive outcomes" (CGF Forest Positive Coalition of Action 2021, 22). There is a risk that big-brand companies, eager to demonstrate bold action in light of past failings, greatly underestimate the complexity of these processes and the time and resources needed to develop them.

Persistence of Exclusionary Practices The jurisdictional approach community of practice highlights the promotion of social inclusion as an important policy objective. This includes the empowerment of indigenous people and local community-based conservation (Hovani et al. 2018, 31). But existing research on community-based natural resource governance in the Global South shows that power asymmetries and exclusionary practices are very difficult to overcome. In complex multistakeholder settings, imbalances in power and resources between stakeholders often lead to political compromises being imposed in a top-down manner (Ponte, Noe, and Mwamfupe 2021). This also poses a challenge for the jurisdictional approach and its theory of change. While the attempt to "recenter the state" in sustainability governance is one of the most celebrated features of these programs, it is important not to forget the history of state formation in the global tropics. In Brazil, Indonesia, and other parts of the tropical world, state formation is deeply entangled with colonial histories and legacies, and often involves the development of powerful state-industrial agricultural complexes (Cramb and McCarthy 2016b; Giacomin 2018). As described by McCarthy (2000, 103), "the colonial regime set up a regulatory order that overlaid a pre-existing customary regime with its own concepts of property rights. The scene was set for conflict in the post-colonial period between elites using national law to justify access to local resources, and local people seeking to preserve their own tenure systems." Indeed, in modern times, transnational and national elites have continued to impose hegemonic notions of legality, land ownership, and land use on local communities in the Global South, often ignoring their customary claims to land (Myers et al. 2020). Hence, when placed in the historical context, the jurisdictional approach's focus on public law and state-led multistakeholder governance becomes more controversial. There is a risk that it perpetuates a dynamic in which powerful government and business actors and their transnational partners impose their visions of sustainable land use and political compromises on local communities in a top-down manner. For example, in Mato Grosso, there was little participation from local communities and small-scale producers in the design phase of the PCI strategy, which undermined support and trust in the state's jurisdictional program (Fishman, Oliveira, and Gamble 2017). In Central Kalimantan, protracted conflict over land rights between government officials, palm oil companies, and local communities has cast doubt on the government's plan to make Seruyan a model district for "jurisdictional sustainability" (Gecko Project 2017). There also is more systematic evidence to suggest that social inclusion is a weak spot of the jurisdictional approach. In this regard, a study, examining how jurisdictional programs across eleven tropical forest jurisdictions protect the rights of local communities and indigenous people, finds that the rights of these groups are often not formally recognized and that this limits their ability to participate in policy formulation (DiGiano, Stickler, and David 2020).

Conclusion

As part of a forward-looking research agenda, this chapter explores the jurisdictional turn in sustainability governance. Jurisdictional programs are state-led multistakeholder initiatives with jurisdiction-wide sustainability goals. They differ from programs centered on supply chains, among others, through their larger scale, broader scope, and longer timeframe. In the context of polycentric trade, they promise to strengthen governance system at the supply side of global, regional, and local production networks. Moreover, what makes these programs so intriguing is that they resonate with recent calls by academics to recenter the state in sustainability governance (Bartley 2018a), to resolve the disconnects between transnational and domestic actors (Cashore et al. 2021; Pacheco et al. 2018), and to prioritize the poor in earth system governance (Kashwan et al. 2020).

Against this background, this chapter explores the potential and limits of the jurisdictional approach to contribute to sustainability transitions in tropical forest landscapes. I debate the opportunities and challenges of the approach and conclude that jurisdictional programs have potential to address gaps and limitations in the regime complex for tropical deforestation. At the same time, the explorations in this chapter suggest that these programs do not constitute a paradigm shift for sustainability governance. The jurisdictional approach is not a radical change project, striving to fundamentally reform the ways in which natural resources are produced, traded, and consumed. Instead, it is a reformist project, which, conforming to dominant global discourses on sustainable development, aims to reconcile economic, environmental, and social-inclusion objectives in rural areas. How progressive the reform agendas of these programs will be is ultimately a political question, which needs to be answered by the actors involved. Worryingly, recent developments in advanced jurisdictional programs in Brazil and Indonesia suggest that transnational and local elites are compromising on a rather conservative version of the approach. In this version, marginalized groups are excluded from the design phase of these programs, economic concerns often take precedence over environmental ones, and important human rights issues are not addressed. Moreover, private market-driven instruments are increasingly central to the overall approach, as practitioners seek to deliver global value propositions to local businesses and political elites. If these tendencies prevail, the jurisdictional approach is unlikely to become a catalyst for progressive reform in tropical forest countries. Instead, the approach risks to reify existing policy paradigms, modes of governance, and their power asymmetries and exclusionary practices.

7 Conclusion

I began this book with an anecdote about a partnership between environmentalists and Ben & Jerry's and the emergence of rainforest marketing in the late 1980s. Rainforest marketing, while commercially successful, was soon discontinued because its conservation effects were deemed too insignificant. Nonetheless, in the absence of strong international and domestic regulation, the idea to leverage the power of global supply chains to eliminate commodity-driven deforestation became the dominant policy approach in the decades that followed. The 2000s saw the creation of industry roundtables in major forest-risk commodity sectors. In the 2010s, these certification-based mechanisms were complemented by a wave of corporate no-deforestation commitments by powerful lead firms in agricultural supply chains.

The starting point for the present analysis was the observation that this supply chain movement has not brought about a global market transformation. The 2010 have been called a "lost decade" for tropical forests (Butler 2019), and many analysts agree that the zero-deforestation movement missed its policy targets by a large margin (Chagas et al. 2018; Climate Focus 2018; Taylor and Streck 2018). To understand the role of supply chain initiatives in reducing deforestation, research into their effectiveness has burgeoned (e.g., Carlson et al. 2018; Garrett et al. 2019; Lambin et al. 2018; Smith et al. 2019; van der Ven, Rothacker, and Cashore 2018), with analysts identifying design deficiencies, low adoption rates, and spillover effects as key explanatory factors. The importance of these immediate causes notwithstanding, this book offers a broader analysis. Beyond traditional concerns with institutional effectiveness, it explores the shifting terrain of sustainability governance in a time of major structural change in the world economy.

Concluding the analysis, this chapter has three objectives. First, it revisits the main findings of this book. Second, it considers implications for practice. Finally, it outlines emerging global trends and identifies avenues for future research in these areas. I close the chapter with a reflection on the COVID-19 pandemic, and the war in Ukraine and its implications for the politics and governance of sustainability in the world food economy.

A Shifting Terrain: Governing Sustainability in a Changing World Economy

Sustainability emerged as a policy issue on the global governance agenda in the second half of the twentieth century. The 1972 United Nations Conference on the Environment was the first global conference to address the issue. In 1987, the Brundtland Commission defined sustainability as "meeting the needs of the present without compromising the ability of future generations to meet their own needs" (United Nations n.d.), which policymakers translated into an international action agenda at the 1992 Rio Earth Summit. The so-called Agenda 21 included the promotion of sustainable development through trade and making trade and the environment mutually supportive as important program areas (United Nations 1992). Ten years on, the 2002 World Summit on Sustainable Development in Johannesburg, South Africa, focused attention on questions of implementation. Then UN secretary-general Kofi Anan identified the business world and civil society as "vital partners" in advancing "responsible globalization" (United Nations 2006). The endorsement of nonstate actors by the UN and leading states ushered in an era of transnational new governance for sustainability (Abbott 2012b). As shown in chapter 1, also the governance of agriculture and forests was transformed by a wave of private sustainability standards during this period.

These transformations in governance have been accompanied by a new politics of global supply chains (Macdonald 2014), characterized by multiple cleavages. One such cleavage is linked to broader debates about economic globalization, environmental protection, and the appropriate means of regulation. Liberal environmentalism, which emphasizes the reconcilability of economic growth and environmental protection (Bernstein 2002), has long dominated this debate in international and domestic policy arenas. From this perspective, market-based instruments and corporate self-regulation are seen as promising tools to govern sustainability in global agriculture (e.g., Carlson et al. 2017; Smith et al. 2019). In stark contrast to the liberal environmentalist position, the limits-to-growth paradigm emphasizes the existence of planetary boundaries and the limited carrying capacity of planet Earth (Meadows et al. 1972). To prevent catastrophic environmental change, its proponents call for state intervention and far-reaching economic reforms, such as de-globalization and a return to more localized systems of food production and consumption (e.g., Clapp 2012; Dauvergne 2008). In addition to these high-level controversies, globalizing food supply chains created a new "private politics" as civil society actors started to "knock on firms' doors" to make their concerns about sustainability heard (see den Hond and de Bakker 2012). New partnerships for sustainability between once-antagonistic actors have emerged, and, ever since, firms and NGOs have been engaged in complex legitimation politics over the design, content, and control of transnational business governance (Bartley 2007; Fransen 2012; Pattberg 2007). However, it would be a mistake to assume that the spheres of private and public authority are distinct or static. Instead, transnational business governance is fuzzy and dynamic, as public and private governors interact in both complementary and conflicting ways (Cashore et al. 2021; Eberlein et al. 2014; Macdonald 2014; Renckens 2020). Another important cleavage in the politics of sustainable production and trade runs along North-South lines. Concerned that the outsourcing of production to low-cost jurisdictions would undercut wages and harm the environment, states and social movement actors in the Global North have demanded environmental and social safeguards for global supply chains, often in the form of private standards. This has been met with opposition from government and industry actors in the Global South, who view such standards as barriers to trade and a threat to their economic development (Thorstensen, Weissinger, and Sun 2015).

These and other issues continue to define the politics and governance of global supply chains in the agriculture sector and other sectors. However, as this book shows, the political dynamics around existing issues are changing and new issues are emerging. In the age of advanced globalization, major structural shifts in the world food economy have far-reaching implications for power, governance, and environmental issues. Surprisingly, however, these trends have long been sidelined in mainstream academic and policy debates on the governance of sustainability in the sector. All too often, scholars and practitioners focus on questions of institutional design and narrowly defined environmental benefits, with too little attention being paid to changing global political economy structures and processes and their consequences.

This book set out to address this gap. With a focus on global shifts in agricultural markets, my goal is to tackle these big picture questions and thus to advance understanding of the deeper causes of ecological crisis and governance failure in a changing world food economy. My contention is that a political economy perspective can help us achieve this goal. Such a perspective does not rely on institutional boundaries as the defining parameters within which effectiveness should be analyzed (Kütting 2005), nor does it limit itself to a narrow assessment of the environmental benefits of transnational business governance. Instead, this line of research casts a much wider analytical net, starting with the incongruence of a worsening ecological crisis despite unprecedented degrees of sustainability governance (Newell 2012, 34–60). However, as discussed in chapter 2, political economy research on transnational business governance remains too disconnected (Graz and Nölke 2008), with little exchange and cross-fertilization between scholars working in the traditions of international political economy, comparative political economy, and GVC analysis. To overcome these divides and to leverage the full spectrum of political economy scholarship, this book puts forward a multilevel framework of analysis. In the empirical chapters of this book, this framework guides a layered analysis into the environmental and institutional consequences of twenty-first-century globalization in the agriculture sector. The following sections synthesize the main findings from the empirical chapters. Based on this, I develop a set of descriptive and causal claims, which begin to reveal the shifting terrain of sustainability governance in the modern world food economy.

It is important to note that these claims are mainly of an inductive nature, which was an important element of the research strategy underlying this book. This means that they are context specific and cannot simply be generalized to other empirical settings. However, there is good reason to believe that they are not unique to the issue area of commodity-driven deforestation and the industries studied in this book. For example, there is ample evidence to suggest that processes of contemporary globalization are driving environmental degradation across a wide range of industries and issue areas (Hopewell 2019; Mol 2011). It also is evident that global market and power shifts are restructuring value chains throughout the world economy, not just in the agriculture sector (Cattaneo, Gereffi, and Staritz 2010; Pasquali, Godfrey, and Nadvi 2020). Therefore, the claims developed here may serve as hypotheses to guide research beyond the empirical scope of this book.

Global-Level Findings

The relationship between environmental degradation and economic globalization is an important theme in the literature on international political economy (Christoff and Eckersley 2013; Dauvergne 2005; Newell 2012). With a focus on the agriculture sector and the problem of commodity-driven deforestation, chapter 3 revisits this relationship in the age of advanced globalization. It shows how global shifts in agricultural markets are reshaping the geography of trade in the sector. The analysis of international trade data reveals a steady shift in trade flows from North-South to South-South for the entire sector. However, the data also show significant variation between individual sectors. While the advanced economies of the Global North continue to be the main importers of commodities like coffee or cocoa, trade flows have shifted strongly for other forest-risk commodities (e.g., palm oil and soy). The global deforestation footprint of large emerging economies has increased accordingly. Between, 2005 and 2017, deforestation risks linked to Chinese and Indian imports of palm oil and soy increased by 159 percent, from 108,000 hectares to 280,000 hectares. In the same period, the combined imports of deforestation linked to these commodities of the EU and the United States fell by 35 percent, from 210,000 hectares to 136,000 hectares (analysis of data from Pendrill, Persson, and Kastner 2020). Another important source of demand is domestic markets. In Indonesia, domestic palm oil consumption grew from less than four MMT in 2002 to over fifteen MMT in 2020 (data from Index Mundi). These figures illustrate that in the current phase of globalization emerging economies are increasingly replacing advanced economies as the main drivers of agricultural expansion and commodity-driven deforestation in these industries. This leads to a first claim: *Driven by fast-growing emerging economies, the link between globalization and environmental degradation remains strong in twenty-first-century agricultural trade.*

The rise of South-South trade also reconfigures dynamics of power and authority in the world food economy, with important consequences for governance. At the global level, chapter 3 explores how the emerging regime complex for forest-risk commodities adapts and changes in response to global power shifts. Tracing the history of regime formation in the sector, it shows how the regime's most established schemes are the product of the politics of late-twentieth-century globalization, dominated by North-South trade and a Western-led development paradigm (Horner and Nadvi 2018;

Pieterse 2012). In this context, private sustainability standards disseminated in the sector's global supply chains, growing the size of "sustainable markets" in the Global North (Willer et al. 2019). However, a problem arises as many of the established transnational schemes remain anchored in this world of late-twentieth-century trade. In the modern world food economy, this creates a growing mismatch between their market coverage and the "new geography of international economic relations" (UNCTAD 2004). This leads to a second claim: *In the age of advanced globalization, there is a growing incongruence between the location of sustainable markets and the new geography of agricultural trade.*

Turning from the question of regime adaptation to the ways in which the overarching governance architecture is shaped by processes of contemporary globalization, the analysis examines how global power shifts contribute to institutional fragmentation, a key variable in the literature on regime effectiveness (Biermann et al. 2009; Zelli and van Asselt 2013). Invoking Abbott and Snidal's (2009) metaphor of a "regulatory standards bargaining game," chapter 3 identifies global market power as an important background condition that shapes bargaining dynamics between demand-side and supply-side actors in the transnational regulatory space. In this context, shifts in end markets have increased Southern actors' "go it alone power" (i.e., their ability to establish a regulatory scheme that meets some or all of their objectives). This finding complements existing work on Southern standards in agricultural value chains, which mainly focuses on domestic factors to explain their emergence (e.g., Schouten and Bitzer 2015; Hospes, van der Valk, and Mheen-Sluijer 2012). It also increases understanding of the conditions under which the interactions between Southern and transnational standards oscillate between conflict and cooperation. This leads to a third claim: *Global power shifts have increased institutional fragmentation in the regime complex for forest-risk commodities.*

Sector-Level Findings

The comparative political economy perspective of chapter 4 allows for a more fine-grained analysis of how shifts in global markets interact with other political economy factors and how this shapes the authority of transnational business governance across commodity sectors and over time. In the major forest-risk commodity sectors, the proportion of global production that is certified by third-party certification schemes, the most robust private governance institutions (Bloomfield 2017, 16–18), is highest for timber (13 percent), followed by palm oil (11 percent). Conversely, with 1.5 percent and less than 1 percent, respectively, certification uptake remains very low in the soy and beef sectors. The uptake of company-level deforestation commitments largely mirrors this cross-sectoral distribution. This shows that in none of the major forest-risk commodities are private regulatory programs currently close to attaining a market share that would allow them to transform global markets, as envisioned by their theory of change (WWF 2012). The analysis also reveals that the uptake of the most advanced private regulatory schemes (e.g., the RSPO) has stagnated in recent years. This leads to a fourth claim: *Transnational business governance has progressed differently across forest-risk commodity sectors, but market uptake remains too low overall.*

The comparative political economy analysis explains why transnational business governance has been at least moderately successful in some sectors, whereas it gained hardly any uptake in others. Comparing the palm oil and soy sectors, chapter 4 shows how contemporary globalization is reconfiguring the political economies in both industries, but to different degrees. In the soy sector, the volume of the Brazil-China trade rose from 6.2 MMT in 2003 to 61 MMT in 2020 (+884 percent) (analysis of data from ITC n.d.). The trade in palm oil also experienced significant shifts. However, unlike in the soy sector, Global North countries retained more of their market share. Although important, global market power also is not the only factor that matters. The analysis reveals how European actors retained substantial agenda-setting power in the palm oil industry due to the interplay of several market and nonmarket conditions, which reinforced one another. Specifically, private regulators benefited from a high level of support from global buyers, a powerful transnational advocacy network, and endorsement from state actors in Europe. This allowed the RSPO to diffuse its standards in the industry's North-South supply chain. In comparison, with less support from European firms, civil society, and state actors, the almost identical RTRS failed to achieve the same level of success. This leads to a fifth claim: *The interplay of political economy forces emanating from advanced economies allowed transnational business governance to achieve moderate coverage in some forest-risk commodity sectors but less favorable conditions have limited uptake in others.*

The analysis of changes in the political economy context of the RSPO and the RTRS also highlights some important commonalities between the two sectors. Confronted with global market shifts, a lack of support from emerging market buyers, and antagonism from powerful state and industry actors in the producer countries, private regulators in both industries saw themselves confronted with an increasingly challenging environment. As previously mentioned, favorable conditions allowed the RSPO to achieve large-scale coverage in the European market. However, political economy conditions have been very challenging for both schemes in fast-growing regional and domestic markets in the Global South. This leads to a sixth claim: *The scope conditions of transnational business governance have become less favorable across forest-risk commodity sectors, limiting its global coverage and thus impact.*

Value Chain-Level Findings
Scholars of transnational business governance often link its effectiveness to the ways in which sustainability standards disseminate through GVCs. Chapter 5 draws on conceptual innovations in the GVC literature on polycentric trade (Horner and Nadvi 2018) and multipolar governance (Ponte 2014) to explore the evolutionary dynamics of the value chains of the "post-Washington Consensus world" (Gereffi 2014). Global shifts in trade and the role of emerging economies as new sources of demand are hypothesized to have dramatic consequences for value chain organization, governance, and upgrading (Gereffi 2014). With a focus on the palm oil supply chain, a front-runner industry in the zero-deforestation supply chain movement (Donofrio, Leonard, and Rothrock 2017), chapter 5 examines these consequences. The analysis reveals that the palm oil value chain does not resemble the buyer-driven model that is common to other tropical commodity sectors, such as coffee. For example, Unilever, the world's largest palm oil buyer, accounts for only 4 percent of global demand (Pacheco et al. 2017, 13), whereas Nestlé controls over 20 percent of the global coffee retail market (Grabs 2020a, 10). Instead, corporate concentration is highest in the refining (upstream) and trading segments (midstream) of the palm oil supply chain, making it a producer- and trader-driven chain. Another defining feature is its distinct polycentric structure. Shifts in the geography of palm oil trade have been accompanied by a relocation of its production networks, with regional and domestic supply chains and the actors that control them gaining in importance (e.g., the biofuel industry in Indonesia). This leads to a seventh claim: *Global shifts in the geography of trade and consumption are reconfiguring the structure of forest-risk supply chains, with important implications for power and governance in these chains.*

Conclusion

This restructuring of value chains has important implications for the distribution of corporate power in the world food economy and hence for any "theory of change" (WWF 2012) attempting to use the supply chain "as a conduit for influencing the social and environmental conditions of production and consumption" (Bush et al. 2015, 13). The GVC literature has long focused on the role of Northern lead firms as the main drivers of environmental upgrading processes (Jeppesen and Hansen 2004; Khattak and Stringer 2017; Poulsen, Ponte, and Lister 2016). However, in the post–Washington Consensus World the limits of "unipolar" big-brand sustainability are increasingly clear (see Dauvergne and Lister 2012), raising questions about the potential of "multipolar" governance. Through value chain mapping, chapter 5 identifies the main drivers of environmental upgrading in the industry's global, regional, and domestic production networks. This includes governance actors that are private and public, internal, and external, and linked to different positions in the chain. This leads to an eighth claim: *In the context of polycentric trade, the governance of sustainability in forest-risk supply chains is increasingly multipolar in nature, comprising global, regional, and domestic drivers.*

The in-depth investigation of multipolar governance in the palm oil value chain shows how standard-driven environmental upgrading is reaching a point of market transformation in the industry's North-South network, with close to 90 percent of Europe's palm oil imports verified by private sustainability standards (IDH and EPOA 2020). Plans for mandatory due diligence regulation for deforestation-free products in the European Union could further "harden" corporate accountability in this supply chain setting (Moser and Leipold 2021; Schilling-Vacaflor and Lenschow 2021). However, important gaps in the on-the-ground implementation of sustainability standards persist, particularly in Indonesia's fast-expanding smallholder sector. Certification programs have long struggled to include small-scale producers in their systems (Brandi et al. 2015) and analysts fear that the EU's plans for full traceability in its no-deforestation regulation could cut them out entirely from European supply chains, with negative livelihood implications for this group of vulnerable producers (ISEAL 2022). In comparison to Europe, the regulatory agenda on sustainability in the industry's largest regional markets (China and India) remains at an early stage. The emergence of a public policy agenda on green supply chains and the creation of new emerging market-centered sustainability schemes are promising recent developments. However, constrained by bureaucratic politics and other factors, regulatory coalitions powerful enough to steer these supply chains toward sustainable sourcing have yet to emerge. There is a different dynamic in the producer countries. Here, powerful regulatory coalitions have emerged to take back control of the industry's sustainability agenda. In principle, stronger public regulation in the producer countries is to be desired. Based on hard law, national sustainability schemes are mandatory for all producers in a country. However, in the case of the ISPO program, weak regulatory capacity and a lack of global market acceptance undermine its effectiveness (Hidayat, Offermans, and Glasbergen 2018). Moreover, the interactions between domestic and transnational regulatory coalitions in this industry remain characterized by disconnects and antagonisms between transnational private and domestic public governance (Pacheco et al. 2018). This leads to a ninth claim: *Global, regional, and domestic drivers are unevenly developed and disconnects and antagonisms between demand-side and supply-side regulatory coalitions undermine multipolar governance in forest-risk supply chains.*

Is Place-Based Governance the Answer?

As part of a forward-looking research agenda, chapter 6 explores the opportunities and challenges of newly emerging, place-based programs to govern agricultural commodity production in Brazil and Indonesia. These so-called jurisdictional programs differ from traditional supply chain initiatives through their scale, scope, and governance. They focus on entire jurisdictions as opposed to individual supply chains, pursue integrated sustainable development agendas, and are led by local change coalitions. Exploring the approach and its emerging features, chapter 6 identifies three pathways through which jurisdictional programs can strengthen natural resource governance at the supply side of global, regional, and domestic supply chains. First, through a high level of local government involvement, jurisdictional programs create opportunities to harness the power of public authority to scale sustainability in the producing countries. Second, as experimental arenas, jurisdictional programs create opportunities for policy coordination to enhance institutional complementarities and resolve disconnects between transnational and domestic governance actors (Nepstad et al. 2013; Pacheco et al. 2018). Third, a focus on local communities and indigenous people in the rhetoric and design of these programs creates opportunities to include these otherwise often marginalized actors (Hovani et al. 2018, 31). While these features show

Conclusion

that jurisdictional programs have great potential to drive innovations in natural resource governance, the approach is not without challenges. One of these challenges is answered by this book's analysis of global market shifts, which casts a critical light on recent efforts by sustainability practitioners to use "jurisdictional sourcing" (Boshoven et al. 2021) and "jurisdictional certification" (RSPO 2021) to generate "global value propositions" for local stakeholders. This and other developments suggest that transnational and local elites are compromising on a conservative agenda for these programs. Addressing the challenges identified in chapter 6, will be important to make the jurisdictional approach a more progressive and promising governance project.

Implications for Practice

As global markets shift, what are the implications for policy and practice? Based on the theoretical and empirical insights of this book, this section offers some reflections for practitioners. My main point concerns the need to critically rethink theories of change in the age of advanced globalization. Practitioners in particular need to overcome deeply entrenched assumptions about North-South dependencies and power and interest constellations, which are increasingly at odds with the realities of the modern world economy. I also discuss the value of political economy analysis and how it can help policymakers and practitioners develop a better understanding of global trends and their environmental and institutional consequences.

As the analysis of this book has shown, major structural shifts in the world food economy have important implications for power, governance, and sustainability. Surprisingly, however, these developments remain at the margins of policy debates on the use of supply chain initiatives and other trade instruments to advance environmental and social policy objectives in the producing countries. One example discussed at length in this book is the market transformation strategy of the World Wide Fund for Nature (WWF 2012). Based on faulty assumptions about the structure and governance of agricultural value chains, it greatly overestimates the power of (Northern) big-brand companies in these industries. Despite growing evidence of their faulty nature, many of these assumptions remain central to practitioners' thinking on the ways in which global supply chains can be leveraged to provide economic incentives to local stakeholders. As described in the previous section, a recent example is proposals to use jurisdictional sourcing and jurisdictional certification to generate global value propositions for rural jurisdictions to produce deforestation-free commodities. Beyond supply chain initiatives, practitioners are calling on government actors in advanced economies for "getting the incentives right" (Ozinga 2020). Trade incentives should be used as leverage to move producer countries toward sustainability. Such agreements may work in some sectors where North-South trade dependencies remain strong. For example, in the cocoa sector, the EU remains in a powerful position. It is the world's largest importer of cocoa, and many of the leading chocolate companies are headquartered in Europe (Fern 2020). However, in the post–Washington Consensus World, this is the exception and not the rule. Policymakers and practitioners in the Global North need to be realistic about their leverage and ability to provide economic incentives to government and industry actors in the Global South.

Political economy analysis can help policymakers and practitioners better understand the context of their planned interventions. Going beyond a narrow focus on policy design and technoeconomic environmental impact assessments, the framework developed in this book offers powerful analytical tools to better understand global trends, differences in domestic and sectoral political economies, and the structure and governance of supply chains. In this regard, the lens of international political economy focuses on the deeper causes of ecological crises by revealing the global political, economic, and historical forces that contribute to their emergence and persistence. This "big picture" perspective is of key importance, if conservation interventions are meant to achieve more than merely addressing a problem's symptoms. Moreover, the comparative political economy perspective allows for a structured analysis of differences in the "favorability" of a sector or country for a planned governance intervention. To give a concrete example, the Tropical Forest Alliance recently published a "Collective Action Agenda" to accelerate the shift to sustainable agriculture and remove deforestation from commodity production (Tropical Forest Alliance 2020). The document envisages a broad coalition of actors, including supply chain actors, civil society organization, producer country governments, demand-side country governments, and the financial sector. Similarly, others have called for a "smart mix" of measures to achieve deforestation-free industries (Fripp and Brack 2020). However, when and where are such coalitions likely to form? The method of comparative political economy can help practitioners answer these questions by identifying enabling and constraining conditions, and showing how these vary across contexts and over time. The framework developed in this book also allows for a better understanding of the economic networks through which sustainability governance disseminates. As shown above, global supply chains remain central to practitioners' theories of change. However, these theories are often based on faulty assumptions about the structure and governance of value chains, and how supply chains are evolving in the current phase of globalization.

Emerging Global Trends and Future Research

This book examines the consequences of global economic shifts for the governance and politics of sustainability in the agriculture sector. However, economic shifts from North to South are not the only large-scale trend transforming the world economy. There are other economic, technological, and normative trends that call for scholarly attention, including the rise of green finance, new technologies, and new normative discourses. In the remainder of this section, I discuss some of these trends and suggest avenues for future research in these areas. Sustainability in global agriculture is my reference point in this discussion. However, the themes explored in this section are of relevance to other issue areas as well.

Green Private Investment
International climate finance was meant to be a game changer for tropical forests. However, analysts criticize that it has been "too low, too slow, and too encumbered by bureaucratic processes" (Seymour and Busch 2016, 390). In recent years, shifts in global financial markets have created hopes that private investors could help fill the gap. Indeed, major private investors are beginning to recognize climate risks tied to deforestation and are adopting policies for investing in companies linked to forest-risk supply chains. This includes BlackRock, the world's largest asset manager, which adopted a new investment stewardship approach for its engagement with agribusiness corporations. The policy outlines how the company will incorporate sustainable agricultural practices in its board oversight functions (BlackRock 2020). Similarly, Rabobank, BNP Paribas, and other major banks require agribusiness companies to adopt no-deforestation policies for their supply chains (BNP Paribas 2019; Rabobank 2018). Private and public investors have also made collective statements calling on companies to act on tropical deforestation.

The biggest yet brings together 251 investment organizations, representing approximately US$18 trillion in globally managed assets (Ceres 2019). In response to these developments, global financial flows are increasingly redirected to "green assets." According to the Global Sustainable Investment Alliance (2020), private green investments grew from US$23 billion to over US$35 billion between 2016 and 2020.

These figures show that green private investment is a large-scale trend in the global financial system. However, it remains poorly understood. One area for future research is the contentious politics of green private investment (Ayling and Gunningham 2017). Recent years saw the formation of new transnational advocacy networks, such as BlackRock's Big Problem.[1] Important questions for scholars to answer in this area include: What are the characteristics and strategies employed by these networks? Under what conditions can advocacy groups achieve policy change in some of the world's most powerful and secretive companies? Another area for future research concerns the ways in which green investment policies disseminate through global supply chains. What governance systems are put in place? How are these polices received and implemented by supply chain actors? What are the impacts of these policies on the ground? Finally, with attention increasingly focused on "green investment," what is the political economy of "brown investment." Public and private investors around the world continue to invest large sums of money into businesses that drive deforestation (Forests & Finance 2021). Why do these practices persist, and how can barriers to reform be overcome?

Technological Change

Technological change creates opportunities but also challenges for sustainability. Techno-optimists argue that so-called Smart Earth technologies hold significant potential to transform environmental governance (Bakker and Ritts 2018). Derived from the Smart City concept (Zubizarreta, Seravalli, and Arrizabalaga 2016), Smart Earth deploys new information and communication technologies to monitor, analyze, and increasingly predict socioecological processes. This includes advanced satellite technology, "internet of things" applications (e.g., environmental sensor networks), and other emerging technologies (e.g., artificial intelligence). A reduction in the cost of cloud computing, improved digital infrastructure, and new machine-learning tools is driving the proliferation of these technologies around the world. In the governance of tropical deforestation, Smart Earth technologies are applied in multiple settings. Most advanced is the use of remote sensing to track forest

Conclusion

cover changes in almost real time through digital platforms such as Global Forest Watch.[2] Also, the use of artificial intelligence interventions is increasingly widespread. Applications include new technology start-ups such as Satelligence[3] and Overstory,[4] which develop machine-learning algorithms to provide companies with customized tools to remotely monitor deforestation risks in their supply chains. Other applications include a new program by the Sustainable Trade Initiative that uses artificial intelligence to help smallholders manage the challenges of water management (IDH 2021a). Used by companies to improve the transparency of their supply chain tracking systems, blockchain is another nascent technology (Ledger Insights 2020).

As these examples illustrate, the use of Smart Earth technologies is beginning to transform environmental governance in the world food economy. While some scholars claim these technologies have great potential (Bakker and Ritts 2018), others caution against too much techno-optimism (Arts, van der Wal, and Adams 2015; Dauvergne 2020; Gale, Ascui, and Lovell 2017; Möller 2020). For example, Auld et al. (2010) remind us that technologies influence problem definitions (what is measured matters) and therefore the choice of policy instruments. A focus on technological fixes may thus divert attention away from the underlying root causes of a problem (Huesemann and Huesemann 2011). Similarly, others warn that the microlevel improvements from artificial intelligence will not add up to macrolevel solutions for the negative environmental consequences of global supply chains (Dauvergne 2020). As artificial intelligence and other technologies continue to advance, the debate between techno-optimists and techno-pessimists will remain very important for scholars of transnational business governance in the years to come.

New Normative Discourses

Global discourses on justice and decoloniality are another important development. While concerns with institutional effectiveness have long been a key focus of mainstream governance research, Biermann, Dirth, and Kalfagianni (2020) observe a shift in the debate toward the normative foundations of global environmental governance. This "justice turn" in environmental politics is driven by powerful social movements, notably climate activism but also indigenous rights groups. While scholarship on environmental justice has a rich intellectual tradition (Mohai, Pellow, and Roberts 2009), scholars of earth system governance argue that this debate requires a new conceptual framing in the age of the Anthropocene. They propose the concept of "planetary justice" to interrogate the justice implications of profound transformations of the earth system. An important focus of this research agenda is how justice issues are addressed in global environmental institutions (Biermann and Kalfagianni 2020). Connecting to the emerging research agenda on planetary justice, scholars of transnational business governance could use the framework developed by Biermann and Kalfagianni to interrogate the political discourses, programs, and outcomes of major private governance institutions, such as the Forest Stewardship Council, the RTRS, and the Fairtrade Labelling Organization.

In addition to global justice concerns, the Black Lives Matter movement has reinvigorated global discussions on racism and coloniality. These debates are also taking place in the domain of environmental politics, including the governance of sustainable development, biodiversity, and land (DePuy et al. 2021; Hope 2020). As highlighted throughout this book, colonialism and its legacies loom large in global agriculture and its governance (Clapp 2020, 24–57). In Africa, South America, and Asia, European colonial projects included the development export-oriented agricultural industries to supply metropolitan Europe with cheap natural resources and exotic goods. The expansion of these industries in the modern era remains deeply entangled with the history of postcolonial state formation and its dominant development paradigms. Colonial histories and modernist development thinking are thus woven into the fabric of these industries and their institutions. As these themes are brought to the foreground in broader societal discourses on colonialism and racism, students of transnational business governance should use this opportunity to engage more deeply with the colonial legacy of the industries they study. Confronting colonial legacies also creates opportunities to critically interrogate the modernist ontology of current systems of environmental governance. This may open up intellectual space to consider alternatives, including indigenous ideas about human-nature relationships (DePuy et al. 2021). Making these ontologies visible could help imagine institutions that are more attuned to the challenges posed by the Anthropocene, in which old dichotomies that portray the natural world as being distinct from the world of humans are no longer tenable.

Concluding Thoughts

As I finish this book, the world economy is shaken by the COVID-19 pandemic and the war in Ukraine. The pandemic has triggered a global public health emergency on a scale unseen since the Spanish flu outbreak of 1918.

Conclusion

With lockdown measures and travel restrictions heavily disrupting supply chains around the world, the pandemic has caused an economic shock even greater than that of the 2008 global financial crisis. As COVID-19 restrictions are finally lifted in large parts of the world, the war in Ukraine is shaping up to become the largest military conflict in Europe since World War II, with major geopolitical and global economic repercussions. In concluding this book, I would like to offer some reflections on the economic, environmental, and political consequences of these events for the world food economy.

The 2008 financial crisis contributed to a gravitational shift in the global economy from North to South, as emerging economies were less affected by the crisis (Staritz, Gereffi, and Cattaneo 2011). Strong demand for natural resources from fast-growing emerging economies fueled the tropical commodity boom analyzed in this book. How will the COVID-19 pandemic and the war in Ukraine affect this trend? Global economic data from the first year of the pandemic suggests that the coronavirus recession led to divergence between advanced and emerging economies as well as within the group of the BRICS economies (Brazil, Russia, India, China, South Africa) (Brennan 2020). As in the 2008 financial crisis, China was initially less affected by the coronavirus recession than the major advanced economies, further accelerating the country's global economic rise (BBC 2020). In the first phase of the pandemic, China also did better than the other BRICS economies, which could suffer from "long economic Covid" (Wolf 2020), as low vaccinations rates and overburdened public health systems hinder their recovery. However, the medium- to long-term economic consequences of the crisis remain uncertain. China's strict zero-COVID strategy, which saw Shanghai and other major economic centers put under lockdown at a time when many other countries finally lifted their restrictions, could undo some of its economic success early in the crisis. Moreover, as the world recovers from the coronavirus recession, the war in Ukraine is sending new shockwaves through the global economy, including markets for agricultural commodities. Ukraine and the Russian Federation are among the world's top exporters of wheat, maize, rapeseed, sunflower seeds, and sunflower oil. The FAO projects that the conflict will lead to a significant reduction in cereal and oilseed exports by the two countries, with major repercussions for global agricultural markets and food security (FAO 2022). As countries around the world scramble to find alternative suppliers to meet their demand for food, feed, and vegetable oil, world market prices for soft commodities have risen strongly. This includes tropical oil crops, such as palm oil, which saw its price increase by over 60 percent between April 2021 and April 2022 (Trading Economics 2021).

What are the consequences of these global crises for sustainability? There is evidence that the COVID pandemic has undermined conservation efforts around the world, with tropical countries being particularly hard hit. Brancaliona et al. (2020) show that deforestation alerts across the global tropics nearly doubled during the first months of the pandemic. Exploring the links between COVID-19 and tropical deforestation, they describe how deforestation drivers can change rapidly during periods of profound sociopolitical-economic transformations. The pandemic's immediate consequences include opportunistic forest clearing during lockdown periods. As global agricultural markets are shaken up by the war in Ukraine, fast-rising prices for soft commodities could become another driver of deforestation. In response to strong global demand, crisis-ridden tropical countries could further expand their agricultural industries, which are often the most important foreign exchange earners for these countries. There also are fears that the pandemic and the war in Ukraine could undo the progress toward the United Nations Sustainable Development Goals (FAO 2022; United Nations 2021). Among other challenges, food security is a major concern. In the first year of the pandemic, the number of people facing hunger increased by 118 million, making the achievement of the goal to eradicate world hunger and malnutrition in all its forms by 2030 increasingly unlikely (FAO et al. 2021). One reason for the increase is the disruption of food supply chains during lockdowns (Reardon, Bellemare, and Zilberman 2020). The war in Ukraine has caused another shock to global food supply, creating major risks for countries like Eritrea, Egypt, Lebanon, and Somalia, which heavily depend on cereal exports from Ukraine and the Russian Federation (FAO 2022, 10). The two crises thus expose the vulnerabilities of a world food system, in which developing countries are increasingly dependent on the seamless functioning of global supply chains (WFP 2020).

Finally, what are consequences for regulation and governance? The short-term consequences of the pandemic included the disruption of public and private regulatory efforts through lockdown measures and travel restrictions. Researching the response of private regulatory programs to the pandemic, Auld and Renckens (2021) find that ad hoc changes in audit policies, the use of remote audits, and limited transparency exacerbated existing barriers for Global South actors in these programs. There also is evidence to suggest that the pandemic created a window of opportunity to roll back public environmental regulation. One example comes from Brazil, where the Minister of the Environment suggested that the pandemic offers a distraction during which the government should "run the cattle herd through the Amazon" (Gonzales 2020). While the pandemic's short-term consequences become increasingly clear, its medium- to long-term implications remain uncertain. For transnational business governance, Auld and Renckens (2021) speculate about two scenarios. First, the pandemic could accelerate existing evolutionary dynamics among private sustainability schemes, as they expand their nonregulatory activities (e.g., consultancy, capacity building, advocacy) (also see Fransen 2018). Second, market-driven regulatory programs could face a harder time if supply chains shorten, and trade does not return to former levels. At a broader level, the pandemic and the war in Ukraine could have both positive and negative consequences for environmental policy. There is a risk that in a moment of economic crisis government and industry actors will renege on their sustainability commitments. In response to the crisis in Ukraine, Iceland, the British retail giant, announced with "huge regret" a U-turn on its no-palm oil policy (Butler 2022), and the EU is conducting a review of its sustainable food strategy after a concerted push against planned reforms by national governments and the agriculture industry (Bounds 2022). However, in a more optimistic scenario, these crises could also open a window of opportunity to reform what some activists describe as a "very broken food system" (Greenpeace 2022).

Notes

Chapter 1

1. Statement made during a webinar of Innovation Forum, September 22, 2017, https://www.innovationforum.co.uk/articles/accelerating-action-on-deforestation-in-commodity-supply-chains.

2. See Bartley (2007) and Synnott (2005) for detailed accounts of the emergence of private governance in the forestry sector.

3. For more information about the Standards Map Database, see Fiorini et al. (2019).

4. The twelve certification organizations are 4C, Better Cotton Initiative, Bonsucro, Cotton Made in Africa, Fairtrade, Global G.A.P., Organic, ProTerra, the Roundtable on Sustainable Palm Oil, the Roundtable on Responsible Soy, the Rainforest Alliance, and UTZ. For more details on these programs and their certified production areas, see Willer et al. (2019, 14–29).

5. This is based on a conservative estimate. According to the International Trade Centre and its partners, the globally certified area in the commodity sectors depicted in figure 1.2 range from a minimum of 19.7 million hectares and a maximum of 26.4 million hectares. The reason for this large range is that many producers are certified by more than one certification organization, and there is not enough reliable data on the share of multiple certifications.

6. Zero net deforestation allows for forest conversion in one area as long as an equal area is replanted elsewhere. It is a weaker criterion than zero deforestation, which allows no forest clearance or conversion at all.

7. The methods behind the deforestation data shown in figure 1.3 have changed over time. Therefore, caution needs to be exercised when comparing old and new data, especially before and after 2015. See https://www.globalforestwatch.org/blog/data-and-research/tree-cover-loss-satellite-data-trend-analysis/.

8. See https://www.theconsumergoodsforum.com/environmental-sustainability/forest-positive.

9. See https://jaresourcehub.org/resources/webinars/.

Chapter 2

1. Note that market uptake is not a sufficient condition for outcome effectiveness because programs with high membership levels but lenient standards and weak enforcement rules, so-called greenwashes (Prakash and Potoski 2006, 63), are unlikely to induce meaningful behavioral changes beyond a business-as-usual scenario.

2. In the global value chain literature, the term governance refers to the practices and organizational forms through which a specific division of labor between lead firms and their suppliers in global industries is established and managed (Gibbon, Bair, and Ponte 2008, 319).

Chapter 3

1. The members of the original Cairns Group consisted of Argentina, Australia, Brazil, Canada, Chile, Colombia, Fiji, Hungary, Indonesia, Malaysia, New Zealand, the Philippines, Thailand, and Uruguay.

2. In 2018, the EU lowered the proportion of land-based biofuels in the Renewable Energy Directive to 7 percent (EU Commission n.d.).

3. The developing country members of the Cairns group are Argentina, Brazil, Chile, Colombia, Costa Rica, Guatemala, Indonesia, Malaysia, Pakistan, Paraguay, Peru, Philippines, South Africa, Thailand, Uruguay, and Vietnam.

4. The model that is used for attributing deforestation to expanding cropland, pastures and forest plantations is implemented at national level (with the exception of Brazil and Indonesia, where it is run at microregion and province level, respectively). This implies that the deforestation attribution risks mixing direct and indirect drivers of deforestation (i.e., commodities produced directly on deforested land and commodities indirectly causing deforestation by expanding on other land uses, pushing these into forests) and that the deforestation attribution reflects national averages, and does not account for differences in geographical sourcing between importing countries. The estimates of deforestation embodied in imports should therefore be interpreted as a measure of deforestation risk. There are some slight differences between the trade data total and attribution data total. These primarily result from inconsistencies in the input trade data used for the physical trade model, where a country's exports of a commodity were larger than its domestic production and imports (measured in primary equivalents), resulting in negative values for apparent consumption for some specific combinations of countries, commodities, and years. These values have been excluded

and for this reason, the trade data total is slightly higher than the attribution data total (Pendrill, Persson, and Kastner 2020).

5. There are many overlaps between these concepts. See Abbott et al. (2012b); Alter and Raustiala (2018), Orsini, Morin, and Young (2013), and Zelli and van Asselt (2013) for detailed discussions.

6. This includes due diligence regulation for global supply chains in consumer countries and mandatory sustainability standards in producer countries that are at least partially directed at global markets.

7. https://www.sustainabilitymap.org.

8. The members of the Amsterdam Declarations Partnership are Denmark, France, Germany, Italy, the Netherlands, Norway, and the United Kingdom. Initially focused on the trade of deforestation-free palm oil, the Amsterdam Declarations Partnership has been extended to cover other forest-risk commodities, including soy and cocoa.

9. The calculations are based on a basket of tropical commodities (bananas, cocoa, coffee, cotton, oil palm, soybeans, sugarcane, and tea) and the main transnational sustainability schemes in these sectors.

10. There is institutional diversity among the group of Southern standards. In addition to the state-led, top-down model, there are also civil society–led bottom-up approaches and other programs that defy simple geographical categorizations into Northern and Southern standards (see Langford 2019; Sun and van der Ven 2020).

11. In their framework, Biermann et al. (2009) distinguish between three types of fragmentation: synergistic, cooperative, and conflictive. The first type (synergistic) is excluded here as there is no single, core institution in this issue area.

12. See Pacheco et al. (2018) for a notable exception.

Chapter 4

1. "Sustainable markets" is a term used by practitioners and refers to the uptake of private standards in a given sector (see Lernoud et al. 2018). Here, "sustainable" is put in quotation marks to emphasize that the uptake of a standard does not equal sustainability. For example, the adoption of weak standards or standards that lack implementation has no or only very limited effects on sustainability.

2. https://www.forest500.org.

3. https://www.supply-change.org.

4. https://www.sustainabilitymap.org.

5. Forest 500 considers a company to be exposed if it produces, procures, or uses a commodity as part of its core business.

Notes to Pages 75–153

6. The different supply chain segments considered are producers, processors, traders, manufactures, and retailers. In addition to companies, Forest 500 also ranks financial institutions, which are excluded here. For a detailed description of the company selection and assessment methodologies, see Global Canopy Program (2016, 2017).

7. According to Henders, Persson, and Kastner (2015), who investigate land use change between 2000 and 2011 in seven major forest-risk countries, the cattle sector accounts for 2.7 million hectares of annual forest loss, followed by soy (0.5 million hectares), timber (0.4 million hectares), and oil palm (0.3 million hectares).

8. See Chagas et al. (2018, 60–61) for a detailed discussion of the media coverage assessment methodology.

9. The study does not include media outlets from China or India.

Chapter 5

1. In Indonesia, plantation companies are mandated by law to provide 20 percent of their land to plasma smallholders, although many companies do not comply with this requirement (Jelsma et al. 2017, 282).

2. Apical belongs to the Royal Golden Eagle Group.

3. Annual Communication of Progress reports can be accessed at https://rspo.org/members/acop.

4. Statement made by the vice president of sustainability relations of Golden Agri-Resources at the Innovation Forum webinar on 16 March 2017 (https://innovation-forum.co.uk/analysis.php?s=business-and-deforestation-are-companies-going-to-meet-their-supply-chain-commitments).

5. For a detailed description of the RSPO's certification process, see https://rspo.org/certification.

6. Documentation about the conflict settlement process in the case of IOI Group can be downloaded from the RSPO's archives at https://rspo.org/members/complaints/status-of-complaints/view/80.

7. For a detailed analysis, see Sun's (2022) recently published book, *Certifying China: The Rise and Limits of Transnational Sustainability Governance in Emerging Economies*.

Chapter 6

1. http://www.gcftaskforce.org.

2. https://www.kabupatenlestari.org/en/.

Chapter 7

1. https://blackrocksbigproblem.com/#bigproblem.
2. https://www.globalforestwatch.org/.
3. https://satelligence.com/.
4. https://www.overstory.com/.

References

Abbott, Kenneth W. 2012a. Engaging the Public and the Private in Global Sustainability Governance. *International Affairs* 88 (3): 543–564. https://doi.org/10.1111/j.1468-2346.2012.01088.x.

Abbott, Kenneth W. 2012b. The Transnational Regime Complex for Climate Change. *Environment and Planning C: Government and Policy* 30 (4): 571–590. https://doi.org/10.1068/c11127.

Abbott, Kenneth W., and Benjamin Faude. 2021. Choosing Low-Cost Institutions in Global Governance. *International Theory* 13 (3): 397–426. https://doi.org/10.1017/s1752971920000202.

Abbott, Kenneth W., Phillipp Genschel, Duncan Snidal, and Bernhard Zangl. 2015. Orchestration: Global Governance through Intermediaries. In *International Organizations as Orchestrators*, edited by Kenneth W. Abbott, Phillipp Genschel, Duncan Snidal, and Bernhard Zangl, 3–37. Cambridge: Cambridge University Press.

Abbott, Kenneth W., Jessica F. Green, and Robert O. Keohane. 2016. Organizational Ecology and Institutional Change in Global Governance. *International Organization* 70 (2): 247–277. https://doi.org/10.1017/S0020818315000338

Abbott, Kenneth W., and Duncan Snidal. 2009. The Governance Triangle: Regulatory Standards Institutions and the Shadow of the State. In *The Politics of Global Regulation*, edited by Walter Mattli and Ngaire Woods, 44–88. Princeton, NJ: Princeton University Press.

Abram, Nicola K., Erik Meijaard, Kerrie A. Wilson, Jacqueline T. Davis, Jessie A. Wells, Marc Ancrenaz, Sugeng Budiharta, Alexandra Durrant, Afif Fakhruzzi, Rebecca K. Runting, David Gaveau, and Kerrie Mengersen. 2017. Oil Palm–Community Conflict Mapping in Indonesia: A Case for Better Community Liaison in Planning for Development Initiatives. *Applied Geography* 78: 33–44. https://doi.org/10.1016/j.apgeog.2016.10.005.

Adolph, Christopher, Vanessa Quince, and Aseem Prakash. 2017. The Shanghai Effect: Do Exports to China Affect Labor Practices in Africa? *World Development* 89: 1–18. https://doi.org/10.1016/j.worlddev.2016.05.009.

Akoyi, Kevin Teopista, and Miet Maertens. 2018. Walk the Talk: Private Sustainability Standards in the Ugandan Coffee Sector. *Journal of Development Studies* 54 (10): 1792–1818. https://doi.org/10.1080/00220388.2017.1327663.

Alexandratos, Nikos, and Jelle Bruinsma. 2012. World Agriculture towards 2030/2050: The 2012 Revision. ESA Working Paper No. 12–03. Rome: FAO. http://www.fao.org/docrep/016/ap106e/ap106e.pdf.

Alix-Garcia, Jennifer, and Holly K. Gibbs. 2017. Forest Conservation Effects of Brazil's Zero Deforestation Cattle Agreements Undermined by Leakage. *Global Environmental Change* 47: 201–217. https://doi.org/10.1016/j.gloenvcha.2017.08.009.

Alter, Karen J., and Kal Raustiala. 2018. The Rise of International Regime Complexity. *Annual Review of Law and Social Science* 14 (1): 329–349. https://doi.org/10.1146/annurev-lawsocsci-101317-030830.

Amsterdam Declarations Partnership. 2015. The Amsterdam Declaration in Support of a Fully Sustainable Palm Oil Supply Chain by 2020. December 7, 2015. Accessed March 23, 2022. https://www.idhsustainabletrade.com/uploaded/2016/06/declaration-palm-oil-amsterdam.pdf?msclkid=4bd9e6feaaeb11ecb8d4df6f96d90352.

Amsterdam Declarations Partnership. 2016. Strategy AD Partnership. December 1, 2016. Accessed March 23, 2022. https://ad-partnership.org/wp-content/uploads/2018/10/AD-Partnership-Implementation-Strategy-v1Dec2016.pdf.

Anandi, Cut Augusta Mindry, Ida Aju Pradnja Resosudarmo, Mella Komalasari, Andini Desita Ekaputri, and Dian Yusvita Intarin. 2014. TNC's Initiative within the Berau Forest Carbon Program, East Kalimantan, Indonesia. In *REDD+ on the Ground*, edited by Erin O. Sills, Stibniati S. Atmadja, Claudio de Sassi, Amy E. Duchelle, Demetrius L. Kweka, Ida Aju Pradnja Resosudarmo, and William D. Sunderlin, 362–379. Bogor Barat, Indonesia: Center for International Forestry Research (CIFOR). Accessed March 23, 2022. https://www.cifor.org/publications/pdf_files/books/BCIFOR1403.pdf.

Anderson, Christa M., Gregory P. Asner, and Eric F. Lambin. 2019. Lack of Association between Deforestation and either Sustainability Commitments or Fines in Private Concessions in the Peruvian Amazon. *Forest Policy and Economics* 104: 1–8. https://doi.org/10.1016/j.forpol.2019.03.010.

Andonova, Liliana B. 2004. *Transnational Politics of the Environment: The European Union and Environmental Policy in Central and Eastern Europe*. Cambridge, MA: MIT Press.

Andresen, Steinar. 2013. International Regime Effectiveness. In *The Handbook of Global Climate and Environmental Policy*, edited by Robert Falkner, 304–319. Malden, MA: Wiley and Blackwell. https://doi.org/10.1002/9781118326213.ch18.

APROBI. n.d. About Us. Accessed March 23, 2022. https://aprobi.or.id/our-approach/.

References

Arima, Eugenio Y., Peter Richards, Robert Walker, and Marcellus M. Caldas. 2011. Statistical Confirmation of Indirect Land Use Change in the Brazilian Amazon. *Environmental Research Letters* 6 (2): 1–7. https://doi.org/10.1088/1748-9326/6/2/024010.

Arts, Koen, René van der Wal, and William M. Adams. 2015. Digital Technology and the Conservation of Nature. *Ambio* 44 (4): 661–673. https://doi.org/10.1007/s13280-015-0705-1.

Aspinall, Edward, and Ward Berenschot. 2019. *Democracy for Sale: Elections, Clientelism, and the State in Indonesia*. Ithaca, NY: Cornell University Press.

Atmadja, Stibniati S., Yayan Indriatmoko, Nugroho Adi Utomo, Mella Komalasari, and Andini Desita Ekaputri. 2014. Kalimantan Forests and Climate Partnership, Central Kalimantan, Indonesia. In *REDD+ on the Ground*, edited by Erin O. Sills, Stibniati S. Atmadja, Claudio de Sassi, Amy E. Duchelle, Demetrius L. Kweka, Ida Aju Pradnja Resosudarmo, and William D. Sunderlin, 290–309. Bogor Barat, Indonesia: Center for International Forestry Research (CIFOR). Accessed March 23, 2022. https://www.cifor.org/publications/pdf_files/books/BCIFOR1403.pdf.

Auld, Graeme. 2010. Assessing Certification as Governance: Effects and Broader Consequences for Coffee. *Journal of Environment and Development* 19 (2): 215–241. https://doi.org/10.1177/1070496510368506.

Auld, Graeme. 2014. *Constructing Private Governance: The Rise and Evolution of Forest, Coffee, and Fisheries Certification*. New Haven, CT: Yale University Press.

Auld, Graeme, Cristina Balboa, Tim Bartley, Benjamin Cashore, and Kelly Levin. 2007. The Spread of the Certification Model: Understanding the Evolution of Non-State Driven Market Governance. Paper presented at the annual meeting of the International Studies Association 48th Annual Convention, Chicago, IL, February 28 to March 3, 2007.

Auld, Graeme, Benjamin Cashore, Cristina Balboa, Laura Bozzi, and Stefan Renckens. 2010. Can Technological Innovation Improve Private Regulation in the Global Economy? Special issue, *Business and Politics* 12 (3): 1–39. https://doi.org/10.2202/1469-3569.1323.

Auld, Graeme, and Stefan Renckens. 2021. Private Sustainability Governance, the Global South and COVID-19: Are Changes to Audit Policies in Light of the Pandemic Exacerbating Existing Inequalities? *World Development* 139: 105314. https://doi.org/10.1016/j.worlddev.2020.105314.

Austin, Kemen G., Mariano González-Roglich, Danica Schaffer-Smith, Amanda M. Schwantes, and Jennifer J. Swenson. 2017. Trends in Size of Tropical Deforestation Events Signal Increasing Dominance of Industrial-Scale Drivers. *Environmental Research Letters* 12 (5): 054009. https://doi.org/10.1088/1748-9326/aa6a88.

Ayling, Julie M., and Neil Gunningham. 2017. Non-state Governance and Climate Policy: The Fossil Fuel Divestment Movement. *Climate Policy* 17 (2): 131–149. https://doi.org/10.1080/14693062.2015.1094729.

Bäckstrand, Karin. 2006. Democratizing Global Environmental Governance? Stakeholder Democracy after the World Summit on Sustainable Development. *European Journal of International Relations* 12 (4): 467–498. https://doi.org/10.1177/1354066106069321.

Bäckstrand, Karin, Jamil Kahn, Annica Kronsell, and Eva Lövbrand, eds. 2010. *Environmental Politics and Deliberative Democracy: Examining the Promise of New Modes of Governance*. Cheltenham: Edward Elgar.

Baines, Joseph, and Sandy Brian Hager. 2021. Commodity Traders in a Storm: Financialization, Corporate Power and Ecological Crisis. *Review of International Political Economy*. https://doi.org/10.1080/09692290.2021.1872039.

Bakker, Karen, and Max Ritts. 2018. Smart Earth: A Meta-Review and Implications for Environmental Governance. *Global Environmental Change* 52: 201–211. https://doi.org/10.1016/j.gloenvcha.2018.07.011.

Barbosa, Luiz C. 2015. *Guardians of the Brazilian Amazon Rainforest: Environmental Organizations and Development*. London: Routledge.

Barham, Bradford L., Mercedez Callenes, Seth Gitter, Jessa Lewis, and Jeremy Weber. 2011. Fair Trade/Organic Coffee, Rural Livelihoods, and the "Agrarian Question": Southern Mexican Coffee Families in Transition. *World Development* 39 (1): 134–145. https://doi.org/10.1016/j.worlddev.2010.08.005.

Barrientos, Stephanie, Gary Gereffi, and Arianna Rossi. 2011. Economic and Social Upgrading in Global Production Networks: A New Paradigm for a Changing World. *International Labour Review* 150 (3–4): 319–340. https://doi.org/10.1111/j.1564-913x.2011.00119.x.

Bartley, Tim. 2007. Institutional Emergence in an Era of Globalization: The Rise of Transnational Private Regulation of Labor and Environmental Conditions. *American Journal of Sociology* 113 (2): 297–351. https://doi.org/10.1086/518871.

Bartley, Tim. 2009. Standards for Sweatshops: The Power and Limits of the Club Approach to Voluntary Labor Standards. In *Voluntary Programs: A Club Theory Perspective*, edited by Matthew Potoski and Aseem Prakash, 107–131. Cambridge, MA: MIT Press.

Bartley, Tim. 2010. Transnational Private Regulation in Practice: The Limits of Forest and Labor Standard Regulation in Indonesia. Special issue, *Business and Politics* 12 (3): 1–34. https://doi.org/10.2202/1469-3569.1321.

Bartley, Tim. 2018a. *Rules without Rights: Land, Labor, and Private Authority in the Global Economy*. Oxford: Oxford University Press.

References

Bartley, Tim. 2018b. Transnational Corporations and Global Governance. *Annual Review of Sociology* 44 (1): 145–165. https://doi.org/10.1146/annurev-soc-060116-053540.

BBC. 2020. Chinese Economy to Overtake US by 2028 Due to Covid. December 26, 2020. Accessed March 23, 2022. https://www.bbc.com/news/world-asia-china-55454146.

Beisheim, Marianne, and Sabine Campe. 2012. Transnational Public-Private Partnerships' Performance in Water Governance: Institutional Design Matters. *Environment and Planning C: Government and Policy* 30 (4): 627–642. https://doi.org/10.1068/c1194.

Beisheim, Marianne, and Andrea Liese, eds. 2014. *Transnational Partnerships: Effectively Providing for Sustainable Development?* Houndmills: Palgrave Macmillan.

Beisheim, Marianne, Andrea Liese, Hannah Janetschek, and Johanna Sarre. 2014. Transnational Partnerships: Conditions for Successful Service Provision in Areas of Limited Statehood. *Governance* 27 (4): 655–673. https://doi.org/10.1111/gove.12070.

Bennett, Elizabeth A. 2013. A Short History of Fairtrade Certification Governance. In *The Processes and Practices of Fair Trade: Trust, Ethics, and Governance*, edited by Brigitte Granville and Janet Dine, 43–79. Abingdon: Routledge.

Berger, K. G., and S. M. Martin. 2000. Palm Oil. In *The Cambridge World History of Food*, edited by Kenneth F. Kiple and Kriemhild Coneè Ornelas, 397–411. Cambridge: Cambridge University Press. https://doi.org/10.1017/CHOL9780521402149.040.

Berliner, Daniel, and Aseem Prakash. 2014. Public Authority and Private Rules: How Domestic Regulatory Institutions Shape the Adoption of Global Private Regimes. *International Studies Quarterly* 58 (4): 793–803. http://doi.org/10.1111/isqu.12166.

Bernstein, Steven. 2002. Liberal Environmentalism and Global Environmental Governance. *Global Environmental Politics* 2 (3): 1–16. http://doi.org/10.1162/152638002320310509.

Biermann, Frank, Elizabeth Dirth, and Agni Kalfagianni. 2020. Planetary Justice as a Challenge for Earth System Governance: Editorial. *Earth System Governance* 6: 100085. https://doi.org/10.1016/j.esg.2020.100085.

Biermann, Frank, and Agni Kalfagianni. 2020. Planetary Justice: A Research Framework. *Earth System Governance* 6: 100049. https://doi.org/10.1016/j.esg.2020.100049.

Biermann, Frank, Phillipp Pattberg, Harro van Asselt, and Fariborz Zelli. 2009. The Fragmentation of Global Governance Architectures: A Framework for Analysis. *Global Environmental Politics* 9 (4): 14–40. https://doi.org/10.1162/glep.2009.9.4.14.

Bitzer, Verena, and Alessia Marazzi. 2021. Southern Sustainability Initiatives in Agricultural Value Chains: A Question of Enhanced Inclusiveness? The Case of Trustea in India. *Agriculture and Human Values* 38: 381–395. https://doi.org/10.1007/s10460-020-10151-4.

Blackman, Allen, Leonard Thomas Goff, and Marisol Rivera Planter. 2018. Does Eco-Certification Stem Tropical Deforestation? Forest Stewardship Council Certification in Mexico. *Journal of Environmental Economics and Management* 89: 306–333. https://doi.org/10.1016/j.jeem.2018.04.005.

Blackman, Allen, and Maria Naranjo. 2012. Does Eco-Certification have Environmental Benefits? Organic Coffee in Costa Rica. *Ecological Economics* 83: 58–66. https://doi.org/10.1016/j.ecolecon.2012.08.001.

BlackRock. n.d. Investment Stewardship's Approach to Engagement with Agribusiness Companies on Sustainable Business Practices. Accessed March 23, 2022. https://www.blackrock.com/corporate/literature/publication/blk-commentary-engaging-on-sustainable-agriculture.pdf.

Bloomberg. 2019a. China Slashed US Soybean Imports in Half in 2018 after Trade War. January 24, 2019. Accessed March 23, 2022.

Bloomberg. 2019b. *EU Sets Limits on Palm Oil in Biofuels as Trade War Looms*. March 13, 2019.

Bloomfield, Michael John. 2014. Shame Campaigns and Environmental Justice: Corporate Shaming as Activist Strategy. *Environmental Politics* 23 (2): 263–281. https://doi.org/10.1080/09644016.2013.821824.

Bloomfield, Michael John. 2017. *Dirty Gold: How Activism Transformed the Jewelry Industry*. Cambridge, MA: MIT Press.

Bloomfield, Michael John. 2020. South-South Trade and Sustainable Development: The Case of Ceylon Tea. *Ecological Economics* 167: 106393. https://doi.org/10.1016/j.ecolecon.2019.106393.

Bloomfield, Michael John, and Philip Schleifer. 2017. Tracing Failure of Coral Reef Protection in Nonstate Market-Driven Governance. *Global Environmental Politics* 17 (4): 127–146. https://doi.org/10.1162/glep_a_00432.

BNP Paribas. 2019. *Global Sustainability Strategy*. Paris: BNP Paribas. Accessed March 23, 2022. https://docfinder.bnpparibas-am.com/api/files/1FC9FC6C-0DA8-468E-90B3-016DDB5CD270.

Borneo Post. 2016. IOI Group Reaches Settlement with Aidenvironment. December 3, 2016. Accessed March 23, 2022. https://www.theborneopost.com/2016/12/03/ioi-group-reaches-settlement-with-aidenvironment-issues/.

Boshoven, Judy, Leonardo C. Fleck, Sabine Miltner, Nick Salafsky, Justin Adams, Andreas Dahl-Jørgensen, Gustavo Fonseca, Dan Nepsted, Kevin Rabinovitch, and Frances Seymour. 2021. Jurisdictional Sourcing: Leveraging Commodity Supply Chains to Reduce Tropical Deforestation at Scale. A Generic Theory of Change for a Conservation Strategy, v 1.0. *Conservation Science and Practice* 3 (5): e383. https://doi.org/10.1111/csp2.383.

References

Boström, Magnus, and Kristina Tamm Hallström. 2010. NGO Power in Global Social and Environmental Standard-Setting. *Global Environmental Politics* 10 (4): 36–59. http://doi.org/10.1162/GLEP_a_00030.

Boucher, Doug, Sarah Roquemore, and Estrellita Fitzhugh. 2013. Brazil's Success in Reducing Deforestation. *Tropical Conservation Science* 6 (3): 426–445. https://doi.org/10.1177/194008291300600308.

Bounds, Andy. 2022. EU Reviews Sustainable Food Plans as Ukraine War Disrupts Imports. *Financial Times*, March 20, 2022. Accessed April 23, 2022. https://www.ft.com/content/f99d784c-0448-4552-ab8b-e77ed68ea173.

Boyd, William, Claudia Stickler, Amy E. Duchelle, Frances Seymour, Daniel Nepstad, Nur H. A. Bahar, and Dawn Rodriguez-Ward. 2018. Jurisdictional Approaches to REDD+ and Low Emissions Development: Progress and Prospects. World Resources Institute, Working Paper, June 2018. Accessed March 23, 2022. https://wriorg.s3.amazonaws.com/s3fs-public/ending-tropical-deforestation-jurisdictional-approaches-redd.pdf.

Brancaliona, Pedro H. S., Eben N. Broadbent, Sergio de-Miguel, Adrián Cardil, Marcos R. Rosa, Catherine T. Almeida, Danilo R. A. Almeida, Shourish Chakravarty, Mo Zhou, Javier G. P. Gamarrah, Jingjing Liang, Renato Crouzeilles, Bruno Hérault, Luiz E. O. C. Aragão, Carlos Alberto Silva, and Angelica M. Almeyda-Zambranos. 2020. Emerging Threats Linking Tropical Deforestation and the COVID-19 Pandemic. *Perspectives in Ecology and Conservation* 18 (4): 243–246. https://doi.org/10.1016/j.pecon.2020.09.006.

Brandi, Clara. 2017. Sustainability Standards and Sustainable Development—Synergies and Trade-Offs of Transnational Governance. *Sustainable Development* 25 (1): 25–34. https://doi.org/10.1002/sd.1639.

Brandi, Clara. 2021. The Interaction of Private and Public Governance: The Case of Sustainability Standards for Palm Oil. *European Journal of Development Research* 33:1574–1595. https://doi.org/10.1057/s41287-020-00306-8.

Brandi, Clara, Tobia Cabani, Christoph Hosang, Sonja Schirmbeck, Lotte Westermann, and Hannah Wiese. 2015. Sustainability Standards for Palm Oil: Challenges for Smallholder Certification Under the RSPO. *Journal of Environment & Development* 24 (3): 292–314. https://doi.org/10.1177/1070496515593775.

Branford, Sue, and Thais Borges. 2019. Brazil on the Precipice: From Environmental Leader to Despoiler (2010–2020). Mongabay, December 23, 2019. Accessed March 23, 2022. https://news.mongabay.com/2019/12/brazil-on-the-precipice-from-environmental-leader-to-despoiler-2010-2020/.

Breitmeier, Helmut, Oran R. Young, and Michael Zürn. 2006. *Analyzing International Environmental Regimes: From Case Study to Database*. Cambridge, MA: MIT Press.

Brennan, Peter. 2020. COVID-19 Magnifies BRICS Divergence as China Solidifies Lead. S&P Global Market Intelligence, November 5, 2020. Accessed March 23, 2022.

https://www.spglobal.com/marketintelligence/en/news-insights/latest-news-headlines/covid-19-magnifies-brics-divergence-as-china-solidifies-lead-61053247.

Brown-Lima, Carrie, Melissa Cooney, and David Cleary. 2009. An Overview of the Brazil-China Soybean Trade and Its Strategic Implications for Conservation. Arlington, VA: Nature Conservancy.

Bush, Simon R., Peter Oosterveer, Megan Bailey, and Arthur P. J. Mol. 2015. Sustainability Governance of Chains and Networks: A Review and Future Outlook. *Journal of Cleaner Production* 107: 8–19. https://doi.org/10.1016/j.jclepro.2014.10.019.

Büthe, Tim, and Walter Mattli. 2011. *New Global Rulers: The Privatization of Regulation in the Global Economy*. Princeton, NJ: Princeton University Press.

Butler, Rhett A. 2019. Tropical Forests' Lost Decade: The 2010s. Mongabay, December 17, 2019. Accessed March 23, 2022. https://news.mongabay.com/2019/12/tropical-forests-lost-decade-the-2010s/.

Butler, Sarah. 2022. Iceland Reverts to Palm Oil "With Regret" as Ukraine War Hits Food Prices. *The Guardian*, March 26, 2022. Accessed April 23, 2022. https://www.theguardian.com/business/2022/mar/28/iceland-reverts-to-palm-oil-with-regret-as-ukraine-war-hits-food-prices.

Byerlee, Derek, and Klaus W. Deininger. 2010. The Rise of Large Farms: Drivers and Development Outcomes. Tokyo: United Nations University. December 2010. Accessed March 23, 2022. http://www.wider.unu.edu/publications/newsletter/articles-2010/en_GB/article-11-12-2010/.

Byerlee, Derek, Walter P. Falcon, and Rosamond Naylor, eds. 2016. *The Many Dimensions of the Tropical Oil Crop Revolution*. Oxford: Oxford University Press.

Byrne, Jane. 2017. EU and Brazilian Players Act to Foster "More Sustainable" Soy Production and Trade. FeedNavigator, January 24, 2017. Accessed March 23, 2022. https://www.feednavigator.com/Article/2017/01/24/EU-and-Brazilian-players-act-to-foster-more-sustainable-soy-production-and-trade.

Cannon, John C. 2016. "This Is Not Empty Forest": Africa's Palm Oil Surge Builds in Cameroon. Mongabay, March 30, 2016. Accessed March 23, 2022. https://news.mongabay.com/2016/03/this-is-not-empty-forest-africas-palm-oil-surge-builds-in-cameroon/.

Carazo, Felipe, and Duncan Brack. 2020. TFA Roundtables to Discuss EU Action to Protect Forests, June 26, 2020. Tropical Forest Alliance. Accessed March 23, 2022. https://www.fern.org/fileadmin/uploads/fern/Documents/Presentations/TFA_Roundtables_260620.pdf.

Carlson, Kimberly M., Robert Heilmayr, Holly K. Gibbs, Praveen Noojipady, David N. Burns, Douglas C. Morton, Nathalie F. Walker, Gary D. Paoli, and Claire Kremen. 2017. Effect of Oil Palm Sustainability Certification on Deforestation and Fire in

Indonesia. *Proceedings of the National Academy of Sciences* 115 (1): 121–126. https://doi.org/10.1073/pnas.1704728114.

Cashore, Benjamin. 2002. Legitimacy and the Privatization of Environmental Governance: How Non-State Market-Driven (NSMD) Governance Systems Gain Rule-Making Authority. *Governance* 15 (4): 503–529. https://doi.org/10.1111/1468-0491.00199.

Cashore, Benjamin, Graeme Auld, and Deanna Newsom. 2004. *Governing through Markets: Forest Certification and the Emergence of Non-State Authority*. New Haven, CT: Yale University Press.

Cashore, Benjamin, Elizabeth Egan, Graeme Auld, and Deanna Newsom. 2007. Revising Theories of Nonstate Market-Driven (NSMD) Governance: Lessons from the Finnish Forest Certification Experience. *Global Environmental Politics* 7 (1): 1–44. https://doi.org/10.1162/glep.2007.7.1.1.

Cashore, Benjamin, Jette Steen Knudsen, Jeremy Moon, and Hamish van der Ven. 2021. Private Authority and Public Policy Interactions in Global Context: Governance Spheres for Problem Solving. *Regulation & Governance* 15 (4): 1166–1182. https://doi.org/10.1111/rego.12395.

Cattaneo, Olivier, Gary Gereffi, and Cornelia Staritz, eds. 2010. *Global Value Chains in a Postcrisis World: A Development Perspective*. Washington, DC: World Bank. Accessed March 23, 2022. https://documents1.worldbank.org/curated/en/432691468332065846/pdf/569230PUB0glob1C0disclosed010151101.pdf?msclkid=04395db0aafe11ec95591f18096aa568.

Cattau, Megan E., Miriam E. Marlier, and Ruth DeFries. 2016. Effectiveness of Roundtable on Sustainable Palm Oil (RSPO) for Reducing Fires on Oil Palm Concessions in Indonesia from 2012 to 2015. *Environmental Research Letters* 11 (10): 1–11.

Cattelan, Alexandre José, and Amélio Dall'Agnol. 2018. The Rapid Soybean Growth in Brazil. *OCL* 25 (1): D102. https://doi.org/10.1051/ocl/2017058.

CCICED. *See* China Council for International Cooperation on Environment and Development

CEC. *See* Commission on Environmental Cooperation

Center for International Forestry Research (CIFOR). 2022. Atlas of Deforestation and Industrial Plantations in Borneo. Accessed March 23, 2022. https://nusantara-atlas.org.

Centre for Responsible Business. 2014. Responsible Business Practices in the Indian Palm Oil Sector. Accessed March 23, 2022. https://www.isealalliance.org/get-involved/resources/report-responsible-business-practices-indian-palm-oil-sector?msclkid=691cf375aaff11ecab6bb83e4c6519fc.

Centre for Responsible Business. 2018. Improving Uptake of Sustainable Palm Oil in India. Research report. March 2018. Accessed March 23, 2022. https://c4rb.org

/insights/ResearchReport/Improving-uptake-of-sustainable-palm-oil-in-India-Mar18.pdf?msclkid=927d8829aaff11ec938df99f8c5deab2.

Ceres. 2019. Investor Statement on Deforestation and Forest Fires in the Amazon. Accessed March 23, 2022. https://www.ceres.org/sites/default/files/Investor%20statement%20on%20deforestation%20and%20forest%20fires%20in%20the%20Amazon.pdf?msclkid=d9256131aaff11ec961ef1fd435c3c0f.

Chagas, Thiago, Charlotte Streck, Hilda Galt, Steve Zwick, Ingrid Schulte, Alan Kroeger, and Ashley Thompson. 2018. Impacts of Supply Chain Commitments on the Forest Frontier. Climate Focus, Tropical Forest Alliance 2020, and Forest Trends, July 17, 2018. Accessed March 23, 2022. https://www.forest-trends.org/publications/impacts-of-supply-chain-commitments-on-the-forest-frontier/.

Chain Reaction Research. 2018a. Cattle-Driven Deforestation: A Major Risk to Brazilian Retailers. September 6, 2018. Accessed March 23, 2022. https://chainreactionresearch.com/report/cattle-driven-deforestation-a-major-risk-to-brazilian-retailers/.

Chain Reaction Research. 2018b. Shadow Companies Present Palm Oil Investor Risks and Undermine NDPE efforts. June 21, 2018. Accessed March 23, 2022. https://chainreactionresearch.com/wp-content/uploads/2018/06/Shadow-Company-June-22-2018-Final-for-sharepoint.pdf.

Chain Reaction Research. 2020a. The Chain: Food Shortages in China May Increase Reliance on Brazil. April 1, 2020. Accessed March 23, 2022. https://chainreactionresearch.com/the-chain-food-shortages-in-china-may-increase-reliance-on-brazil/.

Chain Reaction Research. 2020b. The Chain: Repeat Offenders Continue to Clear Forests for Oil Palm in Southeast Asia. February 21, 2020. Accessed March 23, 2022. https://chainreactionresearch.com/the-chain-repeat-offenders-continue-to-clear-forests-for-oil-palm-in-southeast-asia/.

Cheyns, Emmanuelle. 2011. Multi-Stakeholder Initiatives for Sustainable Agriculture: Limits of the "Inclusiveness" Paradigm. In *Governing through Standards: Origins, Drivers and Limitations*, edited by Stefano Ponte, Peter Gibbon, and Jakob Vestergaard, 318–354. Houndmills: Palgrave Macmillan.

Cheyns, Emmanuelle. 2014. Making "Minority Voices" Heard in Transnational Roundtables: The Role of Local NGOs in Reintroducing Justice and Attachments. *Agriculture and Human Values* 31 (3): 439–453. http://doi.org/10.1007/s10460-014-9505-7.

China Council for International Cooperation on Environment and Development (CCICED). 2020. Global Green Value Chains: Greening China's Soft Commodity Value Chains. CCICED, September 2020. Accessed March 23, 2022. https://cciced.eco/wp-content/uploads/2020/09/SPS-4-2-Global-Green-Value-Chains-1.pdf.

China Daily. 2018. Top 10 Retailers with Largest Market Shares in China. September 20, 2018. Accessed March 23, 2022. https://www.chinadaily.com.cn/a/201809/20/WS5ba2d03fa310c4cc775e7272_10.html.

References

China Dialogue. 2019. *Tracking China's Soy and Beef Imprint on South America*. London: Diálogo Chino. Accessed March 23, 2022. https://dialogochino.net/wp-content/uploads/2019/12/China-soy-beef-South-America.pdf.

Christoff, Peter, and Robyn Eckersley. 2013. *Globalization and the Environment*. London: Rowman and Littlefield.

CIFOR. *See* Center for International Forestry Research

Confederation of Indian Industry, and Sedex. 2020. Integrating Sustainability into Indian Supply Chains. September 2020. Accessed March 23, 2022. https://sustainabledevelopment.in/wp-content/uploads/2020/09/Integrating-Sustainability-Into-Indian-Supply-Chains-CII-and-Sedex-FINAL.pdf.

Clapp, Jennifer. 1998. The Privatization of Global Environmental Governance: ISO 14000 and the Developing World. *Global Governance* 4 (3): 295–316. http://doi.org/10.1163/19426720-00403004.

Clapp, Jennifer. 2005. Global Environmental Governance for Corporate Responsibility and Accountability. *Global Environmental Politics* 5 (3): 23–34. http://doi.org/10.1162/1526380054794916.

Clapp, Jennifer. 2012. *Food*, 2nd ed. Cambridge: Polity.

Clapp, Jennifer. 2020. *Food*, 3rd ed. Cambridge: Polity.

Clapp, Jennifer, and Doris Fuchs, eds. 2009. *Corporate Power in Global Agrifood Governance*. Cambridge, MA: MIT Press.

Clapp, Jennifer, and Eric Helleiner. 2012. International Political Economy and the Environment: Back to the Basics? *International Affairs* 88 (3): 485–501. https://doi.org/10.1111/j.1468-2346.2012.01085.x.

Clay, Jason. 2004. *World Agriculture and the Environment: A Commodity-by-Commodity Guide to Impacts and Practices*. Washington, DC: Island.

Clay, Jason. 2010. How Big Brands Can Help Save Biodiversity. Filmed July 10, 2010, at University of Oxford. TED Video, 19:13. Accessed March 23, 2022. http://blog.ted.com/2010/08/16/how-big-brands-can-save-biodiversity-jason-clay-on-ted-com/.

Climate Focus. 2016. Progress on the New York Declaration on Forests: Eliminating Deforestation from the Production of Agricultural Commodities—Goal 2 Assessment Report. Accessed March 23, 2022. https://www.forest-trends.org/wp-content/uploads/2018/09/2016-NYDF-Goal-2-Assessment-Report.pdf.

Climate Focus. 2018. Assessing the Zero-Deforestation Supply Chain Movement. Accessed March 23, 2022. https://climatefocus.com/projects/assessing-the-zero-deforestation-supply-chain-movement/.

Coase, R. H. 1960. The Problem of Social Cost. *Journal of Law and Economics* 3: 1–44.

Coca, Nithin. 2020. As Palm Oil for Biofuel Rises in Southeast Asia, Tropical Ecosystems Shrink. *China Dialogue*, April 15, 2020. Accessed March 23, 2022. https://chinadialogue.net/en/energy/11957-as-palm-oil-for-biofuel-rises-in-southeast-asia-tropical-ecosystems-shrink/.

Colchester, Marcus, Emil Kleden, Djayu Sukma, Norman Jiwan, Hannah Storey, and Lourdes Barragán Alvarado. 2020. Upholding Human Rights in Jurisdictional Approaches: Some Emerging Lessons. Forest Peoples Programme, June 2020. Accessed March 23, 2022. https://www.forestpeoples.org/sites/default/files/documents/Upholding%20Human%20Rights%20in%20Jurisdictional%20Approaches%20Jun2020.pdf.

Commission on Environmental Cooperation (CEC). 2017. Alliance of Green Consumption and Green Supply Chain Established in Beijing. Accessed March 23, 2022. http://en.mepcec.com/news/show-2217.html.

Committee on Sustainability Assessment (COSA). 2013. The COSA Measuring Sustainability Report: Coffee and Cocoa in 12 Countries. Accessed March 23, 2022. https://thecosa.org/wp-content/uploads/2014/01/The-COSA-Measuring-Sustainability-Report.pdf.

Consumer Goods Forum. 2010. Consumer Goods Industry Announces Initiatives on Climate Protection. November 29, 2010. Accessed March 23, 2022. https://www.theconsumergoodsforum.com/press_releases/consumer-goods-industry-announces-initiatives-on-climate-protection/.

COSA. *See* Committee on Sustainability Assessment

Coxhead, Ian, and Sisira Jayasuriya. 2010. China, India and the Commodity Boom: Economic and Environmental Implications for Low-Income Countries. *World Economy* 33 (4): 525–551. https://doi.org/10.1111/j.1467-9701.2009.01232.x.

Cramb, Rob, and John F. McCarthy. 2016a. Characterising Oil Palm Production in Indonesia and Malaysia. In *The Oil Palm Complex: Smallholders, Agribusiness and the State in Indonesia and Malaysia*, edited by Rob Cramb and John F. McCarthy, 27–78. Singapore: National University of Singapore Press.

Cramb, Rob, and John F. McCarthy, eds. 2016b. *The Oil Palm Complex: Smallholders, Agribusiness and the State in Indonesia and Malaysia*. Singapore: National University of Singapore Press.

Crevello, Stacy. 2004. Dayak Land Use Systems and Indigenous Knowledge. *Journal of Human Ecology* 16 (1): 69–73. https://doi.org/10.1080/09709274.2004.11905718.

Cuff, Madeleine. 2016. Palm Oil Giant IOI Group Regains RSPO Sustainability Certification. *The Guardian*, August 8, 2016. Accessed March 23, 2022. https://www.theguardian.com/environment/2016/aug/08/palm-oil-giant-ioi-group-regains-rspo-sustainability-certification.

References

Curtis, Philip G., Christy M. Slay, Nancy L. Harris, Alexandra Tyukavinaand, and Matthew C. Hansen. 2018. Classifying Drivers of Global Forest Loss. *Science* 361 (6407): 1108–1111. https://doi.org/10.1126/science.aau3445.

Cutler, A. Claire, Virginia Haufler, and Tony Porter. 1999a. Private Authority and International Affairs. In *Private Authority and International Affairs*, edited by A. Claire Cutler, Virginia Haufler, and Tony Porter, 3–28. Albany: State University of New York Press.

Cutler, A. Claire, Virginia Haufler, and Tony Porter, eds. 1999b. *Private Authority and International Affairs*. Albany: State University of New York Press.

Darnall, Nicole, Hyunjung Ji, and Matthew Potoski. 2017. Institutional Design of Ecolabels: Sponsorship Signals Rule Strength. *Regulation & Governance* 11 (4): 438–450. https://doi.org/10.1111/rego.12166.

Dashwood, Hevina S. 2012. *The Rise of Global Corporate Social Responsibility: Mining and the Spread of Global Norms*. Cambridge: Cambridge University Press.

Dauvergne, Peter. 2005. Globalization and the Environment. In *Global Political Economy*, edited by John Ravenhill, 448–478. Oxford: Oxford University Press.

Dauvergne, Peter. 2008. *The Shadows of Consumption: Consequences for the Global Environment*. Cambridge, MA: MIT Press.

Dauvergne, Peter. 2016. *Environmentalism of the Rich*. Cambridge, MA: MIT Press.

Dauvergne, Peter. 2017. Is the Power of Brand-Focused Activism Rising? The Case of Tropical Deforestation. *Journal of Environment & Development* 26 (2): 135–155.

Dauvergne, Peter. 2020. Is Artificial Intelligence Greening Global Supply Chains? Exposing the Political Economy of Environmental Costs. *Review of International Political Economy* 29 (3): 1–23. https://doi.org/10.1080/09692290.2020.1814381.

Dauvergne, Peter, and Jennifer Clapp. 2016. Researching Global Environmental Politics in the 21st Century. *Global Environmental Politics* 16 (1): 1–12. https://doi.org/10.1162/GLEP_e_00333.

Dauvergne, Peter, and Jane Lister. 2010. The Power of Big Box Retail in Global Environmental Governance: Bringing Commodity Chains Back into IR. *Millennium* 39 (1): 145–160. https://doi.org/10.1177/0305829810371018.

Dauvergne, Peter, and Jane Lister. 2012. Big Brand Sustainability: Governance Prospects and Environmental Limits. *Global Environmental Change* 22 (1): 36–45. https://doi.org/10.1016/j.gloenvcha.2011.10.007.

Dauvergne, Peter, and Jane Lister. 2013. *Eco-Business: A Big-Brand Takeover of Sustainability*. Cambridge, MA: MIT Press.

De Búrca, Gráinne, Robert O. Keohane, and Charles Sabel. 2014. Global Experimentalist Governance. *British Journal of Political Science* 44 (3): 477–486. http://doi.org/10.1017/S0007123414000076.

DeFries, Ruth S., Jessica Fanzo, Pinki Mondal, Roseline Remans, and Stephen A. Wood. 2017. Is Voluntary Certification of Tropical Agricultural Commodities Achieving Sustainability Goals for Small-Scale Producers? A Review of the Evidence. *Environmental Research Letters* 12 (3): 033001. http://doi.org/10.1088/1748-9326/aa625e.

De Marchi, Valentina, Eleanora Di Maria, Aarti Krishnan, Stefano Ponte, and Stephanie Barrientos. 2019. Environmental Upgrading in Global Value Chains. In *Handbook on Global Value Chains*, edited by Stefano Ponte, Gary Gereffi, and Gale Raj-Reichert, 310–322. Cheltenham: Edward Elgar.

De Marchi, Valentina, Eleanora Di Maria, and Stefano Micelli. 2013. Environmental Strategies, Upgrading and Competitive Advantage in Global Value Chains. *Business Strategy and the Environment* 22 (1): 62–72. http://dx.doi.org/10.1002/bse.1738.

den Hond, Frank, and Frank de Bakker. 2012. Boomerang Politics: How Transnational Stakeholders Impact Multinational Corporations in the Context of Globalization. In *A Stakeholder Approach to Corporate Social Responsibility: Pressures, Conflicts, and Reconciliation*, edited by Adam Lindgreen, Philip Kotler, Joëlle Vanhamme, and François Maon, 275–292. Aldershot: Gower.

DePuy, Walker, Jacob Weger, Katie Foster, Anya M. Bonanno, Suneel Kumar, Kristen Lear, Raul Basilio, and Laura German. 2021. Environmental Governance: Broadening Ontological Spaces for a More Livable World. *Environment and Planning E: Nature and Space* 5 (2): 947–975. https://doi.org/10.1177/25148486211018565.

Dermawan, Ahmad, and Otto Hospes. 2018. When the State Brings Itself Back into GVC: The Case of the Indonesian Palm Oil Pledge. *Global Policy* 9 (S2): 21–28. https://doi.org/doi:10.1111/1758-5899.12619.

Dietz, Thomas, Janina Grabs, and Andrea Estrella Chong. 2019. Mainstreamed Voluntary Sustainability Standards and Their Effectiveness: Evidence from the Honduran Coffee Sector. *Regulation & Governance* 15 (2): 333–355. https://doi.org/10.1111/rego.12239.

DiGiano, Maria, Claudia Stickler, and Olivia David. 2020. How Can Jurisdictional Approaches to Sustainability Protect and Enhance the Rights and Livelihoods of Indigenous Peoples and Local Communities? *Frontiers in Forests and Global Change* 3 (40). https://doi.org/10.3389/ffgc.2020.00040.

Dingwerth, Klaus. 2007. *The New Transnationalism: Transnational Governance and Democratic Legitimacy*. Houndmills: Palgrave Macmillan.

Dingwerth, Klaus, and Phillipp Pattberg. 2009. Word Politics and Organizational Fields: The Case of Transnational Sustainability Governance. *European Journal of International Relations* 15 (4): 707–744. https://doi.org/10.1177/1354066109345056.

Distelhorst, Greg, Richard M. Locke, Timea Pal, and Hiram Samel. 2015. Production Goes Global, Compliance Stays Local: Private Regulation in the Global Electronics Industry. *Regulation & Governance* 9 (3): 224–242. http://doi.org/10.1111/rego.12096.

Dolan, C., and J. Humphrey. 2000. Governance and Trade in Fresh Vegetables: The Impact of UK Supermarkets on the African Horticulture Industry. *Journal of Development Studies* 37 (2): 147–176. https://doi.org/10.1080/713600072.

Domask, J. 2003. From Boycotts to Global Partnership: NGOs, the Private Sector, and the Struggle to Protect the World's Forests. In *Globalization and NGOs: Transforming Business, Government, and Society*, edited by Jonathan P. Doh and Hildy Teegen, 157–186. Westport, CT: Praeger.

Donofrio, Stephen, Jonathan Leonard, and Philip Rothrock. 2017. Supply Change: Tracking Corporate Commitments to Deforestation-Free Supply Chains, 2017. Forest Trends, March 2017. Accessed March 23, 2022. http://www.forest-trends.org/documents/files/doc_5521.pdf.

Duboua-Lorsch, Lucie. 2020. The EU's Imported Deforestation Problem: A Closer Look. EURACTIV France, November 17, 2020. Accessed March 23, 2022. https://www.euractiv.com/section/energy-environment/news/the-eus-imported-deforestation-problem-a-closer-look.

Earth Innovation Institute. 2018. Jurisdictional Sustainability: A Primer for Practitioners. Accessed March 23, 2022. https://www.gcftf.org/wp-content/uploads/2020/12/jurisdictional_sustainability_primer_en.pdf.

Earth System Governance Project. 2018. Earth System Governance: Science Implementation Plan of the Earth System Governance Project. Utrecht, Netherlands.

Easton, David. 1965. *A Systems Analysis of Political Life*. New York: John Wiley.

Eberlein, Burkard, Kenneth W. Abbott, Julia Black, Errol Meidinger, and Stepan Wood. 2014. Transnational Business Governance Interactions: Conceptualization and Framework for Analysis. *Regulation & Governance* 8 (1): 1–21. http://dx.doi.org/10.1111/rego.12030.

EIA. *See* Environmental Investigation Agency

Elder, Sara D., Hisham Zerriffi, and Philippe Le Billon. 2012. Effects of Fair Trade Certification on Social Capital: The Case of Rwandan Coffee Producers. *World Development* 40 (11): 2355–2367. https://doi.org/10.1016/j.worlddev.2012.06.010.

Environmental Investigation Agency (EIA). 2015. Who Watches the Watchmen? Auditors and the Breakdown of Oversight in the RSPO. November 2015. Accessed March 23, 2022. https://eia-international.org/wp-content/uploads/EIA-Who-Watches-the-Watchmen-FINAL.pdf.

Environmental News Network. 2005. Greenpeace Gives Golden Chainsaw to Brazil Tycoon. June 21, 2005. Accessed March 23, 2022. https://www.enn.com/articles/1843-greenpeace-gives-golden-chainsaw-to-brazil-tycoon.

Espach, Ralph H. 2005. Private Regulation Amid Public Disarray: An Analysis of Two Private Environmental Regulatory Programs in Argentina. *Business and Politics* 7 (2): 1–36. https://doi.org/10.2202/1469-3569.1113.

Espach, Ralph H. 2009. *Private Environmental Regimes in Developing Countries: Globally Sown, Locally Grown*. New York: Palgrave Macmillan.

EU Commission. *See* European Union Commission

European Biotechnology. 2017. GMO Acreage Growing. May 8, 2017. Accessed March 23, 2022. https://european-biotechnology.com/up-to-date/latest-news/news/gmo-acreage-growing.html.

European Environment Agency. 2011. Global Governance and the Rise of Non-State Actors: A Background Report for the SOER 2010 Assessment of Global Megatrends. Publications Office. Accessed March 23, 2022. https://data.europa.eu/doi/10.2800/7633.

European Union (EU). 2009. Directive 2009/28/EC of the European Parliament and of the Council of 23 April 2009 on the Promotion of the Use of Energy from Renewable Sources and Amending and Subsequently Repealing Directives 2001/77/EC and 2003/30/EC. *Official Journal of the European Union* L140 (16). Accessed March 23, 2022. https://eur-lex.europa.eu/legal-content/EN/TXT/PDF/?uri=CELEX%3a32009L0028&msclkid=4799af48ab9411eca9b042f7da7525ce.

European Union (EU) Commission. 2006. Communication from the Commission: An EU Strategy for Biofuels. Brussels, February 8, 2006. Accessed March 23, 2022. https://eur-lex.europa.eu/legal-content/EN/TXT/PDF/?uri=CELEX%3a52006DC0034&msclkid=5bd6cac7ab8c11ecb8f39b18a2c450b7.

European Union (EU) Commission. 2007. Communication from the Commission to the Council of the European Parliament: Renewable Energy Roadmap. Brussels, January 10, 2007. Accessed March 23, 2022. https://eur-lex.europa.eu/LexUriServ/LexUriServ.do?uri=COM%3a2006%3a0848%3aFIN%3aEN%3aPDF&msclkid=8639fbf1ab8c11ec8692b6a27ea7d888.

European Union (EU) Commission. 2021. Proposal for a Regulation on Deforestation-Free Products, COM (2021) 706 final, Brussels, 17.11.2021.

European Union (EU) Commission. n.d. Renewable Energy: Recast to 2030 (RED II). Accessed March 23, 2022. https://ec.europa.eu/jrc/en/jec/renewable-energy-recast-2030-red-ii.

Evans, Peter. 1997. The Eclipse of the State? Reflections on Stateness in an Era of Globalization. *World Politics* 50 (1): 62–87. http://www.jstor.org/stable/25054027.

Eyes on the Forest. 2016. No One Is Safe: Illegal Indonesian Palm Oil Spreads through Global Supply Chains despite Global Sustainability Commitments and Certification. April 2016. Accessed March 23, 2022. https://www.eyesontheforest.or.id/uploads/default/report/Eyes-on-the-Forest-Investigative-Report-No-One-is-Safe-April-20161.pdf.

Eyes on the Forest. 2018. Investigative Report: Enough Is Enough: Time for the Palm Oil Market to Start the Real Work to Stop Driving Deforestation. June 2018. Accessed March 23, 2022. https://www.eyesontheforest.or.id/uploads/default/report/EoF_(08Jun18)_Enough_is_Enough.pdf.

Fahamsyah, Ermanto. 2020. Observations on Presidential Regulation Number 44 of 2020 on ISPO. *Palm Scribe*, March 24, 2020. Accessed March 23, 2022.

Fairbairn, Madeleine. 2015. Finance and the Food System. In *Handbook of the International Political Economy of Agriculture and Food*, edited by Alessandro Bonanno and Lawrence Busch, 232–249. Cheltenham: Edward Elgar. https://doi.org/10.4337/9781782548263.00020.

Falkner, Robert. 2003. Private Environmental Governance and International Relations: Exploring the Links. *Global Environmental Politics* 3 (2): 72–87. https://doi.org/10.1162/152638003322068227.

Falkner, Robert. 2008. *Business Power and Conflict in International Environmental Politics*. London: Palgrave Macmillan.

Falkner, Robert. 2009. The Troubled Birth of the "Biotech Century": Global Corporate Power and Its Limits. In *Corporate Power in Global Agrifood Governance*, edited by Jennifer Clapp and Doris Fuchs, 225–285. Cambridge, MA: MIT Press. https://doi.org/10.7551/mitpress/9780262012751.003.0008.

FAO. 2022. Information Note: The Importance of Ukraine and the Russian Federation for Global Agricultural Markets and the Risks Associated with the Current Conflict. Rome, March 25, 2022. Accessed April 22, 2022. https://www.fao.org/3/cb9236en/cb9236en.pdf.

FAO, IFAD, UNICEF, WFP, and WHO. 2021. In Brief to the State of Food Security and Nutrition in the World: Transforming Food Systems for Food Security, Improved Nutrition and Affordable Healthy Diets for All. Rome: FAO. https://doi.org/10.4060/cb5409en.

FAOSTAT. n.d. a. Crops and Livestock Products. Accessed March 23, 2022. https://www.fao.org/faostat/en/#data/QCL.

FAOSTAT. n.d. b. Trade: Crops and Lifestock Products. Accessed March 23, 2022. https://www.fao.org/faostat/en/#data/TCL.

Fearnside, Philip M., and Adriano M. R. Figueiredo. 2015. China's Influence on Deforestation in Brazilian Amazonia: A Growing Force in the State of Mato Grosso.

Discussion Paper 2015–3. Boston, MA: Global Economic Governance Initiative. Accessed March 23, 2022. http://www.bu.edu/pardeeschool/files/2014/12/Brazil1.pdf.

Fern. 2020. Key Elements for an Agreement between the EU and Cocoa-Producing Countries to Ensure Sustainability in the Cocoa Sector. September 22, 2020. Accessed March 23, 2022. https://www.fern.org/publications-insight/key-elements-for-an-agreement-between-the-eu-and-cocoa-producing-countries-to-ensure-sustainability-in-the-cocoa-sector-2207/.

Financial Express. 2020. Modi's Atmanirbhar Bharat: How Palm Oil Cultivation Can Make India Self-Reliant in Edible Oil. July 28, 2020. Accessed March 23, 2022. https://www.financialexpress.com/economy/modis-atmanirbhar-bharat-how-palm-oil-cultivation-can-make-india-self-reliant-in-edible-oil/2037185/.

Fiorini, Matteo, Bernard Hoekman, Marion Jansen, Philip Schleifer, Olga Solleder, Regina Taimasova, and Joseph Wozniak. 2019. Institutional Design of Voluntary Sustainability Standards Systems: Evidence from a New Database. *Development Policy Review* 37 (S2): 193–212. https://doi.org/10.1111/dpr.12379.

Fishbein, Greg, and Donna Lee. 2015. Early Lessons from Jurisdictional REDD+ and Low Emissions Development Programs. Nature Conservancy, January 2015. Accessed March 23, 2022. https://www.forestcarbonpartnership.org/sites/fcp/files/2015/January/REDD%2B_LED_web_high_res.pdf.

Fishman, Akiva, Edgar Oliveira, and Lloyd Gamble. 2017. Tackling Deforestation through a Jurisdictional Approach: Lessons from the Field. WWF, September 2017. Accessed March 23, 2022. https://www.worldwildlife.org/publications/tackling-deforestation-through-a-jurisdictional-approach.

Fitri, Ofra Shinta. 2016. Tracing Smallholders in Palm Oil Supply Chains: Evidence from Collaborative Jurisdictional and Mapping Initiatives. Presentation by INOBU at the 14th Roundtable Conference of the RSPO, Bangkok, November 7–10, 2016. Accessed March 23, 2022. https://rt14.rspo.org/ckfinder/userfiles/files/PC4_1%20Ofra%20Shinta%20Fitri.pdf.

Forest 500. 2016. Company Selection Methodology. Global Canopy Program. Accessed March 23, 2022. https://forest500.org/sites/default/files/company_selection_methodology.pdf.

Forest 500. 2017. Company Assessment Methodology. Global Canopy Program. Accessed March 23, 2022. https://forest500.org/sites/default/files/2017_company_assessment_methodology.pdf

Forest 500. 2019a. 2019 Annual Report. Accessed March 23, 2022. https://forest500.org/sites/default/files/forest500_annualreport2019_final_0.pdf.

Forest 500. 2019b. Company Trends. Accessed March 23, 2022. https://forest500.org/analysis/company-trends.

Forest 500. 2021. Company Rankings. Accessed March 23, 2022. https://forest500.org/rankings/companies.

Forest Declaration. 2017. New York Declaration on Forests: Progress Assessment. October 2017. Accessed March 23, 2022. https://forestdeclaration.org/wp-content/uploads/2021/10/2017NYDFReport.pdf?msclkid=8020306fab9811ec8a658a8246a0f728.

Forests & Finance. 2021. Finance's Role in Deforestation. June 2021. Accessed March 23, 2022. https://forestsandfinance.org/wp-content/uploads/2021/06/FF-Briefing_2021_June.pdf.

Fransen, Luc. 2012. Multi-Stakeholder Governance and Voluntary Programme Interactions: Legitimation Politics in the Institutional Design of Corporate Social Responsibility. *Socio-Economic Review* 10 (1): 163–192. https://doi.org/10.1093/ser/mwr029.

Fransen, Luc. 2018. Beyond Regulatory Governance? On the Evolutionary Trajectory of Transnational Private Sustainability Governance. *Ecological Economics* 146: 772–777. https://doi.org/10.1016/j.ecolecon.2018.01.005.

Fransen, Luc, Kendra Dupuy, Marja Hinfelaar, and Sultan Mohammed Zakaria Mazumder. 2021. Tempering Transnational Advocacy? The Effect of Repression and Regulatory Restriction on Transnational NGO Collaborations. *Global Policy* 12 (S5): 11–22. https://doi.org/10.1111/1758-5899.12972.

Fransen, Luc, and Ans Kolk. 2007. Global Rule-Setting for Business: A Critical Analysis of Multi-Stakeholder Standards. *Organization* 14 (5): 667–684.

Fransen, Luc, Jelmer Schalk, and Graeme Auld. 2016. Work Ties Beget Community? Assessing Interactions among Transnational Private Governance Organizations in Sustainable Agriculture. *Global Networks* 16 (1): 45–67. http://doi.org/10.1111/glob.12097.

Friends of the Earth. 2010. Too Green to be True. March 19, 2010. Accessed March 23, 2022. https://www.foei.org/publication/too-green-to-be-true/.

Friends of the Earth. 2013. Commodity Crimes: Illicit Land Grabs, Illegal Palm Oil, and Endangered Orangutans. November 2013. Accessed March 23, 2022. http://www.foeeurope.org/sites/default/files/news/commodity_crimes_nov13_01.pdf

Fripp, Emily, and Duncan Brack. 2020. The Need for Smart a Smart Mix of Measures. Presentation given at the TFA webinar on Raising Ambition for Effective EU Policy to Protect the World's Forests. July 23, 2020. Accessed March 23, 2022. https://www.tropicalforestalliance.org/assets/Slide-Deck_TFA-Virtual-Dialogue_Raising-Ambition-for-Effective-EU-Policy-to-Protect-the-Worlds-Forests-v2.pdf.

Fuchs, Doris. 2005. Commanding Heights? The Strength and Fragility of Business Power in Global Politics. *Millennium Journal of International Studies* 33 (3): 771–801. https://doi.org/10.1177/03058298050330030501.

Fuchs, Doris. 2007. Business and Governance: Transnational Corporations and the Effectiveness of Private Governance. In *Globalization: State of the Art and Perspectives*, edited by Stefan A. Schirm, 122–142. Abingdon: Routledge.

Fuchs, Doris, and Agni Kalfagianni. 2010. The Causes and Consequences of Private Food Governance. *Business and Politics* 12 (3): 1–34. https://doi.org/10.2202/1469-3569.1319.

Fuchs, Doris, and Agni Kalfagianni. 2012. The Effectiveness of Private Environmental Governance. In *Handbook of Global Environmental Politics*, edited by Peter Dauvergne, 298–307. Cheltenham: Edward Elgar.

Fuchs, Richard, Peter Alexander, Calum Brown, Frances Cossar, Roslyn C. Henry, and Mark Rounsevell. 2019. Why the US-China Trade War Spells Disaster for the Amazon. *Nature* 567: 451–454. https://www.nature.com/articles/d41586-019-00896-2.

Funbio. 2017. REM Mato Grosso. Accessed March 23, 2022. https://www.funbio.org.br/en/programas_e_projetos/rem-mato-grosso/.

Gale, Fred, Francisco Ascui, and Heather Lovell. 2017. Sensing Reality? New Monitoring Technologies for Global Sustainability Standards. *Global Environmental Politics* 17 (2): 65–83. https://doi.org/10.1162/GLEP_a_00401.

Garrett, Rachael D., Kimberly M. Carlson, Ximena Rueda, and Praveen Noojipady. 2016. Assessing the Potential Additionality of Certification by the Round Table on Responsible Soybeans and the Roundtable on Sustainable Palm Oil. *Environmental Research Letters* 11 (4): 045003. https://doi.org/10.1088/1748-9326/11/4/045003.

Garrett, R. D., S. Levy, K. M. Carlson, T. A. Gardner, J. Godar, J. Clapp, P. Dauvergne, R. Heilmayr, Y. le Polain de Waroux, B. Ayre, R. Barr, B. Døvre, H. K. Gibbs., S. Hall, S. Lake, J. C. Milder., L. L. Rausch, R. Rivero, X. Rueda, R. Sarsfieldp, B. Soares-Filho, and N. Villoria. 2019. Criteria for Effective Zero-Deforestation Commitments. *Global Environmental Change* 54: 135–147. https://doi.org/10.1016/j.gloenvcha.2018.11.003.

Garrett, Rachael D., Samuel A. Levy, Florian Gollnow, Leonie Hodel, and Ximena Rueda. 2021. Have Food Supply Chain Policies Improved Forest Conservation and Rural Livelihoods? A Systematic Review. *Environmental Research Letters* 16 (3): 033002. https://doi.org/10.1088/1748-9326/abe0ed.

Gaud, William S. 1968. The Green Revolution: Accomplishments and Apprehensions. Speech given before the Society for International Development, Washington, DC, March 8, 1968. Accessed March 23, 2022. http://www.agbioworld.org/biotech-info/topics/borlaug/borlaug-green.html.

Gaveau, David L. A., Sean Sloan, Elis Molidena, Husna Yaen, Doug Sheil, Nicola K. Abram, Marc Ancrenaz, Robert Nasi, Marcela Quinones, Niels Wielaard, Erik Meijaard. 2014. Four Decades of Forest Persistence, Clearance and Logging on Borneo. *PLOS ONE* 9 (7): e101654. https://doi.org/10.1371/journal.pone.0101654.

References

Gaworecki, Mike. 2015. An Alternative to Help Companies Fulfill Zero Deforestation Pledges. Mongabay, September 28, 2015. Accessed March 23, 2022. https://news.mongabay.com/2015/09/an-alternative-to-help-companies-fulfill-zero-deforestation-pledges/.

GCFTF. *See* Governors' Climate and Forest Task Force

Gecko Project. 2017. The Palm Oil Fiefdom. Mongabay, October 10, 2017. https://news.mongabay.com/2017/10/the-palm-oil-fiefdom/.

George, Alexander L., and Andrew Bennett. 2005. *Case Studies and Theory Development in the Social Sciences*. Cambridge, MA: MIT Press.

Gereffi, Gary. 1994. The Organization of Buyer-Driven Global Commodity Chains: How US Retailers Shape Overseas Production Networks. In *Commodity Chains and Global Capitalism*, edited by Gary Gereffi, 95–133. Westport, CT: Greenwood.

Gereffi, Gary. 1999. International Trade and Industrial Upgrading in the Apparel Commodity Chain. *Journal of International Economics* 48 (1): 37–70. https://doi.org/10.1016/S0022-1996(98)00075-0.

Gereffi, Gary. 2014. Global Value Chains in a Post-Washington Consensus World. *Review of International Political Economy* 21 (1): 9–37. http://doi.org/10.1080/09692290.2012.756414.

Gereffi, Gary, and Karina Fernandez-Stark. 2016. *Global Value Chain Analysis: A Primer*. 2nd ed. Durham, NC: Center on Globalization Governance and Competitiveness, Duke University. Accessed March 23, 2022. https://hdl.handle.net/10161/12488.

Gereffi, Gary, John Humphrey, and Timothy Sturgeon. 2005. The Governance of Global Value Chains. *Review of International Political Economy* 12 (1): 78–104. https://doi.org/10.1080/09692290500049805.

Gereffi, Gary, and Olga Memedovic. 2003. *The Global Apparel Value Chain: What Prospects for Upgrading for Developing Countries*. Vienna: United Nations Industrial Development Organization. http://www.hubrural.org/IMG/pdf/unido_global_apparel_value_chain.pdf.

Giacomin, Valeria. 2018. The Transformation of the Global Palm Oil Cluster: Dynamics of Cluster Competition between Africa and Southeast Asia (c.1900–1970). *Journal of Global History* 13 (3): 374–398. https://doi.org/10.1017/S1740022818000207.

Gibbon, Peter. 2001. Upgrading Primary Production: A Global Commodity Chain Approach. *World Development* 29 (2): 345–363. https://doi.org/10.1016/S0305-750X(00)00093-0.

Gibbon, Peter, Jennifer Bair, and Stefano Ponte. 2008. Governing Global Value Chains: An Introduction. *Economy and Society* 37 (3): 315–338. https://doi.org/10.1080/03085140802172656.

Gibbon, Peter, Stefano Ponte, and Evelyne Lazaro, eds. 2010. *Global Agro-Food Trade and Standards: Challenges for Africa*. Houndmills: Palgrave Macmillan. https://doi.org/10.1057/9780230281356.

Gibbs, David, Nancy Harris, and Frances Seymour. 2018. By the Numbers: The Value of Tropical Forests in the Climate Change Equation. World Resources Institute, October 4, 2018. Accessed March 23, 2022. https://www.wri.org/insights/numbers-value-tropical-forests-climate-change-equation.

Gibbs, Holly K., Lisa Rausch, J. Munger, Ian H. Schelly, Douglas C. Morton, Praveen Noojipady, Britaldo Silveira Soares-Filho, Paulo Barreto, L. Micol, and Fourdan Nathalie Walker. 2015. Brazil's Soy Moratorium. *Science* 347 (6220): 377–378. https://doi.org/10.1126/science.aaa0181.

Gibbs, Holly K., A. S. Ruesch, F. Achard, M. K. Clayton, P. Holmgren, N. Ramankutty, and J. A. Foley. 2010. Tropical Forests Were the Primary Sources of New Agricultural Land in the 1980s and 1990s. *Proceedings of the National Academy of Sciences* 107 (38): 16732–16737. https://doi.org/10.1073/pnas.0910275107.

Giessen, Lukas, Sarah Burns, Muhammad Alif K. Sahide, and Agung Wibowo. 2016. From Governance to Government: The Strengthened Role of State Bureaucracies in Forest and Agricultural Certification. *Policy and Society* 35 (1): 71–89. https://doi.org/10.1016/j.polsoc.2016.02.001.

Global Forest Watch. 2020. Dashboard. Accessed March 23, 2022. https://www.globalforestwatch.org/dashboards/global/.

Global Resource Initiative. 2020. Final Recommendations Report: Executive Summary. March 2020. Accessed March 23, 2022. https://partnershipsforforests.com/wp-content/uploads/2020/03/GRI-Taskforce-Final-Recomendations-Report-Executive-summary.pdf.

Global Sustainable Investment Alliance (GSIA). 2020. Global Sustainable Investment Review 2020. Accessed March 23, 2022. http://www.gsi-alliance.org/wp-content/uploads/2021/08/GSIR-20201.pdf.

Gonzales, Jenny. 2020. Brazil Minister Advises Using COVID-19 to Distract from Amazon Deregulation. Mongabay, May 26, 2020. Accessed March 23, 2022. https://news.mongabay.com/2020/05/brazil-minister-advises-using-covid-19-to-distract-from-amazon-deregulation/.

Governors' Climate and Forest Task Force (GCFTF). 2019. Governor's Climate and Forest Task Force Knowledge Database: Central Kalimantan Overview. Accessed March 23, 2022. Link no longer active. http://www.gcftaskforce-database.org/StateOverview/indonesia.central_kalimantan.

Governors' Climate and Forest Task Force (GCFTF). 2021. Governors' Climate and Forest Task Force Knowledge Database: Mato Grosso Overview. Accessed March 23,

References

2022. Link no longer active. http://www.gcftaskforce-database.org/StateOverview/brazil.mato_grosso.

Government Central Kalimantan. 2015. Central Kalimantan: Moving towards Green Growth. Provincial Government of Central Kalimantan, Ministry of National Development Planning/Bappenas, and Global Green Growth Institute, January 2015. Accessed March 23, 2022. http://greengrowth.bappenas.go.id/wp-content/uploads/2018/05/20151020220943.Central_Kalimantan_Green_Growth_Report_ENGLISH.pdf.

Grabs, Janina. 2017. The Rise of Buyer-Driven Sustainability Governance: Emerging Trends in the Global Coffee Sector. ZenTra Working Paper in Transnational Studies 73. Rochester, NY: SSRM. https://ssrn.com/abstract=3015166.

Grabs, Janina. 2020a. Assessing the Institutionalization of Private Sustainability Governance in a Changing Coffee Sector. *Regulation & Governance* 14 (2): 362–387. https://doi.org/10.1111/rego.12212.

Grabs, Janina. 2020b. *Selling Sustainability Short: The Private Governance of Labor and the Environment in the Coffee Sector.* Cambridge, MA: Cambridge University Press.

Grabs, Janina, and Sophia Louise Carodenuto. 2021. Traders as Sustainability Governance Actors in Global Food Supply Chains: A Research Agenda. *Business Strategy and the Environment* 30 (2): 1314–1332. https://doi.org/10.1002/bse.2686.

Graz, Jean-Christophe. 2021. Grounding the Politics of Transnational Private Governance: Introduction to the Special Section. *New Political Economy* 27 (2): 177–187. https://doi.org/10.1080/13563467.2021.1881472.

Graz, Jean-Christophe, and Andreas Nölke. 2008. *Transnational Private Governance and Its Limits.* Abingdon: Routledge. https://doi.org/10.4324/9780203939338.

Green, Jessica F. 2014. *Rethinking Private Authority: Agents and Entrepreneurs in Global Environmental Governance.* Princeton, NJ: Princeton University Press.

Green, Jessica F., and Graeme Auld. 2017. Unbundling the Regime Complex: The Effects of Private Authority. *Transnational Environmental Law* 6 (2): 259–284. https://doi.org/10.1017/S2047102516000121.

Greenpeace. 2006. *Eating Up the Amazon.* Amsterdam: Greenpeace International. Accessed March 23, 2022. https://www.greenpeace.org/usa/wp-content/uploads/legacy/Global/usa/report/2010/2/eating-up-the-amazon.pdf.

Greenpeace. 2008. *How Unilever Palm Oil Suppliers Are Burning up Borneo.* Amsterdam: Greenpeace International. Accessed March 23, 2022. http://www.greenpeace.nl/Global/nederland/report/2010/5/burningupborneo.pdf.

Greenpeace. 2012. *Frying the Forest: How India's Use of Palm Oil Is Having a Devastating Impact on Indonesia's Rainforests, Tigers and the Global Climate.* Richmond Town,

Bengaluru: Greenpeace India. Accessed March 23, 2022. http://www.greenpeace.org/india/Global/india/docs/palm_oil_report_2012.pdf.

Greenpeace. 2016. *Why IOI's Destruction in Ketapang Is a Burning Issue for the RSPO and the Palm Oil Industry*. Amsterdam: Greenpeace International. Accessed March 23, 2022. http://www.greenpeace.org/archive-international/Global/international/publications/forests/2016/Burning%20Issue.pdf.

Greenpeace. 2017. *How the Palm Oil Industry Is Still Cooking the Climate*. Amsterdam: Greenpeace International. Accessed March 23, 2022. https://storage.googleapis.com/planet4-southeastasia-stateless/2019/04/0a48e8fb-0a48e8fb-still-cooking-the-climate.pdf.

Greenpeace. 2022. How the Invasion of Ukraine Broke the World's Fragile Food System—and How We Can Fix It. Greenpeace, March 29, 2022. Accessed April 23, 2022. https://www.greenpeace.org.uk/news/ukraine-invasion-food-crisis/.

Greenpeace International. 2018. Breakthrough as World's Largest Palm Oil Trader Gives Forest Destroyers Nowhere to Hide. December 10, 2018. Accessed March 23, 2022. https://www.greenpeace.org/international/press-release/19898/worlds-largest-palm-forest-destroyers-nowhere-to-hide/.

Greenpeace Southeast Asia. 2019. Greenpeace Halts Engagement with Wilmar-Unilever-Mondelez over Continued Failure to Take Necessary Action to Cut Deforestation from Their Supply Chains. Greenpeace, September 3, 2019. Accessed March 23, 2022. https://www.greenpeace.org/southeastasia/press/2973/greenpeace-halts-engagement-with-wilmar-unilever-mondelez-over-continued-failure-to-take-necessary-action-to-cut-deforestation-from-their-supply-chains/.

Grupo de Reflexión Rural. 2005. Final Document of the Iguazú Counter Conference on the Impacts of Soya and Monocultures. San Miguel de Iguazú, Brazil, March 16–18, 2005.

GSIA. *See* Global Sustainable Investment Alliance

Guarín, Alejandro, and Peter Knorringa. 2014. New Middle-Class Consumers in Rising Powers: Responsible Consumption and Private Standards. *Oxford Development Studies* 42 (2): 151–171. http://doi.org/10.1080/13600818.2013.864757.

Gulbrandsen, Lars H. 2006. Creating Markets for Eco-Labelling: Are Consumers Insignificant? *International Journal of Consumer Studies* 30 (5): 477–489. https://doi.org/10.1111/j.1470-6431.2006.00534.x.

Gulbrandsen, Lars H. 2008. Organizing Accountability in Transnational Standards Organizations: The Forest Stewardship Council as a Good Governance Model. In *Organizing Transnational Accountability*, edited by Magnus Boström and Christina Garsten, 61–79. Cheltenham: Edward Elgar. https://doi.org/10.4337/9781848442726.

Gulbrandsen, Lars H. 2010. *Transnational Environmental Governance: The Emergence and Effects of the Certification of Forests and Fisheries*. Cheltenham: Edward Elgar.

Hale, Thomas. 2020. Transnational Actors and Transnational Governance in Global Environmental Politics. *Annual Review of Political Science* 23: 203–220. https://doi.org/10.1146/annurev-polisci-050718-032644.

Hale, Thomas, and David Held, eds. 2011. *Handbook of Transnational Governance: Institutions and Innovations*. Cambridge: Polity.

Hale, Thomas, and David Held. 2017. *Beyond Gridlock*. Cambridge, MA: Wiley.

Hall, Rodney Bruce, and Thomas J. Biersteker. 2002. *The Emergence of Private Authority in Global Governance*. Cambridge: Cambridge University Press.

Hansen, M. C., Peter V. Potapov, R. Moore, M. Hancher, S. A. Turubanova, A. Tyukavina, D. Thau, S. V. Stehman, S. J. Goetz, T. R. Loveland, A. Kommareddy, A. Egorov, L. Chini, C. O. Justice, and J. R. G. Townshend. 2013. High-Resolution Global Maps of 21st-Century Forest Cover Change. *Science* 342 (6160): 850–853. https://doi.org/10.1126/science.1244693.

Hanson, Arthur. 2019. Ecological Civilization in the People's Republic of China: Values, Action, and Future Needs. ADB East Asia Working Paper Series No. 21, December 2019. Manila: Asian Development Bank. Accessed March 23, 2022. https://www.adb.org/sites/default/files/publication/545291/eawp-021-ecological-civilization-prc.pdf.

Hatte, Sophie, and Pamina Koenig. 2018. The Geography of NGO Activism against Multinational Corporations. *World Bank Economic Review* 34 (1): 143–163. https://doi.org/10.1093/wber/lhy007.

Haufler, Virginia. 2009. The Kimberley Process, Club Goods, and Public Enforcement of a Private Regime. In *Voluntary Programs: A Club Theory Perspective*, edited by Matthew Potoski and Aseem Prakash, 89–105. Cambridge, MA: MIT Press. https://doi.org/10.7551/mitpress/9780262162500.001.0001.

Heilmayr, Robert, and Eric F. Lambin. 2016. Impacts of Nonstate, Market-Driven Governance on Chilean Forests. *Proceedings of the National Academy of Sciences* 113 (11): 2910. https://doi.org/10.1073/pnas.1600394113.

Henders, Sabine, U. Martin Persson, and Thomas Kastner. 2015. Trading Forests: Land-Use Change and Carbon Emissions Embodied in Production and Exports of Forest-Risk Commodities. *Environmental Research Letters* 10 (12): 125012. https://doi.org/10.1088/1748-9326/10/12/125012.

Henderson, Jeffrey, Peter Dicken, Martin Hess, Neil Coe, and Henry Wai-Chung Yeung. 2002. Global Production Networks and the Analysis of Economic Development. *Review of International Political Economy* 9 (3): 436–464. https://doi.org/10.1080/09692290210150842.

Hidayat, Nia Kurniawati, Astrid Offermans, and Pieter Glasbergen. 2016. On the Profitability of Sustainability Certification: An Analysis among Indonesian Palm Oil Smallholders. *Journal of Economics and Sustainable Development* 7 (18): 45–61. https://iiste.org/Journals/index.php/JEDS/article/view/33228.

Hidayat, Nia Kurniawati, Astrid Offermans, and Pieter Glasbergen. 2018. Sustainable Palm Oil as a Public Responsibility? On the Governance Capacity of Indonesian Standard for Sustainable Palm Oil (ISPO). *Agriculture and Human Values* 35 (1): 223–242. https://doi.org/10.1007/s10460-017-9816-6.

Higgins, Vaughan, and Geoffrey Lawrence. 2005. *Agricultural Governance: Globalization and the New Politics of Regulation*. Abingdon: Routledge. https://doi.org/10.4324/9780203698907.

Higgott, Richard A., Geoffrey R. D. Underhill, and Andreas Bieler, eds. 2000. *Non-State Actors and Authority in the Global System*. London: Routledge. https://doi.org/10.4324/9780203165041.

Hillson, Mark. 2020. Tendrils of Hope amid Huge Setbacks for Sustainable Soy in Brazil. Reuters Events, March 7, 2020. https://www.reutersevents.com/sustainability/tendrils-hope-amid-huge-setbacks-sustainable-soy-brazil.

Hochstetler, Kathryn. 2012. South-South Trade and the Environment: A Brazilian Case Study. *Global Environmental Politics* 13 (1): 30–48. https://doi.org/10.1162/GLEP_a_00152.

Hope, Jessica. 2020. Globalising Sustainable Development: Decolonial Disruptions and Environmental Justice in Bolivia. *Area* 54 (2): 176–184. https://doi.org/10.1111/area.12626.

Hopewell, Kristen. 2019. How Rising Powers Create Governance Gaps: The Case of Export Credit and the Environment. *Global Environmental Politics* 19 (1): 34–52. https://doi.org/10.1162/glep_a_00490.

Horner, Rory. 2016. New Economic Geography of Trade and Development? Governing South–South Trade, Value Chains and Production Networks. *Territory, Politics, Governance* 4 (4): 400–420. https://doi.org/10.1080/21622671.2015.1073614.

Horner, Rory, and Khalid Nadvi. 2018. Global Value Chains and the Rise of the Global South: Unpacking Twenty-First Century Polycentric Trade. *Global Networks* 18 (2): 207–237. https://doi.org/10.1111/glob.12180.

Hospes, Otto. 2014. Marking the Success or End of Global Multi-Stakeholder Governance? The Rise of National Sustainability Standards in Indonesia and Brazil for Palm oil and Soy. *Agriculture and Human Values* 31 (3): 425–437. https://doi.org/10.1007/s10460-014-9511-9.

Hospes, Otto, Olga van der Valk, and Jennie van der Mheen-Sluijer. 2012. Parallel Development of Five Partnerships to Promote Sustainable Soy in Brazil: Solution or

References

Part of Wicked Problems? Special issue, *International Food and Agribusiness Management Review* 15 (B): 29–52. http://edepot.wur.nl/242793.

Hovani, Lex, Rane Cortez, Herlina Hartanto, Ian Thompson, Greg Fishbein, Erin Myers Madeira, and Justin Adams. 2018. The Role of Jurisdictional Programs in Catalyzing Sustainability Transitions in Tropical Forest Landscapes. Nature Conservancy. Accessed March 23, 2022. https://www.nature.org/content/dam/tnc/nature/en/documents/TNC_Role_Jurisdictional_Programs_Sustainability_Transitions_2018.pdf.

Howard, Jennifer, Jennifer Nash, and John Ehrenfeld. 2000. Standard or Smokescreen? Implementation of a Voluntary Environmental Code. *California Management Review* 42 (2): 63–82. https://doi.org/10.2307/41166033.

Huesemann, Michael, and Joyce Huesemann. 2011. *Techno-Fix: Why Technology Won't Save Us or the Environment*. Gabriola Island, BC: New Society.

Humphrey, John. 2018. The Position and Potential of Developing Country Suppliers in Global Value Chains: A Review of the Literature. Institute of Developing Economies Japan External Trade Organization. Accessed March 23, 2022. https://www.ide.go.jp/library/English/Publish/Reports/InterimReport/2018/pdf/2018_2_40_005_ch01.pdf.

Huseh, Roselyn. 2011. *China's Regulatory State: A New Strategy for Globalization*. Ithaca, NY: Cornell University Press. https://doi.org/10.7591/cornell/9780801449956.001.0001.

IDH. 2021a. AI Holds Water: A Case for AI-enabled Water Management in Agriculture. White Paper, May 2021. Accessed March 23, 2022. https://www.idhsustainabletrade.com/uploaded/2021/05/WIAI-IDH-DD-AI-holds-water-white-paper-May-2021.pdf.

IDH. 2021b. European Soy Monitor: Insights on the European Uptake of Responsible and Deforestation-free Soy in 2019. Accessed March 23, 2022. https://www.idhsustainabletrade.com/publication/european-soy-monitor-report-2019/.

IDH and EPOA. 2020. Sustainable Palm Oil for Europe in 2019. Accessed March 23, 2022. https://palmoilalliance.eu/wp-content/uploads/2020/09/New-Palm-IG-6.5.pdf.

Index Mundi. n.d. Indonesia Palm Oil Domestic Consumption by Year. Accessed March 23, 2022. https://www.indexmundi.com/agriculture/?country=id&commodity=palm-oil&graph=domestic-consumption.

Indonesian Palm Oil Conference (IPOC). 2018. GAPKI Profile. Accessed March 24, 2021. http://www.gapkiconference.org/about-event/gapki-profile.

Intergovernmental Panel on Climate Change (IPCC). 2019. Climate Change and Land. Special Report, August 2019. Accessed March 23, 2022. https://www.ipcc.ch/srccl/

International Palm Oil Sustainability Framework (IPOS). 2021. About Us. Accessed March 23, 2022. https://iposindia.in/about-us/.

International Trade Centre (ITC). 2021. The State of Sustainable Markets 2021. Accessed March 23, 2022. https://standardsmap.org/en/trends.

International Trade Centre (ITC). n.d. International Trade in Goods 2001–2021. Accessed March 23, 2022. https://www.trademap.org/tradestatistics/.

International Tropical Timber Organization (ITTO). n.d. Biennial Review Statistics. Last updated March 9, 2022. https://www.itto.int/biennal_review/?mode=searchdata.

IOI Group. 2009. Environmental Sustainability. December 31, 2009. Link no longer active. http://www.ioigroup.com/corporateresponsibility/environment_plantation.cfm.

IOI Group. 2021. Our Businesses. Accessed March 23, 2022. https://www.ioigroup.com/Content/BUSINESS/B_Plantation#:~:text=Our%20current%20total%20planted%20area,palm%20age%20is%2013%20years.

IPCC. *See* Intergovernmental Panel on Climate Change

IPOC. *See* Indonesian Palm Oil Conference

IPOS. *See* International Palm Oil Sustainability

ISEAL. 2021. Jurisdictional Monitoring and Claims. Accessed March 23, 2022. https://www.isealalliance.org/about-iseal/our-work/jurisdictional-monitoring-and-claims.

ISEAL. 2022. Recommendations for Strengthening the European Union's Deforestation-free supply Chains Proposal. February 2022. Accessed March 23, 2022. https://www.isealalliance.org/sites/default/files/resource/2022-02/ISEAL-EU%20Deforestation-Position%20Paper_02-2022_ISEAL.pdf.

ISPOC. *See* Sustainable Palm Oil Coalition for India

ITC. *See* International Trade Centre

ITTO. *See* International Tropical Timber Organization

Jakarta Post. 2011. GAPKI Withdraws from RSPO to Support ISPO. October 5, 2011. Accessed March 23, 2022. https://www.thejakartapost.com/news/2011/10/05/gapki-withdraws-rspo-support-ispo.html.

Jelsma, Idsert. 2019. In Search of Sustainable and Inclusive Palm Oil Production: The Role of Smallholders in Indonesia. PhD diss., University of Utrecht. Accessed March 23, 2022. https://www.cifor.org/knowledge/publication/7399/.

Jelsma, Idsert, and G. C. Schoneveld. 2016. Towards More Sustainable and Productive Independent Oil Palm Smallholders in Indonesia: Insights from the Development of a Smallholder Typology. CIFOR Working Paper 210. Bogor Barat, Indonesia: Center for International Forestry Research (CIFOR). https://doi.org/10.17528/cifor/006222.

Jelsma, Idsert, G. C. Schoneveld, Annelies Zoomers, and A. C. M. van Westen. 2017. Unpacking Indonesia's Independent Oil Palm Smallholders: An Actor-Disaggregated

Approach to Identifying Environmental and Social Performance Challenges. *Land Use Policy* 69: 281–297. https://doi.org/10.1016/j.landusepol.2017.08.012.

Jeppesen, Soeren, and Michael W. Hansen. 2004. Environmental Upgrading of Third World Enterprises through Linkages to Transnational Corporations: Theoretical Perspectives and Preliminary Evidence. *Business Strategy and the Environment* 13 (4): 261–274. https://doi.org/10.1002/bse.410.

Jepson, Nicholas. 2020. *In China's Wake: How the Commodity Boom Transformed Development Strategies in the Global South*. New York: Columbia University Press.

Jong, Hans Nicholas. 2020a. Indonesia Aims for Sustainability Certification for Oil Palm Smallholders. Mongabay, April 29, 2020. https://news.mongabay.com/2020/04/indonesia-aims-for-sustainability-certification-for-oil-palm-smallholders/.

Jong, Hans Nicholas. 2020b. Indonesia's Biofuel Bid Threatens More Deforestation for Oil Palm Plantations. Mongabay, December 21, 2020. https://news.mongabay.com/2020/12/indonesia-biofuel-deforestation-oil-palm-plantation-b30/.

Jong, Hans Nicholas. 2020c. Watchdogs Lament Palm Oil Giant Wilmar's Exit from Forest Conservation Alliance. Mongabay, April 8, 2020. https://news.mongabay.com/2020/04/palm-oil-wilmar-hcsa-deforestation-forest-carbon/.

Jordan, Andrew, Dave Huitema, Harro van Asselt, and Johanna Forster, eds. 2018. *Governing Climate Change: Polycentricity in Action?* Cambridge: Cambridge University Press. https://doi.org/10.1017/9781108284646.

Kalfagianni, Agni, and Phillipp Pattberg. 2011. The Effectiveness of Transnational Rule-Setting Organisations in Global Sustainability Politics: An Analytical Framework. Global Governance Working Paper No. 43, February 2011. Amsterdam: Global Governance Project. https://citeseerx.ist.psu.edu/viewdoc/download?doi=10.1.1.661.3120&rep=rep1&type=pdf.

Kalfagianni, Agni, and Phillipp Pattberg. 2013. Fishing in Muddy Waters: Exploring the Conditions for Effective Governance of Fisheries and Aquaculture. *Marine Policy* 38: 124–132. https://doi.org/10.1016/j.marpol.2012.05.028.

Kaplinsky, Raphael, Anne Terheggen, and Julia Tijaja. 2011. China as a Final Market: The Gabon Timber and Thai Cassava Value Chains. *World Development* 39 (7): 1177–1190. https://doi.org/10.1016/j.worlddev.2010.12.007.

Kashwan, Prakash, Frank Biermann, Aarti Gupta, and Chukwumerije Okereke. 2020. Planetary Justice: Prioritizing the Poor in Earth System Governance. *Earth System Governance* 6: 100075. https://doi.org/10.1016/j.esg.2020.100075.

Kaup, Felix. 2015. *The Sugarcane Complex in Brazil: The Role of Innovation in a Dynamic Sector on Its Path toward Sustainability*. Cham: Springer.

Keck, Margaret E., and Kathryn Sikkink. 1998. *Activists beyond Borders: Advocacy Networks in International Politics*. Ithaca, NY: Cornell University Press.

Keck, Margaret E., and Kathryn Sikkink. 1999. Transnational Advocacy Networks in International and Regional Politics. *International Social Science Journal* 51 (159): 89–101. https://doi.org/10.1111/1468-2451.00179.

Keohane, Robert O., and David G. Victor. 2011. The Regime Complex for Climate Change. *Perspectives on Politics* 9 (1): 7–23. http://dx.doi.org/10.1017/S1537592710004068.

Kharas, Homi. 2010. The Emerging Middle Class in Developing Countries. Working Paper No. 285, OECD Development Centre. http://www.oecd.org/dev/44457738.pdf.

Khattak, Amira, and Christina Stringer. 2017. Environmental Upgrading in Pakistan's Sporting Goods Industry in Global Value Chains: A Question of Progress? *Business & Economic Review* 9 (1): 43–64. http://bereview.pk/index.php/BER/article/view/140.

Khattak, Amira, Christina Stringer, Maureen Benson-Rea, and Nigel Haworth. 2015. Environmental Upgrading of Apparel Firms in Global Value Chains: Evidence from Sri Lanka. *Competition & Change* 19 (4): 317–335. https://doi.org/10.1177/1024529415581972.

Kim, Dong-Shik, Mohammadmatin Hanifzadeh, and Ashok Kumar. 2018. Trend of Biodiesel Feedstock and Its Impact on Biodiesel Emission Characteristics. *Environmental Progress & Sustainable Energy* 37 (1): 7–19. https://doi.org/doi:10.1002/ep.12800.

Korten, David C. 1995. *When Corporations Rule the World*. West Hartford, CT: Kumarian.

Krasner, Stephen D. 1983. *International Regimes*. Ithaca, NY: Cornell University Press.

Krishnan, Aarti. 2017. Re-thinking the Environmental Dimensions of Upgrading and Embeddedness in Production Networks: The Case of Kenyan Horticulture Farmers. PhD diss., University of Manchester. https://www.research.manchester.ac.uk/portal/files/84024566/FULL_TEXT.PDF.

Kütting, Gabriela. 2005. *Globalization and the Environment: Greening Global Political Economy*. Albany: State University of New York Press.

Kütting, Gabriela. 2014. Rethinking Global Environmental Governance: Coordinating Ecological Policy. *Critical Policy Studies* 8 (2): 227–234. https://doi.org/10.1080/19460171.2014.904236.

Lambin, Eric F., Holly K. Gibbs, Robert Heilmayr, Kimberly M. Carlson, Leonardo C. Fleck, Rachael D. Garrett, Yann le Polain de Waroux, Constance L. McDermott, David McLaughlin, Peter Newton, Christoph Nolte, Pablo Pacheco, Lisa L. Rausch, Charlotte Streck, Tannis Thorlakson, and Nathalie F. Walker. 2018. The Role of Supply-Chain Initiatives in Reducing Deforestation. *Nature Climate Change* 8 (2): 109–116. https://doi.org/10.1038/s41558-017-0061-1.

Lambin, Eric F., and Tannis Thorlakson. 2018. Sustainability Standards: Interactions Between Private Actors, Civil Society, and Governments. *Annual Review of Environment and Resources* 43 (1): 369–393. https://doi.org/10.1146/annurev-environ-102017-025931.

Langford, Natalie J. 2019. The Governance of Social Standards in Emerging Markets: An Exploration of Actors and Interests Shaping Trustea as a Southern Multi-Stakeholder Initiative. *Geoforum* 104: 81–91. https://doi.org/10.1016/j.geoforum.2019.06.009.

Langford, Natalie J. 2021. From Global to Local Tea Markets: The Changing Political Economy of Tea Production within India's Domestic Value Chain. *Development and Change* 52 (6): 1445–1472. https://doi.org/10.1111/dech.12652.

Langford, Natalie J., Khalid Nadvi, and Corinna Braun-Munzinger. 2022. The Shaping of "Southern" Sustainability Standards in a Value Chain World: Comparative Evidence from China and India. *Review of International Political Economy: 1–26*. https://doi:10.1080/09692290.2022.2089713.

Larsen, Rasmus Kløcker, Maria Osbeck, Elena Dawkins, Heidi Tuhkanen, Ha Nguyen, Agus Nugroho, Toby Alan Gardner, Zulfahm, and Paul Wolvekamp. 2018. Hybrid Governance in Agricultural Commodity Chains: Insights from Implementation of "No Deforestation, No Peat, No Exploitation" (NDPE) Policies in the Oil Palm Industry. *Journal of Cleaner Production* 183: 544–554. https://doi.org/10.1016/j.jclepro.2018.02.125.

Lawson, Sam. 2021. Relying on Green Labels to Address our Thirst for the Products of Deforestation Would be a Disaster (Commentary). Mongabay, November 8, 2021. https://news.mongabay.com/2021/11/relying-on-green-labels-to-address-our-thirst-for-the-products-of-deforestation-would-be-a-disaster-commentary/.

LeBaron, Genevieve, and Andreas Rühmkorf. 2017. Steering CSR Through Home State Regulation: A Comparison of the Impact of the UK Bribery Act and Modern Slavery Act on Global Supply Chain Governance. *Global Policy* 8 (S3): 15–28. https://doi.org/10.1111/1758-5899.12398.

Lederer, Markus, and Chris Höhne. 2021. Max Weber in the Tropics: How Global Climate Politics Facilitates the Bureaucratization of Forestry in Indonesia. *Regulation & Governance* 15 (1): 133–151. https://doi.org/10.1111/rego.12270.

Lederer, Markus, Chris Höhne, Fee Stehle, Thomas Hickmann, and Harald Fuhr. 2020. Multilevel Climate Governance in Brazil and Indonesia. In *Climate Governance across the Globe: Pioneers, Leaders, and Followers*, edited by Rüdiger K. W. Wurzel, Mikael Skou Andersen, and Paul Tobin, 101–120. Abingdon: Routledge.

Ledger Insights. 2020. Ben & Jerry's Owner Unilever to Use Blockchain to Tackle Deforestation, Invests $1 Billion in Climate Change. June 15, 2020. https://www.ledgerinsights.com/unilever-blockchain-deforestation-climate-change-ben-jerrys/.

Lenox, Michael J., and Jennifer Nash. 2003. Industry Self-Regulation and Adverse Selection: A Comparison across Four Trade Association Programs. *Business Strategy and the Environment* 12 (6): 343–356. http://dx.doi.org/10.1002/bse.380.

Lernoud, Julia, Jason Potts, Gregory Sampson, Bernhard Schlatter, Gabriel Huppe, Vivek Voora, Helga Willer, Joseph Wozniak, and Duc Dang. 2018. *The State of Sustainable Markets: Statistics and Emerging Trends 2018*. Geneva: International Trade Centre. https://intracen.org/media/file/2616.

Li, Tania Murray. 2016. Situating Transmigration in Indonesia's Oil Palm Labour Regime. In *The Oil Palm Complex: Smallholders, Agribusiness and the State in Indonesia and Malaysia*, edited by Rob Cramb and John F. McCarthy, 378–409. Singapore: National University of Singapore Press. https://doi.org/10.2307/j.ctv1xz0km.16.

Lingkar Temu Kabupaten Lestari [Sustainable District Meeting Circle] (LTKL). 2021. Member Districts. Accessed March 23, 2022. http://kabupatenlestari.org/.

Lingkar Temu Kabupaten Lestari [Sustainable District Meeting Circle] (LTKL), and Tropical Forest Alliance. 2020. Mapping Commitment of Subnational Government to Sustainable Land use in Southeast Asia. Final Report, December 2020. Accessed March 23, 2022. https://jaresourcehub.org/wp-content/uploads/2021/02/Buku_LTKL-TFA-Report_Final.pdf.

Lister, Jane, and Peter Dauvergne. 2014. Voluntary Zero Net Deforestation: The Implications of Demand-Side Retail Sustainability for Global Forests. In *Forests and Globalization: Challenges and Opportunities for Sustainable Development*, edited by William Nikolakis and John Innes, 65–77. Abingdon: Routledge.

Locke, Richard, Matthew Amengual, and Akshay Mangla. 2009. Virtue Out of Necessity? Compliance, Commitment, and the Improvement of Labor Conditions in Global Supply Chains. *Politics & Society* 37 (3): 319–351. http://pas.sagepub.com/content/37/3/319.abstract.

Lockeretz, William, ed. 2007. *Organic Farming: An International History*. Wallingford: CABI.

LTKL. *See* Lingkar Temu Kabupaten Lestari [Sustainable District Meeting Circle]

Ludwig, Kathrin. 2018. *The Emerging Governance Landscape around Zero Deforestation Pledges: Insights into Dynamics and Effects of Zero Deforestation Pledges. Background Report*. The Hague: Netherlands Environmental Assessment Agency. Accessed March 23, 2022. https://www.pbl.nl/sites/default/files/downloads/2354_Ludwig_ZeroNetDeforestation.pdf.

Lukes, Steven. 1974. *Power: A Radical View*. London: Macmillan.

Macdonald, Kate. 2014. *The Politics of Global Supply Chains: Power and Governance Beyond the State*. Cambridge: Polity.

Mafria, Tiza, Randy Rakhmadi, and Cherika Novianti. 2018. Towards a More Sustainable and Efficient Palm Oil Supply Chain in Berau, East Kalimantan. Climate Policy Initiative Report, July 2018. Accessed March 23, 2022. https://climatepolicyinitiative

.org/wp-content/uploads/2018/07/Towards-a-more-sustainable-and-efficient-palm-oil-supply-chain-in-Berau-East-Kalimantan-Full-publication.pdf.

Mahbubani, Kishore. 2008. *The New Asian Hemisphere: The Irresistible Shift of Global Power to the East*. New York: Public Affairs.

Malets, Olga. 2015. When Transnational Standards Hit the Ground: Domestic Regulations, Compliance Assessment and Forest Certification in Russia. *Journal of Environmental Policy & Planning* 17 (3): 332–359. http://doi.org/10.1080/1523908X.2014.947922.

Margono, Belinda Arunarwati, Peter V. Potapov, Svetlana Turubanova, Fred Stolle, and Matthew C. Hansen. 2014. Primary Forest Cover Loss in Indonesia over 2000–2012. *Nature Climate Change* 4 (8): 730–735. http://doi.org/10.1038/nclimate2277.

Marques, José Carlos, and Burkard Eberlein. 2020. Grounding Transnational Business Governance: A Political-Strategic Perspective on Government Responses in the Global South. *Regulation & Governance* 15 (4): 1209–1229. https://doi.org/10.1111/rego.12356.

Marx, Axel, and Dieter Cuypers. 2010. Forest Certification as a Global Environmental Governance Tool. What Is the Macro-Impact of the Forest Stewardship Council? *Regulation & Governance* 4 (4): 408–434. https://doi.org/10.1111/j.1748-5991.2010.01088.x.

Mathiesen, Karl. 2016. Malaysian Palm Oil Giant IOI Drops Lawsuit against Green Group. *The Guardian*, June 7, 2016. Accessed March 23, 2022. https://www.theguardian.com/sustainable-business/2016/jun/07/palm-oil-ioi-rspo-unilever-nestle-kelloggs-mars-deforestation-indonesia.

Mayer, Frederick W., and Gary Gereffi. 2010. Regulation and Economic Globalization: Prospects and Limits of Private Governance. Special issue, *Business and Politics* 12 (3): 1–25. https://doi.org/10.2202/1469-3569.1325.

Mayer, Frederick W., and Nicola Phillips. 2017. Outsourcing Governance: States and the Politics of a "Global Value Chain World." *New Political Economy* 22 (2): 134–152. https://doi.org/10.1080/13563467.2016.1273341.

McCarthy, John F. 2000. The Changing Regime: Forest Property and Reformasi in Indonesia. *Development and Change* 31 (1): 91–129. https://doi.org/https://doi.org/10.1111/1467-7660.00148.

McCarthy, John F. 2012. Certifying in Contested Spaces: Private Regulation in Indonesian Forestry and Palm Oil. *Third World Quarterly* 33 (10): 1871–1888. https://doi.org/10.1080/01436597.2012.729721.

McInnes, Angus. 2017. *A Comparison of Leading Palm Oil Certification Standards*. Forest Peoples Programme, Moreton-in-Marsh: Forest Peoples Programme. Accessed March 23, 2022. https://www.forestpeoples.org/sites/default/files/documents/Palm%20Oil%20Certification%20Standards_lowres_spreads.pdf.

Meadows, Donella H., Dennis L. Meadows, Jergen Randers, and William W. Behrens. 1972. *The Limits to Growth*. New York: Universe.

Meckling, Jonas. 2015. Oppose, Support, or Hedge? Distributional Effects, Regulatory Pressure, and Business Strategy in Environmental Politics. *Global Environmental Politics* 15 (2): 19–37. https://doi.org/10.1162/GLEP_a_00296.

Meier, C., G. Sampson, C. Larrea, B. Schlatter, V. Voora, D. Dang, S. Bermudez, J. Wozniak, and H. Willer. 2020. The State of Sustainable Markets 2020: Statistics and Emerging Trends. Evidensia. https://www.evidensia.eco/resources/329/the-state-of-sustainable-markets-2020-statistics-and-emerging-trends/.

Mena, Sébastien, and Guido Palazzo. 2015. Input and Output Legitimacy of Multi-Stakeholder Initiatives. *Business Ethics Quarterly* 22 (3): 527–556. https://doi.org/10.5840/beq201222333.

Mera-Gomez, Laura, Jean-Frédéric Morin, and Thijs Van de Graaf. 2020. Regime Complexes. In *Architectures of Earth System Governance: Institutional Complexity and Structural Transformation*, edited by Frank Biermann and Rakhyun E. Kim, 137–157. Cambridge: Cambridge University Press. https://doi.org/10.1017/9781108784641.007.

Miles, Edward L., Steinar Andresen, Elaine M. Carlin, Jon Birger Skjærseth, Arild Underdal, and Jørgen Wettestad. 2002. *Environmental Regime Effectiveness: Confronting Theory with Evidence*. Cambridge, MA: MIT Press.

Milhorance, Caroline, and Marcel Bursztyn. 2018. Emerging Hybrid Governance to Foster Low-Emission Rural Development in the Amazon Frontier. *Land Use Policy* 75: 11–20. https://doi.org/10.1016/j.landusepol.2018.03.029.

Ministry of Agriculture and Farmers Welfare. 2018. Brief Note on Oil Palm. Accessed March 24, 2022. https://www.nfsm.gov.in/ReadyReckoner/Oilseeds/BriefNote_OS2018.pdf.

Ministry of Corporate Affairs. 2019. India's National Action Plan on Business and Human Rights. Accessed March 23, 2022. https://www.mca.gov.in/Ministry/pdf/NationalPlanBusinessHumanRight_13022019.pdf.

Ministry of Corporate Affairs. 2020. Report of the Committee on Business Responsibility Reporting. Government of India. Accessed March 23, 2022. https://www.mca.gov.in/Ministry/pdf/BRR_11082020.pdf.

Mitchell, Ronald B. 1994. Regime Design Matters: International Oil Pollution and Treaty Compliance. *International Organization* 48 (3): 425–458.

Mohai, Paul, David Pellow, and J. Timmons Roberts. 2009. Environmental Justice. *Annual Review of Environment and Resources* 34 (1): 405–430. https://doi.org/10.1146/annurev-environ-082508-094348.

Mol, Arthur P. J. 2011. China's Ascent and Africa's Environment. *Global Environmental Change* 21 (3): 785–794. https://doi.org/10.1016/j.gloenvcha.2011.03.015.

Molenaar, J. W., J. Dallinger, J. Gorter, L. Heilbron, L. Simons, E. Blackmore, and B. Vorley. 2015. The Role of Voluntary Sustainability Standards in Scaling Up Sustainability in Smallholder-Dominated Agricultural Sectors. White Paper 4, International Finance Corporation. Accessed March 23, 2022. https://pubs.iied.org/sites/default/files/pdfs/migrate/16586IIED.pdf.

Möller, Ina. 2020. Political Perspectives on Geoengineering: Navigating Problem Definition and Institutional Fit. *Global Environmental Politics* 20 (2): 57–82. https://doi.org/10.1162/glep_a_00547.

Morgans, Courtney L., Erik Meijaard, Truly Santika, Elizabeth Law, Sugeng Budiharta, Marc Ancrenaz, and Kerrie A. Wilson. 2018. Evaluating the Effectiveness of Palm Oil Certification in Delivering Multiple Sustainability Objectives. *Environmental Research Letters* 13 (6): 064032. https://doi.org/10.1088/1748-9326/aac6f4.

Moser, Christine, and Sina Leipold. 2021. Toward "Hardened" Accountability? Analyzing the European Union's Hybrid Transnational Governance in Timber and Biofuel Supply Chains. *Regulation & Governance* 15 (1): 115–132. https://doi.org/10.1111/rego.12268.

MSI Integrity. 2020. Not Fit-for-Purpose: The Grand Experiment of Multi-Stakeholder Initiatives in Corporate Accountability, Human Rights and Global Governance. July 2020. Accessed March 23, 2022. https://www.msi-integrity.org/wp-content/uploads/2020/07/MSI_SUMMARY_REPORT.FORWEBSITE.FINAL_.pdf.

Mukpo, Ashoka. 2020. California Lawmakers Introduce Legislation to Fight Tropical Deforestation. Mongabay, February 24, 2020. Accessed March 23, 2022. https://news.mongabay.com/2020/02/california-lawmakers-introduce-legislation-to-fight-tropical-deforestation/.

Myers, Rodd, Rebecca L. Rutt, Constance McDermott, Ahmad Maryudi, Emmanuel Acheampong, Marisa Camargo, and Hoàng Cẩm. 2020. Imposing Legality: Hegemony and Resistance under the EU Forest Law Enforcement, Governance, and Trade (FLEGT) Initiative. *Journal of Political Ecology* 27 (1): 125–149. https://doi.org/10.2458/v27i1.23208.

Nadvi, Khalid. 2014. "Rising Powers" and Labour and Environmental Standards. *Oxford Development Studies* 42 (2): 137–150. http://dx.doi.org/10.1080/13600818.2014.909400.

Nadvi, Khalid. 2017. Rising Powers, Labour Standards and the Governance of Global Production Networks. *Impact 2017* (9): 22–27. https://doi.org/10.21820/23987073.2017.9.22.

Nepstad, Daniel, Silvia Irawan, Tathiana Bezerra, William Boyd, Claudia Stickler, João Shimada, Oswaldo Carvalho, Katie MacIntyre, Alue Dohong, Ane Alencar, Andrea Azevedo, David Tepper, and Sarah Lowery. 2013. More Food, More Forests, Fewer Emissions, Better Livelihoods: Linking REDD+, Sustainable Supply Chains and

Domestic Policy in Brazil, Indonesia and Colombia. *Carbon Management* 4 (6): 639–658. https://doi.org/10.4155/cmt.13.65.

Nepstad, Daniel, David McGrath, Claudia Stickler, Ane Alencar, Andrea Azevedo, Briana Swette, Tathiana Bezerra, Maria Digiano, João Shimada, Ronaldo Seroa Da Motta, Eric Armijo, Leandro Castello, Paulo Brando, Matt C. Hansen, Max McGrath-Horn, Oswaldo Carvalho, and Laura Hess. 2014. Slowing Amazon Deforestation through Public Policy and Interventions in Beef and Soy Supply Chains. *Science* 344 (6188): 1118–1123. https://doi.org/10.1126/science.1248525.

Nepstad, Lucy S., James S. Gerber, Jason D. Hill, Lívia C. P. Dias, Marcos H. Costa, and Paul C. West. 2019. Pathways for Recent Cerrado Soybean Expansion: Extending the Soy Moratorium and Implementing Integrated Crop Livestock Systems with Soybeans. *Environmental Research Letters* 14 (4): 044029. https://doi.org/10.1088/1748-9326/aafb85.

Neville, Kate J. 2021. *Fueling Resistance: The Contentious Political Economy of Biofuels and Fracking.* New York: Oxford University Press. https://doi.org/10.1093/oso/9780197535585.001.0001.

Newell, Peter. 2012. *Globalization and the Environment: Capitalism, Ecology, and Power.* Cambridge: Cambridge University Press.

Newell, Peter, Philipp Pattberg, and Heike Schroeder. 2012. Multiactor Governance and the Environment. *Annual Review of Environment and Resources* 37 (1): 365–387. https://doi.org/10.1146/annurev-environ-020911-094659.

NGO Coalition. 2016. Civil Society Recommendations to Brands and Traders Regarding the Cancellation of IOI Group as a Global Supplier of Palm Oil. Public Letter. May 12, 2016. Accessed March 23, 2022. https://25tdel2721up1vm6qbzkbca2-wpengine.netdna-ssl.com/wp-content/uploads/rainforestactionnetwork/pages/15920/attachments/original/1464047398/Coalition_Ltr_DropIOI_0612202016_4.pdf?1464047398.

Nikkhah, Hedayat Allah, and Ma'rof Bin Redzuan. 2010. The Role of NGOs in Promoting Empowerment for Sustainable Community Development. *Journal of Human Ecology* 30 (2): 85–92. https://doi.org/10.1080/09709274.2010.11906276.

Nölke, Andreas, ed. 2014. *Multinational Corporations from Emerging Markets: State Capitalism 3.0.* London: Palgrave Macmillan.

Noss, Reed F. 1983. A Regional Landscape Approach to Maintain Diversity. *BioScience* 33 (11): 700–706. https://doi.org/10.2307/1309350.

NYDF Assessment Partners. 2019. Protecting and Restoring Forests: A Story of Large Commitments yet Limited Progress. New York Declaration on Forests Five-Year Assessment Report, Climate Focus. Accessed March 23, 2022. https://climatefocus.com/wp-content/uploads/2022/06/2019NYDFReport.pdf.

References

NYDF Global Platform. 2019. Endorsers of the New York Declaration on Forests. Accessed March 23, 2022. https://forestdeclaration.org/about/endorsers/.

Nyman, Mikaela. 2006. *Democratizing Indonesia: The Challenges of Civil Society in the Era of Reformasi*. Copenhagen: NIAS Press.

O'Neil, Jim. 2001. Building Better Global BRICs. Global Economics Paper No. 66, Goldman Sachs, November 30, 2001. Accessed March 23, 2022. http://www.goldmansachs.com/our-thinking/archive/archive-pdfs/build-better-brics.pdf.

Odell, John S. 2003. Case Study Methods in International Political Economy. *International Studies Perspectives* 2 (2): 161–176. https://doi.org/10.1111/1528-3577.00047.

Organisation for Economic Co-operation and Development (OECD). 2016. Brazil: Federal Country. October 2016. Accessed March 23, 2022. https://www.oecd.org/regional/regional-policy/profile-Brazil.pdf.

Orsini, Amandine. 2013. Multi-Forum Non-State Actors: Navigating the Regime Complexes for Forestry and Genetic Resources. *Global Environmental Politics* 13 (3): 34–55. https://doi.org/10.1162/GLEP_a_00182.

Orsini, Amandine, Jean-Frédéric Morin, and Oran Young. 2013. Regime Complexes: A Buzz, a Boom, or a Boost for Global Governance? *Global Governance: A Review of Multilateralism and International Organizations* 19 (1): 27–39. http://journals.rienner.com/doi/abs/10.5555/1075-2846-19.1.27.

Overdevest, Christine. 2010. Comparing Forest Certification Schemes: The Case of Ratcheting Standards in the Forest Sector. *Socio-Economic Review* 8 (1): 47–76.

Overdevest, Christine, and Jonathan Zeitlin. 2014. Assembling an Experimentalist Regime: Transnational Governance Interactions in the Forest Sector. *Regulation & Governance* 8 (1): 22–48. https://doi.org/10.1111/j.1748-5991.2012.01133.x.

Overdevest, Christine, and Jonathan Zeitlin. 2018. Experimentalism in Transnational Forest Governance: Implementing European Union Forest Law Enforcement, Governance and Trade (FLEGT) Voluntary Partnership Agreements in Indonesia and Ghana. *Regulation & Governance* 12 (1): 64–87. https://onlinelibrary.wiley.com/doi/abs/10.1111/rego.12180.

Oya, Carlos, Florian Schaefer, and Dafni Skalidou. 2018. The Effectiveness of Agricultural Certification in Developing Countries: A Systematic Review. *World Development* 112: 282–312. https://doi.org/10.1016/j.worlddev.2018.08.001.

Ozinga, Saskia. 2020. Getting the Incentives Right: Why Partnership Agreements Should Be at the Heart of EU Efforts to End Deforestation. Fern, October 2020. Accessed March 23, 2022. https://www.fern.org/publications-insight/getting-the-incentives-right-2236/.

Pacheco, Pablo, Sophia Gnych, Ahmad Dermawan, Heru Komarudin, and Beni Okarda. 2017. The Palm Oil Value Chain: Implications for Economic Growth and Social and Environmental Sustainability. CIFOR Working Paper 220. Bogor Barat, Indonesia: Center for International Forestry Research (CIFOR). https://doi.org/10.17528/cifor/006405.

Pacheco, Pablo, George Schoneveld, Ahmad Dermawan, Heru Komarudin, and Marcel Djama. 2018. Governing Sustainable Palm Oil Supply: Disconnects, Complementarities, and Antagonisms between State Regulations and Private Standards. *Regulation & Governance* 14 (3): 568–598. https://doi.org/10.1111/rego.12220.

Pacheco-Vega, Raul, and Amanda Murdie. 2021. When Do Environmental NGOs Work? A Test of the Conditional Effectiveness of Environmental Advocacy. *Environmental Politics* 30 (1–2): 180–201. https://doi.org/10.1080/09644016.2020.1785261.

Palm Oil Investigations (POI). 2018. POI Withdrawal of Support from RSPO. September 12, 2016. Accessed March 23, 2022. http://www.palmoilinvestigations.org/poi-position-statement-on-the-rspo.html.

Panlasigui, Stephanie, Jimena Rico-Straffon, Alexander Pfaff, Jennifer Swensona, and Colby Loucks. 2018. Impacts of Certification, Uncertified Concessions, and Protected Areas on Forest Loss in Cameroon, 2000 to 2013. *Biological Conservation* 227: 160–166. https://doi.org/10.1016/j.biocon.2018.09.013.

Paoli, Gary, Blair Palmer, Jim Schweithelm, Godwin Limberg, and Lindsay Green. 2016. *Jurisdictional Approaches to Reducing Palm Oil Driven Deforestation in Indonesia: Scoping Study of Design Considerations and Geographic Priorities*. Bogor Barat, Indonesia: Daemeter. November 2016. http://daemeter.org/new/uploads/20161105170630.Daemeter_JA_2016_Full_Report_ENG.compressed.pdf.

Paris, R. 2015. Global Governance and Power Politics: Back to Basics. *Ethics & International Affairs* 29 (4): 407–418. https://doi.org/10.1017/S0892679415000428.

Park, Susan, and Teresa Kramarz, eds. 2019. *Global Environmental Governance and the Accountability Trap*. Cambridge, MA: MIT Press.

Partiti, Enrico. 2020. Private Processes and Public Values Tackling Global Deforestation and Ecosystem Conversion via Non-Financial Due Diligence. TILEC Discussion Paper No. DP 2020-017, June 17, 2020. http://dx.doi.org/10.2139/ssrn.3629272.

Partzsch, Lena. 2020. *Alternatives to Multilateralism: New Forms of Social and Environmental Governance*. Cambridge, MA: MIT Press.

Pasquali, Giovanni, Shane Godfrey, and Khalid Nadvi. 2020. Understanding Regional Value Chains through the Interaction of Public and Private Governance: Insights from Southern Africa's Apparel Sector. *Journal of International Business Policy* 4: 368–389. https://doi.org/10.1057/s42214-020-00071-9.

Pattberg, Phillipp. 2005. The Institutionalization of Private Governance: How Business and Nonprofit Organizations Agree on Transnational Rules. *Governance* 18 (4): 589–610. https://doi.org/10.1111/j.1468-0491.2005.00293.x.

Pattberg, Phillipp. 2007. *Private Institutions and Global Governance: The New Politics of Environmental Sustainability*. Cheltenham: Edward Elgar.

Pattberg, Phillipp, Frank Biermann, Sander Chan, and Aysen Mert, eds. 2012. *Public-Private Partnerships for Sustainable Development: Emergence, Influence, and Legitimacy*. Cheltenham: Edward Elgar.

Pattberg, Phillipp, and Oscar Widerberg. 2016. Transnational Multistakeholder Partnerships for Sustainable Development: Conditions for Success. *Ambio* 45 (1): 42–51. https://doi.org/10.1007/s13280-015-0684-2.

PCI. *See* Produce, Conserve, Include

PCI Monitor. 2021. The Mato Grosso PCI Strategy. Accessed March 23, 2022. https://pcimonitor.org/.

PCI Monitoring Committee. 2019. Balance of Goals: 2015 to 2019. Accessed March 23, 2022. https://www.pcimt.org/images/balancodasmetaspciano420152019english.pdf.

Pendrill, Florence, U. Martin Persson, and Thomas Kastner. 2020. Deforestation Risk Embodied in Production and Consumption of Agricultural and Forestry Commodities 2005–2017, version 1.0 data set. Zenodo, November 9, 2020. https://doi.org/10.5281/zenodo.4250532.

Phillips, Nicola. 2005. Bridging the Comparative/International Divide in the Study of States. *New Political Economy* 10 (3): 335–343. https://doi.org/10.1080/13563460500204209.

Phillips, Nicola, and Anthony Payne. 2014. Introduction: The International Political Economy of Governance. In *Handbook of the International Political Economy of Governance*, edited by Anthony Payne and Nicola Phillips, 1–13. Cheltenham: Edward Elgar.

Pickles, John, Stephanie Barrientos, and Peter Knorringa. 2016. New End Markets, Supermarket Expansion and Shifting Social Standards. *Environment and Planning A: Economy and Space* 48 (7): 1284–1301. https://doi.org/10.1177/0308518X16631540.

Pieterse, Jan N. 2012. Twenty-First Century Globalization: A New Development Era. *Forum for Development Studies* 39 (3): 367–385. https://doi.org/10.1080/08039410.2012.688859.

Plantation Office Central Kalimantan. 2013. The Central Kalimantan Roadmap to Low-Deforestation Rural Development that Increases Production and Reduces Poverty. Link no longer active. https://fayllar.org/the-central-kalimantan-roadmap-to-low-deforestation-rural-deve.html.

Plantation Office Central Kalimantan. 2015. Meeting Minutes. Jurisdiction-Based Certification Working Group Central Kalimantan, May 29, 2015. On file with author.

POI. *See* Palm Oil Investigations

Ponte, Stefano. 2008. Greener than Thou: The Political Economy of Fish Ecolabeling and Its Local Manifestations in South Africa. *World Development* 36 (1): 159–175. https://doi.org/10.1016/j.worlddev.2007.02.014.

Ponte, Stefano. 2014. The Evolutionary Dynamics of Biofuel Value Chains: From Unipolar and Government-Driven to Multipolar Governance. *Environment and Planning A: Economy and Space* 46 (2): 353–372. https://doi.org/10.1068/a46112.

Ponte, Stefano. 2019. *Business, Power and Sustainability in a World of Global Value Chains*. New York: Zed Books.

Ponte, Stefano, and Joachim Ewert. 2009. Which Way is "Up" in Upgrading? Trajectories of Change in the Value Chain for South African Wine. *World Development* 37 (10): 1637–1650. https://doi.org/10.1016/j.worlddev.2009.03.008.

Ponte, Stefano, Christine Noe, and Asubisye Mwamfupe. 2021. Private and Public Authority Interactions and the Functional Quality of Sustainability Governance: Lessons from Conservation and Development Initiatives in Tanzania. *Regulation & Governance* 15 (4): 1270–1285. https://doi.org/10.1111/rego.12303.

Ponte, Stefano, and Timothy Sturgeon. 2014. Explaining Governance in Global Value Chains: A Modular Theory-Building Effort. *Review of International Political Economy* 21 (1): 195–223. https://doi.org/10.1080/09692290.2013.809596.

Potoski, Matthew, and Aseem Prakash, eds. 2009. *Voluntary Programs: A Club Theory Perspective*. Cambridge, MA: MIT Press.

Poulsen, René Taudal, Stefano Ponte, and Jane Lister. 2016. Buyer-Driven Greening? Cargo-Owners and Environmental Upgrading in Maritime Shipping. *Geoforum* 68:57–68. https://doi.org/10.1016/j.geoforum.2015.11.018.

Poulsen, René Taudal, Steafno Ponte, and Henrik Sornn-Friese. 2018. Environmental Upgrading in Global Value Chains: The Potential and Limitations of Ports in the Greening of Maritime Transport. *Geoforum* 89:83–95. http://www.sciencedirect.com/science/article/pii/S0016718518300174.

Pradipta, T. 2018. More Smallholders Get ISPO Certified. *Palm Scribe*, December 11, 2018. Accessed March 23, 2022. https://thepalmscribe.id/more-smallholders-get-ispo-certified/.

Prakash, Aseem, and Jeffrey A. Hart. 2000. *Coping with Globalization*. London: Routledge. https://doi.org/10.4324/9780203466162.

References

Prakash, Aseem, and Matthew Potoski. 2006. *The Voluntary Environmentalist: Green Clubs, ISO 14001, and Voluntary Environmental Regulations*. Cambridge: Cambridge University Press.

Prakash, Aseem, and Matthew Potoski. 2007. Collective Action through Voluntary Environmental Programs: A Club Theory Perspective. *Policy Studies Journal* 35 (4): 773–792. http://dx.doi.org/10.1111/j.1541-0072.2007.00247.x.

Prakash, Aseem, and Matthew Potoski. 2009. Voluntary Clubs: Future Prospects. In *Voluntary Programs: A Club Theory Perspective*, edited by Matthew Potoski and Aseem Prakash, 281–296. Cambridge, MA: MIT Press.

Prakash, Aseem, and Matthew Potoski. 2012. Voluntary Environmental Programs: A Comparative Perspective. *Journal of Policy Analysis and Management* 31 (1): 123–138. https://doi.org/10.1002/pam.20617.

Produce, Conserve, Include (PCI). 2019. Strategy. Accessed March 24, 2022. http://pci.mt.gov.br/.

Pro Sampit. 2019. Palm Oil Farmers in Seruyan towards ISPO Certification. (Translated by Google Translate). February 14, 2019. Accessed March 23, 2022. http://sampit.prokal.co/read/news/21289-petani-sawit-di-seruyan-menuju-sertifikasi-ispo.html.

Purnomo, Herry, Bayuni Shantiko, Soaduon Sitorusa, Harris Gunawan, Ramadhani Achdiawan, Hariadi Kartodihardjob, and Ade Ayu Dewayania. 2017. Fire Economy and Actor Network of Forest and Land Fires in Indonesia. *Forest Policy and Economics* 78:21–31. https://doi.org/10.1016/j.forpol.2017.01.001.

Quack, Sigrid. 2020. From the Hope of Transcendence to Dreams of Domestication? Review Symposium: On Tim Bartley's, Rules without Rights: Land, Labor and Private Authority in the Global Economy, Oxford, Oxford University Press, 2018. *Socio-Economic Review* 18 (1): 295–308. https://doi.org/10.1093/ser/mwz035.

Rabobank Group. 2018. Global Standard on Sustainable Development. Accessed March 23, 2022. https://www.rabobank.com/en/images/sustainability-policy-framework.pdf.

Ragin, Charles C. 2008. *Redesigning Social Inquiry: Fuzzy Sets and Beyond*. Chicago: University of Chicago Press.

Ramos, Gian D. 2020. International Political Economy and the Environment. In *The Routledge Handbook to Global Political Economy*, edited by Ernesto Vivares, 813–828. New York: Routledge. https://doi.org/10.4324/9781351064545-53.

Rainforest Action Network (RAN). 2016a. Human Cost of Conflict Palm Oil. April 2016. Accessed March 23, 2022. https://www.ran.org/wp-content/uploads/rainforestactionnetwork/pages/15889/attachments/original/1467043668/The_Human_Cost_of_Conflict_Palm_Oil_RAN.pdf?msclkid=03f3b551abcd11ecaf706923cbbe9eb3.

Rainforest Action Network (RAN). 2016b. RSPO Puts Credibility on the Line by Lifting IOI Suspension. August 5, 2016. Accessed March 23, 2022. https://www.ran.org/press-releases/statement_on_ioi_rspo/.

RAN. *See* Rainforest Action Network

Raustiala, Kal, and David G. Victor. 2004. The Regime Complex for Plant Genetic Resources. *International Organization* 58 (2): 277–309.

Reardon, Thomas, Marc F. Bellemare, and David Zilberman. 2020. How COVID-19 May Disrupt Food Supply Chains in Developing Countries. International Food Policy Research Institute, April 2, 2020. Accessed March 23, 2022. https://www.ifpri.org/blog/how-covid-19-may-disrupt-food-supply-chains-developing-countries.

Reed, James, Amy Ickowitza, Colas Chervier, Houria Djoudi, Kaala Moombe, Mirjam Ros-Tonen, Malaika Yanou, LindaYuliani, and Terry Sunderland. 2020. Integrated Landscape Approaches in the Tropics: A Brief Stock-Take. *Land Use Policy* 99: 104822. https://doi.org/10.1016/j.landusepol.2020.104822.

Reed, James, Josh Van Vianen, Elizabeth L. Deakin, Jos Barlow, and Terry Sunderland. 2016. Integrated landscape Approaches to Managing Social and Environmental Issues in the Tropics: Learning from the Past to Guide the Future. *Global Change Biology* 22 (7): 2540–2554. https://doi.org/10.1111/gcb.13284.

Reinsberg, Bernhard, and Oliver Westerwinter. 2019. The Global Governance of International Development: Documenting the Rise of Multi-Stakeholder Partnerships and Identifying Underlying Theoretical Explanations. *Review of International Organizations* 16: 59–94. https://doi.org/10.1007/s11558-019-09362-0.

Renckens, Stefan. 2020. *Private Governance and the Public Sector: Regulating Sustainability in the Global Economy*. Cambridge: Cambridge University Press.

Reuters. 2018. European Move to Ban Palm Oil from Biofuels Is "Crop Apartheid"—Malaysia. January 17, 2018. https://www.reuters.com/article/malaysia-palmoil-eu-idUSL3N1PD1NJ.

Riisgaard, Lone. 2009. Global Value Chains, Labor Organization and Private Social Standards: Lessons from East African Cut Flower Industries. *World Development* 37 (2): 326–340. https://doi.org/10.1016/j.worlddev.2008.03.003.

Rio Branco Declaration. 2014. Building Partnerships and Securing Support for Forests, Climate, & Livelihoods. Rio Branco, August 11, 2014. Governors' Climate and Forest Task Force (GCF). https://www.gcftf.org/wp-content/uploads/2020/12/Rio_Branco_Declaration_ENG.pdf.

Risse, Thomas. 2013. Transnational Actors and World Politics. In *Handbook of International Relations*, edited by Walter Carlsnaes, Thomas Risse and Beth A. Simmons, 426–452. Thousand Oaks, CA: Sage.

Risse, Thomas, Stephen C. Roop, and Kathyrn Sikkink, eds. 1999. *The Power of Human Rights: International Norms and Domestic Change.* Cambridge: Cambridge University Press.

Robinson, Elizabeth, and Herry Purnomo. 2019. Palm Oil: An EU Ban Won't Save Asian Rainforests, but Here's What Might Help. The Conversation, May 3, 2019. Accessed March 23, 2022. http://theconversation.com/palm-oil-an-eu-ban-wont-save-asian-rainforests-but-heres-what-might-help-110519.

Rodríguez Fernández-Blanco, Carmen, Sarah L. Burns, and Lukas Giessen. 2019. Mapping the Fragmentation of the International Forest Regime Complex: Institutional Elements, Conflicts and Synergies. *International Environmental Agreements: Politics, Law and Economics* 19 (2): 187–205. https://doi.org/10.1007/s10784-019-09434-x.

Rodrik, Dani. 2011. *The Globalization Paradox: Democracy and the Future of the World Economy.* New York: W. W. Norton.

Roger, Charles, and Peter Dauvergne. 2016. The Rise of Transnational Governance as a Field of Study. *International Studies Review* 18 (3): 415–437. https://doi.org/10.1093/isr/viw001.

Rosenau, James N., and Ernst-Otto Czempiel, eds. 1992. *Governance without Government, Order and Change in World Politics.* Cambridge: Cambridge University Press.

Round Table on Responsible Soy Association (RTRS). 2009. Minutes of the Executive Board. May 25, 2009. On file with author.

Round Table on Responsible Soy Association (RTRS). 2020. Members. Accessed March 24, 2022. http://www.responsiblesoy.org/about-rtrs/members/?lang=en.

Round Table on Responsible Soy Association (RTRS). 2021a. Certified Volumes and Producers. Accessed March 24, 2022. http://www.responsiblesoy.org/mercado/volumenes-y-productores-certificados/?lang=en.

Round Table on Responsible Soy Association (RTRS). 2021b. RTRS Managing Report 2020. August 2021. Accessed March 24, 2022. https://responsiblesoy.org/management-report-2020?lang=en.

Roundtable on Sustainable Palm Oil (RSPO). 2011a. BOG [Board of Governors'] Meeting Minutes: July 13 & 14, 2011. Accessed March 23, 2022. https://rspo.org/resources/rspo-meeting-minutes/board-of-governors-meeting-minutes/2011.

Roundtable on Sustainable Palm Oil (RSPO). 2011b. BOG [Board of Governors'] Meeting Minutes: March 31 & April 1, 2011. Accessed March 23, 2022. https://rspo.org/resources/rspo-meeting-minutes/board-of-governors-meeting-minutes/2011.

Roundtable on Sustainable Palm Oil (RSPO). 2012. Dispute between IOI and the Community of Lond Teran Kanan, Miri, Sarawak Malaysia. Letter from RSPO to IOI and Complainants, May 3, 2012. Accessed March 23, 2022. https://www.rspo.org/file/RSPO%20letter%20to%20IOI%20LTK%20sNGO%2020120503.pdf.

Roundtable on Sustainable Palm Oil (RSPO). 2014. Transforming the Market to Make Sustainable Palm Oil the Norm. Accessed March 23, 2022. https://www.rspo.org/publications/download/16f4adeec882eb2.

Roundtable on Sustainable Palm Oil (RSPO). 2017a. RSPO Annual Communication of Progress 2017: AAA Oils & Fats Pte. Ltd. Accessed March 23, 2022. https://rspo.org/file/acop2017/submissions/aaa%20oils%20fats%20pte.%20ltd.-ACOP2017.pdf.

Roundtable on Sustainable Palm Oil (RSPO). 2017b. RSPO Annual Communication of Progress 2017: Golden Agri-Resources Ltd. Accessed March 23, 2022. https://rspo.org/file/acop2017/submissions/golden%20agri-resources%20ltd-ACOP2017.pdf.

Roundtable on Sustainable Palm Oil (RSPO). 2017c. RSPO Annual Communication of Progress 2017: PT. Musim Mas. Accessed March 23, 2022. https://rspo.org/file/acop2017/submissions/pt.%20musim%20mas-ACOP2017.pdf.

Roundtable on Sustainable Palm Oil (RSPO). 2017d. RSPO Annual Communication of Progress 2017: Wilmar International Limited. Accessed March 23, 2022. https://rspo.org/file/acop2017/submissions/wilmar%20international%20limited-ACOP2017.pdf.

Roundtable on Sustainable Palm Oil (RSPO). 2017e. RSPO Smallholder Strategy. Accessed March 23, 2022. https://rspo.org/smallholders/rspo-smallholder-strategy.

Roundtable on Sustainable Palm Oil (RSPO). 2018a. Calling for Participation and Nomination of Jurisdictional Approach Working Group Members. Announcements, March 30, 2018. Accessed March 23, 2022. https://rspo.org/news-and-events/announcements/calling-for-participation-and-nomination-of-jurisdictional-approach-working-group-members.

Roundtable on Sustainable Palm Oil (RSPO). 2018b. Principles and Criteria Review. Accessed March 24, 2022. https://rspo.org/principles-and-criteria-review.

Roundtable on Sustainable Palm Oil (RSPO). 2018c. Smallholders Working Group. Accessed March 24, 2022. https://rspo.org/about/who-we-are/working-groups/smallholders.

Roundtable on Sustainable Palm Oil (RSPO). 2020a. What Is RSPO PalmTrace? Accessed March 24, 2022. https://rspo.org/palmtrace.

Roundtable on Sustainable Palm Oil (RSPO). 2020b. RSPO Smallholders. Accessed March 24, 2022. https://rspo.org/smallholders.

Roundtable on Sustainable Palm Oil (RSPO). 2021a. Impact. Accessed March 24, 2022. http://www.rspo.org/about/impacts.

References

Roundtable on Sustainable Palm Oil (RSPO). 2021b. New Planting Procedure (NPP), 2021. Accessed March 24, 2022. https://rspo.org/certification/new-planting-procedure.

Roundtable on Sustainable Palm Oil (RSPO). 2021c. RSPO Jurisdictional Approach Pilot Framework. Accessed March 24, 2022. https://jaresourcehub.org/wp-content/uploads/2021/10/rspo-jurisdictional-approach-piloting-framework-eng.pdf.

Roundtable on Sustainable Palm Oil (RSPO). 2022. Search Members. Accessed March 24, 2022. https://rspo.org/members/all.

RSPO. *See* Roundtable on Sustainable Palm Oil

RTRS. *See* Round Table on Responsible Soy Association

Samora, Roberto. 2019a. Brazil Agriculture Minister Calls Amazon Soy Moratorium "Absurd." Reuters, November 13, 2019. Accessed March 24, 2022. https://www.reuters.com/article/us-brazil-soy-moratorium/brazil-agriculture-minister-calls-amazon-soy-moratorium-absurd-idUSKBN1XN2LM.

Samora, Roberto. 2019b. Brazil Farmers Push Traders to End Amazon Soy Moratorium. Reuters, November 5, 2019. Accessed March 24, 2022. https://www.reuters.com/article/us-brazil-soybeans-moratorium/brazil-farmers-push-traders-to-end-amazon-soy-moratorium-idUSKBN1XF2J6.

Samuel, Jency. 2021. Can India Make Palm Oil Sustainable? Third Pole, May 17, 2021. Accessed March 24, 2022. https://www.thethirdpole.net/en/food/can-india-make-palm-oil-sustainable/.

Samuels, David, and Fernando Luiz Abrucio. 2000. Federalism and Democratic Transitions: The "New" Politics of the Governors in Brazil. *Publius* 30 (2): 43–61. https://www.jstor.org/stable/3331087.

Saragih, Bungaran. 2017. Oil Palm Smallholders in Indonesia: Origin, Development Strategy and Contribution to the National Economy. Presentation held at the World Plantation Conference and Exhibition, October 18–20, 2017, Jakarta. Accessed March 24, 2022. https://www.iopri.org/wp-content/uploads/2017/10/WPLACE-17-1.1.-OIL-PALM-SMALLHOLDER-Bungaran-Saragih.pdf.

Sawit Watch. 2020. Profile. Accessed March 24, 2022. https://sawitwatch.or.id/profil/.

Schilling-Vacaflor, Almut, and Andrea Lenschow. 2021. Hardening Foreign Corporate Accountability through Mandatory Due Diligence in the European Union? New Trends and Persisting Challenges. *Regulation & Governance*. https://doi.org/10.1111/rego.12402.

Schleifer, Philip. 2013. Orchestrating Sustainability: The Case of European Union Biofuel Governance. *Regulation & Governance* 7 (4): 533–546. http://dx.doi.org/10.1111/rego.12037.

Schleifer, Philip. 2016a. Let's Bargain: Setting Standards for Sustainable Biofuels. In *Sustainability Politics and Limited Statehood: Contesting the New Modes of Governance*, edited by Aljeandro Esguerra, Nicole Helmerich, and Thomas Risse, 47–73. New York: Springer.

Schleifer, Philip. 2016b. Private Governance Undermined: India and the Roundtable on Sustainable Palm Oil. *Global Environmental Politics* 16 (1): 38–58.

Schleifer, Philip. 2017. Private Regulation and Global Economic Change: The Drivers of Sustainable Agriculture in Brazil. *Governance* 30 (4): 687–703. http://dx.doi.org/10.1111/gove.12267.

Schleifer, Philip. 2019. Varieties of Multi-Stakeholder Governance: Selecting Legitimation Strategies in Transnational Sustainability Politics. *Globalizations* 16 (1): 50–66. https://doi.org/10.1080/14747731.2018.1518863.

Schleifer, Philip, Matteo Fiorini, and Graeme Auld. 2019. Transparency in Transnational Governance: The Determinants of Information Disclosure of Voluntary Sustainability Programs. *Regulation & Governance* 13 (4): 488–506. https://doi.org/10.1111/rego.12241.

Schleifer, Philip, Matteo Fiorini, and Luc Fransen. 2019. Missing the Bigger Picture: A Population-level Analysis of Transnational Private Governance Organizations Active in the Global South. *Ecological Economics* 164: 106362. https://doi.org/10.1016/j.ecolecon.2019.106362.

Schleifer, Philip, and Yixian Sun. 2018. Emerging Markets and Private Governance: The Political Economy of Sustainable Palm Oil in China and India. *Review of International Political Economy* 25 (2): 1–25. https://doi.org/10.1080/09692290.2017.1418759.

Schleifer, Philip, and Yixian Sun. 2020. Reviewing the impact of sustainability certification on food security in developing countries. *Global Food Security* 24: 100337. https://doi.org/10.1016/j.gfs.2019.100337.

Schlesinger, Sergio. 2010. Sugar Cane and Land Use Change in Brazil: Biofuel Crops, Indirect Land Use Change and Emissions. Friends of the Earth Europe, August 2010. Accessed March 24, 2022. https://www.foeeurope.org/sites/default/files/publications/foee_biofuels_briefing_sugarcane_0810.pdf?msclkid=0933a635ab9a11ecaf9011e84120fe76.

Schmidt, Vivien A., and Mark Thatcher, eds. 2013. *Resilient Liberalism in Europe's Political Economy*. Cambridge: Cambridge University Press.

Schnepf, Randall D., Erik Dohlman, and Christine Bolling. 2001. Agriculture in Brazil and Argentina: Developments and Prospects for Major Field Crops. Market and Trade Economics Division, Economic Research Service, U.S. Department of Agriculture, Agriculture and Trade Report. WRS-01-3. Accessed March 24, 2022. https://www.ers.usda.gov/webdocs/outlooks/40339/15069_wrs013fm_1_.pdf?v=5286.8&msclkid=8e25ac79abd811ec91305b1011836a6e.

References

Scholte, Jan Aaart. 2020. Multistakeholderism Filling the Global Governance Gap? Research Overview for the Global Challenges Foundation, April 2020. Accessed March 24, 2022. https://globalchallenges.org/multistakeholderism-filling-the-global-governance-gap/.

Schouten, Greetje, and Verena Bitzer. 2015. The Emergence of Southern Standards in Agricultural Value Chains: A New Trend in Sustainability Governance? *Ecological Economics* 120: 175–184. https://doi.org/10.1016/j.ecolecon.2015.10.017.

Schouten, Greetje, and Pieter Glasbergen. 2011. Creating Legitimacy in Global Private Governance: The Case of the Roundtable on Sustainable Palm Oil. *Ecological Economics* 70 (11): 1891–1899. https://doi.org/10.1016/j.ecolecon.2011.03.012.

Schouten, Greetje, and Otto Hospes. 2018. Public and Private Governance in Interaction: Changing Interpretations of Sovereignty in the Field of Sustainable Palm Oil. *Sustainability* 10 (12): 4811. https://www.mdpi.com/2071-1050/10/12/4811.

Schouten, Greetje, Pieter Leroy, and Pieter Glasbergen. 2012. On the Deliberative Capacity of Private Multi-Stakeholder Governance: The Roundtables on Responsible Soy and Sustainable Palm Oil. *Ecological Economics* 83: 42–50. https://doi.org/10.1016/j.ecolecon.2012.08.007.

Schwartzman, Stephan, and Molly Kingston. 1997. *Global Deforestation, Timber, and the Struggle for Sustainability*. New York: Environmental Defense Fund.

Serdijn, Merel, Ans Kolk, and Luc Fransen. 2020. Uncovering Missing Links in Global Value Chain Research and Implications for Corporate Social Responsibility and International Business. *Critical Perspectives on International Business* 17 (4): 619–636. https://doi.org/10.1108/cpoib-01-2020-0002.

Seruyan Regency. 2016. Working Group on Jurisdictional Certification of Palm Oil in Seruyan District. Meeting Minutes, March 11, 2016. On file with author.

Setzer, Joana. 2017. How Subnational Governments are Rescaling Environmental Governance: The Case of the Brazilian State of São Paulo. *Journal of Environmental Policy & Planning* 19 (5): 503–519. https://doi.org/10.1080/1523908X.2014.984669.

Seymour, Frances. 2020. Insider: 4 Reasons Why a Jurisdictional Approach for REDD+ Crediting Is Superior to a Project-Based Approach. World Resources Institute, May 5, 2020. Accessed March 24, 2022. https://www.wri.org/insights/insider-4-reasons-why-jurisdictional-approach-redd-crediting-superior-project-based.

Seymour, Frances J., Leony Aurora, and Joko Arif. 2020. The Jurisdictional Approach in Indonesia: Incentives, Actions, and Facilitating Connections. *Frontiers in Forests and Global Change* 3 (124). https://doi.org/10.3389/ffgc.2020.503326.

Seymour, Frances, and Jonah Busch. 2016. *Why Forests? Why Now? The Science, Economics, and Politics of Tropical Forests and Climate Change*. Washington, DC: Center for Global Development. Accessed March 24, 2022. https://www.cgdev.org/sites/default/files/Seymour-Busch-why-forests-why-now-full-book.PDF.

Shirotori, Miho, and Ana Cristina Molina. 2009. South-South Trade: The Reality Check. United Nations Conference on Trade and Development, Geneva. Accessed March 24, 2022. https://unctad.org/en/docs/ditctab20081_en.pdf.

Shiva, Vandana. 2016. *The Violence of the Green Revolution: Third World Agriculture, Ecology, and Politics*. Lexington: University Press of Kentucky.

Singh, Kalpana. 2014. Retail Sector in India: Present Scenario, Emerging Opportunities and Challenges. *Journal of Business and Management* 16 (4): 72–81. https://doi.org/10.9790/487X-16417281.

Singh, Vijaita. 2015. Greenpeace India's Registration Cancelled. *The Hindu*, September 4, 2015. Accessed March 24, 2022. https://www.thehindu.com/news/national/greenpeace-indias-registration-cancelled/article7613184.ece.

Slavin, Terry. 2018. Deadline 2020: "We Won't End Deforestation through Certification Schemes," Brands Admit. Reuters Events, November 1, 2018. Accessed March 24, 2022. https://www.reutersevents.com/sustainability/deadline-2020-we-wont-end-deforestation-through-certification-schemes-brands-admit.

Smith, W. K., E. Nelson, J. A. Johnson, S. Polasky, J. C. Milder, J. S. Gerber, P. C. West, S. Siebert, K. A. Brauman, K. M. Carlson, M. Arbuthnot, J. P. Rozza, and D. N. Pennington. 2019. Voluntary Sustainability Standards Could Significantly Reduce Detrimental Impacts of Global Agriculture. *Proceedings of the National Academy of Sciences* 116 (6): 2130–2137. https://doi.org/10.1073/pnas.1707812116.

SMP. *See* Sustainable Municipalities Program

Soares-Filho, Britaldo, Raoni Rajão, Marcia Macedo, Arnaldo Carneiro, William Costa, Michael Coe, Hermann Rodrigues, and Ane Alencar. 2014. Cracking Brazil's Forest Code. *Science* 344 (6182): 363–364. https://doi.org/10.1126/science.1246663.

Solidaridad. 2019. Drafting China's Sustainable Soy Guidelines. November 8, 2019. Accessed March 24, 2022. https://www.solidaridadnetwork.org/news/drafting-chinas-sustainable-soy-guidelines.

Song, Xiao-Peng, Matthew C. Hansen, Peter Potapov, Bernard Adusei, Jeffrey Pickering, Marcos Adami, Andre Lima, Viviana Zalles, Stephen V. Stehman, Carlos M. Di Bella, Maria C. Conde, Esteban J. Copati, Lucas B. Fernandes, Andres Hernandez-Serna, Samuel M. Jantz, Amy H. Pickens, Svetlana Turubanova, and Alexandra Tyukavina. 2021. Massive Soybean Expansion in South America since 2000 and Implications for Conservation. *Nature Sustainability*, June 7, 2021. https://doi.org/10.1038/s41893-021-00729-z.

Staritz, Cornelia, Gary Gereffi, and Olivier Cattaneo. 2011. Editorial: Special Issue on Shifting End Markets and Upgrading Prospects in Global Value Chains.

International Journal of Technological Learning, Innovation and Development 4 (1/2/3): 1–12.

Stickler, Claudia M., Amy E. Duchelle, Juan Pablo Ardila, Daniel C. Nepstad, Olivia David, C. Chan, Juan Guillermo Rojas, Rafael Vargas, T. Bezzera, Lowell Pritchard, J. Simmonds, Joanna C. Durbin, Gabriela Simonet, Swetha Peteru, Mella Komalasari, Maria DiGiano, and Matthew Warren. 2018. The State of Jurisdictional Sustainability: Synthesis for Practitioners and Policymakers. Center for International Forestry Research, Governors' Climate and Forest Task Force. Accessed March 24, 2022. https://www.cifor.org/knowledge/publication/6999/.

Strange, Susan. 1982. Cave! Hic Dragones: A Critique of Regime Analysis. *International Organization* 36 (2): 479–496. http://www.jstor.org/stable/2706530.

Strange, Susan. 1988. *States and Markets*. London: Pinter.

Strange, Susan. 1996. *The Retreat of the State: The Diffusion of Power in the World Economy*. Cambridge: Cambridge University Press.

Sun, Yixian. 2022. *Certifying China: The Rise and Limits of Transnational Sustainability Governance in Emerging Economies*. Cambridge, MA: MIT Press.

Sun, Yixian, and Hamish van der Ven. 2020. Swimming in Their Own Direction: Explaining Domestic Variation in Homegrown Sustainability Governance for Aquaculture in Asia. *Ecological Economics* 167: 106445. https://doi.org/10.1016/j.ecolecon.2019.106445.

Supply Change. 2020a. Commercial Agriculture Drives At Least Two-thirds of Tropical Deforestation. Supply Chain: Commitments that Count. Accessed March 24, 2022. http://www.supply-change.org/#remove.

Supply Change. 2020b. Global Market Overview: A Summary of Key Indicators on Global Commodity Commitments. Accessed March 24, 2022. https://supply-change.org/#market-overview.

Sustainable Municipalities Program (SMP). 2019. Mato Grosso's Sustainable Municipalities Program. Accessed March 24, 2022. http://municipiossustentaveis.mt.gov.br/#!programa/plano-de-metas.

Sustainable Palm Oil Coalition for India (ISPOC). 2021a. Members. Accessed March 23, 2022. http://www.indiaspoc.org/member.

Sustainable Palm Oil Coalition for India (ISPOC). 2021b. Steering Committee. Accessed March 23, 2022. http://www.indiaspoc.org/steering.

Sustainable Palm Oil Coalition for India (ISPOC). 2021c. Working Groups. Accessed March 23, 2022. http://www.indiaspoc.org/working.

Synnott, Timothy. 2005. Some Notes on the Early Years of FSC. Accessed March 24, 2022. https://ic.fsc.org/preview.notes-on-the-early-years-of-fsc.a-798.pdf.

Szulecki, Kacper, Philipp Pattberg, and Frank Biermann. 2011. Explaining Variation in the Effectiveness of Transnational Energy Partnerships. *Governance* 24 (4): 713–736. http://dx.doi.org/10.1111/j.1468-0491.2011.01544.x.

Taylor, Rod, and Charlotte Streck. 2018. The Elusive Impact of the Deforestation-Free Supply Chain Movement. World Resources Institute, Working Paper, June 2018. Washington, DC: World Resources Institute. http://wriorg.s3.amazonaws.com/s3fs-public/ending-tropical-deforestation-supply-chain-movement.pdf.

Thorstensen, Vera, Reinhard Weissinger, and Xinhua Sun. 2015. Private Standards: Implications for Trade Development, and Governance, E15 Initiative. International Centre for Trade and Sustainable Development and World Economic Forum, Geneva. Accessed August 12, 2022. http://e15initiative.org/wp-content/uploads/2015/07/E15-Regulatory-Thorstensen-et-al.-final.pdf.

Trading Economics. 2021. Commodities. Accessed March 24, 2022. https://tradingeconomics.com/

Transport and Environment. 2020. Why Is Palm Oil Biodiesel Bad? Accessed March 24, 2022. https://www.transportenvironment.org/challenges/energy/biofuels/why-is-palm-oil-biodiesel-bad/#:~:text=Palm%20oil%20biodiesel%20is%20the,be%20needed%20to%20quench%20it.

Trase. 2018. Trase Yearbook 2018, Sustainability in Forest-Risk Supply Chains: Spotlight on Brazilian Soy. Accessed March 24, 2022. http://resources.trase.earth/documents/TraseYearbook2018.pdf.

Trase. 2019. New Insights on Indonesian Palm Oil Exports, 2013–2018. *Infobrief* 7. Accessed March 24, 2022. http://resources.trase.earth/documents/infobriefs/Trase%20Infobrief%207_En.pdf.

Trase. 2020a. Corporate Ownership and Dominance of Indonesia's Palm Oil Supply Chains, *Infobrief* 9. January 2020. Accessed March 24, 2022. http://resources.trase.earth/documents/infobriefs/infobrief09EN.pdf.

Trase. 2020b. The State of Forest Risk Supply Chains: Executive Summary. Trase Yearbook 2020. Accessed March 24, 2022. https://insights.trase.earth/yearbook/highlights/expansion-and-deforestation/.

Trase. 2021. Trase Data Highlights EU's Role in Deforestation. Trase Insights, April 14, 2021. Accessed March 24, 2022. https://insights.trase.earth/insights/trase-data-highlights-eus-role-in-deforestation.

Trase. n.d. Supply Chain Data Explorer. Accessed March 23, 2022. https://explore.trase.earth.

Tropical Forest Alliance. 2018. Emerging Market Consumers and Deforestation: Risks and Opportunities of Growing Demand for Soft Commodities in China and Beyond. Geneva: World Economic Forum. Accessed March 24, 2022. https://www

References

.tropicalforestalliance.org/assets/Uploads/47530_Emerging-markets_consumers_and_deforestation_report_2018.pdf.

Tropical Forest Alliance. 2020. Collective Action Agenda. Accessed March 24, 2022. https://www.tropicalforestalliance.org/assets/Uploads/Collective-Action-Agenda-Four-Pager.pdf.

Trustea. 2020. Trustea Year Book 2020. Accessed March 24, 2022. https://trustea.org/wp-content/uploads/2021/04/trustea-Yearbook-2020-1.pdf.

Tscharntke, Teja, Jeffrey C. Milder, Götz Schroth, Yann Clough, Fabrice DeClerck, Anthony Waldron, Robert Rice, and Jaboury Ghazoul. 2015. Conserving Biodiversity Through Certification of Tropical Agroforestry Crops at Local and Landscape Scales. *Conservation Letters* 8 (1): 14–23. https://doi.org/10.1111/conl.12110.

UNCTAD. *See* United Nations Conference on Trade and Development

Underdal, Arild. 2008. Determining the Causal Significance of Institutions: Accomplishments and Challenges. In *Institutions and Environmental Change*, edited by Oran R. Young, Leslie A. King, and Heike Schroeder, 49–78. Cambridge: Cambridge University Press. https://10.7551/mitpress/9780262240574.001.0001.

UNFCCC. *See* United Nations Framework Convention on Climate Change

UNFSS. *See* United Nations Forum on Sustainability Standards

Unilever. 2017. Driving a New Approach to Sustainable Palm Oil. Press Release, January 17, 2017. Accessed March 24, 2022. https://www.unilever.com/news/news-and-features/Feature-article/2017/We-are-driving-a-new-approach-to-sustainable-palm-oil.html.

United Nations. 1992. Agenda 21, United Nations Conference on Environment and Development, Rio de Janeiro, Brazil, June 3–14, 1992. Accessed March 24, 2022. https://sustainabledevelopment.un.org/content/documents/Agenda21.pdf.

United Nations. 2006. Annan Stresses "Vital" UN Partnership with Business to Advance Responsible Globalization, October 23, 2006. Accessed March 24, 2022. https://news.un.org/en/story/2006/10/197022-annan-stresses-vital-un-partnership-business-advance-responsible-globalization.

United Nations. n.d. Sustainability. Accessed March 24, 2022. https://www.un.org/en/academic-impact/sustainability.

United Nations Conference on Trade and Development (UNCTAD). 2004. The New Geography of International Economic Relations. Trade and Development Board, September 17, 2004. Accessed March 24, 2022. https://unctad.org/en/docs//tdb51d6_en.pdf.

United Nations Department of Economic and Social Affairs. 2021. Top Economists Warn COVID-19 Impacts Will Be Severe and Long-Lasting for Developing Countries.

Accessed March 24, 2022. https://www.un.org/en/desa/top-economists-warn-covid-19-impacts-will-be-severe-and-long-lasting-developing-countries.

United Nations Forum on Sustainability Standards (UNFSS). 2013. Voluntary Sustainability Standards. Accessed March 24, 2022. https://unfss.org/wp-content/uploads/2012/05/unfss-report-initiatives-2_draft_lores.pdf.

United Nations Framework Convention on Climate Change (UNFCCC). 2021. Presidency Event: Facing the Facts Unpacking the Forest, Agriculture and Commodity Trade Dialogue to Tackle Deforestation. Filmed November 6, 2021, at Plenary Cairn Gorm. Video, 2:49:24. Accessed March 24, 2022. https://unfccc-cop26.streamworld.de/webcast/presidency-event-facing-the-facts-unpacking-the-fo.

United States Department of Agriculture (USDA). 2020. Brazil: Soybean Production. Accessed March 24, 2022. https://ipad.fas.usda.gov/rssiws/al/crop_production_maps/Brazil/Municipality/Brazil_Soybean_Production_Municipality.jpg.

Utting, Peter, and Ann Zammit. 2008. United Nations-Business Partnerships: Good Intentions and Contradictory Agendas. *Journal of Business Ethics* 90 (1): 39. https://doi.org/10.1007/s10551-008-9917-7.

van der Ven, Hamish. 2018. Gatekeeper Power: Understanding the Influence of Lead Firms over Transnational Sustainability Standards. *Review of International Political Economy* 25 (5): 624–646. https://doi.org/10.1080/09692290.2018.1490329.

van der Ven, Hamish, and D. Barmes. 2019. Learning to Live Together: Competition and Complementarity in Public and Private Land Use Governance. Paper presented at the 4th International Conference on Public Policy, Montreal, Canada, June 28, 2019.

van der Ven, Hamish, Catherine Rothacker, and Benjamin Cashore. 2018. Do Eco-Labels Prevent Deforestation? Lessons from Non-State Market Driven Governance in the Soy, Palm Oil, and Cocoa Sectors. *Global Environmental Change* 52: 141–151. https://doi.org/10.1016/j.gloenvcha.2018.07.002.

van Houten, Heloïse, and Peter de Koning. 2018. Jurisdictional Approaches for Deforestation-Free and Sustainable Palm Oil. Mekon Ecology, December 2018. Accessed March 24, 2022. https://mekonecology.net/wp-content/uploads/2018/12/Mekon-Ecology-2018-Jurisdictional-Approaches-Borneo.pdf.

Varns, Theodore, Rane Cortez, Lex Hovani, and Paul Kingsbury. 2018. *São Félix do Xingu, Brazil: A Jurisdictional Approach to Conserving the Amazon*. Arlington, VA: Nature Conservancy. Accessed March 24, 2022. https://www.nature.org/content/dam/tnc/nature/en/documents/TNC_JurisdictionalApproaches_CaseStudies_Brazil.pdf.

Vickers, Adrian. 2013. *A History of Modern Indonesia*. 2nd ed. Cambridge: Cambridge University Press.

Vit, Jonathan. 2016. Under Government Pressure, Palm Oil Giants Disband Green Pledge. Mongabay, July 1, 2016. Accessed March 24, 2022. https://news.mongabay.com/2016/07/under-government-pressure-palm-oil-giants-disband-green-pledge/.

Vogel, David. 2009. The Private Regulation of Global Corporate Conduct: Achievements and Limitations. *Business & Society* 49 (1): 68–87. https://doi.org/10.1177/0007650309343407.

von Essen, Marius, and Eric F. Lambin. 2021. Jurisdictional Approaches to Sustainable Resource Use. *Frontiers in Ecology and the Environment* 19 (3): 159–167. https://doi.org/10.1002/fee.2299.

Watts, John D., and Silvia Irawan. 2018. Oil Palm in Indonesia. LEAVES (Leveraging Agricultural Value Chains to Enhance Tropical Tree Cover and Slow Deforestation), Background Paper. Accessed March 24, 2022. https://www.profor.info/sites/profor.info/files/Oil%20Palm_Case%20Study_LEAVES_2018.pdf.

West, Paul C., Deepak K. Ray, and James S. Gerber. 2020. Improving the Broader Effectiveness of Zero-Deforestation Commitments and Commodity Standards, Meridian Institute, Washington, DC. Accessed March 24, 2022. https://www.evidensia.eco/resources/930/improving-the-broader-effectiveness-of-zero-deforestation-commitments-and-commodity-standards/.

WFP. *See* World Food Programme

Whelan, Glen, and Judy Muthuri. 2015. Chinese State-Owned Enterprises and Human Rights: The Importance of National and Intra-Organizational Pressures. *Business & Society* 56 (5): 738–781. https://doi.org/10.1177/0007650315612399.

Wicke, Birka, Richard Sikkema, Veronika Dornburg, and Andre Faaij. 2011. Exploring Land Use Changes and the Role of Palm Oil Production in Indonesia and Malaysia. *Land Use Policy* 28 (1): 193–206. https://doi.org/10.1016/j.landusepol.2010.06.001.

Wijaya, Arief, Tjokorda Nirarta "Koni" Samadhi, and Juliane Reidinar. 2019. Indonesia Is Reducing Deforestation, but Problem Areas Remain. World Resources Institute, July 24, 2019. Accessed March 24, 2022. https://www.wri.org/insights/indonesia-reducing-deforestation-problem-areas-remain.

Wijaya, Atika, and Pieter Glasbergen. 2016. Toward a New Scenario in Agricultural Sustainability Certification? The Response of the Indonesian National Government to Private Certification. *Journal of Environment & Development* 25 (2): 219–246. https://doi.org/10.1177/1070496516640857.

Willer, H., G. Sampson, V. Voora, D. Dang, and J. Lernoud. 2019. The State of Sustainable Markets 2019: Statistics and Emerging Trends. Evidensia. Accessed March 24, 2022. https://www.evidensia.eco/resources/900/state-of-sustainable-markets-2019-statistics-and-emerging-trends/.

Wilmar. 2013. No Deforestation, No Peat, No Exploitation Policy. December 5, 2013. Accessed March 24, 2022. https://www.wilmar-international.com/sustainability/wp-content/uploads/2012/11/No-Deforestation-No-Peat-No-Exploitation-Policy.pdf.

Wilmar. 2018. Action Plan to Improve and Accelerate NDPE Implementation. October 5, 2018. Accessed March 24, 2022. https://www.wilmar-international.com/sustainability/wp-content/uploads/2018/10/Wilmar-Action-Plan-Announcement-Final-5-Oct-2018.pdf.

Wilmar. 2020. Deforestation-Free Palm Oil: Our Pledge, Our Progress. March 2020. Accessed March 24, 2022. https://www.wilmar-international.com/docs/default-source/default-document-library/sustainability/wilmar_deforestationprogressreport_mar20_final.pdf?sfvrsn=69b278b1_2.

Wolf, M. 2020. The Threat of Long Economic Covid Looms. *Financial Times*, October 20, 2020. Accessed March 24, 2022. https://www.ft.com/content/f9a0c784-712e-4bf9-b994-55f8d63316d9.

World Bank. 2004. Implementation Mechanisms for Codes of Conduct: Study Prepared for the CSR Practice Foreign Investment Advisory Service, Washington, DC.

World Economic Forum. 2019. We Can Feed the World in a Sustainable Way, but We Need to Act Now. January 24, 2019. Accessed March 24, 2022. https://www.weforum.org/agenda/2019/01/we-can-feed-the-world-in-a-sustainable-way-but-we-need-to-act-now/.

World Food Programme (WFP). 2020. COVID-19: Potential Impact on the World's Poorest People. April 2020. Accessed March 24, 2022. https://docs.wfp.org/api/documents/WFP-0000114040/download/.

World Resource Institute (WRI). 2017. Drivers of Deforestation in Indonesia, Inside and Outside Concession Areas. July 19, 2017. Accessed March 24, 2022. http://www.wri.org/blog/2017/07/drivers-deforestation-indonesia-inside-and-outside-concessions-areas.

Worster, Donald. 2004. *Dust Bowl: The Southern Plains in the 1930s*. Oxford: Oxford University Press.

WRI. *See* World Resource Institute

WTO. *See* World Trade Organization

World Trade Organization (WTO). 2019. Indonesia Initiates WTO Dispute Complaint against EU Biofuels Measures. December 16, 2019. Accessed March 24, 2022. https://www.wto.org/english/news_e/news19_e/ds593rfc_16dec19_e.htm.

WWF. 2004. Some Thoughts on and Lessons Learned from Commodity-Specific Dialogues. Memo by Jason Clay, June 11, 2004.

References

WWF. 2005. Oil Palm, Soy and Tropical Forests: A Strategy for Life. Forest Conversion Initiative, September 2005.

WWF. 2010. Certification and Roundtables: Do They Work? September 2010. Accessed March 24, 2022. http://assets.wwf.org.uk/downloads/wwf_certification_and_roundtables_briefing.pdf.

WWF. 2012. Market Transformation Strategy. Accessed March 24, 2022. http://awsassets.panda.org/downloads/market_transformation_initiative_strategy_1.pdf.

WWF. 2017. Credible Certification: Agriculture. Accessed March 24, 2022. http://wwf.panda.org/what_we_do/how_we_work/our_global_goals/markets/mti_solutions/certification/agriculture/.

WWF. 2021a. Deforestation Fronts: Drivers and Responses in a Changing World. Accessed March 24, 2022. https://wwfint.awsassets.panda.org/downloads/deforestation_fronts___drivers_and_responses_in_a_changing_world___full_report_1.pdf.

WWF. 2021b. Sustainable Palm Oil Uptake in Asia: Where Do We Go from Here? September 2021. Accessed March 24, 2022. https://wwfint.awsassets.panda.org/downloads/sustainable_palm_oil_uptake_in_asia_sept_2021.pdf.

Yaap, Betsy, and Gary Paoli. 2014. A Comparison of Leading Palm Oil Certification Standards Applied in Indonesia: Towards Defining Emerging Norms of Good Practices. *Daemeter*, May 2014. Accessed March 24, 2022. http://daemeter.org/new/uploads/20140505064302.Daemeter_Comparison_of_Palm_Oil_Certification_Standards_FullReport_Eng.pdf

Yasmin, Nur, and Ridho Syukra. 2020. Indonesia's Thirst for Biodiesel May Undercut Global Palm Oil Supply. *Jakarta Globe*, February 4, 2020. Accessed March 24, 2022. https://jakartaglobe.id/business/indonesias-thirst-for-biodiesel-may-undercut-global-palm-oil-supply

Yifan, Jiang. 2021. Stalemate: Sustainable Palm Oil Struggles to Take Off in China. *China Dialogue*, April 27, 2021. Accessed March 24, 2022. https://chinadialogue.net/en/food/stalemate-sustainable-palm-oil-struggles-to-take-off-in-china/.

Young, Oran R., ed. 1999. *The Effectiveness of International Environmental Regimes: Causal Connections and Behavioral Mechanisms*. Cambridge, MA: MIT Press.

Young, Oran R. 2002. *The Institutional Dimensions of Environmental Change: Fit, Interplay, and Scale*. Cambridge, MA: MIT Press.

Yulian, Bayu Eka, Arya Hadi Dharmawan, Endriatmo Soetarto, and Pablo Pacheco. 2020. Silent Expansion of Oil Palm Plantation: The Tragedy of Access Between Bundle of Right and Power. *Journal of Economics and Sustainable Development* 11 (6): 71–80. https://doi.org/10.7176/JESD/11-6-08.

Zanon, Silvestrin, Raquel Saes, and Maria Sylvia Macchione. 2010. Soybean Production in Brazil: Main Determinants of Property Sizes. *Proceedings in System Dynamics and Innovation in Food Networks*: 292–306. https://doi.org/10.22004/ag.econ.100476.

Zeitlin, Jonathan, and Christine Overdevest. 2019. Experimentalist Interactions: FLEGT and the Transnational Timber Legality Regime. Amsterdam Centre for European Studies, SSRN Research Paper 2019/4. https://doi.org/10.2139/ssrn.3406065.

Zeitlin, Jonathan, and Christine Overdevest. 2021. Experimentalist Interactions: Joining up the Transnational Timber Legality Regime. *Regulation & Governance* 15 (3): 686–708. https://doi.org/10.1111/rego.12350.

Zelli, Fariborz, Karin Bäckstrand, Naghmeh Nasiritousi, Jakob Skovgaard, and Oscar Widerberg, eds. 2020. *Governing the Climate-Energy Nexus: Institutional Complexity and Its Challenges to Effectiveness and Legitimacy*. Cambridge: Cambridge University Press. https://doi.org/10.1017/9781108676397.

Zelli, Fariborz, and Harro van Asselt. 2013. Introduction: The Institutional Fragmentation of Global Environmental Governance: Causes, Consequences, and Responses. *Global Environmental Politics* 13 (3): 1–13. http://dx.doi.org/10.1162/GLEP_a_00180.

Zen, Zahari, Colin Barlow, Ria Gondowarsito, and John F. McCarthy. 2016. Interventions to Promote Smallholder Oil Palm and Socio-Economic Improvement in Indonesia. In *The Oil Palm Complex: Smallholders, Agribusiness and the State in Indonesia and Malaysia*, edited by Rob Cramb and John F. McCarthy, 78–108. Singapore: National University of Singapore Press.

Zubizarreta, Iker, Alessandro Seravalli, and Saioa Arrizabalaga. 2016. Smart City Concept: What It Is and What It Should Be. *Journal of Urban Planning and Development* 142 (1): 04015005. https://doi.org/(ASCE)UP.1943-5444.0000282.

Zu Ermgassen, Erasmus K. H., Javier Godar, Michael J. Lathuillière, Pernilla Löfgren, Toby Gardner, André Vasconcelos, and Patrick Meyfroidt. 2020. The Origin, Supply Chain, and Deforestation Footprint of Brazil's Beef Exports. *Proceedings of the National Academy of Sciences* 117 (50): 31770–31779. https://doi.org/10.1073/pnas.2003270117.

Index

AAA Oils & Fats Pte, 118
ABIOVE (Brazilian Association of Vegetable Oils), 97–98
Accountability Framework Initiative, 59, 61
Action Plan for Prevention and Control of Deforestation and Burning (Mato Grosso, Brazil), 147
ADM, 10
Africa. *See also specific countries*
 agricultural support programs in, 48
 colonial legacies in, 106, 180
 palm oil sector in, 106
Agricultural sector. *See also specific sectors (e.g., palm oil sector)*
 certification programs in (*see* Certification programs)
 deforestation by (*see* Commodity-driven deforestation)
 fair trade in, 2, 5–6, 30
 Green Revolution in, 48, 153
 organic certification in, 2, 5–6, 30
 political economy context for (*see* Political economy analysis)
 subsidies for, 49
 supply chains in (*see* Supply chains)
 transformations in global, 47–50, 169–170
 transnational governance in (*see* Transnational business governance)
 tropical commodity boom in, 52–55, 64–65
 Tropical Oil Crop Revolution in, 1–2, 11, 47, 48–50, 52
Aidenvironment, 122, 123
AKK Kamani, 129
Albani, Marco, 3
Aliança da Terra, 99
Alliance of Consumption and Green Supply Chains, 126
Amazon Soy Moratorium, 31–32, 61, 69, 98, 99
Amsterdam Declaration on Deforestation, 63, 96
Amsterdam Declarations Partnerships, 88, 187n8
Amsterdam Palm Oil Declaration, 88
Apical Group, 111, 114, 118–119, 188n5 (chap. 5)
Aprosoja (Brazilian Association of Soy Producers), 97–98
Artificial intelligence, 179. *See also* Technology
Asda, 40
Asia. *See also specific countries*
 agricultural support programs in, 48
 colonial legacies in, 106–107, 180
 commodity-driven deforestation in, 11
 palm oil industry history in, 106–108
 Tropical Oil Crop Revolution in, 49, 50
Associação Amigos da Terra, 99

Astra Agro Lesarti, 110
Audits, 82, 119–122, 134, 182
Australia, 154
Automotive industry, 40

B&Q, 6
Bangladesh, 85
Basel Criteria for Responsible Soy Production, 60
Beef or cattle sector
 certification programs in, 171
 deforestation by, 11, 146, 188n8
 exports of, 78
 imports of, 63
 soy sector displacing, 2
 sustainable markets for, 74–78, 103
Beidahuang Group, 94
Ben & Jerry's, 1, 165
Berau Forest Carbon Program, 151–152
Biodiversity loss, 10–11, 31, 49, 79, 108, 139
Biofuels
 agricultural transformation with demand for, 50
 palm oil in, 50, 52, 84, 86, 112, 114
 soy in, 92
 sustainability regulations on, 37, 50, 52, 86, 138, 186n2 (chap. 3)
Black Lives Matter, 180
BlackRock, 177, 178
Blockchain, 179
BNP Paribas, 177
Bogor Agricultural University, 22
Bolsonaro, Jair, 98–99
Bonsucro Production Standard, 9, 31, 37
Bootcamps, 30
Borneo, 10–11
Brazil
 agricultural trade by, 51–52 (*see also specific products*)
 agricultural transformation in, 50
 beef or cattle sector in, 2, 78, 146

 COVID-19 pandemic effects on, 181
 deforestation in, 18, 55, 92, 97–99, 143–147, 149
 domestic consumption in, 52, 78
 Governors' Climate and Forest Task Force in, 145, 146, 147
 jurisdictional approach in, 140, 143–151, 159, 160, 163
 Mato Grosso's Produce, Conserve, and Include Strategy in, 145–151, 159, 160, 163
 soy sector in, 2, 52, 55, 62, 66, 69, 78, 92–100, 146, 171
 subnational governments in, 144–151
 sugarcane production standard in, 37
 sustainability governance in, 20, 62, 140, 143–151, 159, 160, 163
Brazilian Association of Soy Producers (Aprosoja), 97–98
Brazilian Association of Vegetable Oils (ABIOVE), 97–98
BRICS (Brazil, Russia, India, China, South Africa) economies, 51–52, 181. *See also specific countries*
Bright Food Company, 113
British Soil Association, 5
Bunge, 10
Businesses
 agricultural (*see* Agricultural sector; *specific sectors*)
 markets for (*see* Markets)
 power of (*see* Corporate power)
 supply chains for (*see* Supply chains)
 transnational governance by (*see* Transnational business governance)
Business Responsibility and Sustainability Report framework (India), 127

Cairns Group of Fair Trading Nations, 49, 51, 186nn1, 3
Captive value chains, 40
Cargill, 2, 10, 117
Carrefour, 150

Index

Cattle sector. *See* Commodity-driven deforestation, beef or cattle sector
CCICED (China Council for International Cooperation on Environment and Development), 126
Center for International Forestry Research, 22
Central Kalimantan's Roadmap to Low-Deforestation Rural Development, 153–158, 159–160, 161, 163
Centre for International Forestry Research, 11, 86
Centre for Responsible Business, 20, 22, 87, 127
Certification programs
  fair trade, 2, 5–6, 30
  impact evaluation of, 30–32, 74
  institutionalist perspective on, 29
  jurisdictional approach and, 155, 157
  mainstreaming of, 6–8
  organic, 2, 5–6, 30
  palm oil sector, 7–8, 31–32, 65, 79, 84–91, 100–102, 117–124, 132, 155, 157, 171, 173
  regulatory authority of, 36–37
  soy sector, 65, 79, 92–102, 171
  sustainable markets and, 74–80, 84–103, 170–171
  zero-deforestation regime complex and, 61, 65, 69, 117
CGF. *See* Consumer Goods Forum
China
  agricultural trade by, 51–52, 94
    (*see also specific products*)
  civil society pressure in, 83
  commodity-driven deforestation and, 35, 54–55, 87, 101
  COVID-19 pandemic effects on, 181
  Ecological Civilization policy in, 20, 126
  palm oil sector and, 52, 54–55, 64, 65–66, 85–86, 87, 89, 100, 113, 115–116, 125–127, 129–130, 169
  soy sector and, 20, 52, 54–55, 64, 65–66, 69, 93–95, 96, 100, 169, 171
  sustainability governance changes in, 20, 125–126, 129–130
  timber sector and, 70
  transnational business governance-domestic governance clash in, 38
China Council for International Cooperation on Environment and Development (CCICED), 126
China Environmental United Certification Center, 126
China Forest Certification Council, 89
China Sustainable Palm Oil Alliance, 66, 127, 130
Civil society pressure, 82–83, 91, 99–100. *See also* Social movement pressure; Transnational advocacy pressure
Clay, Jason, 1, 2, 10
Climate Policy Alliance, 152
Climate Policy Institute, 155
Club theory, 29–30
Cocoa sector, 30, 52, 63, 64, 176
COFCO, 65, 94, 101, 129, 151
Coffee sector, 30, 52, 63–64, 74, 76, 112, 172
Cohen, Ben, 1
Colgate-Palmolive, 128
Colonialism, legacies of, 17, 106–107, 163, 180
Commodity-driven deforestation
  beef or cattle sector, 11, 146, 188n8
  climate change and, 14
  COVID-19 pandemic effects on, 182
  globalization and, 18–19, 43–44, 47, 55
  green private investment to address, 177–178
  impact evaluation on reducing, 31–32
  jurisdictional approach to, 140, 143–147, 149, 151–158, 160, 161
  overview of, 10–15

Commodity-driven deforestation (cont.)
  palm oil sector, 2, 11, 31–32, 54–55, 78–79, 87–89, 101, 108, 118, 121–123, 152–158, 169, 188n8 (chap. 4) (*see also* Palm oil sector)
  political economy context for, 25–26, 35–36
  quantification of, 11–13, 54, 186n4
  soy sector, 2, 11, 31–32, 54–55, 78–79, 92, 95, 97–99, 101, 146, 169, 188n8 (*see also* Soy sector)
  timber and pulp sector, 2, 11, 188n8
  Tropical Oil Crop Revolution effect on, 2, 11, 49–50
  Ukraine war effects on, 182
  zero-deforestation regime complex (*see* Zero-deforestation regime complex)
Comparative political economy
  comparative findings in, 100–102, 171–172
  contextual conditions for, 79
  demand-side conditions for, 79, 80–81, 83, 85–89, 93–96, 100–102
  framework for analysis, 43, 44
  institutional conditions for, 79
  overview of, 26, 36–38, 73–74, 102–103, 170–172
  practitioner and policymaker analysis of, 176–177
  research on, 17–18
  RSPO analysis, 73–74, 79–80, 83, 84–91, 100–103, 171–172
  RTRS analysis, 73–74, 79–80, 83, 92–103, 171–172
  supply-side conditions for, 79, 81–83, 89–91, 97–102
  sustainable markets analysis, 73–74, 79–103, 170–172
  temporal dimension of, 80, 84
Conflictive fragmentation, 68–70

Conservation
  biodiversity, 139
  COVID-19 pandemic effects on, 182
  impact evaluation of, 31, 32
  jurisdictional approach to, 148–149, 159, 162
  rainforest marketing and, 165
Consumer Goods Forum (CGF)
  Forest Positive Coalition of Action, 14, 61, 144, 159, 162
  zero-deforestation pledge of, 3, 12, 57, 61, 73, 77, 162
Cooperative fragmentation, 68, 70
COP26 Climate Summit, 14, 36, 62, 144
Corporate power
  concentration of, 10, 14, 82, 113, 120, 172
  exclusionary practice persistence with, 162–163
  of lead firms in GVCs, 39–40, 41, 80, 86–87, 94–95, 105, 114–115, 173
  political economy analysis of, 33–35, 39–40, 41
  in sustainable markets, 75, 80, 82, 86–87, 90, 94–95, 97–98
Council of Palm Oil Producing Countries, 85–86, 91
Country clubs, 30
COVID-19 pandemic, 180–183

Deforestation. *See* Commodity-driven deforestation
Demand-side actors
  in buyer-driven GVCs, 39–40, 41
  in sustainable markets, 79, 80–81, 83, 85–89, 93–96, 100–102
  in zero-deforestation regime complex, 56–57, 59, 60–63
Demeter, 5
Denmark, 88
Developing countries. *See* Emerging economies

Index

Domestic industry structure, 81–82, 89–90, 97
Dust Bowl, 48

Earth Innovation Institute, 144, 148, 150, 155
Earth Summit (Rio, 1992), 166
East Hope Group, 94
Economic upgrading, 40
Economies of scale, 81–82, 111
Emerging economies. *See also* Global South; *specific countries*
  agricultural support programs in, 48
  agricultural trade and demand in, 49, 51–53, 169
  consumption growth in, 51–53
  COVID-19 pandemic effects on, 181
  export dependency of, 37–38
  globalization and, 35, 51, 55
  global value chain implications for, 39–40
  sustainable markets and, 80–81, 85–86
  2008 financial crisis in, 181
  zero-deforestation regime complex and, 65–70
Emerging global trends, 177–180
Employees. *See* Labor
Environmental impact evaluation. *See* Impact evaluation
Environmental justice, 179–180
Environmental Research Institute, 148
Environmental upgrading, 20, 40–42, 105–106, 114–115, 117, 129, 173
EU-Brazil Sustainable Soy Partnership, 96
European Commission, 22
European Palm Oil Alliance, 61, 65
European Soy Monitor, 65
European Union (EU). *See also specific countries*
  agricultural trade by, 51, 52 (*see also specific products*)
  biofuel sustainability regulation in, 37, 50, 86, 186n2 (chap. 3)
  cocoa sector and, 176
  colonial legacies of, 17, 106–107, 180
  commodity-driven deforestation and, 17, 54, 63, 65, 88–89, 117
  Forest Law Enforcement, Governance, and Trade framework, 70
  jurisdictional approach in, 138
  palm oil sector and, 61, 65, 85–86, 87, 88–89, 100–101, 107, 113, 115, 117, 169, 171–172, 173
  Renewable Energy Directive in, 50, 186n2 (chap. 3)
  soy sector and, 65, 93, 95–96, 100–101, 169
  Timber Regulation of 2013, 63, 70
  in zero-deforestation regime complex, 63, 65, 69–70
Exports
  beef or cattle, 78
  Global South, 38, 51
  palm oil, 50, 78, 85–86, 105, 107
  soy, 50, 69, 78, 93–94, 96
  taxes on agricultural, 49
  timber, 37, 70
  transnational business governance adoption and dependency on, 37–38, 78, 80, 85
Eyes on the Forest, 120

Fairtrade International, 6
Fairtrade Labelling Organization, 180
Fairtrade Mark, 5
Fair trade programs, 2, 5–6, 30
Falkner, Robert, 5
Fern, 22
Financialization, 33, 34
Food insecurity, 182
Forest, Agriculture, and Commodity Trade Dialogue to Tackle Deforestation, 36
Forest Conversion Initiative (FCI), 2–3, 11, 61, 79, 92, 93, 100
Forest fires, 31, 122

Forest 500 Index, 74–75, 76, 78, 86, 102, 129, 187–188nn5–6
Forest Positive Coalition of Action, 14, 61, 144, 159, 162
Forest Stewardship Council
  certification programs of, 78, 80
  in China, 83, 89
  competitors to, 70
  formation of, 6
  planetary justice discourse on, 180
  praise for, 9
  rule-making authority of, 37
Forest Trends
  Supply Change Initiative, 74–75, 76, 78, 86, 102
  on zero-deforestation commitments, 12
France, 63, 88

GAPKI (Indonesian Palm Oil Association), 90, 131–132
General Agreement on Tariffs and Trade, 49
Genetically modified organisms, 50, 95
Geospatial analysis, 16, 31
German International Cooperation Agency, 152
Germany, 5, 63, 88, 152
Ghana, 63
Glasgow Leaders Declaration, 62
Global Canopy Program's Forest 500 Index, 74–75, 76, 78, 86, 102, 129, 187–188nn5–6
Global Forest Watch, 179
Globalization
  agricultural trade and, 49, 51–52, 169–170
  commodity-driven deforestation and, 18–19, 43–44, 47, 55
  comparative politics of sustainable markets and, 73, 171
  environmental degradation link to, 18, 169
  hyper-, 35
  palm oil value chain and, 105, 115
  political economy analysis of, 33–35, 37, 39, 42–43
  South-South trade and, 51–52, 55, 169–170
  transnational business governance and, 4–8, 14–19, 25, 59, 166–167
  zero-deforestation regime complex effects of, 64, 66–67, 70, 170
Global North. *See also specific countries*
  biofuel demand in, 50
  colonial legacies of, 17, 106–107, 163, 180
  Global South opposition to demands of, 167
  palm oil value chain in, 115, 117, 173
  practice implications of shifts in, 175–176
  2008 financial crisis in, 181
  zero-deforestation regime complex and, 19, 57, 59, 61–63, 64–66, 68, 70
Global South. *See also specific countries*
  agricultural transformation in, 50
  consumption growth in, 51–53
  exports by, 38, 51
  Global North demand opposition by, 167
  jurisdictional approach in (*see* Jurisdictional approach)
  location of end markets in, 80, 85–86, 111, 170
  palm oil value chain in, 112–114, 115–116, 125–130
  practice implications of shifts in, 175–176
  South-South trade, 15, 18, 35–36, 41, 51–55, 63–64, 66, 69, 85–86, 103, 161–162, 169–170
  2008 financial crisis in, 181
  zero-deforestation regime complex and, 19, 57, 62, 63–70

Index

Global value chains (GVCs)
  buyer-driven, 39–40, 41
  defined, 39
  economic upgrading in, 40
  environmental upgrading in, 20, 40–42, 105–106, 114–115, 117, 129, 173
  framework for analysis, 43, 44
  lead firms in, 39–40, 41, 80, 86–87, 94–95, 105, 114–115, 172–173
  mapping and analysis of, 42
  multipolar, 20, 41–42, 114–116, 173
  palm oil sector, 105–136, 172–174 (*see also* Palm oil value chain)
  political economy analysis, 17–18, 26, 38–42, 43, 44
  producer-driven, 39–40, 41
  research on, 17–18
  social upgrading in, 40
  sustainability governance of, 59
  unipolar, 41, 114–115, 173
Golden Agri-Resources, 111, 118
Governance. *See* Regulatory authority; Sustainability governance; Transnational business governance
Government actors
  agricultural expansion policies of, 50
  exclusionary practice persistence by, 162–163
  in global value chains, 41
  in jurisdictional approach (*see* Jurisdictional approach)
  in palm oil value chain, 107, 110–111, 116, 131–133
  recentering of, with jurisdictional approach, 158–159, 161, 162
  sustainable market support by, 81, 82, 88–89, 90–91, 95–96, 98–99
  transnational regulatory pressure by, 37–38, 81, 96 (*see also* Regulatory authority)
  in zero-deforestation regime complex, 56, 57, 59, 61, 62–63, 66, 67–70

Government-controlled palm oil estates, 110–111
Governors' Climate and Forest Task Force (Brazil), 145, 146, 147
Governors' Climate Task Force (Indonesia), 152–153, 154
Greenhouse gas emissions, 9, 11, 31, 131–132
"Greening China's Soft Commodity Value Chains" study, 126, 130
Greenpeace, 12, 22, 61, 87–88, 91, 118–119, 146
Green private investment, 177–178
Green Revolution, 48, 153
Greenwashes, 29, 161, 186n1 (chap. 2)
Grupo de Reflexión Rural, 99
GVCs. *See* Global value chains

Hindustan Unilever, 128, 129
Home Depot, 6
HSBC, 60

Iceland (retailer), 183
IDH (Sustainable Trade Initiative), 60, 128, 144, 150–151, 159, 179
Impact evaluation, 16, 26, 30–32, 37, 74
Imports
  agricultural, global shifts in, 51–55
  beef or cattle, 63
  biofuel, 50
  cocoa, 52, 63, 176
  coffee, 52, 63
  palm oil, 53–55, 65, 85–86, 112–113
  soy, 53–55, 65, 93–94
  taxes on agricultural, 49
  timber, 63
India
  agricultural trade by, 51–52 (*see also specific products*)
  agricultural transformation in, 48
  commodity-driven deforestation and, 35, 54–55, 87–88
  COVID-19 pandemic effects on, 181

India (cont.)
  palm oil sector and, 20, 52, 54–55, 64, 65–66, 85–86, 87–88, 100, 112–113, 115–116, 125–129, 169
  soy sector and, 54, 64, 169
  sustainability governance changes in, 20, 126–127, 129
  tea sector in, 127–128
India Sustainable Palm Oil Coalition (ISPOC), 20, 66, 116, 125, 127–129
Indigenous peoples
  civil society support for, 99
  commodity-driven deforestation effects on, 11
  environmental justice driven by, 179
  jurisdictional approach inclusion of, 143, 160, 162, 174
  zero-deforestation regime complex and, 62
Indonesia
  agricultural transformation in, 50
  Berau Forest Carbon Program in, 151–152
  Central Kalimantan's Roadmap to Low-Deforestation Rural Development in, 153–158, 159–160, 161, 163
  certification program impact evaluation in, 31, 32
  deforestation in, 18, 31, 55, 108, 118, 121–123, 151–158
  domestic consumption in, 52, 85–86, 113–114, 169
  forest fires in, 122
  Govenors' Climate Task Force, 152–153, 154
  jurisdictional approach in, 140, 143–144, 151–158, 159–160, 161, 163
  Lingkar Temu Kabupaten Lestari in, 153
  palm oil industry history in, 106–108
  palm oil sector in, 2, 52, 55, 62, 66, 67, 68–69, 78, 84–86, 89–91, 106–124, 128, 130–136, 152–158, 169, 173–174, 188n1 (chap. 5)
  palm oil value chain in, 108–114
  rice sector in, 153, 154
  "silent" palm oil expansion in, 123–124
  subnational governments in, 151–158
  sustainability governance in, 20, 62, 130–133, 140, 143–144, 151–158, 159–160, 161, 163
  timber and pulp sector in, 63, 69–70, 152, 153
  transnational business governance–domestic governance clash in, 38
Indonesian Biofuel Producer Association, 114
Indonesian Ecolabelling Program, 69–70
Indonesian Palm Oil Association (GAPKI), 90, 131–132
Indonesia Palm Oil Pledge, 69, 91, 133
Indonesia Sustainable Palm Oil (ISPO) program
  implementation of, 133–135
  jurisdictional approach with, 155
  in palm oil value chain, 116, 130–131, 133–135, 174
  sustainable markets and, 90
  zero-deforestation regime complex and, 62, 66, 67
Industry structure, 81–82, 89–90, 97
Inobu, 91, 155, 157
Institutional conditions, 79
Institutional fragmentation, 19, 64, 66–70, 170, 187n11 (chap. 3)
Institutionalist perspective, 16, 26, 27–30
International political economy
  framework for analysis, 43–44
  global agriculture transformations and, 47–50, 169–170
  global market and power shifts and, 47–71, 169–170
  overview of, 26, 33–36, 70–71, 169–170
  practitioner and policymaker analysis of, 176

Index

research on, 17–18
South-South trade and, 35–36, 41, 51–55, 63–64, 66, 69, 169–170
tropical commodity boom and, 52–55, 64–65
zero-deforestation regime complex and, 55–70, 71, 169–170
International Trade Centre
Standards Map, 7
Sustainability Map, 75–77, 78, 102
Trade for Sustainability Forum, 22
International Tropical Timber Organization, 62
Investments, green private, 177–178
IOI Group, 117, 121–123
ISEAL Alliance, 22, 159
ISPO. *See* Indonesia Sustainable Palm Oil (ISPO) program
ISPOC (India Sustainable Palm Oil Coalition), 20, 66, 116, 125, 127–129
Italy, 88

Jokowi administration, 135
Jurisdictional approach
big-brand sustainability limits and, 161–162
in Brazil, 140, 143–151, 159, 160, 163
Central Kalimantan's Roadmap to Low-Deforestation Rural Development as, 153–158, 159–160, 161, 163
challenges of, 21, 158, 160–163, 175
conceptual and institutional antecedents for, 139–140
conservation objectives in, 148–149, 159, 162
economic development objectives in, 137, 148–149
emerging features of, 140–143
exclusionary practice persistence with, 162–163
governance mode in, 141–142
in Indonesia, 140, 143–144, 151–158, 159–160, 161, 163
Mato Grosso's Produce, Conserve, and Include Strategy as, 144–151, 159, 160, 163
number of, 143
opportunities with, 21, 158–160, 174–175
overview of, 137–138, 163–164, 174–175
palm oil value chain and, 135–136
public-private complementarities in, 159–160
recentering government actors with, 158–159, 161, 162
research on, 20–21
scale of, 141, 142
scope of, 141, 143
social inclusion objectives in, 137, 139, 143, 148–149, 160, 162, 174
succumbing to "dreams of domestication" with, 160–161
supply chain initiatives and, 137, 139, 141, 159–160
in sustainability governance debate, 138–139
Jurisdictional Certification Working Group (Indonesia), 155

Kalimantan Forests and Climate Partnership, 154
Kellogg's, 122

Labor
palm oil sector, 107–108, 153
social upgrading in GVCs, 40
Latin America, 48. *See also specific countries*
Lever Brother's Company, 106. *See also* Unilever
Liby, 113
Life Centre Institute, 148
Limits-to-growth paradigm, 166–167

Lingkar Temu Kabupaten Lestari (Sustainable Districts Platform, LTKL), 153
Location or place
 of end markets, 80, 85–86, 93–94, 111, 170
 jurisdictional approach specific to (*see* Jurisdictional approach)
L'Oréal, 128
Louis Dreyfus, 10

Maggi, Blair, 147
Malaysia, 50, 62, 66, 68, 84, 107
Malaysia Sustainable Palm Oil program, 62, 66
Mandarins, 30
Market adoption. *See* Market uptake or adoption
Markets
 governance driven by (*see* Transnational business governance)
 sustainable (*see* Sustainable markets)
 for tropical oil crops, 50 (*see also* Palm oil sector; Soy sector)
Market uptake or adoption
 comparative political economy analysis of, 36–37, 171
 explanation of, 78–79
 impact evaluation on, 37, 74
 outcome effectiveness and, 37, 186n1 (chap. 2)
 sustainable markets and, 65, 73–79, 83, 84–85, 92, 171
Market value chains, 40
Mars, 60, 122
Mato Grosso's Produce, Conserve, and Include (PCI) Strategy, 145–151, 159, 160, 163
Max Havelaar label, 5
Mega Rice Project (Indonesia), 153, 154
Mendes, Governor, 147–148
Mills, palm oil, 119–121

Municipal Pact to End Illegal Deforestation of São Félix do Xingu (Brazil), 145
Musim Mas, 111, 114, 118–119

Narang, Teras, 154, 155, 157
National Action Plan on Business and Human Rights (India), 127
National Forest Code (Brazil), 99
National Guidelines on Responsible Business Conduct (India), 126–127
Nature Conservancy, 140, 144, 145, 151–152
Neoliberalism, 15, 49–50, 59
Nestlé, 10, 12, 60–61, 112, 120, 122, 172
Netherlands, 5, 63, 88, 95–96
New Hope Group, 94
New normative discourses, 179–180
Nice Group, 113
Nongovernmental organizations (NGOs). *See also specific organizations*
 compliance tracing and accountability requirements of, 120, 121–123
 in global value chains, 41
 in jurisdictional approach, 140, 144, 145–146, 148, 150, 151–152, 153, 155
 sustainable markets support by, 81, 82–83, 87–88, 91, 95, 97, 99
 transnational advocacy pressure by, 6–7, 10, 12, 81, 87–88, 95
 transnational governance role of, 5–7, 25, 59, 167
 in zero-deforestation regime complex, 56, 59–61, 65
Nonstate market-driven governance. *See* Transnational business governance
North. *See* Global North
Norway, 88

Oil industries. *See* Palm oil sector; Soy sector
Organic certification programs, 2, 5–6, 30

Index

Overconsumption, 8, 33, 161
Overstory, 179

Palm Oil Agribusiness Strategic Policy Institute, 89
Palm oil sector
  biofuels from, 50, 52, 84, 86, 112, 114
  certification programs in, 7–8, 31–32, 65, 79, 84–91, 100–102, 117–124, 132, 155, 157, 171, 173
  civil society pressure in, 91
  comparative findings on, 100–102, 125, 171–172
  deforestation by, 2, 11, 31–32, 54–55, 78–79, 87–89, 101, 108, 118, 121–123, 152–158, 169, 188n8 (*see also* Commodity-driven deforestation)
  demand-side conditions for, 85–89, 100–102
  domestic industry structure in, 89–90
  exports in, 50, 78, 85–86, 105, 107
  global value chain analysis of, 105–136, 172–174 (*see also* Palm oil value chain)
  government actor influence in, 88–89, 90–91, 107, 110–111, 116, 131–133
  imports in, 53–55, 65, 85–86, 112–113
  industry history, 106–108
  jurisdictional approach to, 152–158
  lead firms in GVCs influence on, 86–87, 105, 114–115, 172–173
  location of end markets for, 85–86, 111
  producer groups in, 90, 111, 114, 117
  RSPO for (*see* Roundtable on Sustainable Palm Oil)
  supply-side conditions for, 89–91, 100–102, 116
  sustainable markets for, 73–80, 83, 84–91, 100–103, 171–172
  transnational advocacy pressure on, 87–88
  tropical commodity boom for, 52–55, 64–65
  Tropical Oil Crop Revolution in, 2, 11, 49–50, 52
  Ukraine war effects on, 181–182
  zero-deforestation focus on, 57, 60, 65, 69, 75, 84, 91, 117, 118–119, 133 (*see also* Zero-deforestation regime complex)
Palm oil value chain
  accountability in, politics of, 121–123, 173
  China and India market changes for, 125–127
  compliance tracing and audits in, 119–122, 134, 173
  domestic issues in, 113–114, 130–131
  downstream segment of, 108–109, 112–114, 129
  environmental upgrading in, 114–115, 117, 129, 173
  Global North drivers in, 115, 117, 173
  Global South drivers in, 112–114, 115–116, 125–130
  India Sustainable Palm Oil Coalition and, 116, 125, 127–129
  Indonesian, 108–114
  industry history, 106–108
  IOI Group in, 117, 121–123
  ISPO program and, 116, 130–131, 133–135, 174
  jurisdictional approach and, 135–136
  lead firms in, 105, 114–115, 172–173
  market transformation with loopholes for, 117
  midstream segment of, 108–109, 111–112
  multipolar governance in, 114–116, 173–174
  overview of, 105–106, 136, 172–174
  regulatory authority and, 115, 126–127, 129–130, 131–133, 134, 173–174
  renationalization of sustainability governance for, 131–133

Palm oil value chain (cont.)
  roadblocks to sustainability in, 129–130
  "silent" palm oil expansion in, 123–124
  smallholders in, 110–111, 123–124, 135, 173, 188n1 (chap. 5)
  traders/trading companies in, 111–112, 117–119
  upstream segment of, 108–109, 110–111
PALM (Production and Protection Approach to Landscape Management) program, 155
Paris Agreement on Climate Change/Paris Climate Conference, 88, 145, 148
PCI (Mato Grosso's Produce, Conserve, and Include) Strategy, 145–151, 159, 160, 163
PepsiCo, 10, 14
Place. *See* Location or place
Place-based sustainability governance. *See* Jurisdictional approach
Planetary justice, 179–180
Plantations, private palm oil, 110–111, 121–123, 131, 153, 188n1 (chap. 5)
Political economy analysis, 25–45
  commodity-driven deforestation and, 25–26, 35–36
  comparative (*see* Comparative political economy)
  framework for multilevel, 42–44, 168, 176–177
  global value chain, 17–18, 26, 38–42, 43, 44
  impact evaluation and, 16, 26, 30–32, 37
  institutionalist perspective and, 16, 26, 27–30
  international (*see* International political economy)
  overview of, 25–27, 44–45
  practitioner and policymaker use of, 176–177
  research developments and, 16–20, 27, 42–44, 168
  varieties of, 33
Polycentric trade, 19, 63–66, 112, 115, 161
Practice implications, 175–177
Procter & Gamble, 128
Producer groups, 82, 90, 97–98, 111, 114, 117. *See also* Supply-side actors
Production and Protection Approach to Landscape Management (PALM) program, 155
Program for the Endorsement of Forest Certification, 78
Program on Reducing Emissions from Deforestation and Forest Degradation (REDD+), 140, 145, 147, 153–154, 155, 159
PTPN III, 110
PT SNA, 121
Public-private complementarities, 139, 159–160

Rabobank, 60, 177
Rainforest Action Network, 123
Rainforest Alliance, 60, 66, 128
Rainforest marketing, 1, 165
REDD+ (Program on Reducing Emissions from Deforestation and Forest Degradation), 140, 145, 147, 153–154, 155, 159
Regime complex theory, 56. *See also* Zero-deforestation regime complex
Regulatory authority
  defined, 36
  in jurisdictional approach, 137, 138–139, 158–159, 162–163
  palm oil value chain and, 115, 126–127, 129–130, 131–133, 134, 173–174

Index

political economy analysis of, 20, 36–38
sustainable markets and, 81, 82, 88–89, 90–91, 95–96, 98–99
transnational regulatory pressure and, 37–38, 81, 96
zero-deforestation regime complex and, 57, 59–63, 67–70
Remote-sensing technology, 31, 178–179
Research
  data and methodology, 21–23
  future, 177–180
  impact evaluation, 16, 26, 30–32, 37, 74
  on jurisdictional approaches, 20–21
  political economy analysis and, 16–20, 27, 42–44, 168
  on transnational business governance, 4–8, 15–23, 27
  on zero-deforestation regime complex, 3–4, 55–56
Retail Soy Group, 61
Rice sector, 153, 154
Rising Powers and Global Standards research network, 16
Roundtable on Responsible Soy (RTRS)
  certification program of, 65, 79, 92–102, 171
  comparative findings on, 100–102, 171–172
  comparative political economy analysis of, 73–74, 79–80, 83, 92–103, 171–172
  demand-side conditions for, 93–96, 100–102
  launch of, 2–3
  market uptake of, 92
  planetary justice discourse on, 180
  research data from, 22
  supply-side conditions for, 97–102
  in zero-deforestation regime complex, 12, 60, 61, 65, 69
Roundtable on Sustainable Biomaterials, 60

Roundtable on Sustainable Palm Oil (RSPO)
  accountability to standards of, 121–123
  certification program of, 8, 31, 65, 79, 84–91, 100–102, 117–124, 132, 155, 171
  comparative findings on, 100–102, 171–172
  comparative political economy analysis of, 73–74, 79–80, 83, 84–91, 100–103, 171–172
  compliance with standards of, 119–121
  critiques of, 8
  demand-side conditions for, 85–89, 100–102
  dispute settlement system of, 121–122
  impact evaluation of, 31, 32
  jurisdictional approach with, 155, 159
  launch of, 2–3
  market uptake of, 84–85
  New Planting Procedure, 131–132
  palm oil value chain standards, 115, 117–123, 131–132
  renationalization of sustainability governance and withdrawal from, 131–133
  research data from, 22
  Smallholder Working Group/Strategy, 124
  supply-side conditions for, 89–91, 100–102
  traders in, 118–119
  in zero-deforestation regime complex, 12, 60, 61, 65, 84
RSPO. *See* Roundtable on Sustainable Palm Oil
RTRS. *See* Roundtable on Responsible Soy
Russia, 51–52, 181. *See also* Ukraine, war in

Sainsbury's, 40
São Félix do Xingu, Municipal Pact to End Illegal Deforestation of (Brazil), 145
Satelligence, 179
Sawit Watch, 91
Sime Darby, 110
Sinar Mas, 110
Singapore Sustainable Palm Oil Alliance, 61, 66, 127
Sinograin, 94
Smallholders
　jurisdictional approach inclusion of, 143, 150, 157, 160
　palm oil sector, 110–111, 123–124, 135, 157, 173, 188n1 (chap. 5)
　tea sector, 128
Smart Earth technologies, 178–179
Social inclusion objectives, 137, 139, 143, 148–149, 160, 162, 174
Social movement pressure. *See also* Transnational advocacy pressure
　for environmental/planetary justice, 179–180
　sustainable markets influence via, 82–83, 91, 99–100
　transnational business governance adoption and, 37–38
Social upgrading, 40
Société Générale de Surveillance, 121
Soft Commodities Forum, 61
Soja Plus Program, 62, 66, 69, 96, 98
Solidaridad, 5, 60, 91, 96
Solvent Extractor Association of India, 129
Sorriso, PCI Compact (Brazil), 150–151
South. *See* Global South
South Africa, 51–52, 181
South America. *See also specific countries*
　agricultural support programs in, 48
　colonial legacies in, 180
　commodity-driven deforestation in, 11
　Tropical Oil Crop Revolution in, 49

Soy sector
　Amazon Soy Moratorium on, 31–32, 61, 69, 98, 99
　biofuels from, 92
　certification programs in, 65, 79, 92–102, 171
　civil society pressure in, 99–100
　comparative findings on, 100–102, 171–172
　deforestation by, 2, 11, 31–32, 54–55, 78–79, 92, 95, 97–99, 101, 146, 169, 188n8 (*see also* Commodity-driven deforestation)
　demand-side conditions for, 93–96, 100–102
　domestic industry structure in, 97
　exports in, 50, 69, 78, 93–94, 96
　government actor influence in, 95–96, 98–99
　imports in, 53–55, 65, 93–94
　lead firms in GVCs influence on, 94–95
　location of end markets for, 93–94
　producer groups in, 97–98
　RTRS for (*see* Roundtable on Responsible Soy)
　supply-side conditions for, 97–102
　sustainable markets for, 73–80, 83, 92–103, 171–172
　transnational advocacy pressure on, 95
　tropical commodity boom for, 52–55, 64–65
　Tropical Oil Crop Revolution in, 2, 11, 49–50, 52
　zero-deforestation focus on, 57, 60, 65, 75, 98 (*see also* Zero-deforestation regime complex)
SPIKEBUN, 157
Sponsorships
　in jurisdictional approach, 154
　in voluntary programs, 30
　in zero-deforestation regime complex, 56, 57, 60–61, 66
State actors. *See* Government actors

Index

Sugarcane sector, 9, 31, 37
Suharto regime, 91, 107, 110, 131, 151
Sun Art Retail Group, 113
Supply Change Initiative, 74–75, 76, 78, 86, 102
Supply chains
  agricultural, 49
  corporate power in, 34, 39, 41
  COVID-19 pandemic effects on, 182
  global value chains and (*see* Global value chains)
  history of initiatives focused on, 2–3
  impact evaluation of initiatives in, 31–32
  jurisdictional approach and, 137, 139, 141, 159–160
  Ukraine war effects on, 182
  zero-deforestation regime complex for (*see* Zero-deforestation regime complex)
Supply Change, 61, 65
Supply-side actors. *See also* Producer groups
  in jurisdictional approach, 138–139
  in palm oil value chain, 116
  in producer-driven GVCs, 39–40, 41
  in sustainable markets, 79, 81–83, 89–91, 97–102
  in zero-deforestation regime complex, 56–57, 60, 62
Sustainability governance. *See also* Transnational business governance
  certification programs for (*see* Certification programs)
  environmental upgrading and, 20, 40–42, 105–106, 114–115, 117, 129, 173
  global economic changes affecting, 166–168
  global value chains and (*see* Global value chains)
  place-based (*see* Jurisdictional approach)
  political economy context for (*see* Political economy analysis)
  renationalization of, 20, 131–133
  sustainability defined for, 166
  sustainable markets and (*see* Sustainable markets)
  zero-deforestation regime complex for (*see* Zero-deforestation regime complex)
Sustainable Districts Platform (Lingkar Temu Kabupaten Lestari), 153
Sustainable markets
  comparative findings on, 100–102, 171–172
  comparative political economy analysis of, 73–74, 79–103, 170–172
  demand-side conditions for, 79, 80–81, 83, 85–89, 93–96, 100–102
  market uptake and, 65, 73–79, 83, 84–85, 92, 171
  overview of, 73–74, 102–103
  for palm oil, 73–80, 83, 84–91, 100–103, 171–172
  for soy, 73–80, 83, 92–103, 171–172
  state of, 8, 74–78
  supply-side conditions for, 79, 81–83, 89–91, 97–102
  terminology for, 187n1
Sustainable Municipalities Program (Mato Grosso, Brazil), 147–148
Sustainable Soy Trade Platform, 20, 66, 127
Sustainable Trade Initiative (IDH), 60, 128, 144, 150–151, 159, 179
Synergistic fragmentation, 187n11

Taques, Governor, 147, 148
Tata, 128
Tea sector, 127–128
Technology
  agricultural transformation with, 47–48, 50
  artificial intelligence, 179

Technology (cont.)
  blockchain, 179
  changes in, opportunities and challenges of, 178–179
  political economy analysis of, 33, 34
  remote-sensing, 31, 178–179
  Smart Earth, 178–179
  sustainable markets and access to, 82
Tesco, 40
Tetley Group, 128
Timber and pulp sector
  certification programs in, 78, 171
  deforestation by, 2, 11, 188n8
  exports in, 37, 70
  imports in, 63
  jurisdictional approach to, 152
  regulatory authority in, 69–70
  sustainability regulations on, 138
  sustainable markets for, 74–78
  transnational advocacy pressure on, 6
Timber Legality Assurance System (Indonesia), 70
Trade
  agricultural, global shifts in, 49–55, 169–170
  exports and (*see* Exports)
  fair, 2, 5–6, 30
  free, 49
  imports and (*see* Imports)
  incentives for, 176
  polycentric, 19, 63–66, 112, 115, 161
  South-South, 15, 18, 35–36, 41, 51–55, 63–64, 66, 69, 85–86, 103, 161–162, 169–170
  tariffs, quotas, subsidies, and barriers to, 49, 94
Trading companies, palm oil, 111–112, 117–119
Transaction costs, 81–82
Transfair, 5
Transnational advocacy pressure, 6–7, 10, 12, 81, 87–88, 95. *See also* Social movement pressure

Transnational business governance. *See also* Sustainability governance
  certification programs for (*see* Certification programs)
  critiques of, 8–10, 14
  defined, 5
  domestic governance clashes with, 20, 38, 82
  environmental degradation despite, 8–10
  global economic changes affecting, 166–168
  globalization and, 4–8, 14–19, 25, 59, 166–167
  global value chains and (*see* Global value chains)
  history of, 4–8, 15, 19, 25, 59, 166–167
  impact evaluation perspective on, 16, 26, 30–32, 37, 74
  institutionalist perspective on, 16, 26, 27–30
  jurisdictional approach vs (*see* Jurisdictional approach)
  legitimacy of, 9, 34–36, 66
  political economy context for (*see* Political economy analysis)
  regulatory authority of, 36–38 (*see also* Regulatory authority)
  research on, 4–8, 15–23, 27
  terminology for, 5
  transnational factors affecting, 37–38
  zero-deforestation regime complex as (*see* Zero-deforestation regime complex)
Transnational regulatory pressure, 37–38, 81, 96
Tropical commodity boom, 52–55, 64–65
Tropical commodity-driven deforestation. *See* Commodity-driven deforestation

Index

Tropical Forest Alliance, 3, 22, 61, 176
Tropical Oil Crop Revolution, 1–2, 11, 47, 48–50, 52
Trustea program, 125, 127–128
2008 financial crisis, 15, 181

Ukraine, war in, 180–183
Unilever
  market control by, 10
  in palm oil sector, 106, 112, 120, 122, 129, 157, 172
  in tea sector, 128
  in zero-deforestation regime complex, 60, 66
United Kingdom, 5, 63, 88, 138
United Nations Climate Change Summit (New York), 133
United Nations Climate Conference (Bali), 147
United Nations Climate Conference (Paris), 148. *See also* Paris Agreement on Climate Change/Paris Climate Conference
United Nations Conference on the Environment, 166
United Nations Conference on Trade and Development, 51
United Nations Environmental Program, 157
United Nations Forum on Sustainability Standards, 22
United Nations Framework Convention on Climate Change, 140
United Nations Guiding Principles on Business and Human Rights, 126
United Nations New York Declaration on Forests, 12, 62, 88, 91, 94
United Nations Program on Reducing Emissions from Deforestation and Forest Degradation, 62
United Nations Sustainable Development Goals, 139, 182

United States
  agricultural trade by, 51, 52, 94 (*see also specific products*)
  agricultural transformations in, 47–48
  commodity-driven deforestation and, 54
  Dust Bowl in, 48
  jurisdictional approach in, 138
  palm oil sector and, 169
  soy sector in, 54, 94, 100, 169
  timber sector and, 70
  in zero-deforestation regime complex, 61, 70
University of Palangka Raya, 155

Value chains. *See* Global value chains
Vanguard Group, 113
Via Campensina, 99
Voluntary programs, 29–30, 37, 74. *See also* Certification programs

Walmart, 10
Wilmar, 110, 111, 114, 118–119
Workforce. *See* Labor
World Bank, 50, 107
World Resource Institute, 11, 60, 153
World Summit on Sustainable Development, 166
World Trade Forum, 22
World Trade Organization, 49, 86, 88
World Wide Fund for Nature (WWF)
  certification mainstreaming by, 7
  Forest Conversion Initiative, 2–3, 11, 61, 79, 92, 93, 100
  Markets Institute, 1, 12, 117
  market transformation strategy, 175
  roundtables of, 2–3, 10, 11, 60 (*see also specific roundtables*)
  on sustainable markets, 78
  in zero-deforestation regime complex, 11, 59–60, 61, 66

Yonghui Group, 113

Zero-deforestation regime complex, 55–70
  collaboratives in, 60, 69
  demand-side actors in, 56–57, 59, 60–63
  global economic changes affecting, 63–70
  globalization effects on, 64, 66–67, 70, 170
  global power shifts and, 66–70, 169–170
  governance triangle and, 56, 67
  government actors in, 56, 57, 59, 61, 62–63, 66, 67–70
  history of, 11–14
  impact evaluation of, 31–32, 37
  institutional fragmentation and, 19, 64, 66–70, 170
  jurisdictional approach and, 155, 162
  mapping of, 56–57, 58–59
  overview of, 55–56, 71
  pledges for zero net deforestation in, 3, 12, 57, 61, 69, 73, 77, 91, 118–119, 133, 162
  polycentric trade adaptation and, 63–66
  research and scholarship on, 3–4, 55–56
  sponsorships in, 56, 57, 60–61, 66
  supply-side actors in, 56–57, 60, 62
  sustainable markets and, 75, 77, 84, 91, 170
  targets not reached by, 3, 12, 77, 137, 144, 159, 162, 165
  time periods for, 13, 57, 58–59, 60–61
  transnational regulatory space for, 57, 59–63, 67–70